WITHDRAWN
HARVARD LIBRARY
WITHDRAWN

STUDIES IN BAPTIST HISTORY AND THOUGHT
VOLUME 11

Recycling the Past or Researching History?

Studies in Baptist Historiography and Myths

STUDIES IN BAPTIST HISTORY AND THOUGHT

A full listing of all titles in this series
appears at the close of this book

STUDIES IN BAPTIST HISTORY AND THOUGHT
VOLUME 11

Recycling the Past or Researching History?

Studies in Baptist Historiography and Myths

Edited by
Philip E. Thompson and Anthony R. Cross

Foreword by Stephen Brachlow

PATERNOSTER

Copyright © Philip E. Thompson, Anthony R. Cross
and the Contributors 2005

First published 2005 by Paternoster

Paternoster is an imprint of Authentic Media
9 Holdom Avenue, Bletchley, Milton Keynes, MK1 1QR, UK
and
PO Box 1047, Waynesboro, GA 30830–2047, USA

11 10 09 08 07 06 05   7 6 5 4 3 2 1

The right of Philip E. Thompson and Anthony R. Cross to be
identified as the Editors of this Work has been asserted by them
in accordance with the Copyright, Designs
and Patents Act 1988

All rights reserved. No part of this publication may be reproduced, stored in a retrieval system, or transmitted in any form by any means, electronic, mechanical, photocopying, recording or otherwise, without the prior permission of the publisher or a license permitting restricted copying. In the UK such licenses are issued by the Copyright Licensing Agency, 90 Tottenham Court Road, London W1P 9HE.

British Library Cataloguing in Publication Data
A catalogue record for this book is available from the British Library

ISBN 1-84227-122-9

Typeset by A.R. Cross
Printed and bound in Great Britain
for Paternoster Press
by Nottingham Alphagraphics

Series Preface

Baptists form one of the largest Christian communities in the world, and while they hold the historic faith in common with other mainstream Christian traditions, they nevertheless have important insights which they can offer to the worldwide church. Studies in Baptist History and Thought will be one means towards this end. It is an international series of academic studies which includes original monographs, revised dissertations, collections of essays and conference papers, and aims to cover any aspect of Baptist history and thought. While not all the authors are themselves Baptists, they nevertheless share an interest in relating Baptist history and thought to the other branches of the Christian church and to the wider life of the world.

The series includes studies in various aspects of Baptist history from the seventeenth century down to the present day, including biographical works, and Baptist thought is understood as covering the subject-matter of theology (including interdisciplinary studies embracing biblical studies, philosophy, sociology, practical theology, liturgy and women's studies). The diverse streams of Baptist life throughout the world are all within the scope of these volumes.

The series editors and consultants believe that the academic disciplines of history and theology are of vital importance to the spiritual vitality of the churches of the Baptist faith and order. The series sets out to discuss, examine and explore the many dimensions of their tradition and so to contribute to their on-going intellectual vigour.

A brief word of explanation is due for the series identifier on the front cover. The fountains, taken from heraldry, represent the Baptist distinctive of believer's baptism and, at the same time, the source of the water of life. There are three of them because they symbolize the Trinitarian basis of Baptist life and faith. Those who are redeemed by the Lamb, the book of Revelation reminds us, will be led to 'fountains of living waters' (Rev. 7.17).

Studies in Baptist History and Thought

Series Editors

Anthony R. Cross   Centre for Baptist History and Heritage,
                          Regent's Park College, Oxford, England
Curtis W. Freeman   Duke University, North Carolina, USA
Stephen R. Holmes   University of St Andrews, Scotland
Elizabeth Newman   Baptist Theological Seminary at
                          Richmond, Virginia, USA
Philip E. Thompson   North American Baptist Seminary, Sioux
                          Falls, South Dakota, USA

Series Consultants

David Bebbington   University of Stirling, Stirling, Scotland
Paul S. Fiddes   Regent's Park College, Oxford, England
Stanley J. Grenz   Carey Theological College, Vancouver,
                          British Columbia, Canada
Stanley E. Porter   McMaster Divinity College, Hamilton,
                          Ontario, Canada

*In memory of
Dale Moody
and
W.M.S. West
(two Baptist churchmen who cared deeply
for Baptist memory and who helped us to the study of the subject)
with love and gratitude*

Contents

Contributors xi

Foreword
Stephen Brachlow xiii

Introduction: Caring for Baptist Memory
Philip E. Thompson and Anthony R. Cross xv

Chapter 1
John H.Y. Briggs
Confessional Identity, Denominational Institutions and Relations
with Others: A Study in Changing Contexts 1

Chapter 2
Stanley K. Fowler
Churches and the Church 25

Chapter 3
Elizabeth Newman
The Priesthood of All Believers and the Necessity of the Church 50

Chapter 4
Mike Broadway
The Roots of Baptists in Community, and therefore, Voluntary
Membership not Individualism, or, the High-Flying Modernist,
Stripped of his Ontological Assumptions, Appears to Hold the
Ecclesiology of a Yaho 67

Chapter 5
Mark S. Medley
A Good Walk Spoiled?: Revisiting Baptist Soteriology 84

Chapter 6
Ian M. Randall
The Myth of the Missing Spirituality: Spirituality among English
Baptists in the Early Twentieth Century 106

Chapter 7
Anthony R. Cross
The Myth of English Baptist Anti-Sacramentalism 128

Chapter 8
Karen E. Smith
Forgotten Sisters: The Contributions of Some Notable but
Un-noted British Baptist Women..163

Chapter 9
Philip E. Thompson
'As It Was in the Beginning'(?): The Myth of Changelessness in
Baptist Life and Belief...184

Chapter 10
Larry J. Kreitzer
1653 or 1656: When did Oxford Baptists Join the Abingdon
Association?...207

Chapter 11
Larry J. Kreitzer
The Fifth Monarchist John Pendarves (d.1656): A Victim of
'Studious Bastard Consumption'?..220

Chapter 12
Clive Jarvis
The Myth of High Calvinism?...231

Chapter 13
Michael A.G. Haykin
Eighteenth-Century Calvinistic Baptists and the Political Realm,
with Particular Reference to the Thought of Andrew Fuller.............264

Chapter 14
Valdis Teraudkalns
Episcopacy in the Baptist Tradition..279

Chapter 15
Tim Grass
Strict Baptists and Reformed Baptists in England, 1955–76..............294

General Index..317

Contributors

Stanley K. Fowler, Professor of Theology, Heritage Theological Seminary, Cambridge, Ontario, Canada.

Michael A.G. Haykin, Principal, The Toronto Baptist Seminary and Bible College, and Senior Fellow, The Jonathan Edwards Centre for Reformed Spirituality, Toronto, Ontario, Canada.

Larry J. Kreitzer, Tutor of New Testament and Tutor for Graduates, Regent's Park College, University of Oxford, UK.

Valdis Teraudkalns, Lecturer in History of Christianity, Faculty of Theology, University of Latvia, Riga, and Docent in Philosophy, Faculty of Humanities and Law, Rezekne Higher Educational Institution, Rezekne, Latvia.

Ian M. Randall, Deputy Principal and Lecturer in Church History and Spirituality, Spurgeon's College, London, UK.

Philip E. Thompson, Associate Professor of Systematic Theology and Christian Heritage, North American Baptist Seminary, Sioux falls, South Dakota, USA.

Anthony R. Cross, Fellow of the Centre for Baptist History and Heritage, Regent's Park College, University of Oxford, UK.

Karen E. Smith, Tutor in Church History and Spirituality at South Wales Baptist College and in Cardiff University, and the Pastor of Orchard Place Baptist Church, Neath, South Wales, UK

Mike Broadway, Assistant Professor of Theology and Ethics, Shaw University Divinity School, Raleigh, North Carolina, USA

Elizabeth Newman, Professor of Theology and Ethics, Baptist Theological Seminary at Richmond, Virginia, USA.

Clive Jarvis, Minister, Dorford Baptist Church, Dorchester, UK.

Tim Grass, Associate Lecturer in Church History, Spurgeon's College, London, UK

John H.Y. Briggs, Senior Research Fellow in Ecclesiastical History and Director of the Centre for Baptist History and Heritage, Regent's Park College, University of Oxford, UK.

Mark S. Medley, Associate Professor of Theology, Campbellsville University, Campbellsville, Kentucky, USA.

Foreword

Each spring I take a handful of students from Baptist Theological Seminary at Richmond, Virginia, on an extended retreat in the magnificent wilderness setting of the nearby Blue Ridge Mountains. The idea is to take the time and open our eyes to catch a glimpse of that divine glory which the psalmists of ancient Israel saw with such effortless clarity in the wilderness that surrounded them. But because most of us are not very skilled at this ancient contemplative work, we often fail to recognize the prophetic significance of mountain, stream and forest. We see the beauty, but as urban novices in an unfamiliar spiritual context, we too easily miss the sacred freight it carries. So we have discovered the value of paying attention to the guidance provided by more seasoned observers. Poets, theologians and naturalists--from Wendell Berry and Annie Dillard to the abbas and ammas of the desert in fourth-century Egypt-often enable us to see something of the holy mystery in creation that we otherwise miss.

In a similar way, this collection of fifteen essays written by highly qualified Baptist scholars offers a refreshingly new and, at times, challenging perspective on issues vital to Baptist identity today. Through the clarifying lens of history, this collaboration of a remarkably diverse cadre of theologians and historians brings into focus a vision of Baptist faith and life that is informed by the theological wisdom of earlier Baptists. Built on careful examination of church records, sermons, pamphlets, confessions of faith, personal diaries and other valuable sources of Baptist views throughout the past four centuries, a picture emerges that is complex, theologically compelling and ecclesial-oriented. It is the product of meticulous research by Baptist scholars who know the sources of the tradition and their contexts intimately. Perhaps more importantly, they also recognize the theological significance of language and themes in the old literature that current, more popular versions of Baptist identity--especially those originating North America--either ignore or radically reduce to a handy shortlist of five or six distinctive Baptist principles.

Published on the occasion of the 2005 Centennial Celebration of the Baptist World Alliance in Manchester, England, this collection is written with an eye to a global Baptist readership, as much as for scholarly consumption.

While the essays hew to high standards of academic scholarship, they are nevertheless accessible and thoroughly engaging for non-specialists interested in a thoughtful dialogue with the past about issues that affect

Baptist identity today. Finally, while there is often an iconoclastic edge in these essays aimed at dispelling prevailing myths about Baptist individualism, congregational autonomy and anti-sacramental, the real value of this study is the constructive and historically more satisfying reading of the Baptist tradition that emerges. Through the fresh perspectives offered in these superbly crafted essays, what becomes clearer is a picture of Baptist ecclesial convictions that requires a larger canvas than usual, one that is as rich in composition, shading and texture as it is theologically coherent and convincing.

Stephen Brachlow
Professor of Spirituality,
Baptist Theological Seminary at Richmond,
Richmond, Virginia,
USA

Introduction:
Caring for Baptist Memory

Philip E. Thompson and Anthony R. Cross

A decade ago, patristics scholar Robert Louis Wilken published a collection of essays titled collectively *Remembering the Christian Past*.[1] The first essay was Wilken's 1989 presidential address to the American Academy of Religion. Here he sounded a principal concern of his. In the context of an academy dominated by the 'objective' study of religion and religious phenomena, he asked emphatically, 'Who Will Speak *for* the Religious Traditions?'[2] This essay signals the programme for the entire volume. Christian thinkers, Wilken contends, are the bearers of a tradition, and as such bear responsibility both to and for a particular tradition of life and thought. They bear the burden of caring for the Christian past.[3] He follows with essays that examine early Christian reckoning with other religions, Trinitarian theology, exegesis, the life of virtue, and the cultivation of holiness. The final essay offers an explanation for Wilken's effort to speak for Christian tradition by engaging its earliest thinkers and practitioners. In 'Memory and the Christian Intellectual Life', Wilken develops at some length a perception that may be stated concisely in the words of American essayist Wendell Berry: '[M]emory is the ancestor of consciousness.'[4]

Indeed, the burden of Wilken's project is that the cultivation of genuine Christian consciousness and conscience rests upon fidelity to Christian memory, to tradition.[5] This is because tradition alone, he contends, enables genuine learning.

> In most things in life—learning to speak, making cabinets, playing the violin—the only way to learn is by imitation, by letting someone else guide our movements until we learn to do the thing on our own. I am not sure why this is so, but I suspect a chief reason is that only in the act of doing and participating do we

---

[1] R.L. Wilken, *Remembering the Christian Past* (Grand Rapids, MI: Eerdmans, 1995).
[2] Wilken, *Remembering*, pp. 1-23.
[3] Wilken, *Remembering*, p. 170.
[4] W. Berry, *The Hidden Wound* (New York: North Point Press, 1989), p. 49.
[5] Wilken, *Remembering*, pp. 170-71.

truly know and understand. To do something well, we have to give ourselves over to it.[6]

That is, to learn to think and live as Christians, we are to give ourselves up as apprentices to earlier masters of Christian reason and speech. When methodological commitments bring about a departure from tradition, however, scholars risk inviting a 'willful amnesia'; a 'self-imposed affliction that would rob our lives of depth and direction'.[7] Christian memory, in other words, is at risk, and precisely to the degree that this is so Christian identity is likewise at risk.

Baptists seem to grasp this importance of memory for faithfulness on an intuitive level and apply it with rigour, even if covertly, to the question of Baptist identity. Notwithstanding frequent overt rejection of tradition's authority in Baptist life, expressed perhaps most commonly in anti-creedalism, Baptists are keen to preserve what they take to be their historic identity and principles.[8] The cultivation of a consciousness of what it is to be Baptist is important. Yet herein resides a quandary that Baptists sense with particular keenness and at times regard with particular uneasiness. Baptists face numerous obstacles to faithful consciousness, to a clear understanding of their identity, and this is so because their memory is at risk. The distinctive Baptist form of this problem is not rooted so much in questions of methodology within the centres of Baptist training, though there is doubtless an element of this. No, the roots of the Baptist question lie still more deeply—in Baptists' beginnings and the ethos that has characterized them throughout much of their history. American Baptist historian Edwin Scott Gaustad has thus noted that 'Baptists appear to have more problems than most as we endeavor to locate that distillation, that essence, that defining difference which constitutes being Baptist.'[9]

There are two principal reasons for this. First, the debate on Baptist origins remains to some degree open, and with it the question of what influences are strongest in their beginnings.[10] They additionally have more than one point of origin. Contemporary Baptists are as such heirs of

---

[6] Wilken, *Remembering*, p. 171.
[7] Wilken, *Remembering*, p. 170.
[8] See the essay by P.E. Thompson, '"As It Was in the Beginning"(?): The Myth of Changelessness in Baptist Life and Belief ', pp. 184-206.
[9] E.S. Gaustad, 'Toward a Baptist Identity in the Twenty-first Century', in W.H. Brackney (ed.), *Discovering Our Baptist Heritage* (Valley Forge, PA: American Baptist Historical Society, 1985), p. 85. The title of the volume itself indicates the situation. Baptist heritage is something that requires discovery, and so is not generally known.
[10] Cf. H.L. McBeth, *The Baptist Heritage: Four Centuries of Baptist Witness* (Nashville, TN: Broadman Press, 1987), pp. 49-60.

no single tradition, and so have been affected by diverse influences.[11] Baptist evolution has followed multiple and widely divergent trajectories, and so their development has aptly been described as 'diffuse'.[12] There is no normative benchmark by which to evaluate the various expressions of Baptist life. Baptists have not been inclined to think of their earliest forebears as 'masters' to which later generations must be apprenticed, even if the forebears are accorded a certain respect. Baptists have generally felt at liberty to depart from those who have gone before, though this is sometimes done unwittingly.[13] Thus, within Baptist life there is an enormous variety of beliefs and practices, many of which are mutually exclusive. The United States, for instance, is home both to the ardently Calvinistic Primitive Baptists, and also the Pentecostal Freewill Baptists. This diversity is repeated around the globe.[14]

The fact of this multiplicity stems as well from our second factor. Also contributing to crises in Baptist identity has been the temperament that has characterized many in this part of the Christian family. 'We are a practical people...', noted Southern Baptist historian C. Penrose St. Amant, 'theological and historical interests have not been paramount'.[15] This is perhaps the more serious factor, and when it is coupled with an increasing pragmatism which is evident in Baptist life and thought, the situation is compounded.[16] Wilken's work cautions us that at stake in this general lack of theological and historical interest is the Baptist memory. With Baptist memory at risk, so too is the hope of helpful engagement of the question of Baptist consciousness and Baptist identity.

Since these two factors, especially the first, create a persistent difficulty in the development of Baptist memory, they also create a need for persistent attentiveness to the status of that memory. Yet this attentiveness is often absent. While one would suspect that this would lead to greater uncertainty about their identity, the opposite has ironically been true. Rather often, Baptists rest claims about their identity upon accepted articulations of Baptist memory and consciousness stemming from only

---

[11] Cf. W.S. Hudson, 'By Way of Perspective', in W.S. Hudson (ed.), *Baptist Concepts of the Church* (Philadelphia, PA: Judson Press, 1959), p. 11; and B.J. Leonard, *Baptist Ways: A History* (Valley Forge, PA: Judson Press, 2003), pp. 1-15.

[12] W.H. Brackney, '"Commonly (Though Falsely) Called...": Reflections on the Search for Baptist Identity', *Perspectives in Religious Studies* 13.4 (Winter, 1986), p. 68.

[13] See again the essay in the current volume by Thompson.

[14] E.g., V. Teraudkalns, 'Episcopacy in the Baptist Tradition', in the current volume provides a striking example of this diversity in Eastern European Baptist life.

[15] C.P. St. Amant, 'Southern Baptists: Unity in Diversity', *Baptist History and Heritage* 7.1 (January, 1972), p. 20.

[16] On such pragmatism in the United Kingdom, see P. Shepherd, 'The Baptist Ministers' Journal, 1946–1992', *Baptist Quarterly* 35.5 (January, 1994), pp. 253-54.

certain segments of the Baptist past without delving into the story to discover other possibilities. The result has been the confinement of Baptist memory and consciousness in clichés that, while perhaps containing an undeniable element of truthfulness, over generalize and so truncate the rich complexity that lies at the heart of Baptist heritage. Baptists thus fictionalize their past and, in creating a stable and controllable identity for their forebears, over simplify them.[17] Thus Eric Ohlmann's lament remains appropriate: 'Not knowing what rightfully belongs to our heritage, we are inadvertently and recklessly discarding some priceless heirlooms.'[18]

This is one of many reasons for the necessity of the on-going work of critical historical study. The comments of two eminent twentieth-century British historians highlight this and set out clearly what this collection of essays is striving to do. A.J.P. Taylor, in his 'Foreword: Second Thoughts' to his provocative and controversial *The Origins of the Second World War*, dismisses the reaction to the first edition, stating, 'it is the fault of previous legends which have been repeated by historians without examination'.[19] Historical research, as every one knows who has labored to practice it, depends on the interpretation of the extant sources and also the mastering of the work of previous scholars on the subject. In fact, historical research combines interaction with both primary and secondary sources. Yet an inherent danger in all historical study is that the contemporary historian over-relies on the secondary sources and repeats any errors or weaknesses in them.

Similarly, in his re-examination of the historiography of the origins of the Seven Years War, the great Cambridge historian and Methodist, Herbert Butterfield, shows that many scholars had simply repeated the mistaken assumptions of their predecessors. Butterfield speaks of the 'historian's blind eye' whereby he or she overlooks evidence which does not fit into the story they want to tell.[20] Further, historians can also fall into the trap of trying 'to poke the new evidence into the old structure of story, instead of reducing the whole narrative to its primary materials and then putting the pieces together again in a genuine work of

---

[17] See Berry, *The Hidden Wound*, pp. 49-50.

[18] E.H. Ohlmann, 'The Essence of the Baptists: A Reexamination', *Perspectives in Religious Studies* 13.4 (Winter, 1986), p. 83.

[19] A.J.P. Taylor, *The Origins of the Second World War* (London: Penguin, 2nd edn, 1964), pp. 8-9.

[20] H. Butterfield, 'The Reconstruction of an Historical Episode: The History of the Enquiry into the Origins of the Seven Years War', in *Man on His Past: The Study of the History of Historical Scholarship* (Cambridge: Cambridge University Press, 1955), pp. 158-59.

reconstruction'.[21] He warns of the danger of relying uncritically on the work of previous historians—and we might add, however eminent they might be and how highly we might respect them—and 'adding [any] new facts to the old ones, poking them into the acquired structure, pushing them into the margin of the old story, or leaving them as particles, only to be noted in parenthesis'. In short, it is incumbent on historians not to accept uncritically the work of their predecessors: 'It is easy to think that we are being faithful and merely transcribing the evidence when unconsciously we are running the evidence into an ancient mould. The moulds themselves tend to become the most rigid parts of our history. It is necessary to remember that they need to be constantly re-examined.'[22]

We might say that the majority of Baptist theological and historical projects are to some degree quests for a discovery and articulation of Baptist identity. Yet with this attenuated Baptist memory, and so consciousness, Baptists risk their work taking on the characteristics Berry attributes to the art of a divided person.

> The art of a man divided within himself and against his neighbors, no matter how sophisticated its techniques or how beautiful its forms and textures, will never have the communal *power* of the simplest tribal song.[23]

This volume of essays seeks to recover a sense of communal power through an interrogation of certain portions of the Baptist past. We cannot approach exhaustiveness, but hope rather to '(enact) a small fragment of an endless process',[24] and so create a new awareness in order to form and inform Baptist memory and consciousness. Taylor was too good a historian not to realize that his own work was also open to revision in the light of new evidence. He realistically remarked, 'These legends have a long life. I suspect I have repeated some.'[25] Likewise, the essays presented here are not offered as the final word on any of the subjects explored, but as a combined exercise in re-examining Baptist history, life and thought.

The goal is not, and cannot be, the identification or definition of a normative Baptist historical identity. To attempt this would be to

---

[21] Butterfield, 'Reconstruction', p. 159. One of the best known examples of this work of historical reconstruction within the field of church history is in the study of the English reformations. See C. Haig (ed.), *The English Reformation Revised* (Cambridge: Cambridge University Press, 1987); E. Duffy, *The Stripping of the Altars: Traditional Religion in England c.1400–c.1580* (New Haven, CT: Yale University Press, 1992); and C. Haigh, *English Reformation: Religion, Politics, and Society under the Tudors* (Oxford: Clarendon Press, 1993).

[22] Butterfield, 'Reconstruction', p. 162.

[23] Berry, *The Hidden Wound*, p. 49. Italics original.

[24] Berry, *The Hidden Wound*, p. 50.

[25] Taylor, *Origins of the Second World War*, p. 9.

perpetuate the oversimplification of Baptist existence. We attempt, rather, to engage the complexity on several levels, and so offer some degree of redress of the second factor noted above. In the process, the essays will offer clarifications, corrections, and even challenges to some of the clichés, the legends, regarding the Baptist past that are often perpetuated. This we will do on several, often overlapping, levels. These very levels, though, reflect the range of questions concerning the Baptist past.

We are grateful to Larry J. Kreitzer for allowing us to use as the title for this book a title of an as yet unpublished essay,[26] for in brief compass it sets out exactly the aim of this volume. The essays address basic questions and ideas concerning various aspects of Baptist existence. Taylor's 'legends' and Butterfield's 'moulds' are what we have termed 'myths'. Taylor is also credited with having once said that 'History does not repeat itself; historians repeat each other.'[27] This is how the legends/moulds/myths are perpetuated, but '[d]estroying these legends', whatever they might be, 'is a service to historical truth'.[28] While many of the chapters examine various myths within the Baptist tradition, they also deal with areas on which little work has, to date, been done. This is the area of 'historiography'.

The essays are historiographical in that they address basic questions of historical development, while others explore what we might call the 'shape' of Baptist life, the practices in which Baptists have engaged and the ways in which these practices have shaped their life. Finally, and as a corollary of their congregational polity, Baptists have maintained that persons are important in their own right, not simply as a part of a larger collective identity. Thus Baptists care about their forebears personally, wanting to know them as well as possible, much as members of families research and learn their family trees. Thus engagement with historiography and myths permeates the chapters offered here. It would have been possible to arrange them in a variety of different ways, but the basic pattern followed has been to move from the broader views which address Baptist life on a larger scale from historical, theological and philosophical perspectives, to more specific and strictly historiographical studies.

We wish to thank all the contributors for the time they have spent in research and writing and we hope that the result will be a stimulus to further work in Baptist history, life and thought.

---

[26] L. Kreitzer, 'Recycling History or Researching History?: Baptist Beginnings in Oxford according to Roger Hayden—An Assessment' (2004). This is part of a larger project Dr Kreitzer is working on into the origins and history of Baptists in Oxford.

[27] Michael Stanford, *A Companion to the Study of History* (Oxford: Blackwell, 1994), p. 150.

[28] Taylor, *Origins of the Second World War*, p. 9.

CHAPTER 1

Confessional Identity, Denominational Institutions and Relations with Others: A Study in Changing Contexts

John H.Y. Briggs

In a world which is claimed to be post-denominational it is surprising how enduring the reality of denomination is. In Britain, the nomination of a priest who lives in a same sex partnership, albeit now celibately, to a suffragan bishopric has led to much discussion of both the fragility of the Anglican Communion and how that communion can be saved from schism.[1] Last year I found myself in the strange position for a Baptist of being the rapporteur of the World Council of Churches' Special Commission on relations with the Orthodox. Two perceptions of the Orthodox mind struck me forcefully. The first was that since most Protestants seemed to be able to participate in one another's celebrations of the Lord's Supper, they were *de facto* one denomination, or as our Orthodox friends put it 'one communion', whereas they, the Orthodox—because as yet there is not inter-communion between the Eastern and the Oriental—were two families!

The other perception related to post-denominationalism. It was their total inability to develop a sympathetic understanding of how modern Protestants will move from one denomination to another, with little searching of conscience, in their search for a pattern of satisfying worship, an affirming congregation and a preaching ministry they find nurturing, particularly when they move locations. But this we know to be true. You can test it out in any congregation you care to choose, and almost certainly you will find a large part of the congregation have moved into that fellowship from other traditions.

---

[1] Since first writing this the debate in the Anglican Communion has moved on, as large and expanding provinces in the south have questioned developments in North America, in terms of the consecration of a bishop living in a homosexual relationship in the USA and the development of a liturgy for blessing same-sex unions in Canada. Such differences threaten to divide the Anglican Communion at a time when the Baptist World Alliance has witnessed the withdrawal of the Southern Baptist Convention from its fellowship over alleged liberalism in the world body.

Learning the faith of your fathers and developing loyalty to that faith tradition seems to count for very much less today that it did fifty or a hundred years ago. A certain mobility between traditions, however, has always existed, and one of the major complaints of Dissenters who valued their inherited Puritan high churchmanship was that the evangelical revival was bringing into their churches, and perhaps more significantly into their pulpits, those who were not schooled in Puritan theology or ecclesiology.

Jaroslav Pelikan long ago put the problem of the inter-relationship between Spirit and structure within the history of the church into sharp focus: 'Spirit there was, or at any rate could be', he affirmed, 'in the structures of the church; but when the distinction between spirit and structure was blurred, as it had been both by medieval prelates and by medieval theologians, those very structures were crushed by a literalism that was death dealing as well as dead.' Notwithstanding this affirmation, he shows that Luther had to learn that there could be no church which was only Spirit without structures. The need for structures was inevitable: either existing structures had to be renewed or new ones created.[2] But such structures had to serve the energies of the Spirit and not be deployed to imprison them. An example of spirit without structure might be seen in the dissipation of the Revival energies of George Whitefield. Its present day heir, the Countess of Huntingdon Connexion, is small beer when compared with world Methodism, that Methodism which was afforded effective governance by Jabez Bunting.

Early Confessions, Assemblies and Associations

My principal concern is to disengage the story of those confessing the name of Baptist as part of their spiritual obedience, from the institutional organizations and networks—the structures—which have from time to time served groups of believers within this confession. Indeed, in more recent times when organization has become ever more sophisticated there has developed the danger of confusing the two phenomena: the confession and spiritual experience on the one hand, and the institutional apparatus which seeks to promote their interests on the other.

The problem of developing a common identity might be thought to have existed from the earliest years because Baptists had a fractured disposition from the very beginning, which made for difficulty in developing a sense of common mission and fellowship. Older historians stressed differences concerning the doctrines of grace and election, but more recent studies have noted the divisions that existed around the issue

---

[2] J. Pelikan, *Spirit Versus Structure: Luther and the Institutions of the Church* (London: Collins, 1968), pp. 8 and 31.

of how to re-establish right baptismal practice when all existing church officers had abandoned apostolic practice. Thus, for these historians, the issue becomes one about succession of ministry.[3] The issue was whether any kind of respect was due to pre-existing institutions or whether radical rediscoveries of what was believed to be apostolic practice justified wholly new beginnings. So, initially, John Smyth and Thomas Helwys were of the latter persuasion, and hence Smyth's se-baptism before baptizing the other members of his expatriate congregation. Later, Smyth came to question the rightness of such action. Thus the revisionist Smyth joined the Waterlander church in Amsterdam to the consternation of Helwys who continued to uphold the rightness of Smyth's new beginning. Interestingly when the Particular Baptists adopted immersion as the proper mode of baptism in January of 1641/2 they too proceeded by way of se-baptism, deploying similar justification for their initiative.[4]

But from the early years some need for structures was seen to exist. In the seventeenth century provision was made by the General Baptists in their confession of 1678 for the convoking of General Councils or Assemblies. Such gatherings, it was argued, provided 'the best means under heaven to preserve unity, to prevent heresy, and [provide] superintendency among or in any congregation whatsoever within its own limits, or jurisdiction'.[5] The Particular Baptists also jointly expressed their faith in a succession of confessions from the *London Confession* of 1644 onwards with the 1689 variation reaffirmed by the representatives of 107 churches in England and Wales. Ernest Payne's comment is well targeted when he deduces, 'Associations, Synods, Unions and Assemblies of churches are not to be regarded as optional and secondary. They are the necessary expression of Christian fellowship, a necessary manifestation of the church visible. The local congregation is not truly a church if it lives an entirely separate life.'[6]

Payne goes on to cite John Owen's *True Nature of a Gospel Church* (1689) on the argument that it was widely influential amongst Baptists. Owen very clearly indicates the need for local churches to engage in mutual communion, one with another. But beyond that, he asserts that

---

[3] See S. Wright, 'Baptist Alignments and the Restoration of Immersion, 1638-44': 'Part 1', *Baptist Quarterly* 40.5 (January, 2004), pp. 261-83, 'Part 2': *Baptist Quarterly* 40.6 (April, 2004), pp. 346-68.
[4] J.H.Y. Briggs, 'The Influence of Calvinism on Seventeenth-Century Baptists', *Baptist History and Heritage* 39.2 (Spring, 2004), p. 15.
[5] *The Orthodox Creed* of the General Baptists of the Midlands, Buckinghamshire, Hertfordshire, Bedfordshire and Oxford, 1678, as cited by E.A. Payne, *The Fellowship of Believers: Baptist Thought and Practice Yesterday and Today* (London: Carey Kingsgate Press, enlarged edn, 1952), p. 27.
[6] Payne, *Fellowship of Believers*, p. 31.

No Church therefore is so Independent, as that it can always, and in all Cases, observe the Duties it owes unto the Lord Christ and the Church Catholick, by all those Powers which it is able to act in itself distinctly, without conjunction with others. And the Church that confines its Duty unto the Acts of its own Assemblies, cuts itself off from the Church Catholick; nor will it be safe for any Man to commit the Conduct of his Soul to such a Church.

The point is still further reinforced: 'And every Principle, Opinion, or Persuasion, that inclines any Church to confine its Care and Duty unto its own Edification only; yea, or of those only which agree with it in some peculiar practice, making it neglective of all due means of the Edification of the Church Catholick is Schismatical'.[7] Not only, then, was it necessary for local congregations to associate together with those of the same confession and polity, but more than that the need was perceived for some even wider instrument to express the unity of the church. Our seventeenth-century ancestors were already aware of the significance of the ecumenical question challenging their relationship with other groups of believers.

The Early Articulation of Aspirations towards Wider Relationships

One Baptist who gave particular shape to that question was the General Baptist messenger, Thomas Grantham, who as early as 1678 opined, 'When it shall please God to put into the Hearts of the Rulers of the Nations, to permit a Free and General Assembly, of the differing Professors of Christianity, for the finding out of Truth, we trust that some of the Baptized Churches will (if permitted) readily make their appearance with others to help on that needful work.'[8] This was clearly a concern that did not die as illustrated by Carey's 1805 often repeated 'pleasing dream' proposal for a conference of Christians of all denominations to meet in Cape Town in 1810 and every few years thereafter. This proposal was spelt out in greater detail in a letter to Andrew Fuller in 1806 in which Carey posed the question,

> Would it not be possible to have a general association of all denominations of Christians, from the four corners of the world, kept there [the Cape of Good Hope] once in about ten years? I earnestly recommend this plan, let the first meeting be in the Year 1810, or 1812 at furthest. I have no doubt it would be attended with very important effects; we could understand one another better, and more entirely enter

---

[7]   John Owen, *The True Nature of a Gospel Church* (1689 edn), pp. 234 and 251, quotations from p. 251, cited by Payne, *Fellowship of Believers*, pp. 31-32.

[8]   Thomas Grantham, *Christianus Primitivus* (1678), Book II, Ch 10, p. 143, cited by H. Leon McBeth, *The Baptist Heritage: Four Centuries of Baptist Witness* (Nashville, TN: Broadman Press, 1987), p. 518.

into one another's views by two hour conversations than by two or three years of epistolary correspondence.[9]

Fuller was not impressed by such an idealistic proposal. He was much more in tune with the realist Carey who argued that the urgency of the missionary vision suggested that 'in the present divided state of Christendom, it would be more likely for good to be done by each denomination engaging separately in the work, than if thy were to embark upon it conjointly'.[10] Initially the Baptist Missionary Society was happy to receive general evangelical support from London Independents and Anglican evanglicals such as William Wilberforce, Henry Thornton, Thomas Scott and John Newton. The saintly John Broadly Wilson, the society's treasurer from 1826 to 1834, although baptized as a believer by Isaiah Birt at Plymouth Dock, was a member of Rowland Hill's congregation, and therefore strictly speaking remained an Anglican. While Joseph Butterworth, son of the Rev. John Butterworth, Baptist minister in Coventry but himself a leading Methodist layman, and therefore presumably Arminian in theology, played a leading role in early BMS assemblies. Fuller rebuffed J.D.G. Pike of the New Connexion on two occasions when he offered support to the infant missionary society. The first was when he suggested that the BMS might accept a candidate from the New Connexion to serve with the society, the second when he suggested that the New Connexion might form an auxiliary to provide financial and prayer support to the society. The BMS's position as the *Particular* Baptist Missionary Society was not to be compromised in this way. Fuller could not afford to let it be suggested that Fullerism was crypto-Arminianism.[11] Happily the Serampore missionaries were more welcoming and encouraged the General Baptist Missionary Society to develop their work in neighbouring Orissa. Even within the early history of the missionary society there was a debate going on between a wider and a narrower understanding of denomination: were the Baptists one denomination or two?

Not only, then, did the life of the people of God require structures both for the good governance of the local church but for the mutual

---

[9] William Carey to Andrew Fuller, Calcutta, 15 May 1806, cited by Kenneth Scott Latourette, 'Ecumenical Bearings of the Missionary Movement and the International Missionary Council', in Ruth Rouse and Stephen C. Neill (eds), *A History of the Ecumenical Movement, 1517-1948*. Volume 1 (Geneva: World Council of Churches, 3rd edn, 1986), p. 355 n. 2. The original is preserved in the vestry of St Mary's Baptist Church, Norwich.
[10] B. Stanley, *The History of the Baptist Missionary Society, 1792-1992* (Edinburgh: T&T Clark, 1992), p. 20.
[11] J.H.Y. Briggs, *The English Baptists of the Nineteenth Century* (A History of the English Baptists, 3; Didcot: Baptist Historical Society, 1994), p. 100.

relationship of those churches. From the beginning, also, there existed a consciousness of the need to relate beyond denominational boundaries with other Christian bodies. Attempts to secure national means of relating were complemented by the establishment of a series of regional associations amongst both Particular and General Baptists from the 1650s onwards, though most of them were running into difficulties by the middle of the eighteenth century.[12] The Eastern Association Letter of 1777 took upon itself not only the task of defending the 'primitive discipline [of] Associating', which, it confessed, had of recent years 'been degraded from its pristine dignity', but also of suggesting that regional associations, each comprised of about ten to fifteen churches, become the building bricks out of which a national organization could be constructed. Beyond that they also pressed the issue of a general assembly of all the Nonconformist churches in the United Kingdom. This was a proposal that was to lie on the table for over a hundred years until the formation of the National Free Church Council in 1892.[13] For many years, co-operation in mission within the family of the Free Churches seemed the most promising way forward for ecumenical co-operation in England. Much has been achieved, with a widespread acceptance of one another's memberships and ministries, and a long history of sharing in one another's ordinations. Today these things are rather cast into the shadow by wider ecumenical relationships even though these have not the depth of history or acceptance that the older Free Church relationship offered, and indeed still offers.[14]

The Impact of the Evangelical Revival at Home and Abroad

The Evangelical Revival, both through its direct impact on English Christendom and in giving birth to the modern missionary movement, profoundly changed denominational relationships in England. It was, for example, at one of the founding meetings of the [London] Missionary Society that David Bogue preached his famous sermon in which he declared that the crossing of denominational divides in founding the

---

[12] W.T. Whitley, 'Association Life till 1815', *Transactions of the Baptist Historical Society* 5.1 (1916), pp. 19-34.

[13] Payne, *Fellowship of Believers*, pp. 34-35. On the origins of the National Free Church Council and Baptist involvement in it, see E.K.H. Jordan, *Free Church Unity: History of the Free Church Council Movement 1896–1941* (London: Lutterworth Press, 1956), pp. 17-76; D.W. Bebbington, *The Nonconformist Conscience: Chapel and Politics 1870–1914* (London: George Allen & Unwin, 1982), pp. 61-83; Anthony R. Cross, 'Service to the Ecumenical Movement: The Contribution of British Baptists', *Baptist Quarterly* 38.3 (July, 1999), pp. 108-109.

[14] The author writes as the currently serving Convener of the Free Churches Group in England.

society had witnessed 'the funeral of bigotry'.[15] On the mission field the same kind of language was in vogue. An editorial in the *Friend of India*, under the title of 'Union among Christians', stressed the importance of Christian unity if the gospel was to make any impact on heathen India: 'shame, indeed will it be for us, if we waste on the unimportant questions of party strife, those energies which ought to be employed against the common enemy'.[16] In Calcutta Baptist and Congregationalist missionaries and Anglican chaplains regularly met for united prayer at Henry Martyn's pagoda on the Hooghly: 'As the shadow of bigotry never falls upon us here, we take sweet counsel and go together to God's house as friends'. This was privileged experience: 'The utmost harmony prevails and a unity of hearts unknown between persons of different denominations in England.'[17] But even this produces its problems for it enabled William Ward to persuade the other Serampore missionaries to open the communion table at Serampore, to the consternation of the closed communionist Andrew Fuller at home.[18]

On his arrival in India, the newly consecrated Bishop Heber wrote to Marshman a letter which combined ecumenical aspirations with realism as to actual differences of doctrine. Referring to a copy of a college report he had received, Heber writes, 'I have seldom felt more painfully than while reading your appeal on the subject of Serampore College, the unhappy divisions of those who are the servants of the same Great Master! Would to God, my honoured brethren, the time were arrived when not only in heart and hope, but visibly we shall be one fold, as well as under one shepherd!' Notwithstanding these aspirations the bishop indicated that in the interim he judged his energies best spent in co-operative action with those with whom he was in total, not partial, agreement. But he added, 'Surely the leading points which keep us asunder are capable of explanation or softening.' These Heber identified as episcopal church

---

[15] Deryck W. Lovegrove, *Established Church, Sectarian People: Itinerancy and the Transformation of English Dissent, 1780-1830* (Cambridge: Cambridge University Press, 1988), p. 37, and J. Bennett, *Memoirs of the Life of the Revd David Bogue, DD* (London: F. Westley and A.H. Davis, 1827), p. 274.

[16] *Friend of India* 7 September 1837, cited by E. Daniel Potts, *British Baptist Missionaries in India: The History of Serampore and its Mission, 1793-1837* (Cambridge: Cambridge University Press, 1967), p. 58.

[17] Ruth Rouse, 'Voluntary Movements and the Changing Ecumenical Climate', in Rouse and Neill (eds), *History of the Ecumenical Movement*, I, p. 311.

[18] Carey personally dissented but accepted the judgment of the majority. Fuller warned that the majority were wandering in 'the mazes of carnal thinking'. Ward wrote to Fuller, 'That it is the duty of all saints to hold communion together at the Lord's Table is as clear a truth to me as that all men are sinners. If this be not the spirit of the whole New Testament, I was never in anything more mistaken.' Cited by Potts, *British Baptist Missionaries*, p. 51.

government and 'the admission of infants to the Gospel Covenants', both of which he believed had either dominical or apostolic authority. Could he not, the bishop asked, discuss with Marshman and Carey 'in the spirit of meekness and conciliation the points which now divide us, convinced that, if a reunion of our churches could be effected, the harvest of the heathen would ere long be reaped, and the work of the Lord would advance among them with a celerity of which we now have no experience'.[19] Carey reported favourably on this to Fuller, rejoicing in 'the utmost harmony between all the ministers of all denominations'. Heber had immediately to travel to other parts of his vast diocese which meant that although the Baptist missionaries replied positively to his invitation it could not be immediately followed up.[20]

Consensus and Conflict amongst Evangelicals

However, ecumenical relations were not quite as amicable as such quotations suggest, and one can quite as easily compose a list of comments evidencing conflict and lack of trust as much as those expressing harmony. The culture of establishment and of dissent were in essential conflict. Potts comments on the great social gulf separating the Oxbridge chaplains of the East India Company from artisan dissenting missionaries like Carey. Carey, himself, commented on the lack of hospitality he initially received from the Anglicans.[21] This was fortified by Fuller warning Marshman that friendship with the chaplain, Claudius Buchanan, might be 'purchased too dear', 'that you are in great danger of being drawn into his worldly, political religion... Beware of the counsel of this Mr Worldly-wise man'.[22] The chaplains also left evidence of their thinly veiled contempt for the scholarship of men like Carey and Marshman. Even Henry Martyn wrote a note in his private journal that he longed for the company of some of his Cambridge friends to engage in Bible translation, as they were 'so much more fit in point of learning than any of the Dissenters are', with their lack of a classical education. Later the Anglican chaplains wanted to put an Anglican clergyman in charge of the Serampore translations. In effect they wanted to requisition the Serampore premises which had been built or purchased entirely at the

---

[19] G. Smith, *The Life of William Carey: Shoemaker and Missionary* (London: John Murray, 1887), p. 281. Also cited in J.C. Marshman, *The Life and Times of Carey, Marshman and Ward: Embracing the History of the Serampore Mission* (2 vols; London: Longman, Brown, Green, Longmans, and Roberts, 1859), II, pp. 292-93.

[20] Smith, *Life of William Carey*, p. 282.

[21] Carey comments on an occasion when Brown offered no refreshment even though he was aware Carey had walked five miles in the sun to meet him. Potts, *British Baptist Missionaries*, p. 51.

[22] Potts, *British Baptist Missionaries*, p. 53.

expense of the Baptist missionaries. The Serampore trio refused to be ousted, and Ward confided to his journal 'a dreadful collision took place' which led Buchanan to deprive Serampore of 'part of the meagre funds he had allowed them from money raised in their name throughout India'.[23]

The Baptist missionary, John Chamberlain, believed that Daniel Corrie, associate of Henry Martyn and later evangelical Archdeacon of Calcutta and first Bishop of Madras, harboured prejudices against the Baptist missionaries and reported in May 1815 to Fuller on what he thought was his attitude: 'We are Dissenters and worse, Baptists, and as we do not support the church we, of course...are Democrats, demagogues and enemies to the state!! More intent on making proselytes than Christians.'[24] Thomas Thomason, local secretary of the Church Missionary Society gave evidence of hostility between Baptist and Anglican missionaries because, he said, the Baptists preach that the Anglican Church was not a 'pure church', which, of course, they would also deduce from Baptist denial of infant baptism as true baptism. This was the context for Robert Hall's championing of open communion, which was how he sought to defend the unity of the evangelical faith, notwithstanding differing views

---

[23] Potts, *British Baptist Missionaries*, pp. 54-56. The whole issue of Bible translation proved fraught with difficulty. The first issue raised was that of the linguistic competence of the Baptist missionaries. Lt Col. Kennedy spoke of the Serampore missionaries as 'a set of narrow-minded, tasteless, money-making bigots' whose work violated every standard of proper translation. Such slanders were, however, condemned by William Greenfield, the Cambridge orientalist and translator who was himself a Congregationalist, who contrariwise argued that Carey's 'stupendous learning' had become 'the theme of admiration and praise from the shores of the Ganges to the banks of the Thames'. Only later did they move to the more particular issue concerned with the way they translated the Greek βαπτίζω to mean immerse. The Bible Society also began employing others to do work that Carey had already done, and poached his native assistants by offering much higher salaries. However, when Buchanan departed in 1810, there was a deliberate attempt to bury the past and act in union in the common cause, with Serampore receiving a just proportion of the funds raised. But in 1818 a new crisis emerged when the Bible Society required that Carey and colleagues would have to submit future translations to a panel of judges. Carey was unprepared to submit years of labour to the transitory judgment of those not wholly expert. Notwithstanding this the BFBS continued to make available some funds to Serampore. In 1821, William Ward is found praising the objectives of the BFBS, arguing that the union amongst Christians it had achieved was 'one of the sublimest spectacles exhibited since the primitive age [of Christianity]', though he did note that difficulties had arisen because of the growth of 'the spirit of party'.

[24] Cited in Timothy George, *Faithful Witness: The Life and Mission of William Carey* (Leicester: Inter-Varsity Press, 1992), p. 164. George omits the last sentence which can be found in Potts, *British Baptist Missionaries*, p. 58.

of baptism. In India, discordant beliefs put in jeopardy cordial cooperation or even sympathy between the two groups.[25]

A common evangelicalism did not hold the Indian missionary community together, notwithstanding all the goodwill with which the enterprise started. Most painful was the crisis relating to the translation of the scriptures already alluded to. Up until 1827 the Bible Society had been happy to support the Serampore missionaries in their translation of the scriptures. During this period they produced some fifteen to sixteen versions which deployed immersionist language. Until this time Paedobaptists were happy to circulate the Serampore version, even though it did not fully accord with their deepest convictions. But there then arose a complaint from the Calcutta auxiliary of the British and Foreign Bible Society, which around 1830 replaced the earlier Corresponding Committee. No missionaries were to participate in the counsels of the new body which now, under, it was said, episcopal pressure, refused to use the Carey-Yates translation, choosing the earlier version of Ellerton. Notwithstanding the objection to immersionist language, the society did not scruple to support versions which translated the baptismal verb by terms such as 'to sprinkle' or 'to pour'. In 1833 the Bible Society replied to a request by BMS missionaries for help with a Bengali New Testament with terms which the Baptist constituency found wholly unacceptable: '"That this Committee would cheerfully afford assistance to the missionaries connected with the Baptist Missionary Society in their translation of the Bengalee New Testament, provided the Greek terms relating to baptism be rendered, either, according to the principle adopted by the translators of the English authorized version, by a word derived from the original, or by such terms as may be considered unobjectionable by the other denominations of Christians composing the Bible Society."'[26]

The very foundation of the Church Missionary Society was itself a rejection of the non-denominational hopes of the London Missionary Society, that is to say it came into being to offer a structure for church-conscious evangelicals in pursuing their missionary endeavours. And as late as 1829 John Henry Newman was elected co-secretary of the Society's Oxford Auxiliary. Anglican evangelicalism was also wrestling with that central issue of spirit and structure, as the 'noisy professors' so

---

[25] Thomas Thomason to Joseph Pratt, 31 August 1815, cited by Potts, *British Baptist Missionaries*, p. 58, who argues that Thomason's harsh judgment was countered by the record of experience.

[26] 'A Letter to the Right Hon. Lord Bexley, President of the British and Foreign Bible Society', in John Howard Hinton, *The Theological Works of the Rev. John Howard Hinton, M.A..* Volume VI: *Lectures, Sermons, and Controversy* (6 vols; London: Houlston & Wright, 1864–65), p. 480. See Marshman, *Life and Times of Carey, Marshman and Ward*, II, pp. 440-47.

called, with their journal *The Morning Watch*, canvassed an emotionally charged evangelicalism. Increasingly fascinated by new revelations and adventist themes, in its radical extremism it frightened the more conservative evangelicals, who expressed their concern in the *Christian Observer*, and increasingly took resort to speaking ever more reverentially of structures, that is to say of church order. David Newsome perceptively comments, 'By the 1820s their anxiety had become so intense that occasionally they seem to use the language of the High Churchmen.'[27] The Albury Circle, with the founding of the Catholic Apostolic Church led even more directly into a revived sacramentalism and a new church order. Whilst such movements may explain why Anglican evangelicals felt a need to distance themselves from dissenting co-religionists, the founding of what was to become the Liberation Society promoted a strenuous anti-establishmentarianism which also strained relationships.

The Pan-Evangelical Thesis and its Critics

Thus difficult relationships in the missionary world were reflected by conflicts at home between Church and Dissent which put a common evangelicalism at a discount. Here two simultaneous truths have to be confessed. On the one hand, a common evangelicalism brought the denominations together, but at the same time denominational structures were developed which kept evangelical Christians in separate camps. Thus, the debate that exists between scholars such as R.H. Martin and W.R. Ward on the one side, and David Thompson, with support from David Hempton, on the other.[28] Ward puts it like this: 'As men cheerfully shouldered the great missionary burden, denominational divisions seemed to crumble... There was great euphoria at the end of bigotry and the triumph of Catholic Christianity.'[29] Martin, believing that whilst theologies could divide, experience could unite, asserts that 'The Gospel World, for all its bickerings, was a cultural and ideological entity.' Even theologically whilst there was agreement about the great doctrines of the

---

[27] D. Newsome, *The Parting of Friends* (London: John Murray, 1966), pp. 9-12.

[28] R.H. Martin, *Evangelicals United: Ecumenical Stirrings in Pre-Victorian Britain, 1795–1830* (Studies of Evangelicalism, 4; Metuchen, NY: Scarecrow Press, 1983); W.R. Ward, *Religion and Society in England, 1790–1850* (London: B.T. Batsford, 1972); D.M. Thompson, *Denominationalism and Dissent, 1795–1835: A Question of Identity* (Friends of Dr Williams's Library, 39th Lecture; London: Dr Williams's Trust, 1985); and David Hempton, *Methodism and Politics in British Society, 1750–1850* (London: Hutchinson, 1984), pp. 89-90 and 97.

[29] Ward, *Religion and Society*, p. 45. By 'Catholic Christianity' he means an evangelicalism that spanned the boundaries of the Church of England and the several dissenting denominations.

faith such as justification, Martin speaks of 'a conflict of mind and heart' amongst Anglican evangelicals. 'They knew in their minds that they were respectable and loyal members of the national establishment, but they also knew in their hearts that they were evangelicals sharing with other evangelicals a common faith and experience that transcended denominational barriers and theological parties.'[30]

Ruth Rouse calls attention to the phenomenon she calls 'Borderland' churches, that is congregations which were neither established nor dissenting. She also quotes from John Newton's diary for 1776 where he makes the following allusion to a meeting of the Northamptonshire Association of Baptist ministers: 'Yesterday ministers remaining in town breakfasted with me. We seemed all mutually pleased. I thank Thee, my Lord, that Thou hast given me a heart to love Thy People of every name: and I am willing to discover Thine image without respect of parties.'[31] Leigh Richmond, the Anglican secretary of the Religious Tract Society (1812–27), said of his committee, 'Although as individuals the Committee belonged to various denominations of Christians and both thought and worshipped accordingly, yet in the common principles of vital religion, in love for the souls of their fellow men, in a disposition to let every lesser consideration merge in the grand effort to promote evangelical piety throughout the world, they constituted but one denomination.'[32]

As in the mission field so at home, joint endeavours and shared experiences argued for an unrestricted communion table, or so argued Daniel Turner, John Colett Ryland and Robert Robinson.[33] They were later followed by men of the stature of Robert Hall and F.A. Cox. Defending a closed table were Abraham Booth amongst the older men, who also included Carey and Fuller in their number, Joseph Ivimey and Joseph Kinghorn, so table fellowship as much as the theology of grace could prove divisive. However, in Martin's judgment the advocacy of an open table was important: 'The Impact of this irenic theological development...was very important for the future pan-evangelical impulse.'[34] But, as indicated, for many Baptists this was an ecumenical

---

[30] Martin, *Evangelicals United*, pp. 14-16.

[31] John Newton, *Newton's Diary* (1776), quoted in William W. Addison, *The English Country Parson* (London: Dent, 1947), p. 118, cited by Rouse, 'Voluntary Movements', p. 315.

[32] Cited by Martin, *Evangelicals United*, pp. 159-60.

[33] Martin refers to the writings of Daniel Turner and John Ryland in pseudonymous tracts whose common text suggests a collaborative authorship of 1772. See R.W. Oliver, 'John Collett Ryland, Daniel Turner and Robert Robinson and the Communion Controversy, 1772–1781', *Baptist Quarterly* 29.2 (April, 1981), pp. 77-80. Rylands' title interestingly refers to communion 'between True Believers of all Denominations'.

[34] Martin, *Evangelicals United*, p. 19

step too far, for so to open the table seemed to offer some kind of legitimacy to infant baptism, and accordingly they stood aloof from the great pan-evangelical endeavours of the 1780s. Even Andrew Fuller campaigned strenuously for closed communion and just before his death achieved much success in closing Baptist communion tables to those not baptized as believers from 1812 onwards, though Thompson questions the evidence for this.[35]

W.R. Ward sets these changes within a secular context. 'The outpouring of undenominational religion at the end of the eighteenth century left a mark upon English popular faith which has never been effaced, but within a generation its institutional mechanism had been broken up by denominations pressing the clan spirit as a counterpoise to the divisive effects of social tension.' As a result, 'the social strains of the 'forties which on the continent toppled the monarchies, in England divided the churches'.[36]

David Thompson questions whether, in contradiction of Martin, 'the growing power of denominationalism', seen in the acquisition of bureaucracies, both official and unofficial, does in fact reflect the rejection of common evangelical experience and aspirations. Instead he asserts that 'the new denominationalism was the result of the Revival and not a reaction against it'. The bureaucracy, argues Thompson, was not bureaucracy for its own sake, but bureaucracy developed for the sake of effective evangelism both at home and overseas. Thus he poses the question, 'is it plausible to suppose that the undenominational spirit of evangelism could have expressed itself on the scale it did, if it had not been carried by agencies largely denominational in character? To emphasise spirit and underestimate institutions is simply romantic.'[37]

When evangelical unity took on a more institutional form in the founding of the Evangelical Alliance in 1846 it did so largely by side stepping difficult issues of ecclesiology and forming a coalition on the basis of individual commitment. Theological issues were not wholly ignored as seen in Spurgeon's attack upon evangelical clergy using Prayer Book language in the baptismal service which they knew to be untrue. In provocative language, he argued, 'Where union and friendship are not cemented by truth, they are an unhallowed confederacy. It is time that there should be put to an end the flirtations of honest men with those who believe one way and swear another.'[38] This called forth from Lord

---

[35] Thompson, *Denominationalism and Dissent*, p. 29 n. 65; cf. Martin, *Evangelicals United*, p. 62.
[36] Ward, *Religion and Society*, pp. 2, 4, cf. pp. 44-53.
[37] Thompson, *Denominationalism and Dissent*, pp. 13-15
[38] C.H. Spurgeon, 'Baptismal Regeneration: A Sermon [1864]', *Metropolitan Tabernacle Pulpit* 10 (Pasadena, TX: Pilgrim Publcations, 1981 [1885]), p. 317.

Shaftesbury the judgment that Spurgeon was 'a very saucy fellow'.[39] On the basis of such sectarian comments, Spurgeon was compelled to withdraw from membership of the Evangelical Alliance for a period of time. Internationally, the most divisive issue was that of slave-holding, which for many made fellowship with slave owning evangelicals in the American South quite impossible.

The Language of Denomination

The use of the word 'denomination' to describe a religious group seems to have been of mid- to late-eighteenth century coinage, and indeed itself the product of the Revival. The earliest usage of the word in this sense cited by the *Oxford English Dictionary* is by James Hervey who, in 1746–47, glosses the *Te Deum* to speak of Christ opening the kingdom of heaven 'to all generations and denominations of the faithful'.[40] The saintly James Hervey, although first influenced by John Wesley at Oxford, under the influence of Whitefield adopted Calvinist views. Ordained in the Church of England, he served as curate to his father at, and subsequently as rector of, Weston Favell in Northamptonshire. This brought him within the circle of Anglican evangelical friends who gave support to those forward-looking Baptist ministers who founded the Northamptonshire Association. By contrast, in another early usage Gladstone distances the Established Church from such voluntary religious associations: in his *The State in Relation to the Church*, he confidently asserted in 1838, 'We have no fear for the Church of England in her competition with the denominational bodies around her.'[41] Alan Gilbert, as we shall see, argues that Gladstone could not have been more fundamentally wrong in his judgment, or at best was exercising a nostalgic view which did little to help the Church of England to resolve its problems in the new urban-industrial world born of the machine.

Following H. Richard Niebuhr, Gilbert sees the 1830s and 40s as marking a movement from church–sect to denominational relationships. Niebuhr sees this as a function of compromise as both sects and established churches, through the processes of history, come to recognize one another as legitimate representations of the Christian faith.[42] It is not

---

[39] See Briggs, *English Baptists of the Nineteenth Century*, p. 49.

[40] *The Oxford English Dictionary*. Interestingly, Charles Grant of the East India Company wrote to Henry Creighton on 6 June 1795 indicating that John Thomas, by obtruding 'his own *denominational* view with offensive pertinacity', alienated himself from other Europeans in India. See Potts, *British Baptist Missionaries*, p. 9.

[41] 'Denomination', in *The Oxford English Dictionary*.

[42] A.D. Gilbert, *Religion and Society in Industrial England: Church, Chapel and Social Change 1740–1914* (Themes in British Social History; London: Longman, 1976), pp. 142-43.

necessary to accept the whole of the Niebuhrian analysis to see the usefulness of such a use of language, namely that a denomination is a church, or indeed for that matter, a sect 'which has accommodated itself to the reality of permanent competition with other "churches" in its territory'.[43] That, I think, is helpful whilst the larger claim that denominationalism 'represents the accommodation of Christianity to the cast-system of human society'[44] would be more difficult to demonstrate, even though it might seem to sanctify some aspects of church-growth theory. When, however, Niebuhr talks about the impact of generational succession on the history of sects he makes a better point. Because of the nature of things, their very existence demands of sects the development of educational and disciplinary instruments. Arguably, too, 'As generation succeeds generation, the isolation of the community from the world becomes more difficult',[45] Niebuhr also points out how an asceticism of expenditure coupled with a strong sense of the seriousness of work causes capital accumulation with all the associated responsibilities of wealth. Administratively he points to the significance of the emergence of a clerical elite who needed to be trained to the task with the consequent need for training institutions—all indicate ways in which 'the sect becomes a church' or at least a 'denomination'.

Notwithstanding Gladstone's protest noted above, Gilbert argues that 'as early as the beginning of the Victorian era Anglicanism had begun to function essentially as a denominational phenomenon'. For this purpose he appeals to Keble's 1833 *Assize Sermon*. In this, Keble frankly confesses, that henceforth the Church of England was 'only to stand, in the eye of the State, as one sect among many, depending for any pre-eminence she might appear to retain, merely upon her having a strong party in the country'.[46] Gilbert further invokes Peter Berger to complete the explanation of what he regards as this critical change in denominational relations. The Church of England, he argues, in the second quarter of the nineteenth century moved towards 'a typically denominational solution to its intolerable situation as an ex-monopolistic institution in a pluralistic society'. For whereas, in Berger's words, a church can behave 'as befits an institution exercising exclusive control over a population of retainers', a denomination must organize itself so as

---

[43] Gilbert, *Religion and Society*, p. 142.
[44] H. Richard Niebuhr, *The Social Sources of Denominationalism* (New York: Meridian Books, 1957 [1929]), p. 6.
[45] Niebuhr, *Social Sources*, p. 20.
[46] From the Advertisement to the first edition of John Keble, *Assize Sermon on National Apostasy* (1833), quoted in D. Bowen, *The Idea of the Victorian Church* (Montreal: McGill University Press, 1968), p. 43, and cited by Gilbert, *Religion and Society*, p. 142.

'to woo a population of consumers, in competition with other groups having the same purpose'.[47]

The Baptist Denomination

Be that as it may, what did it mean for Baptists to adopt denominational forms? The formative date here would seem to be 1832, although the General Union of 1813 provides a pre-history. But Josiah Conder, writing in the *Eclectic Review* for 1837, argued that earlier the Baptist Missionary Society afforded a *de facto* Baptist Union. For many years, he contended, 'the annual meetings of the several missionary societies have exhibited the heart-cheering spectacle of a metropolitan convocation of each denomination; convened, not to decree articles of faith, not to adjust, by usurped authority, intestine controversies, not to issue canons of excommunication, but to convert or to sanction plans for the propagation of the faith of Christ'.[48]

On such a basis the history of the denominations as denominations can be taken back to the 1790s. However, even the union of 1832 was minimalist in the demands it made. The summary Calvinistic headings embodied in the constitution of 1813 were replaced by the basis for union being agreement 'in the sentiments usually denominated evangelical'. The first two articles of the new body concerned the extension of unity and brotherly love, both in relationships, and in promoting the cause of Christ in general and the Baptist denomination in particular. The second two articles had to do with the collection and distribution of information—of churches, societies, colleges and other institutions, the distribution to be through the preparation of an annual report which would include comment on the state of the denomination. This denomination was not to be confined to churches in membership with the Union but was to contain information from all who would supply it. The Suffolk and Norfolk New Association of Baptist Churches [Strict] wrote a minute in 1836: 'The Association respectfully decline joining the Baptist Union but will be ready, at all times, to communicate to the Secretaries statistical information which they may require.'[49] From 1832 to 1844 this information was published in successive *Baptist Union Reports*, and from 1845 to 1859 in a series of *Manuals of the Baptist Denomination*: the language is significant. After 1861 these became

---

[47]   Gilbert, *Religion and* Society, p. 143, citing P.L. Berger, *The Social Reality of Religion* (London: Faber, 1969), pp. 137-38.

[48]   'The Congregational and Baptist Unions', *Eclectic Review* n.s. 1 (1837), pp. 180-81, cited by Thompson, *Denominationalism and Dissent*, pp. 12-13.

[49]   *Circular Letter* (1836), cited by Kenneth Dix, *Strict and Particular: English Strict and Particular Baptists of the Nineteenth Century* (Didcot: Baptist Historical Society/Strict Baptist Historical Society, 2001), p. 129.

Baptist Handbooks and so they remained until 1973 when another change took place and they were replaced by a new series of *The Baptist Union Directory*. This was a significant change of language and format for whereas earlier series had listed churches by geographical county and cross-referenced them to associations, the listing after 1973 is by association. This did not allow for the listing of non-associating churches or those in associations not in membership with the Baptist Union.[50] This might be argued as a move towards administrative tidyness. It could equally be argued as a confusion of vision: to confuse the denomination with the structures of the Union.

Notwithstanding the statistical energies of James Belcher who gave eight years to shaping the new Union, and was responsible for collecting the information, it was an uphill task: in 1834 he gave it as his opinion that less than half of the Baptist churches in the United Kingdom belonged to associations. This, of course, raises the question whether a wholly independent Baptist church was in its life true to Baptist insights as to the nature of the church. Payne notes that the 182 Baptist ministers who attended the meetings of the Anti-Corn Law League in Manchester in 1841 was a larger number than had, to that time, gathered for meetings of the Baptist Union.[51] The Union only slowly secured influence within the denomination, and that from the need for local churches to associate together for mission rather than any top-down synodical authority. The issue was in part a theological one and had to do with the extent to which the church was necessarily mission-orientated. If that were so then absolute independence served it ill. Independence had to be married to associating. Deryck Lovegrove puts it well when he writes: 'In spite of this contemporary emphasis upon the resilience and vitality of the congregational principle, it is impossible to ignore the real movement towards association, interdependence and the growth of external authority: a policy not capable of reversal, arising as it did from the

---

[50] Study of these documents reveal some interesting features. For example, for the whole period that manuals were produced the much-trumpeted Northamptonshire Association was not apparently in membership with the Union, at least it is not so listed, a distinction only shared with Shropshire for the whole period. As late as 1972 full details are given of the Strict Baptist Associations, namely, Cambridgeshire and East Midlands Union; Metropolitan Strict; Suffolk and Norfolk Strict; as well as the Baptist Union of Ireland and its associations. It also saw the loss of information on such historic chapels as the Metropolitan Tabernacle and Charlotte Chapel, Edinburgh. This may be seen as completing a process that Kenneth Dix sees as dating back to 1890. Dix, *Strict and Particular*, p. 3.

[51] E.A. Payne, *The Baptist Union: A Short History* (London: Baptist Union of Great Britain and Ireland, 1959), p. 70, citing R.G. Cowherd, *The Politics of English Dissent: The Religious Aspects of Liberal and Humanitarian Reform Movements from 1815 to 1848* (New York: New York University Press, 1956), pp. 134-35.

confluent pressures of permanent social change and the practicalities of evangelism.'[52]

By contrast, some Strict Baptists, notably William Gadsby and J.C. Philpot, 'were totally opposed to associations of any kind, regarding them as oppressive and dictatorial'.[53] Here the denominational function was fulfilled by the adoption of the Gospel Standard Articles of Faith, subscription to the *Gospel Standard* as a periodical, and the use of *Gadsby's Hymns,* and later access to the Gospel Standard Aid societies.[54]

The General Baptists in the New Connexion were much better organized than their Particular Baptist cousins. Thus, much of the denominational organization with which J.H. Shakespeare sought to strengthen the Baptist denomination during his strategic secretaryship had New Connexion origins. J.B. Pike complained of the Particular Baptists' lack of a denominational consciousness. They were 'a multitude of independent churches—in many instances isolated churches'.[55] John Clifford agreed. The Particular Baptists were 'not one connexion but a series of connexions under one denomination, not a "body" with a well-defined or easily discovered head, speaking with one voice, but three or four "bodies", separated by prodigious differences though agreeing on baptism'. He judged that Particular Baptists came in three varieties: 'Strict', 'Spurgeonic' and 'Miscellaneous', the latter category finding 'their visible centre in the Colleges of Regent's Park, Bristol and Rawdon and the Baptist Missionary Society'.[56]

An important aspect of denominational consciousness was concern first for churches founded by the modern missionary movement in which Baptists were convinced they had played a critical part. No less important were the new Baptist churches emerging across Europe. Most of these—especially those in Denmark and in Germany—were strict communionist and so related to both churches in the Baptist Union and those separate from it. More generally this was to be an important aspect of denominational consciousness, a sense of being part of a worldwide family. This became one dimension of ecumenical relations that needed to be born in mind when responding to initiatives to draw closer to other denominations in the United Kingdom such, for example, as Archbishop Geoffrey Fisher's 1946 invitation to try out something of the idea of regional episcopacy within their own structures.[57] Baptists believed that they ought not to act unilaterally on such issues, indicating that the other

---

[52] Lovegrove, *Established Church, Sectarian People,* p. 29.
[53] Dix, *Strict and Particular,* p. 140.
[54] Dix, *Strict and Particular,* pp. 60 and 109-12.
[55] *Minutes of the Ninety-Third Annual Association of the New Connexion of General Baptists* (1862), pp. 44-45.
[56] *General Baptist Magazine* (January, 1877), p. 2.
[57] See Payne, *Baptist Union,* pp. 219-21 and 292-303.

European Baptist Unions would have to be consulted. Other denominations may speak of their world families, none, I think, have as widespread global relations as do the Baptists, especially through the European Baptist Federation and the Baptist World Alliance.

You will have observed already the increasing use of the language of denomination in the early nineteenth century, followed by the institutional forms which translated denominational consciousness into reality, even to the extent of the officers of the Baptist Union sometimes mistaking the actuality of denomination and union, of confessional family and institution, even an institution whose purposes were essentially missionary.

Baptists and Cognate Groups

John Rippon in his *Baptist Annual Register* for 1793 produces a grand 'Catalogue of the Professors and Ministers among the Baptists within, and out of the United Netherlands...for 1791', to which he added details of churches in Prussia, Poland, Lithuania, Saxony, the Rhineland, Switzerland, France and Russia.[58] The difficulty for the historian is that none of these several hundred listed churches in continental Europe were Baptists; rather they were Mennonite congregations conceptualized by Rippon as part of a larger baptistic cousinage. The same *Baptist Annual Register* carried a dedication printed on an unnumbered page after the title page, 'to all the baptized ministers and people in America, England, Ireland, Scotland, Wales, the United Netherlands, France, Switzerland, Poland, Russia, Prussia and Elsewhere...in serious expectation that before many years elapse (in imitation of other wise men) a deputation from all these climes will meet probably in London to consult the ecclesiastical good to the whole'. Clearly Rippon conceived of continental Mennonites as part of the Baptist family and on this basis the youthful Baptist Missionary Society visited their churches in Holland to secure financial support for the infant society. Rippon also conceived of an international conference embracing all these churches.

When the foundation Congress of the Baptist World Alliance was called together in London in the summer of 1905, Rippon's argument could not be used to make the Mennonites into honorary Baptists, though there were a few representative Mennonites present. The Baptist presence in Europe was now to be found in those communities who owed their existence to the missionary vision of J.G. Oncken and other pioneering Baptists in continental Europe.[59] Mennonite statistics had accordingly to

---

[58] J. Rippon, *Baptist Annual Register* 1 (1790–93), pp. 303-18.

[59] See Richard V. Pierard, 'Germany and Baptist Expansion in Nineteenth-Century Europe', in D.W. Bebbington (ed.), *The Gospel in the World* (Studies in Baptist History and Thought, 1; Carlisle: Paternoster Press, 2002), pp. 190-208; Ian M. Randall, '"Every

be dropped. But nothing daunted, Shakespeare added another group that he thought belonged to the Baptist family, namely the Disciples of Christ, so in his compilation of global Baptist statistics Shakespeare included some one million Disciples of Christ 'who correspond with us in faith and practice'.[60] Several attempts were in fact made to try and effect a closer mode of working together between Baptists and Churches of Christ in Britain in the 1940s and 1950s—but these foundered on the problematic area of open membership in many Baptist churches, even though for many this made for ecumenically-friendly structures.[61] One practical step which received considerable support was the printing of the list of Churches of Christ in the *Baptist Handbook*, but in the end nothing came of these conversations.

'Handbook' ecumenism was achieved with respect to Baptists' Congregational cousins, but here there was a considerable history of common endeavour. There were, for example, the honourable history of some united associations such as the Bedfordshire Union of Christians and the Huntingdonshire Union of Independent and Baptist Churches. There were also a number of union churches of different periods of foundation. In late nineteenth-century Baptist handbooks you will find printed under the heading of 'Ecclesiatical Information' the names of the officers of the Congregational Union, a full list of members of the Congregational Board, and a list of London Congregational ministers, a practice which in part at least continued well into the twentieth century. In some years details of new Congregational churches appeared in the Architectural Appendix. The information on five different Methodist bodies, the Church of England and the Roman Catholic Church was, by contrast, sparse.

In 1886 the two Congregational denominations held united or in part parallel assemblies. These meetings affirmed their essential unity and suggested strategies for joint church planting. Significantly, Charles Williams' presidential address concerned 'A Plea for Union amongst Baptists', pleading for the Calvinist and the evangelical Arminian branches of the family to come closer together, suggesting in particular that Lancashire and Cheshire and the East Midlands experiment in having

---

Apostolic Church a Mission Society": European Baptist Origins and Identity', in Anthony R. Cross (ed.), *Ecumenism and History: Studies in Honour of John H.Y. Briggs* (Carlisle: Paternoster Press, 2002), pp. 281-301.

[60] John Rippon, *Baptist Annual Register*, p. 1. 1.25 million Disciples were included in the list of 'Baptised Believers', in J.H. Shakespeare (ed.), *The Baptist World Congress. London, July 11-19, 1905. Authorised Record of Proceedings* (London: Baptist Union Publication Department, 1905), p. 343.

[61] See Anthony R. Cross, *Baptism and the Baptists: Theology and Practice in the Twentieth Century* (Studies in Baptist History and Thought, 3; Carlisle: Paternoster Press, 2000), pp. 67-68 and 148-50.

associations which embraced both traditions was also proving very successful in London. In 1901, the two bodies again met in joint assembly. Alexander McLaren forthrightly opened the session: 'Fact and logic are both outraged by the names of the two Unions which join in this Assembly. The division into Congregationalists and Baptists is faulty...for all Baptists are Congregationalists. We are the closest of kin among the Free Churches.' Significantly the joint assembly was suspended on the Wednesday morning for the laying of the foundation stone of the new Baptist Church House. Joseph Parker, who in 1887 had spoken on 'The Larger Congregationalism', in 1901 indicated the way some Congregational minds were developing in speaking about 'The United Congregational Church'.[62] That aspiration after a larger churchmanship as over against the essential federalism of both the Baptist and the Congregational Unions perhaps explains why the two branches of the Congregational family failed to meet at the altar. Instead, the two differing polities within the Reformed faith found one another in the formation of the United Reformed Church in 1972, which in 1981 was joined by the larger part of the former Churches of Christ.

If these were groups to court, or with which to claim common interests, one group was in the first place deliberately distanced, namely the Plymouth Brethren. This was not always easy. Scholars studying defences of believers' baptism in the nineteenth century have not always distinguished accurately Baptist from Brethren writings.[63] Dawson Burns, die-hard opponent of wholly merging the New Connexion with the appropriate regional Particular Baptist associations, warned, 'There are high-Calvinistic Baptists, Spurgeonic Baptists, Scotch Baptists, and Plymouth Brethren Baptists, who would not join in any common organization.'[64] In promoting what he thought might be an Evangelical Alliance, the Congregationalist, John Angell James, set before it the fight against infidelity and the three 'Ps'—Popery, Puseyism and Plymouth Brethrenism. But that was a very early comment from the 1840s. The open Brethren at least were soon accepted as a legitimate aspect of evangelical Nonconformity. No great debates, I think, have ever taken place with Brethren leadership; indeed it would be difficult to identify whether anyone had a sufficient mandate to represent them. But if the histories of local congregations are studied, or indeed the obituaries of those who have faithfully served the Baptist ministry, it will become clear that significant numbers of our members have a Brethren background. This, coupled with the weak ecclesiological loyalties of many Baptists, explains why many Baptist churches work with and give support to non-

---

[62]   See Briggs, *English Baptists of the Nineteenth Century*, pp. 238-39.
[63]   E.g., J.R.C. Perkin, 'Baptism in Non-Conformist Theology, 1820–1920, with special reference to the Baptists' (DPhil thesis, Oxford University, 1955).
[64]   *General Baptist Magazine* (January, 1891), pp. 44-45.

denominational missionary societies. Societies like the Overseas Missionary Fellowship, formerly the China Inland Mission, the Sudan Inland Mission and the World Evangelization Crusade, find much of their support in Baptist churches. Such congregations may well be indicating that they put their evangelicalism before their Baptist convictions

The early nineteenth century witnessed the emergence of formal denominational organizations, though these were so weak that it was not until the early-twentieth century that, with the development of more effective institutional instruments both nationally and internationally, denominational consciousness became a commonplace. Shakespeare sought successfully to exploit this in terms of 'Making a Denomination'. This leads Brian Haymes to suggest, in reviewing Peter Shepherd's recent study of Shakespeare's influential General Secretariat, that 'Shakespeare seemed to assume that the denomination and the Union could be equated'.[65]

Defining a denomination is not easy. Richard Niebuhr distinguished it both from a sect and a church. Both the dogmatic exclusiveness of the sect and the parish inclusiveness of the church have had to accommodate to an ecclesiastically pluralist scene. In these senses, denominations are both good and bad in so far as they represent an incomplete unity: whilst they are an instrument for churches associating together, all too often that has been against others. These were issues that J.H. Shakespeare was very aware of in so far as he helped Baptists to discover and serve one another. He would dearly have loved to have brought these same Baptists into a United Free Church,[66] and even that speculative body he came to envisage as a stepping stone to wider unity.

In Shakespeare's world Baptists had recently largely overcome Calvinist–Arminian differences and the terms of communion at the expense of excluding the Strict and Particular Baptists at one extreme, and the Old General [Unitarian] Baptists at the other. In this sense the denomination remained larger than those who accepted denominational disciplines. Shakespeare's effectiveness was in providing those Baptists prepared to associate together with a means of strengthening their *mutual* corporate life. Such churches were also those prepared to enter into wider conversations with other Christians who they acknowledged as also working for God's kingdom. This wider question was also a dividing line for those who found it genuinely hard to admit the legitimacy of non-Calvinist, baptistic, congregational Christian witness, who continued the Strict Baptist tradition. At the same time, Shepherd argues there were new

---

[65] Brian Haymes, 'Shakespeare—the man who shaped our denomination', *Baptist Times* 24 April 2003, p. 17. See Peter Shepherd, *The Making of a Modern Denomination: John Howard Shakespeare and the English Baptists 1898–1924* (Studies in Baptist History and Thought, 4; Carlisle: Paternoster Press, 2002).

[66] Shepherd, *Making of a Modern Denomination*, e.g., pp. 93-138 and *passim*.

denominations, though they often denied the language, emerging which shared Baptist views of baptism, the urgency of the missionary task and congregational polity, who were cut off from Baptist life by the increasing denominationalism associated with Shakespeare's endeavours.[67]

This is the 'crossroads' around which Shakespeare lived his life and which Peter Shepherd so helpfully illuminates. Shakespeare became General Secretary of the Baptist Union in 1898, seven years after the New Connexion had brought to an end its separate existence encouraging its member churches to join with Particular Baptists in forming or joining regional associations which acknowledged no confessional divide. Shakespeare himself came from a broad tradition within the Particular Baptist part of the family, but he soon recognized that the New Connexion had developed better instruments for expressing extra-congregational action. During his secretariat the Baptist Union acquired a new prestigious headquarters, from which a centralized leadership, now full-time in its service, began to operate. He, with the support of able laymen, raised funds to support local ministries which were now accredited and recognized through due procedure by the Union. Funds were also developed to provide pensions for retired ministers, and an adapted form of *episcope* put in place. With all this energy invested in the Union, the denomination became identified with it.

Alongside the older Free Church movement with its regional provincial support provided by local Free Church councils, Shakespeare worked for a federal council which derived its authority directly from denominational councils and synods. This Shakespeare saw as a stage to the securing of a United Free Church, but this was not to be.

No more successful, it is argued here, were his strategies for the denomination in the long term. Shepherd writes: 'The denomination thus embodied itself and became a meaningful ecclesiastical entity under the banner of the Union. As a strategy for dealing with decline this did not succeed.'[68] The need of the times was for more than the co-ordination of effort and resources that Shakespeare supplied. The danger was that the denomination would look to such centralization of endeavour as the answer to their problems: 'It seems unlikely that a denomination that owed its past vigour and growth to the local and the spontaneous could ever recover that vitality by means of institutionalism.'[69] But it is far from clear that denominations with less structure—either nationally or locally—have fared any better. It is also remarkable that within what some see as a post-denominational world, denominationalism is far from dead.

---

[67] Shepherd, *Making of a Modern Denomination*, p. 174. Such were the Brethren, Churches of Christ and Pentecostals.
[68] Shepherd, *Making of a Modern Denomination*, p. 170.
[69] Shepherd, *Making of a Modern Denomination*, p. 172.

Some denominations seek to overcome old schisms and to seek some kind of united church, but as quickly as denominations combine or die, others are brought into being, while loose federations of independent churches discover the need for the structures that serve to perpetuate denominational interests

As in the time of Luther the forces of renewal, born of the Spirit, still need structures and Baptists need the very best that can be devised, that is those most appropriate to missionary need. Such structures must be so constructed that they enable rather than restrict, release and refocus energies rather than impose uniformity. At the same time, *pace* Pelikan, care must be taken not to blur the distinction between structure and Spirit and mistake the one for the other, so that each may receive its proper due.

CHAPTER 2

Churches and the Church

Stanley K. Fowler

Introduction

For twenty-seven years I have served as a pastor and educator within the Fellowship of Evangelical Baptist Churches in Canada.[1] In those years of ministry among Fellowship Baptists, I have often heard leaders say, 'We are not a denomination—we are just a fellowship of autonomous churches.' I confess that I have always found this comment both amusing and frustrating, in that it assumes, contrary to normal usage, that a 'denomination' must be hierarchically-structured. While Fellowship leaders disavowed the label, the 'Historical Sketch' in the *Yearbook* began with these words: 'The Fellowship of Evangelical Baptist Churches in Canada is one of the largest evangelical denominations in Canada.'[2] So why have some of our leaders felt that it was necessary to make such anti-denominational statements? The answer is surely that many Baptists regard congregational autonomy as one of the most crucial elements of Baptist ecclesiology.

There is at least one other way in which this anti-denominational rhetoric has often puzzled me. Frequently the persons who affirm quite vigorously that we are 'not a denomination' but just a 'loose fellowship of independent (autonomous) churches' without any kind of centralized authority are the same persons who desire to restrict inter-church fellowship to those churches that adhere to a rather narrow confessional basis. It is not true in the Canadian context, but in similar Baptist contexts

---

[1] The Fellowship of Evangelical Baptist Churches in Canada was formed in 1953 by a merger of the Union of Regular Baptist Churches of Ontario and Quebec and the Fellowship of Independent Baptist Churches in Canada, two groups which had begun by secession from the Baptist Convention of Ontario and Quebec during the controversies of the 1920s. Initially the Fellowship was composed almost entirely of churches in Ontario and Quebec, but by 1965 it was a fully national body. It presently contains about 500 churches across Canada with a total membership of about 65,000 and an average Sunday attendance closer to 100,000.

[2] *The Fellowship Yearbook* (Guelph, ON: The Fellowship of Evangelical Baptist Churches in Canada, 1992), p. 43.

in the USA the same kind of autonomy-focused mindset is sometimes affirmed by those who withdraw fellowship from churches over something as narrow as the correct chronology of events surrounding the second coming of Christ. One would think that a loose fellowship of autonomous churches could tolerate a fair bit of diversity within the boundaries of basic orthodoxy, but the opposite is often true, and I have often wondered why this should be so.

Over the last few years I have been involved in various dialogues which have given me a new insight into this puzzling connection between a commitment to local autonomy and a commitment to a very narrow doctrinal basis for any formal association with other churches. I think it works something like this: in this ecclesiology, the real church is the local church, and anything beyond this is purely optional and justified on pragmatic grounds. Although there may be a theoretical affirmation of a universal church, this is really just an abstraction which lacks any kind of tangible structure in the real world which we experience. So in this view the burden of proof is on the one who wants to create formal structures beyond the local congregation, and since these structures are completely optional, their doctrinal basis is optional as well. In other words, we can make the basis as narrow as we wish without violating any biblical principles about the unity of the church, because we aren't dividing the real (local) church anyway. On the other hand, if one sees the universal church as a matter of biblical concern, and perhaps even sees the universal church as the primary reality which manifests itself in local expressions, then the burden of proof is on the one who wants to disconnect from other churches.

The idea that a strong doctrine of congregational autonomy or independence is central to Baptist practice is widely held, especially in North America. This can be seen in a recent book produced by conservatives within the Southern Baptist Convention (SBC), a collection of brief chapters explaining why various individuals have remained or become Baptists.[3] One leader of the past, F.H. Kerfoot, asserted 'that every local church has the right to govern itself', but allowed that those local bodies 'may, in mere matters of expediency, associate and co-operate in Christian work if they see fit'.[4] A current leader, James T. Draper, writes, 'A Baptist is one who recognizes the autonomy of the local church. There is no such thing as "the Baptist church."'[5] Paige Patterson, one of the architects of the conservative resurgence in the Southern Baptist Convention over the last two decades and currently the president of Southwestern Baptist Theological Seminary, argues that the

---

[3] T.J. Nettles and R. Moore (eds), *Why I Am a Baptist* (Nashville, TN: Broadman & Holman, 2001).
[4] Nettles and Moore (eds), *Why I Am A Baptist*, p. 50.
[5] Nettles and Moore (eds), *Why I Am A Baptist*, p. 55.

primacy of the local church is crucial as a foundation for reformation. He writes:

> I find in Baptist ecclesiology and polity the possibility for a grassroots referendum. Because Baptists rejected all forms of connectionalism, and Baptist churches, associations, state conventions, and national conventions are independent, autonomous entities, the people in the churches find it possible, though not easy, to rise up and say, 'We do not approve of the direction that our denomination is going, and we want this corrected.'[6]

Fred A. Malone points to the direct communication of the risen Christ to local churches in Revelation 2–3 and draws these inferences:

> This means that each local church has Christ as its head and has all the authority of his Word to govern its life, without being dictated to by another church or association of churches. If churches choose voluntarily to associate with one another, however, they must agree on the doctrines and practices concerning the purposes of their association in missions, literature publishing, ministerial preparation, and so forth (Acts 15).[7]

Al Meredith emphasizes (as do others) that autonomy does not nullify cooperation on a wider scale, but it does define the nature of that cooperation as purely voluntary and rooted in some specific commonality of purpose in mission. As he puts it, it is voluntary and task-related to such an extent that, 'any time we feel led, we can cease to cooperate with any of them and they with us'.[8] To put it another way, there is no permanent, ontological bond between the churches, only a temporary, teleological bond. The church, if it is affirmed at all (and it is not affirmed by all in the Baptist fold, given the impact of Landmarkism[9]), is only a concept in this system, not a tangible reality connected to the life of real churches and members.

The opinions noted above come from Southern Baptist conservatives, but Baptists farther to the left on the theological map affirm their own commitment to a strong doctrine of autonomy.[10] Although Paige

---

[6] Nettles and Moore (eds), *Why I Am A Baptist*, p. 72.
[7] Nettles and Moore (eds), *Why I Am A Baptist*, p. 140.
[8] Nettles and Moore (eds), *Why I Am A Baptist*, p. 148.
[9] For a description of Landmarkism and its impact on Baptists (Southern Baptists in particular), see H.L. McBeth, *The Baptist Heritage: Four Centuries of Baptist Witness* (Nashville, TN: Broadman Press, 1987), pp. 447-61.
[10] See, e.g., C.P. Staton (ed.), *Why I Am a Baptist* (Macon, GA: Smyth & Helwys, 1999). This book, a moderate complement to the conservative volume with the same title (see n. 2 above), features autobiographical answers to the title by twenty-six Baptists, and the contributions are liberally sprinkled with terms like 'soul liberty' or 'voluntarism' or 'freedom'. In general, the contributors seem to see themselves as the

Patterson has argued that the conservative rise to power in the Southern Baptist Convention since 1980 was a result of congregational autonomy and a 'grassroots referendum', others have argued that the takeover was in fact rooted in a *denial* of such autonomy. Alan Neely, for example, has argued cogently that recent events in the SBC have completed a long process which 'moved the Southern Baptist Convention from a voluntary confederation of congregations to being a connectional Church'.[11] The most crucial element in the conservative takeover was no doubt the power vested in the president to appoint the Committee on Committees (who in turn appointed the boards of SBC-owned organizations), and by electing conservative presidents throughout the 1980's the boards of the SBC entities were thoroughly reoriented.[12] It may indeed be true that the move to the right was in line with the sentiments of the grassroots majority, but it could hardly be said that the process emphasized congregational autonomy and the freedom of the minority. The top-down nature of the transformation can be seen in the fact that although the six seminaries (owned by the national convention) have been conservatively reoriented, the colleges and universities (owned by state conventions) have not followed the same path. In fact, several of the colleges and universities have created seminaries as alternatives to the SBC schools.[13] *The Baptist Faith and Message*, the confessional statement of Southern Baptists, was first adopted in 1925 and later revised in 1963 in the aftermath of a doctrinal controversy at Midwestern Baptist Theological Seminary. As one part of the conservative consolidation of power, the statement has been revised in 1998 and 2000, and it now includes affirmations of the submission of wives to husbands in marriage and male-only pastoral ministry, views not held by many moderate Baptists. Although the confession is not technically binding on the congregations, it is now

---

defenders of Baptist freedom against the authoritarian 'fundamentalists' who now lead the Southern Baptist Convention.

[11] A. Neely, 'Denominationalism, Centralization, and Baptist Principles: Observations by a Somewhat Perplexed Baptist', *American Baptist Quarterly* 21.4 (December, 2002), p. 494.

[12] The story of the changes in the SBC has been told from several angles. For an insider account by one of the chief architects, see P. Pressler, *A Hill on Which to Die* (Nashville, TN: Broadman & Holman, 1999); for a conservative analysis and celebration, see Jerry Sutton, *The Baptist Reformation* (Nashville, TN: Broadman & Holman, 2000); for a moderate analysis and lament, see Bill J. Leonard, *God's Last and Only Hope: The Fragmentation of the Southern Baptist Convention* (Grand Rapids, MI: Eerdmans, 1990).

[13] E.g., The Baptist Theological Seminary at Richmond (Virginia), Campbell University Divinity School (North Carolina), Truett Theological Seminary (Baylor University, Texas), M. Christopher White Divinity School (Gardner-Webb University, North Carolina), Wake Forest Divinity School (Wake Forest University, North Carolina), McAfee School of Theology (Mercer University, Georgia), Logsdon School of Theology (Hardin-Simmons University, Texas), and the Baptist Seminary of Kentucky.

being used as a litmus test in the seminaries and mission boards, thus leading to the charge of 'creedalism'.[14]

The fact is that Baptists all along the theological spectrum tend to assert the freedom of the congregation quite vehemently, but those at different places on the spectrum do so for very different reasons. Those on the right seek to preserve the churches from the imposition of a liberal agenda by a connectional church, and they use the motif of autonomy to argue for extensive and binding confessions of faith in whatever supra-congregational structures they choose to adopt. Since there is no such thing as 'the Baptist Church' anyway, they are not splitting the church by such doctrinal commitments. Those on the left end of the spectrum want to preserve the freedom of theologically diverse churches, and they accordingly reject the concept of binding confessions of faith and their imposition of a conservative agenda. The two sides both affirm the principle of association with other churches, but they differ in their choice of fundamental values for this extra-congregational cooperation. On the right doctrinal purity is a fundamental value, while on the left maximal connection is a fundamental value. To put it another way, one side emphasizes the freedom of the churches to create binding confessions for their cooperative ventures, while the other side emphasizes the freedom of the churches from such binding confessions. Still, both are concerned to preserve what they take to be a high view of local church autonomy.

I suggest that it is time to question the assumption shared by most Baptists that a strong doctrine of church autonomy is biblical, historically Baptist, and important for the health of the church. In what follows I want to show first that the idea that Baptists have always laid this kind of stress on church independence is in fact a myth—pervasive, but still a myth; second, that the biblical and theological support for this kind of autonomy is not strong; and third, that this fixation on autonomy is not conducive to the health of the church.

A Look at History

In my experience, many of those who are most vocal about 'Baptist distinctives' are in fact relatively ignorant of the actual history of Baptist thought and practice, notably that of the seventeenth and eighteenth centuries, and this is nowhere more evident than on the point of inter-church connections. Since the nineteenth century in America, one Baptist after another has declared that a commitment to radically independent churches has been an essential component of Baptist identity from the

---

[14] A.W. Wardin, Jr., 'Baptist Confessions: Use and Abuse', *American Baptist Quarterly* 21.4 (December, 2002), pp. 477-81.

beginning, but a brief look at the history of Baptist statements on the question reveals that this idea is in some ways a North American innovation arising out of the soil of American concepts of freedom.

One of the early Baptist associational confessions is the *First London Confession* of 1644, produced by seven Particular Baptist churches in London. The confession recognizes the authority of each congregation over many matters, for example, the appointment of church officers, but there is also a recognition that there ought to be a tangible connection between churches for their mutual benefit:

> And although the particular Congregations be distinct and severall Bodies, every one a compact and knit Citie in it selfe; yet are they all to walk by one and the same Rule, and by all meanes convenient to have the counsel and help one of another in all needful affaires of the Church, as members of one body in the common faith under Christ their onely head.[15]

Clearly there is a strong sense of the spiritual power present in each local church, but at the same time there is an equally clear sense that all the churches are part of one body as well, and that attachment affects more than attitude. Each church is to receive not only assistance as needed to carry on its ministry, but also counsel from other churches concerning the way in which they ought to carry out their ministry. And far from adopting an 'agree to disagree' attitude toward doctrinal differences, there is an affirmation that there is only one body of revealed truth to which the whole church ought to submit, and obedience to this 'Rule' is to be achieved not by each church independently interpreting the scriptures, but by mutual admonition with unity of faith as the goal.

In 1656 *The Somerset Confession* was adopted by a Particular Baptist association in western England, and it asserts

> That it is the duty of the members of Christ in the order of the gospel, tho' in several congregations and assemblies (being one in the head) if occasion be, to communicate each to other, in things spiritual, and things temporal (Rom. 15:26; Acts 11:29; 15:22; 11:22).[16]

This is a brief and modest statement of association with little in the way of details about what inter-church communion entails. Communicating in 'things temporal' has a fairly obvious referent, but it is not clear what would be involved with regard to 'things spiritual'. What is significant about this confession is its affirmation that such communion between churches is a duty, not an optional extra, this being entailed by their being in a real sense 'one' via their common attachment to Christ.

---

[15] W.L. Lumpkin, *Baptist Confessions of Faith* (Philadelphia: Judson Press, 1959), pp. 168-69.

[16] Lumpkin, *Baptist Confessions of Faith*, p. 211.

The most influential confession of early Particular Baptists was the *Second London Confession*, first adopted in 1677 and later republished in 1689 after the Act of Toleration. Chapter XXVI defines ecclesiology in fifteen paragraphs, beginning with an affirmation of the 'Catholick or universal Church' consisting of 'the Elect that have been, are, or shall be gathered into one, under Christ the head thereof'.[17] Local churches are composed of 'Saints by calling, visibly manifesting and evidencing (in and by their profession and walking) their obedience unto that call of Christ'.[18] Paragraph 7 affirms a high view of the spiritual power resident in each church:

> To each of these Churches thus gathered, according to his mind, declared in his word, he hath given all that power and authority, which is any way needful, for their carrying on that order in worship, and discipline, which he hath instituted for them to observe; with commands, and rules for the due and right exerting, and executing of that power.[19]

For many Baptists this high view of the local church is the ultimate word about the church, but in this confession it is penultimate at best. The final two paragraphs of Chapter XXVI spell out in some detail the necessity and benefit of tangible association with the wider body of believers:

> 14. As each Church, and all the Members of it, are bound to pray continually, for the good and prosperity of all the Churches of Christ, in all places; and upon all occasions to further it (every one within the bounds of their places, and callings, in the Exercise of their Gifts and Graces) so the Churches (when planted by the providence of God so as they may injoy opportunity and advantage for it) ought to hold communion amongst themselves for their peace, increase of love, and mutual edification.

> 15. In cases of difficulties or differences, either in point of Doctrine, or Administration; wherein either the Churches in general are concerned, or any one Church in their peace, union, and edification; or any member, or members, of any Church are injured, in or by any proceedings in censures not agreeable to truth, and order; it is according to the mind of Christ, that many Churches holding communion together, do by their messengers meet to consider, and give their advice in, or about that matter in difference, to be reported to all the Churches concerned; howbeit these messengers assembled, are not entrusted with any Church-power properly so called; or with any jurisdiction over the Churches themselves, to

---

[17] Lumpkin, *Baptist Confessions of Faith*, p. 285.
[18] Lumpkin, *Baptist Confessions of Faith*, p. 286.
[19] Lumpkin, *Baptist Confessions of Faith*, pp. 286-87.

exercise any censures either over any Churches, or Persons; or to impose their determination on the Churches, or Officers.[20]

There are several significant points in this confession's declaration concerning the nature and function of the churches. First is its use of the term 'Church' to denote the universal body of believers extended throughout both space and time. Second, there is a clear assertion of the obligation of the churches to participate in a tangible communion with the extended church. Third, there is a wide range of issues which are to be submitted to representatives of the church for discussion and counsel. Such matters may concern either doctrine or the administration of church life. They may involve differences between churches, or they may pertain to disunity within a particular church. They may involve an appeal of disciplinary actions taken by a church which are alleged to be unjust, thus asserting that while each church has power bestowed by Christ to carry out discipline of its members, those actions are not final in the sense that there is no wider body to which the church is accountable.

Now the confession makes it very clear that the decisions of the church at the association level cannot be imposed authoritatively on the individual churches, so we are not dealing here with a full-fledged presbyterian structure. The power of the wider body is that of moral suasion and advice, leaving the local church free to reject the counsel of the wider church. Nevertheless, it is clear that differences between churches or within a church are not to be accepted as final on the basis of local church autonomy, and the counsel of the wider body of Christ is to be respected rather than despised.[21]

In 1678 the General Baptists of England formulated *The Orthodox Creed*, which resembles the *Second London Confession* of the Particular Baptists in many ways but affirms a significantly higher view of the church. Article XXIX affirms the existence of the 'one holy catholick church' as the 'whole number of the elect',[22] and Article XXX defines true local churches as those in which 'the word of God is rightly preached, and the sacraments truly administered, according to Christ's institution, and the practice of the primitive church; having discipline and

---

[20] Lumpkin, *Baptist Confessions of Faith*, pp. 288-89.

[21] For an extended analysis of seventeenth-century Baptist ecclesiology in general and the *Second London Confession* (1677) in particular, see J.M. Renihan (ed.), *Denominations or Associations? Essays on Reformed Baptist Associations* (Amityville, NY: Calvary Press Publishing, 2001), especially the editor's chapters entitled 'A Reformed Baptist Perspective on Associations of Churches' and 'Reformed Baptist Associations: Primitivism, Scripture, and the Confession of Faith', pp. 43-78, 79-116. This book was produced especially for the Association of Reformed Baptist Churches of America, a group that affirms strict subscription to the Second London Confession.

[22] Lumpkin, *Baptist Confessions of Faith*, p. 318.

government duly executed, by ministers or pastors of God's appointing'.[23] These definitions of the church and the churches are essentially the same as those put forward by Baptists in general, but in its definitions of church officers and church councils this creed goes beyond the Baptist norm.

The creed asserts in Article XXXI that the official ministry of the church is threefold: 'Bishops, or Messengers; and Elders, or Pastors; and Deacons, or Overseers of the poor'.[24] While the elders and deacons are responsible for service in just the particular church by which they are chosen, bishops (messengers) 'have the government' of multiple churches, being chosen by vote of the members of those churches. Part of this governing authority is the power to ordain the elders/pastors of the individual churches, and each pastor must be careful that he does not act in such a way that he 'infringe the liberty, or due power, or office of his bishop'.[25] This concept of the office of bishop has never been widespread among Baptists, but it clearly shows that some kind of supra-congregational authority has been present among some Baptists.

Article XXXIX of the creed defines 'general Councils, or Assemblies' in a way which goes far beyond *Second London Confession* as an affirmation of the extended church:

> General councils, or assemblies, consisting of Bishops, Elders, and Brethren, of the several churches of Christ, and being legally convened, and met together out of all the churches, and the churches appearing there by their representatives, make but one church, and have lawful right, and suffrage in this general meeting, or assembly, to act in the name of Christ; it being of divine authority, and is the best means under heaven to preserve unity, to prevent heresy, and superintendency among, or in any congregation whatsoever within its own limits, or jurisdiction. And to such a meeting, or assembly, appeals ought to be made, in case any injustice be done, or heresy, and schism countenanced, in any particular congregation of Christ, and the decisive voice in such general assemblies is the major part, and such general assemblies have lawful power to hear, and determine, as also to excommunicate.[26]

It would be inaccurate to claim that this view of the power inherent in general assemblies has ever been normative among Baptist churches in general, but it stands as one view affirmed among early Baptists as they were finding their way toward a developed ecclesiology. If General Baptists had continued as a viable movement then this high ecclesiology might have become more common among Baptists, but with the decline of the General Baptists in the direction of Unitarianism in the eighteenth

---

[23] Lumpkin, *Baptist Confessions of Faith*, p. 319.
[24] Lumpkin, *Baptist Confessions of Faith*, p. 319.
[25] Lumpkin, *Baptist Confessions of Faith*, p. 320.
[26] Lumpkin, *Baptist Confessions of Faith*, p. 327.

century, the more modest associational views of the Particular Baptists became the norm. However, this more modest sense of the power of the church was still very different from later views which emphasized the radical independence of every church and in some cases lost all sense of the church as a universal body.

In America the first Baptist association was formed in Philadelphia in 1707, and this group of churches adopted the *Philadelphia Confession of Faith* in 1742. This confession was simply the *Second London Confession* with an additional two articles approving hymn-singing and laying on of hands (articles added in England by Benjamin and Elias Keach). Thus the pattern of relatively autonomous congregations with formal ties to associations with advisory powers and a kind of moral (but not formal) authority found its way into American Baptist life in its formative stages. The Philadelphia Association expanded to include churches from several states spanning hundreds of miles and formulated a plan for a national union of associations, but this plan never came to fruition for a variety of reasons, including fears that churches would lose their independence.[27]

Over time the robust evangelical Calvinism of the *Second London/Philadelphia Confession* became less dominant among Baptists in the United States, and in 1833 *The New Hampshire Confession* was produced, embodying a more moderate Calvinism and also a weaker sense of connection between churches and the church. The confession in fact includes no affirmation of the universal church at all, and the entire definition of a church is found in brief in the thirteenth article:

> [We believe] That a visible Church of Christ is a congregation of baptized believers, associated by covenant in the faith and fellowship of the Gospel; observing the ordinances of Christ; governed by his laws; and exercising the gifts, rights, and privileges invested in them by his word; that its only proper officers are Bishops or Pastors, and Deacons, whose qualifications, claims, and duties are defined in the Epistles to Timothy and Titus.[28]

This focus on the local church does not constitute a denial of a universal church (that would soon enter Baptist life via Landmarkism), but it does amount to a denial that tangible association beyond the local church is essential to a proper ecclesiological orientation.

The New Hampshire Confession became widely accepted as a model for later Baptist confessions in America, as can be seen by the adoption of much of its language in some twentieth-century statements of faith. One example is found in the affirmation of faith of the Baptist Bible Union of America, a fundamentalist renewal group founded in 1923 in opposition

---

[27] See McBeth, *Baptist Heritage*, pp. 240-41.
[28] Lumpkin, *Baptist Confessions of Faith*, pp. 365-66.

to liberalizing trends, especially within the Northern Baptist Convention (later American Baptist Convention, now American Baptist Churches). The statement lacks any affirmation of the universal church, the article entitled 'Of the Church' referring entirely to a local congregation in terms drawn almost verbatim from *The New Hampshire Confession*. In addition to the basic New Hampshire definition of a congregation, the article goes on to assert local autonomy in the strongest of terms:

> We hold that the local church has the absolute right of self government, free from the interference of any hierarchy of individuals or organizations; and that the one and only superintendent is Christ, through the Holy Spirit; that it is scriptural for true churches to cooperate with each other in contending for the faith and for the furtherance of the gospel; that every church is the sole and only judge of the measure and method of its cooperation; on all matters of membership of polity, of government, of discipline, of benevolence, the will of the local church is final.[29]

The reference to 'contending for the faith' as part of the content of inter-church cooperation shows the roots of this confession in the modernist–fundamentalist controversy, and the statement indicates that the fundamentalists saw this emphasis on local autonomy as a crucial part of the battle against heterodoxy, an emphasis which I have shown above in the thought of Paige Patterson (a more recent defender of orthodoxy).

The Southern Baptist Convention had been disinclined toward an official denominational confession of faith since its origin in 1845, but in the turmoil of the 1920's (admittedly much less severe in the South) the SBC adopted in 1925 *The Baptist Faith and Message*. It contained no affirmation of the universal church (which would have been impossible, given the influence of Landmarkism in the SBC), and its definition of 'a gospel church' adopted the language of New Hampshire. Although it contained no affirmation of a universal church, the confession devoted a separate article to the subject of 'co-operation' to define inter-church relations in this way:

> Christ's people should, as occasion requires, organize such associations and conventions as may best secure co-operation for the great objects of the Kingdom of God. Such organizations have no authority over each other or over the churches. They are voluntary and advisory bodies designed to elicit, combine and direct the energies of our people in the most effective manner. Individual members of New Testament churches should co-operate with each other, and the churches themselves should co-operate with each other in carrying forward the missionary, educational and benevolent program for the extension of Christ's Kingdom. Christian unity in

---

[29] Lumpkin, *Baptist Confessions of Faith*, p. 388.

the New Testament sense is spiritual harmony and voluntary co-operation for common ends by various groups of Christ's people.[30]

This kind of connection, then, is purely voluntary and pragmatically justified for missional purposes, and the cooperation in view may be rooted in congregational linkage (the 'convention' approach) or individual linkage (the 'society' approach). There is no sense of accountability to the wider church, only a sense of activity with other churches. It should also be noted that all of the wider bodies formed in this way are autonomous, so that a church may be a member of a local association, a state convention, and a national convention, but each of those three bodies is formed directly from the local churches. In this ecclesiology, the national convention is not equivalent to the aggregate of state conventions, or state conventions equivalent to the aggregate of local associations, and a local church may be a member at any one of the three levels without joining the other two. In practice that has never been normal, but that is the theoretical principle.

The Baptist Faith and Message has been updated three times in 1963, 1998 and 2000. Its current form retains virtually all the ecclesiological language of the original confession, both in the article defining the church and in the article defining appropriate cooperation. In the definition of a 'New Testament church', the words 'autonomous local' are added prior to 'congregation of baptized believers', so that if there is any modification at all, it is in the direction of a more emphatic declaration of autonomy.[31]

The Affirmation of Faith (adopted in 1953) of The Fellowship of Evangelical Baptist Churches in Canada (in which I serve) embodies this commitment to autonomy in a very striking way in its statement about the church. There is no affirmation at all of the universal church, and the description of a local church says this: 'We believe it is a sovereign, independent body, exercising its own divinely awarded gifts, precepts and privileges under the Lordship of Christ, the Great Head of the church.'[32] Here the New Hampshire language of 'gifts, rights and privileges' becomes 'gifts, *precepts* and privileges', which looks like an affirmation of unique commands or laws given by the risen Christ to each church. I am confident that no church in the Fellowship affirms that in fact, but no one seems to know exactly what is meant by 'precepts' in this affirmation.

---

[30] Lumpkin, *Baptist Confessions of Faith*, p. 397.
[31] The current form of the statement is found on the web site of the Southern Baptist Convention (www.sbc.net/bfm/bfm2000.asp).
[32] *The Affirmation of Faith* is found on the denominational web site (www.fellowship.ca).

These examples of the growing sense of local church autonomy and the functional insignificance (though generally not the theoretical denial) of the universal church illustrate the trajectory of Baptist ecclesiology in North America, but the trajectory in other anglophone contexts was sometimes very different. For example, a statement on 'The Baptist Doctrine of the Church' was approved by the Council of the Baptist Union of Great Britain and Ireland in 1948, and that statement includes the following affirmation of the universal church:

> Although Baptists have for so long held a position separate from that of other communions, they have always claimed to be part of the one holy catholic Church of our Lord Jesus Christ. They believe in the catholic Church as the holy society of believers in our Lord Jesus Christ, which He founded, of which He is the only Head, and in which He dwells by His Spirit, so that though manifested in many communions, organized in various modes, and scattered throughout the world, it is yet one in Him. The Church is the Body of Christ and a chosen instrument of the divine purpose in history.[33]

The description of local Baptist churches begins in this way:

> It is in membership of a local church in one place that the fellowship of the one holy catholic Church becomes significant. Indeed, such gathered companies of believers are the local manifestation of the one Church of God on earth and in heaven. Thus the church at Ephesus is described, in words which strictly belong to the whole catholic Church, as 'the church of God, which He hath purchased with His own blood' (Acts xx. 28). The vital relationship to Christ which is implied in full communicant membership in a local church carries with it membership in the Church which is both in time and in eternity, both militant and triumphant.[34]

As the description of local churches continues, the (Second London) 'Baptist Confession of 1677' is invoked as an accurate way to describe the way in churches are formed by the activity of Christ and the believing response of those to whom the gospel comes. Thus, the British Baptist Union's view maintained what was lost or submerged in much of North American Baptist thought, namely, the affirmation that there is in some sense one church in all the world, and that the logical movement is from that church to local manifestations in the churches.[35] That is very

---

[33] The statement is 'Appendix X' in E.A. Payne, *The Baptist Union: A Short History* (London: Carey Kingsgate Press, 1959). The section quoted here is found on p. 283.

[34] Payne, *Baptist Union*, p. 284.

[35] This strong sense of connection to the wider church and involvement in ecumenical movements by the British Baptists has been stimulated by various leaders among them, notably J.H. Shakespeare. See Peter Shepherd, *The Making of a Modern Denomination: John Howard Shakespeare and the English Baptists, 1898–1924* (Studies in Baptist History and Thought, 4; Carlisle: Paternoster Press, 2001).

different from the common American affirmation that the church is a purely 'spiritual' reality lacking tangible shape in the world, in that the 'real' church is the local church, and any supra-church associations are purely functional and not to be called 'the Church'.

It should be noted, however, that the official ecclesiology of the Baptist Union statement did not speak for all within the Union. In 1963, four ministers within the Union (Neville Clark, Alec Gilmore, Morris West, and Stephen Winward) co-authored a book entitled *The Pattern of the Church: A Baptist View*,[36] which articulated a high view of the one church and a strong sense of connection between the churches. Indeed, that book interpreted a body like the Baptist Union as simply one current step toward the ultimate goal of a restored and fully re-united church of Christ. That ecclesiology seems congruent with the 1948 statement of the council, but in 1964 a small book entitled *Liberty in the Lord* was produced by the theologically conservative-evangelical Baptist Revival Fellowship within the Baptist Union, and that book was a direct, negative reaction to *The Pattern of the Church*. The very inclusion of 'liberty' in the title indicates that one of the concerns was to oppose the focus on organizational union of the wider church,[37] although the argument of the book does not exhibit the rhetorical extremes sometimes found in North American documents.

In Summary

Baptists have almost always affirmed a relative autonomy of the local church, but earlier Baptist thought (prior to the nineteenth century) and continuing Baptist thought outside of North America has generally tried to emphasize also the necessity of a genuine interdependence in the wider church. In most cases, this did not imply the existence of officers or councils beyond the church with any kind of formal authority over the local congregation, but it did affirm the ecclesiological necessity of some form of inter-church accountability and at least a kind of moral authority of these wider associations which was not to be taken lightly. However, since the nineteenth century there has been a widespread commitment in North American Baptist life to a radical kind of local church independence in which a universal church may be theoretically affirmed but without any functional significance. In that ecclesiology, it *may* be desirable for churches to form various kinds of voluntary associations to

---

[36] A. Gilmore (ed.), *The Pattern of the Church: A Baptist View* (London: Lutterworth Press, 1963).

[37] Baptist Revival Fellowship, *Liberty in the Lord: Comments on Trends in Baptist Thought* Today (London: Carey Kingsgate Press, 1964). The book expresses concern about theological drift toward ecumenism, connectionalism, and sacramentalism, and links all of these to liberal (as opposed to evangelical) theology.

facilitate various forms of activity, but such associations are not necessary, and where they do exist, there is no sense in which the local church is accountable to them. Therefore, in much of the Baptist world it is assumed that every local church is a kingdom unto itself, even though this does not represent the balance of earlier Baptist life and thought. It is a myth to say that Baptists have always been committed to radical congregational independence. I now propose to ask whether this newer focus on autonomy is defensible theologically and whether it promotes the health of the churches and the church universal.

Evaluating the Case for Independence

There is no standard Baptist rationale for a commitment to autonomous churches any more than there is one standard Baptist confession of faith, and, in fact, the concept is often assumed rather than defended. In what follows I will seek to draw together the kinds of supporting arguments that are found in various Baptist sources and assess the cogency of the case for the high view of autonomy.

The Narrative-Historical Argument

This argument, arguably the most common of Baptist arguments, is quite simple: within the New Testament there is no description of any kind of supra-congregational governance structures, and given the authoritative character of the New Testament writings for New Testament churches, no such structures should be created. This is often linked to a Baptist form of what is called in the Reformed tradition 'the regulative principle'. The point of this principle is that God is to be worshiped and served only in the ways that he has commanded, so that the absence of a command to serve him in a particular way amounts to a prohibition of that form of service. Baptists have often used this argument to refute the baptism of infants, but it is also useful as applied to church structures.

Although the heart of this argument concerns the (lack of) evidence within the New Testament, the conclusions of eminent church historians are often invoked as secondary evidence.[38] It is not difficult to find historians who describe the post-apostolic church as congregational in structure, and their testimony is all the more impressive because they typically belong to denominations with other kinds of governance and thus have no bias in a congregationalist direction. This is, of course, the same kind of historical argument that Baptists have often used to support

---

[38] E.T. Hiscox, *The New Directory for Baptist Churches* (Philadelphia, PA: Judson Press, 1894), pp. 156-59.

their view of the subjects and mode of baptism, and even Landmarkist successionism.[39]

Most interpreters of the New Testament would concede the basic premise of this argument, namely, that within the New Testament there is no description of any formal governing structure for the extended church and, apart from the apostles of Christ, no officers with formal authority over multiple churches. However, the argument works only if one assumes as a second premise something like 'the regulative principle', and this is difficult to sustain. The fact is that virtually no Baptist actually assumes that everything absent from the pages of the New Testament is thereby forbidden, and such an assumption would prove far too much. The fact is that it is not just higher-level governance structures that are absent from the New Testament—there are no formal structures for mission or any other cooperative ventures, so the kind of voluntary association envisioned for purposes of evangelism, education, or benevolence would be ruled out as well.[40]

It should also be noted that the absence of explicit New Testament evidence for formal structures of governance proves only a lack of evidence for such—it is not quite the same as proving the actual absence of such. To assert the actual absence of anything in the life of the apostolic church demands reasonably explicit denial of such, given the occasional nature of most of the New Testament writings. Although this argument from the silence of the New Testament is widely used and often thought to be conclusive, it is hard to feel its force.

The Argument from Church Discipline

It is often argued that in the biblical picture of the church it is assumed that the local congregation is competent to carry out church discipline without any supervision from above. In Matthew 18 instruction is given through the teaching of Jesus to deal with a disciple's perceived mistreatment by another disciple. The prescription for this case is individual confrontation first, taking one or two others to confront if necessary, and finally telling the matter to the church. This must be a local church, given its assumed knowledge of these two persons, and each such church ('two or three gathered in my name') is considered competent to render the final judgment. No possibility of appeal beyond the church is envisioned. In Baptist literature Matthew 18 is commonly

---

[39] Tendencies in this sort of historiography has been critiqued by W.M. Patterson, *Baptist Successionism: A Critical View* (Valley Forge, PA: Judson Press, 1969), pp. 30-46.

[40] Some Baptist churches, notably the Primitive Baptist churches, have in fact drawn this inference and have thus rejected mission organizations, theological schools, and other para-church forms of ministry. See McBeth, *Baptist Heritage*, pp. 371-77.

used in this argument, but the same sort of thing can be said about 1 Corinthians 5–6, where the Corinthian church is assumed to have sufficient wisdom to discipline its members.[41]

Here again we encounter a sweeping argument from silence, and it is less than convincing. It is one thing to say that such discipline ought to occur at the level of the local church, but it is another thing entirely to assert that this is the only level at which it may occur. It is not difficult to envision cases in which the discipline of the Christian community would not be adequately served by denying such disciplinary action apart from a single church. What if a member of one church alleges that he has been wronged by a member of another church? At the very least resolution would seem to involve some sort of action by a church court with representatives from both churches, but this is to posit some kind of governance that transcends the local church. Or what if one church alleges that is has been wronged by another church—is there no possibility of appeal? Furthermore, the biblical texts commonly utilized in this argument deal with issues of personal behaviour, but this does not touch on the whole issue of doctrinal accountability to the wider church.

The Argument from Acts 15

The 'Jerusalem Council' has been utilized by defenders of all three common forms of church government—the unique role of James in the decision supporting an episcopal structure, the participation of leaders (elders) from both Antioch and Jerusalem pointing in the direction of presbyterian structure, and the mention of the whole church at Jerusalem serving to support a congregational structure. This diversity of application should warn us against hasty inferences, but on one reading of the text Baptists find support for strong congregational autonomy.

The basic argument is this: the problem in view is the teaching of certain persons from the Jerusalem church who falsely claim to speak for that church to the church in Antioch. The church in Antioch then sends representatives to Jerusalem to inquire as to the actual view of the (original) church in Jerusalem. The resultant meeting hears testimony from Paul, Barnabas and Peter, but the discussion and decision concern the Jerusalem church. The answer given (that Gentiles believers do not need to submit to the Mosaic law to be saved) represents the opinion of the church at Jerusalem, not a decision of a wider council. It is the answer of one local church to a question from another local church, not an authoritative statement of the whole church. It is indeed the response of the whole church at Jerusalem (v. 22), not just the apostles and elders,

---

[41] Hiscox, *Directory*, p. 153.

although those leaders obviously played a special role in arriving at the decision.[42]

Although it may be granted that this episode does not display a full-orbed presbyterian or episcopal structure for the expanding church, it is still difficult to correlate the account with a radical congregational autonomy. First of all, it should be noted that the question was expressly said to be addressed to 'the apostles and elders' (v. 2)—this was not a question dealt with at a meeting of the whole church. The church as a whole 'received' the delegates from Antioch (v. 4) and was involved in selecting the messengers to carry the letter drafted by the apostles and elders (v. 22), but it was representative leaders who pursued and answered the question. But beyond the question of methodology, it is clear that the underlying assumption is that churches everywhere should be united on this matter of doctrine and practice—there is no thought of a Jewish church and a Gentile church with contrasting perspectives on the relevance of the Mosaic law. Furthermore, the answer given in the letter is sent to churches beyond Antioch (v. 23), and the content of the decision is more than a simple answer to one question (vv. 20, 28-29). The idea that autonomous churches may rightly affirm contradictory doctrines is foreign to this account of the developing church, and while the biblical text does not give a blueprint for resolving all doctrinal disputes at all times and in all places, neither does it give any support to an 'agree to disagree' approach as a paradigm.

The Argument from Revelation 2–3

Some Baptists point to the apocalyptic letters to the seven churches of Asia as proof for congregationalism. The point is simple enough: the risen Christ addresses each of the seven churches individually, with no reference to any kind of federation of the churches ('the church in Asia').[43] Assuming the majority view of a late date for the Apocalypse around AD 95-96, one then sees that even at that time not long before the evidences of a monarchical episcopate, there is still no biblical evidence of any extra-congregational structure.

This argument is not found in many Baptist sources, and for very good reason. It is a particularly unconvincing use of the argument from silence. Given the fact that the condition of each of those churches was unique, it comes as no surprise that each needed a unique letter. But this says nothing about the possibility of there being some sort of inter-church accountability—indeed, the fact that each of the letters is

---

[42] Hiscox, *Directory*, pp. 153-55.
[43] Hiscox, *Directory*, pp. 155-56.

contained in a book to be sent to all of the churches might implicitly indicate some sort of mutual accountability.

The Landmark Argument

In the middle of the nineteenth century some Baptists, notably J.R. Graves and J.M. Pendleton, developed a new 'high church' ecclesiology for Baptists which affirmed, among other things, that the Bible contains no concept of a universal church at all.[44] In this novel ecclesiology, the only true church is a local church, indeed, a local Baptist church! Although only held by a minority of Baptists, this viewpoint has had a significant impact on other Baptists, especially Southern Baptists. At a linguistic level, proponents of Landmarkism argue that the vast majority of New Testament references to 'church' clearly denote local bodies, and the other occurrences of the term may plausibly be understood as generic or heavenly/eschatological. (To take an analogy, if I speak of 'the family in contemporary Canada', I do not mean that there is in fact one family in Canada—I am quite clearly speaking of the family as an institution, that is, of 'families'.)

The Landmark ecclesiology is very much a minority view, and for very good reason. In the first place, synthesizing a New Testament ecclesiology is not simply a matter of counting the various uses of *ekklesia*, but even at that simplistic level one cannot easily come to the conclusion that the biblical authors know nothing of a universal church. To go beyond that and assert that the only true local church is a *Baptist* church seems wrong-headed in the extreme, in that it isolates baptismal practice as the ultimately definitive criterion of a true church, in spite of the fact that the biblical images of the church are diverse and allow for multiple ways of identifying a genuine congregation. For example, if the church is 'the temple of the Holy Spirit' (Eph 2.21-22; 1 Cor. 3.16-17), then one might recognize a true church by the manifest presence of the Spirit of God, which is surely a reality even where there may be some confusion about baptism. In the second place, Landmarkism rests upon a fatally flawed historiography.[45]

The Argument from Doctrinal Purity

What I have in view here is not really a biblical-theological argument as such—it is in reality a pragmatically based argument rooted in a

---

[44] For a survey of the theology and the impact of Landmarkism, see McBeth, *Baptist Heritage*, pp. 447-61. The definitive study of this movement remains J. Tull, 'A Study of Southern Baptist Landmarkism in Light of Historical Baptist Ecclesiology' (PhD thesis, Columbia University, 1960).

[45] Cf. Patterson, *Baptist Successionism*.

theological concern. Clearly there is within the New Testament writings a concern for purity of teaching within the church, and many Baptists in North America in the early twentieth century believed that they were obedient to this apostolic concern in their battle against the capture of their denominations by liberal theology in various forms. In some of those cases the denominational elites were liberal in orientation far beyond the proportion of liberals in the denomination as a whole, which prompted an emphasis on congregational autonomy to prevent the dominance of liberalism.

Whatever may be said about this move as a strategy, it fails to substantiate congregationalism as a principle. Furthermore, even if useful as a strategy to protect one's own church, it shows little concern for other churches. Wider structures of doctrinal accountability could in fact be means of defending orthodoxy, and one might argue that radical autonomy allows all sorts of doctrinal deviations to spread freely. If the defense of orthodoxy is the goal, it is not clear that a focus on autonomy is the way to achieve it. Separatist movements among Baptists in North America arising out of theological conflict in the twentieth century have evidenced both a desire for extensive doctrinal uniformity and a rejection of any kind of supra-congregational authority, but it is not likely that the purity is achievable apart from the authority to enforce it. Personal experience within such movements tells me that while the rhetoric may emphasize freedom and autonomy, the reality is that such 'independent' Baptist churches are not nearly so independent in practice.[46]

A Rationale for Connectional Structures

In addition to pointing out the implausibility of the case for radical congregationalism, it is also possible to construct a positive biblical or historical case for a stronger connection between churches and the universal church and to show that such connectionalism has both biblical and Baptist roots. It is also not difficult to point out some of the benefits of such an ecclesiology for the health of the churches.

With regard to the *biblical basis*, we need to ask whether congregational autonomy is actually taught as a principle. As I see it, the

---

[46] I have personally been involved in two such groups: the General Association of Regular Baptist Churches (in the USA) and the Fellowship of Evangelical Baptist Churches in Canada. My comments here pertain for the most part to the GARBC, because the separatist impulse has never become the heart and soul of the Canadian group. The GARBC is a self-described fundamentalist denomination, and while there is a purported emphasis on autonomous congregations within the group, there is little tolerance for those churches that choose to deviate from the unwritten traditions of the group. My observation is that 'independent fundamentalists' may be fearless opponents of liberal theology, but they tend to be afraid of one another.

major argument for autonomy is an argument from silence: the New Testament does not describe any sort of formal accountability structure beyond the local church (aside from apostolic authority). But the same argument from silence might imply that there should be no larger structures *at all*, not even missional structures. Although the Bible may be silent about any *formal* structures of accountability, there is evident concern for unity of faith and practice on important issues. Twice in 1 Corinthians (11.16; 14.33) Paul invokes the consensus of the churches as an argument to rein in the Corinthian church. It seems obvious that these exhortations to get in line with the other churches presuppose a level of mutual accountability which does not view each local church as a 'sovereign, independent' body, or at least these texts demand a major modification of such sovereignty. The Jerusalem council in Acts 15 is rooted in the assumption that Antioch and Jerusalem ought not to teach contradictory views about Gentiles and the law of Moses. In our modern Baptist contexts, we would be prone to terminate any formal connection, and thus end up with Gentile churches and Jewish churches with no tangible linkage to each other. The essence of the New Testament church may well demand wider structures of accountability just as much as wider structures to facilitate mission.

We might also add here the Pauline description of the church as the body of Christ and the related admonitions to affirm our connection to the other members of the body. It seems clear in those biblical texts that the body of Christ is for Paul not just a reference to each local church, but rather to the universal community of believers. In 1 Corinthians 12.13 his use of 'we' shows that both he and his readers in Corinth are incorporated into the same body, but Paul was clearly not a member of the church in Corinth. Later in the same passage he equates the 'body' with the 'church' (12.28) and describes this church as inclusive of both apostles and prophets, thus denoting the universal church. The burden of the intervening material (vv. 14-26) is to argue that every part of that body must maintain its connection to the whole body. Similarly, in Ephesians Paul speaks of 'the church, which is his body' (1.22-23), and argues that there is a tangible unity of the body which must be maintained (4.3). This is the universal body (church) served by the apostles and prophets (4.11), who constitute the foundation of the church (2.20) and are recipients of canonical revelation (3.5). This universal body affirms its given unity while it moves toward a full unity of faith (4.13). That surely implies that present doctrinal divergence between churches cannot be accepted as a final reality. Instead, the churches are called to mutual interaction which leads toward full unity in the truth. This is not an 'agree to disagree (forever)' mindset. Paul does not spell out a specific kind of inter-congregational structure which will facilitate this movement, but it is easy to see that creating such structures may well help the church to be what Christ calls it to be.

Whatever might be said in theory about a stronger kind of connection between local churches, would such a connection at least be something other than Baptist? *Haven't Baptists always promoted autonomy and rejected the necessity of supra-congregational structures?* The answer, in a word, is 'No'. That is just one myth about Baptist history and thought that has been reiterated sufficiently often to become an assumption, but I have shown above that this fixation on autonomy is a fairly recent innovation, not something inherent in historic Baptist ecclesiology.

At the founding of the Abingdon Association in 1652, a positive rationale for association was articulated along the lines of analogy. Baptists of every stripe would agree that individual disciples of Christ ought to be functioning members of a congregation, so that their freedom in Christ is balanced by their interdependent relationship with other disciples. The Abingdon rationale applies this same logic to the relationship between churches and the universal church, arguing that such association provides mutual care among the churches, establishes mechanisms for keeping the various churches pure in doctrine and practice, translates love for others from attitude into action, assists the local churches by wise counsel from the wider body of churches, and facilitates witness to the wider world.[47] In his widely distributed and influential manual for church order, Edward Hiscox took note of this argument by analogy and explicitly rejected it, thus revealing the extent to which American individualism had already in the nineteenth century modified traditional Baptist patterns of thought.[48]

One might also argue pragmatically that the absence of connectional structures is unhealthy for the churches, in that it fails to provide for inter-church discipline which all churches recognize as necessary in extreme situations. Rather than leaving this at an abstract level, I will here give a fictional illustration that could well become reality in my own stream of the church.

Consider this hypothetical scenario: it is the year 2015, and some Baptists are thinking some very new thoughts. Metropolitan Community Baptist Church in Toronto (a church planted in 2010 by the Toronto Association) has adopted a 'welcoming and affirming' attitude toward self-declared homosexuals. Based on teaching done by their pastor, the church believes that the Bible, properly interpreted and taken as a whole,

---

[47] For an analysis of the Abingdon Association perspective and its implications, see B.R. White, 'The Doctrine of the Church in the Particular Baptist Confession of 1644', *Journal of Theological Studies* n.s. 19.2 (October, 1968), p. 589; David Kingdon, 'Independency and Interdependency', in P. Clarke *et al.*, *Our Baptist Heritage* (Leeds: Reformation Today Trust, 1993), pp. 35-39.
[48] Hiscox, *Directory*, pp. 148-50.

would affirm monogamous homosexual relationships. To formalize this principle, they have created a ceremony for homosexual 'marriages', and this has stimulated numerical growth as homosexual couples have come to them for weddings and have then become members of the church. The marriage law had been changed in 2006 to allow for same-sex marriages, and this church has expanded its ministry accordingly. They know that the Bible makes negative statements about homosexual behaviour, but they believe that those statements are directed at homosexual acts rooted in idolatry or promiscuity and would not apply to the unions that they are prepared to celebrate. They understand that their view is very much a minority view within the Fellowship, but they emphasize that they are an autonomous congregation obeying the 'precepts' given them by Christ, the head of the church, through the infallible Bible as they understand it.

The scenario summarized above is not out of the question, however mind-boggling it may seem at present. Several years ago I debated same-sex marriage on a talk show on CFRB radio in Toronto. The defender of such marriages was Brent Hawkes, the Pastor of the Metropolitan Community Church in Toronto. More recently he became famous by conducting two same-sex marriages in his church via publication of banns rather than a provincial licence. The radio host kept referring to our views as the 'evangelical' and the 'liberal' positions, but after about fifteen minutes of that, Brent protested that he was also an evangelical. He affirmed his commitment to the historic gospel and the final authority of the Bible, and he rejected the 'liberal' label. I am not talking about an unthinkable scenario.[49]

What will the rest of our churches do? Some would argue that the church has clearly violated the Fellowship Affirmation of Faith at the point of biblical infallibility, assuming that one can't very well believe that the Bible is infallible and that homosexual behaviour can be morally correct. But in fact one can believe those two things. Belief in biblical infallibility commits one to believe whatever one believes the Bible teaches, but it does not answer any of the questions about what in fact the Bible teaches. Commitment to biblical infallibility may be foundational and significant, but it does not do any of the work of exegesis and hermeneutics. So the (hypothetical) church believes that the Bible is true in all that it teaches, but also that the traditional condemnation of all homosexual behaviour is rooted in a misinterpretation of the Bible. At the end of the day, we would have to admit that our *Affirmation of Faith* does

---

[49] Monogamous homosexual unions are defended by some who hold a high view of biblical authority. See, e.g., L.D. Scanzoni and V.R. Mollenkott, *Is the Homosexual My Neighbor? A Positive Christian Response* (San Francisco: Harper-San Francisco, rev. edn, 1994). R. Blair, an evangelical homosexual who works as a psychotherapist and directs a Homosexual Community Counseling Center in New York City, is a member of the Evangelical Theological Society and thus affirms biblical inerrancy.

not exclude the pro-gay church. Furthermore, although we have at least one non-binding resolution from past conventions that would be relevant, we do not have a binding policy statement which would exclude the church.

If we want to emphasize congregational autonomy, then we may be stuck with a pro-gay church in our non-denomination until we can expand our *Affirmation of Faith* or adopt a binding policy statement. If all this sounds unthinkable, we need to realize that this essential scenario has unfolded recently in more than one Southern Baptist association. In those cases, the offending churches pleaded 'local church autonomy' and 'soul liberty' as the Baptist principles that justify a more inclusive attitude.[50]

Aside from modifying our rhetoric, what might a more connectional view of the church entail in a contemporary Baptist context? I submit just a few possibilities. First, we will not lightly draw doctrinal lines which exclude other true churches. This is not to say that no division is ever justified, only that it must in fact be justified, because the biblical ideal is that we be genuinely linked to the whole body of Christ. This may have little relevance for Baptists in many parts of the world where their numbers are so small as to make it difficult to think of division, but it has obvious relevance for Baptists in the USA. There, where Baptists are numerous and in some places virtually an established church, splits in the church do not always reduce a union of churches to something less than a critical mass. Secondly, we will be willing to refer difficult issues to the wider church for counsel (the congregation to the association, and the associations to whatever levels of union may be above them). Presently this occurs in my context in our ordination councils, but it might be wise to seek counsel of other churches even prior to the pastoral call. Would that resemble closely the relation of the church to the presbytery in a presbyterian structure? Certainly it would, but that would simply admit that Baptists can learn some valuable lessons from the presbyterian stream of the church.[51] Thirdly, our meetings of the extended church at supra-

---

[50] According to Associated Baptist Press, over the last decade the Baptist State Convention of North Carolina has expelled at least three churches for positive attitudes toward practicing homosexuals (McGill Baptist Church in Concord, Pullen Memorial Baptist Church in Raleigh, and Binkley Memorial Baptist Church in Chapel Hill). On 9 February 2004, Pastor Gene Scarborough of North Rocky Mount Baptist Church filed a complaint with the North Carolina Attorney General, charging that the Baptist State Convention's actions 'violate local-church autonomy'. See www.abpnews.com, 20 February 2004.

[51] Southern Baptist theologian D. Moody was calling for this already over a quarter century ago, 'The Shaping of Southern Baptist Polity', *Baptist History and Heritage* 14.3 (July, 1979), pp. 2-11. Moody argued (p. 6) that if Baptists were true to their claim to

congregational levels would include deliberation on some of the difficult issues confronting the churches in general, and we would stop pretending that they can all be resolved by churches in isolation. Fourthly, we will recognize that Baptist denominations can be viewed as steps toward the ultimate goal of one catholic church, and we will accordingly create or strengthen mechanisms for inter-denominational discussions with a view to extending the formal union of the church in the world. For those of us who have been nurtured in anti-ecumenical environments, this will represent a major paradigm shift, not in the direction of unity at any cost but in the direction of unity in the truth which manifests itself in tangible and visible forms. Fifthly, in Baptist denominations like my own, we will consider the possibility of revising our confessional statements, so that they affirm a more balanced view of association and autonomy. Although formal confessional documents may be in one sense the least important area of concern (how often do we read them or even think about them?), the process of revision would force serious thought about our ecclesiology, and that would surely be beneficial.

No doubt the list of applications of a stronger sense of connection between churches and the church could be expanded far beyond the previous paragraph, but I leave that to the sanctified imagination of the reader. If Baptists take this seriously, then the world around us would surely take note, but more importantly it would surely please our Lord, who desired that all who belong to him would indeed be one.

---

follow the New Testament alone, 'associationalism would be upgraded to presbyterianism, and Presbyterianism will function best with a bishop over the elders'.

CHAPTER 3

The Priesthood of All Believers and the Necessity of the Church

Elizabeth Newman

'The good news of God comes to us not directly but indirectly, through the fully human witness, memory, hope and practice of a community of believers.'[1]

In this essay I examine modern Southern Baptist understandings of the 'priesthood of the believer', a term often used interchangeably with 'soul competency' or 'soul liberty'. I argue that the ecclesiology that typically sustains these understandings is inadequate, primarily because it makes the church secondary to human freedom and Christian identity. In a final section, I suggest an alternative way to understand our corporate priesthood, one that not only requires the church but also gives a fuller account of Christian freedom.

Freedom and the 'Priesthood of the Believer'

Most contemporary Southern Baptists—both conservative and moderate—use 'the priesthood of the believer' to locate freedom in the individual and his or her right to have direct access to God. Conservative leader Paul Pressler, for example, writes,

> No individuals could believe more strongly in the priesthood of the believers than do those in the conservative movement...[the] believer... has the right to go to the Word of God and let the Holy Spirit, who wrote it, interpret it to that person. The priesthood of the believer means that a believer can have direct contact with God and does not need to go through any priest, pope, ecclesiastical organization, or anything or anyone else.[2]

---

[1] Daniel Migliore, *Faith Seeking Understanding, An Introduction to Christian Theology* (Grand Rapids, MI: Eerdmans, 1991), p. 35.

[2] Paul Pressler, *A Hill On Which to Die* (Nashville, TN: Broadman & Holman Publishers, 1999), p. 155. One might wonder how Pressler's definition of our priesthood

On the more moderate side, Herschel Hobbs, in *You Are Chosen: The Priesthood of All Believers*, states that the priesthood of the believer (or soul competency) 'excludes human interference of any kind between the individual soul and God. In its deepest sense, religion is a personal matter between the individual and God... On the other hand, soul competency is inclusive. It includes salvation by grace through faith without the need of a human mediator or any institution, ecclesiastical or political.'[3] Both Hobbs and Pressler are following in the tradition of the influential Baptist theologian E.Y. Mullins (1860–1928), who described soul competency as the distinctive contribution of Baptists to the religious world.[4] Mullins defined such competency not in the 'sense of human self-sufficiency';[5] it was rather a competency under God, one that excluded all human interference.

Like Mullins, those who invoke 'the priesthood of the believer' today note that they are not endorsing 'autonomous privatism',[6] 'unbounded individualism',[7] 'individuals apart from churches',[8] or that 'people can believe anything they choose'.[9] Rather, as Walter Shurden states, the priesthood of the believer (or soul competency) indicates that personal

---

as the believer's right to interpret the Bible comports with his advocacy of an inerrantist understanding of the Bible. In response, Pressler states that the conservative concern has had to do with the *nature* of scripture—as being inspired by God and without error—rather than with *interpretation* of scripture. Thus, he argues that the conservative movement allowed for charismatics as well as five-point Calvinists though not all shared those interpretations. Adrian Rogers, conservative Southern Baptist Convention President in 1979, 1986 and 1987, gives a similar endorsement of the priesthood: 'Because I believe so much in the priesthood of the believer and our accountability to God alone, I would never, I hope till I die, compromise conviction on the altar of cooperation', quoted by Bill Leonard, *God's Last and Only Hope* (Grand Rapids, MI: Eerdmans, 1990), p. 149.

[3] Herschel H. Hobbs, *You Are Chosen: The Priesthood of All Believers* (San Francisco: Harper & Row, 1990), p. 3. Hobbs also calls soul competency the 'distinctive contribution of Baptists to the Christian world'.

[4] E.Y. Mullins, *The Axioms of Religion* (Philadelphia: Judson Press, 1908), p. 53. Before Hobbs, Mullins too declared that the competency of the soul in religion is both inclusive and exclusive: it 'excludes at once all human interference, such as episcopacy and infant baptism, and every form of religion by proxy. Religion is a personal matter between the soul and God', pp. 53-54. At the same time it includes the separation of church and state, as well as the justification by faith alone.

[5] Mullins, *Axioms of Religion*, p. 53.

[6] E. Glenn Hinson, 'The Future of the Baptist Tradition' (Union Seminary, Richmond, VA: Reigner Recording Library, 1981), cassette tape.

[7] Grady C. Cothen and James M. Dunn, *Soul Freedom, Baptist Battle Cry* (Macon, GA: Smyth & Helwys, 2000), p. 64. Cothen and Dunn also stress, p. 65, 'Religion is a personal matter between the soul and God'.

[8] Walter Shurden, 'The Baptist Identity and the Baptist *Manifesto*', *Perspectives in Religious Studies* 25.4 (Winter, 1998), p. 324.

[9] Hobbs, *You Are Chosen*, p. 2.

faith is born *'in the privacy of the human heart'*, a conviction Shurden, like Mullins before him, believes lies 'at the essence of both Baptist and Protestant life'.[10] Such 'soul freedom' is the inalienable right and responsibility of every person.[11]

Given this heavy emphasis on the individual soul and God, how, according to this view, are we to think about the church? Mullins argues that the Roman Catholic system is the direct antithesis of soul competency because 'Christ and the soul alone are not equal to the redemptive task'. The seven sacraments illustrate in a 'striking way' that priestly mediation is necessary, thus implying the soul's incompetency.[12] Mullins instead defines the church as 'a group of individuals sustaining to each other important relations, and organized for a great end and mission'.[13] He thus interprets the church as the social dimension of the soul's competency. So understood, the priesthood of all believers implies democracy in the church. In fact, Mullins argued that democracy not only in the church but also in the state was an 'inevitable corollary' of soul competency. As Philip E. Thompson rightly suggests, for Mullins, 'the final outworking of soul competency is seen in the state at least as much as in the church, and perhaps to a greater degree'.[14] For our purposes, we can simply highlight the fact that soul competency clearly *precedes* the church in Mullin's theology.

If we look at present day advocates of soul competency, how do their understandings of our priesthood and its relation to the church comport with that of Mullins? Walter Shurden, in an essay responding to a document that became known as the 'Baptist Manifesto', strongly states that Baptist life 'historically affirms the theme of "the individual *in* community." The Baptist vision of Christianity certainly does not envision individuals apart from churches...'[15] Throughout the essay,

---

[10] Shurden, 'The Baptist Identity', p. 329, my emphasis.

[11] Walter B. Shurden, *The Baptist Identity: Four Fragile Freedoms* (Macon, GA: Smyth & Helwys, 1993), p. 23.

[12] Mullins, *Axioms of Religion*, pp. 60-61. Mullins argues that some forms of Protestantism are also inconsistent with soul competency because even though they insist upon the doctrine of justification by faith alone, they nonetheless adhere to infant baptism and episcopacy

[13] Mullins, *Axioms of Religion*, p. 55.

[14] Philip E. Thompson, 'Sacraments and Religious Liberty: From Critical Practice to Rejected Infringement', in Anthony R. Cross and Philip E. Thompson (eds), *Baptist Sacramentalism* (Studies in Baptist History and Thought, 5; Carlisle: Paternoster Press, 2003), p.53.

[15] Shurden, 'The Baptist Identity', p. 324. The full title of the document to which Shurden is responding is 'Re-Envisioning Baptist Identity: A Manifesto for Baptist Communities in North America', published in *Perspectives in Religious Studies* 24.3 (Fall, 1997), pp. 303-310. I am one of the six authors of the document, the others being Mickael Broadway, Curtis Freeman, Barry Harvey, James W. McClendon and Philip E.

Shurden emphasizes the role of community, even claiming that one may say Baptists have given the world 'an ecclesiology, not a theology'.[16] For my purposes, however, it is important to attend to the way that Shurden describes the importance of the church. He notes, for example, that the biblical heroes are portrayed as people in community; 'they are *in need* of the genuine value of relationships'.[17] Further, he argues that the church is '*an* altogether valid hermeneutical "*core value*" for understanding the Baptist identity as long as one does not ignore the role of the individual'.[18] What gives dynamism to 'the life of a Baptist church', Shurden states, 'is the deep and devoted personal faith the individuals *bring* to the corporate body of believers'.[19] And finally, 'the Manifesto, in its zeal for advocating *a legitimate role* for the community of believers, negates a powerful part of the Baptist heritage concerning the individual'.[20] We can see in these comments two crucial assumptions. First, the church has an important role (for fellowship, for social action, for relationship, etc.) but is not absolutely necessary; the church is subsequent to the faith of the individual that he or she brings to the larger body. Such a belief is made possible by another assumption conveyed throughout the essay: Shurden places Christian Baptist identity on an individual–communal continuum, arguing that these need to be kept in tension (and criticizing the *Manifesto* for collapsing the individual into the communal, and thus sacrificing freedom).[21] On this latter assumption, he echoes E. Glenn Hinson's analysis and Hinson's identification of Baptist identity with the Holy Spirit working in the individual will rather than the corporate institution:

> If you range denominations across a spectrum from voluntarist to its opposite, involuntarist, or as I prefer to designate it, intentionalist, you will find Baptists near the extreme voluntarist end alongside Quakers, and Roman Catholics on the extreme intentionalists end. Intentionalism considers the Spirit to work through

---

Thompson. In it, we argue that North American Baptists have become deeply entrenched in modern notions of freedom. As an alternative, and drawing from earlier Baptist resources, we discuss the call to shared discipleship and the practices necessary to sustain such a common life in Christ.

16 Shurden, 'The Baptist Identity', p. 324.
17 Shurden, 'The Baptist Identity', p. 324, my emphasis.
18 Shurden, 'The Baptist Identity', p. 325, my emphasis.
19 Shurden, 'The Baptist Identity', p. 329, my emphasis.
20 Shurden, 'The Baptist Identity', p. 327, my emphasis.
21 Shurden, 'The Baptist Identity', p. 339, writes: 'Also, I must confess that when reading the *Manifesto*, I get an uneasy feeling about its commitment to Baptist freedom in general. I subtitled my book on Baptist identity *Four Fragile Freedoms*. After studying the *Manifesto*, I quite honestly wonder if Baptist freedom is not more fragile than I first thought.'

composite structures—clergy and sacraments—and thus the Church assumes primary responsibility for the faith and life of the believers.[22]

On this latter point about the church assuming responsibility for the faith of believers, we can hear echoes of Mullin's argument that Catholicism negates soul competency. We also hear in both Shurden and Hinson the positive conviction that discipleship ought not to be coerced; one ought to be free 'to hear and respond in obedience'[23] to the word of God. James McClendon spells out the implication of this conviction when he notes that the theme of liberty so often embraced by Baptists implies 'the rejection of violence as the basis of community'.[24]

At this point, however, we need to consider the pitfalls of analyzing Christian identity along an individual–communal, or voluntarist–corporate continuum. For my purposes, the main difficulty is that the individual stands over against the church. He or she may voluntarily participate in the church because of certain needs for fellowship, for public discipleship, or for worship, but in the final analysis the church is optional, secondary to the individual. Certainly the church remains important, but it becomes *a* core value. If our thinking is conditioned by the individual–communal continuum, then the notion that the church might not be optional will sound like a denial of freedom, since freedom on this view resides in the space of the individual rather than the communal. While I will develop an alternative understanding of our corporate priesthood below, at this point we need to see that any talk about the 'individual' is going to *already* rely upon some prior community and tradition that gives the word 'individual' meaning. Philosopher William H. Poteat makes this point when he states,

> When someone says, 'Language is the instrument of both our individuation and our socialization,' we can immediately see how there is an implicit anthropology at work in this remark because of the theater of solitude in which it is conceived. For here it is assumed that individuation begins when I can use 'we' and 'us.' Of course,

---

[22] James Leo Garrett, Jr, E. Glenn Hinson and James E. Tull, *Are Southern Baptists 'Evangelicals?'* (Macon, GA: Mercer University Press, 1983), p. 186. Shurden, 'The Baptist Identity', p. 331, quotes a similar statement from Hinson in his essay. Unlike Mullins, Hinson acknowledges that Baptists would do well 'to make more room for the Spirit to work through our corporate experience than our forefathers did'. Even so, Hinson describes Baptists (voluntarists) as non- or anti-sacramentalists, and as experientialists rather than institutionalists.

[23] E. Glenn Hinson, 'The Background of the Moderate Movement', in Walter Shurden (ed.), *The Struggle for the Soul of the SBC* (Macon, GA: Mercer University, 1993), p. 3.

[24] J.W. McClendon, *Systematic Theology: Ethics* (Nashville, TN: Abingdon, 1986), p. 30, significantly adds, though, that 'such rejection remains largely unfinished business among Baptists'.

to learn the use of *I*, to learn to *use* it, I must learn simultaneously to use *we*. Individuation and socialization occur in the selfsame moment.[25]

Stated theologically, this means that we cannot separate out the Christian individual from the church, since it is only through the church (and her traditions) that we can understand how to use the Christian 'I'. The framework we ought to draw from, then, is not the priesthood of believer *versus* the church. Or, we ought not place the 'individual' on one end of the continuum and the 'community' on the other. This way of conceiving the matter blinds us to the fact that some prior community or tradition is always and already informing our use of 'individual', 'priesthood', or 'competent soul'. Rather than asking how the individual and communal ought to relate, it would be more accurate to ask the prior question: 'from within the rich resources of the church community, how ought we to understand the priesthood of all believers?' This way of putting the question makes the church not merely important but absolutely necessary. We cannot learn the habits and skills necessary to use, and thus to live and to be, the 'priesthood of all believers' faithfully apart from the church.

Private Interpretation, 'Direct Access', and the Creation of Religion

Before turning to a fuller reconsideration of our priesthood, I want to look more broadly at certain modern influences that shape contemporary understandings of the priesthood of the believer: 1) the individual as a rights bearing creature, 2) the right to private interpretation, and 3) the creation of religion.

First, let us consider the individual as a bearer of rights. Soul freedom, as used today, is typically underwritten by the idea that freedom resides in the individual. Freedom is then understood primarily, if not solely, in terms of self-determination; it consists of the right to choose—to 'make up your own mind'[26]—and any limit to that right becomes a limit or distortion of one's freedom. Baptist ethicist Paul Simmons, for example, uses 'priesthood' to support his pro-choice position on abortion: 'The woman has priestly powers—in her own conscientious obedience to the Creator-Redeemer; she bears his image in making her decision.'[27] For Simmons, priesthood has to do with the subject's ability freely to make

---

[25] William H. Poteat, *A Philosophical Daybook: Post-Critical Investigations* (Columbia: University of Missouri, 1990), p. 21.
[26] Shurden, *Four Fragile Freedoms*, pp. 28 and 31
[27] As quoted by Barry Hankins, *Uneasy in Babylon: Southern Baptist Conservatives and American Culture* (Tuscaloosa, AL: University of Alabama, 2002), p. 176. Earlier Simmons is quoted as saying, 'Religious imperialism and moralistic authoritarianism are contradictory in this Biblical principle'.

decisions before God. 'No other person', argues Simmons, 'may arrogate to themselves the right to stand between the person and God.'[28]

Simmon's position reflects the broader idea that the individual has direct access to God, as well as the right to interpret the Bible for him or herself. Soul competency, so understood, is typically invoked with the familiar saying, 'no creed but the Bible'. This is interpreted to mean that the individual soul is competent or has the right to interpret the Word of God for him or herself: 'the right and responsibility of private interpretation of Scripture is most certainly part of the "politics" of Baptist church polity'.[29]

But what is a private interpretation of Scripture? Ludwig Wittgenstein argues powerfully that there is no such thing as a private language; he means by this that language by its very nature is a social phenomenon. He writes,

> Why can't my right hand give my left hand money?—My right hand can put it into my left hand... But the further practical consequences would not be those of a gift. When the left hand has taken the money from the right, etc., we shall ask: 'well, and what of it?' And the same could be asked if a person had given himself a private definition of a word...[30]

Wittgenstein's point is that there are no private definitions or interpretations of words. Any interpretation—to make sense—is going to draw from a wider context or 'language game'. He did not mean by this that all interpretation is simply aesthetic non-committal 'play', but rather that speaking a language 'is part of an activity, or of a form of life'.[31]

This latter point is extremely important, as our interpretations of Scripture are not simply private or internal phenomena, but activities reflected in concrete practices that constitute a way of life. Thus Stanley Hauerwas rightly argues that 'if we presume that the Bible is its own standard, if we claim "no creed but the Bible," then the authority of the Bible is not privileged. Instead *the authority of our private judgment will prevail.*'[32] By contrast, Hauerwas points to the significance of 'spiritual

---

[28] Hankins, *Uneasy in Babylon*, p. 176.
[29] Shurden, 'The Baptist Identity', p. 326.
[30] Ludwig Wittgenstein, *Philosophical Investigations* (New York: Macmillan Publishing, 1953), p. 94e.
[31] This is a familiar term coined by Wittgenstein. See, for example, *Philosophical Investigations*, p. 11e.
[32] Stanley Hauerwas, *Unleashing the Scripture: Freeing the Bible from Captivity to America* (Nashville, TN: Abingdon, 1993), p. 29, my emphasis. If there can be no private language, however, can there be private judgment? Perhaps it would be better to say that the creeds help us in knowing how to say and live the Christian story; they are like broad guidelines. If we have only the individual and the Bible, then some other story or interpretative lens will easily prevail.

masters': 'the "right" reading of Scripture depends on having spiritual masters who can help the whole Church stand under the authority of God's Word'.[33]

While such a claim may *sound* 'horrendous'[34] to some modern Baptist ears, it is surely not so in practice. Clarence Jordan, founder of the interracial Koinonia Farm,[35] comes to mind as a contemporary Baptist 'spiritual master': one who lived a faithful and masterful interpretation of Scripture. His was not a private interpretation but one recognized by Christians and others as a faithful witness to God. If anything, Jordan's life and words call others *to account* for the way they are interpreting or 'performing' Scripture in their lives. In a well-known story, for example, Robert Jordan, Clarence Jordan's brother, refused to represent Koinonia Farm legally because of his aspirations to be governor of Georgia. As Jordan records it, his brother said,

> 'Clarence, I can't do that. You know my political aspirations... I follow Jesus, Clarence, up to a point.'
>
> 'Could that point by any chance be—the cross?'
>
> 'That's right. I follow him to the cross, but not on the cross. I'm not getting myself crucified.'
>
> 'Then I don't believe you're a disciple. You're an admirer of Jesus, but not a disciple of his. I think you ought to go back to the church you belong to, and tell them you're an admirer not a disciple.'

In regard to the creeds, Timothy George, 'Toward an Evangelical Future', in Nancy Ammerman (ed.), *Southern Baptists Observed: Multiple Perspectives on a Changing Denomination* (Knoxville, TN: University of Tennessee, 1993), pp. 287-88, notes that Baptists have been 'noncreedal' for three reasons: 1) as a protest against religious conformity by the state; 2) as a refusal to elevate doctrinal formulas above scripture; and 3) as a way to avoid promulgating a Baptist confession of faith as infallible. George importantly adds, however, that 'Although in these three senses Baptists have never been creedalistic, the idea that voluntary, conscientious adherence to an explicit doctrinal standard is somehow foreign to the Baptist tradition is a peculiar notion not borne out by a careful examination of our heritage.'

[33] Hauerwas, *Unleashing the Scripture*, p. 16.
[34] Shurden, 'The Baptist Identity', p. 326.
[35] Jordan is well known for his 'Cotton Patch' interpretation of the New Testament. He started Koinonia Farm, an intentional interracial Christian community, in the Southern United States (Georgia) in 1942 and met with a tremendous amount of prejudice and local resistance. For an interesting analysis of his life and work, see James McClendon, 'The Theory Tested: Clarence Leonard Jordan—Radical in Community', in *Biography as Theology* (Philadelphia, PA: Trinity Press International, 1990), pp. 89-113.

'Well now, if everyone who felt like I do did that, we wouldn't *have* a church, would we?'

'The question,' Clarence said, 'is, "Do you have a church?"' [36]

In living a life of cruciform discipleship, Clarence Jordan calls not only his brother but also the whole church to stand more faithfully under the Word of God. His life testifies to the fact that interpreting Scripture is better understood not as a private right, but as part of 'an activity or form of life'.

The fact that soul competency has been identified so overwhelmingly with 'private interpretation' of Scripture and 'direct access' to God reveals the deep influence of modernity's understanding of religion. In an important essay, William Cavanaugh discusses the modern 'creation of religion' as a 'set of beliefs which is defined as personal conviction and which can exist separately from one's public loyalty to the State'. [37] Cavanaugh states that the dawn of the modern concept of religion, which began around the late fifteenth century, identified it as various manifestations of a common impulse. As religion becomes identified with a universal impulse, 'religion is thus interiorized and removed from its particular ecclesial context'.[38] A second major shift occurred through the late sixteenth and seventeenth centuries as religion became identified with an abstract set of beliefs. Thus, 'religion moves from a virtue to a set of propositions'.[39] In both instances, Cavanaugh notes that religion becomes domesticated. 'Religion is no longer a matter of certain bodily practices

---

[36] As quoted in McClendon, 'The Theory Tested', p. 103.

[37] William Cavanaugh, '"A Fire Strong Enough to Consume the House": The Wars of Religion and the Rise of the State,' *Modern Theology* 11.4 (October, 1995), p. 403. Cavanaugh argues more fully that once religion becomes 'domesticated' through either beliefs or interior experience, then it can be easily manipulated by the state. Cavanaugh is in part following Talal Asad who argues that 'religion' was invented so that the state could garner more political power. Asad states: 'Historians of seventeenth- and eighteenth-century Europe have begun to recount how the constitution of the modern state required the forcible redefinition of religion as *belief*, and of religious belief, sentiment and identity as personal matters that belong to the newly emerging space of *private* (as opposed to *public*) life... Scholars are now more aware that religious toleration was a political means to the formation of the strong state power that emerged from the sectarian wars of the sixteenth and seventeenth centuries rather than the benign intention to defend pluralism', quoted by Philip D. Kenneson, *Beyond Sectarianism: Re-Imagining Church and World* (Harrisburg, PA: Trinity Press International, 1999), pp. 54-55, my emphasis.

[38] Cavanaugh, '"A Fire Strong Enough to Consume the House"', p. 404.

[39] Cavanaugh, '"A Fire Strong Enough to Consume the House"', p. 404.

within the Body of Christ, but is limited to the realm of the "soul," and the body is handed over to the State.'[40]

For our purposes, we can see that the modern meanings of religion that Cavanaugh discusses are replicated in the contemporary understanding of 'priesthood'. The individual has direct access to God either through an objective and inerrant Word (a set of beliefs) or through subjective experience (a universal impulse since we are all competent souls).[41] Yet like the domestication of 'religion', so too has the 'the priesthood of the believer' become divorced from the wider ecclesial context and practices of the Body of Christ. It is little wonder then that it has become an undisciplined cipher for all sorts of beliefs. Perhaps one of the most glaring in our context (Southern United States) is the invocation of soul competency to support segregation.[42]

An Alternative Understanding of Priesthood and Freedom

As we have seen, modern Baptists have easily assumed that relating the Holy Spirit to the individual soul, rather than the church and especially ecclesial authority, would enhance the freedom of the individual Christian. Theologian Thomas Grantham (1634–92), however, one of the most significant leaders of General Baptists in England, thought otherwise. He argued that where the 'form of godliness', by which he meant such practices as believer's baptism, the Lord's Table and the laying on of hands, is neglected,

> religion will in a little time either vanish, or become an unknown conceit, every man being at liberty to follow what he supposes to be the motions of the Spirit of God, in which there is so great a probability of being mistaken, as in nothing

---

[40] Cavanaugh, "'A Fire Strong Enough to Consume the House'", p. 405.

[41] In the latter emphasis—the appeal to the subject and to universal experience (soul competency)—we see the influence of Schleiermacher, a theologian especially influential on E.Y. Mullins.

[42] Hankins, *Uneasy in Babylon*, p. 242, refers to Douglas Hudgins, pastor to one of the South's most well known churches (First Baptist, Jackson, Mississippi) in the 1950s and 1960s, as a typical example of Southern Baptist opposition toward desegregation: 'Hudgins used the moderate theology of E.Y. Mullins, with its emphasis on individualism and soul competency, to argue that the Christian faith had nothing to do with a corporate, societal problem like segregation. He, therefore, refused to speak up for African Americans and, in more ways than we could have known, helped inspire a whole generation of Southern Baptists to rest comfortably in their belief that segregation was natural and that the Civil Rights movement was a perversion of the gospel.'

more; for man's ignorance being very great, and Satan very subtle, and the way of the Lord neglected, men lie open to every fancy which pleaseth best...'[43]

To avoid these dangerous mistakes, Grantham endeavors 'plainly to set down the practical way of God's worship, as settled in the Christian Church by Christ our Lord, and his holy Apostles'.[44] Grantham rightly locates freedom in the faithful worship of God, and in the gathered community (he subtitles this section, 'Of the True Way of Gathering Persons into the Church of Christ'). Thus, from Grantham's perspective, worship and the gathered community give shape to our priesthood, which itself is inherently communal. In this final section, we will consider how certain scriptural, liturgical and theological resources can shape an alternative understanding of our corporate priesthood, a priesthood realized most fully in communion with a Triune God.

Against the view that the priesthood has to do individuals, the Old Testament affirms the corporate nature of our priestly identity. In Exodus, for example, God tells Moses to tell the Israelites, 'if you obey my voice and keep my covenant...you shall be for me a priestly kingdom and a holy nation' (Ex. 19.5-6). All of Israel is set apart to be a priestly kingdom, consecrated to serve God. Later, this priestly vocation promised to Israel is extended to the church; in Revelation the new song claims that the Lamb has made saints 'from every tribe and language and people and nation...to be a kingdom and priests serving our God.' (Rev. 5.9-15) Once again, priesthood describes the whole church.[45] God desires a chosen race, a royal priesthood '*in order that* they may be obedient to Jesus Christ and *in order that* they may proclaim the mighty deeds of God'.[46]

From this perspective, priesthood is parasitic on God's calling into existence or 'gathering' both Israel and the church. This fact indicates at least two things. First, in contrast to 'priesthood' referring to an individual's access to God apart from ecclesiastical mediation, Scripture indicates we have no priestly identity apart from Israel and the church.

---

[43] This quotation is taken from a selection from Thomas Grantham's *Christianismus Primitivus: or The Ancient Christian Religion* 1678), II/I/1, in Curtis W. Freeman, James W. McClendon, Jr and C. Rosalee Velloso da Silva (eds), *Baptist Roots: A Reader in the Theology of a Christian People* (Valley Forge, PA: Judson, 1999), p. 89.

[44] Grantham, *Christianismus Primitivus*, cited by Freeman, McClendon and da Silva (eds), *Baptist Roots*, p. 89.

[45] As Paul S. Fiddes, *Tracks and Traces: Baptist Identity in Church and Theology* (Studies in Baptist History and Thought, 13; Carlisle: Paternoster Press, 2003), p. 69, notes about Exodus 19.6, the 'natural rendering of the Greek as "royal priesthood" stresses the corporate nature of this priesthood; the priesthood belongs to the church as a whole, rather than to any individual within it'.

[46] Gerhard Lohfink, *Does God Need the Church? Toward a Theology of the People of God* (Collegeville, MN: Liturgical Press, 1999), p. 38.

Secondly, such royal priesthood is not an individual right, but a gift given to the whole. Whereas 'rights' language indicates we have some claim to our priestly identity, the language of gift indicates that the initiative belongs with God. The use of the passive in 1 Peter 2.4-5 is instructive: 'Come to him, to that living stone, rejected by men but in God's sight chosen and precious; and like living stones be yourselves built into a spiritual house, to be a holy priesthood, to offer spiritual sacrifices acceptable to God through Jesus Christ.' As indicated by the earlier quotation from Wittgenstein—'My right hand can put it into my left hand... But the further practical consequences would not be those of a gift'—a gift must be received. We are to allow ourselves to be made a holy priesthood; this is not an inalienable right but a gift into which we grow.

But, we might ask, how do we receive such a gift? As the reformers well knew,[47] our priesthood can only be received and lived in light of the sole priesthood of Christ. By contrast, when the emphasis is placed on the individual's unmediated access to God, 'the only priesthood is our priesthood...'[48] James Torrance argues, in fact, that this understanding easily leads to Unitarian worship in that worship is understood primarily as something individuals do. This view has no 'understanding of the mediator or sole priesthood of Christ, is human-centered, has no proper doctrine of the Holy Spirit, is too often non-sacramental, and can engender weariness'.[49]

Torrance rightly indicates that our understandings of priesthood and worship go hand in hand. As we saw earlier, Mullins regarded the church as something like a collection of individuals; it is 'the social expression of the spiritual experiences common to a number of individuals'.[50] Worship is an expression of a prior spiritual experience, a view clearly formed by Mullin's understanding of soul competency. Philip Thompson in fact

---

[47] Martin Luther, for example, claimed that 'We are priests as he is Priest', quoted by Timothy George, *Theology of the Reformers* (Nashville, TN: Broadman, 1988), p. 96. According to George, Luther invoked two New Testament claims to support his position, 'You are...a royal priesthood' (1 Pet. 2.9) and 'Thou hast made them a kingdom and priests' (Rev. 1.6). Luther understood the priesthood of all believers to be both a responsibility and a privilege. It meant that Christians were to pray and intercede for each other, and more fully to bear each other's burdens. Luther's position, George points out, serves as an important corrective for the modern tendency to equate 'priesthood of the believer' with individual rights.
[48] James Torrance, *Worship, Community and the Triune God of Grace* (Downers Grove, IL: InterVarsity Press, 1996), p. 20.
[49] Torrance, *Worship*, p. 20.
[50] As quoted in Philip E. Thompson, 'Re-envisioning Baptist Identity: Historical, Theological and Liturgical Analysis', *Perspective in Religious Studies* 27.3 (Fall, 2000), p. 297.

refers to Mullin's view (as well as that of most nineteenth- and twentieth-century Baptists) as a 'subsequentialist' ecclesiology: that church as a gathering of like-minded individuals is 'subsequent to individual salvation'.[51]

Such an understanding stands in radical contrast to Orthodox theologian Alexander Schmemann's description of the church gathered for worship. Liturgy, he states, means 'an action by which a group of people become something corporately which they *had not been as a mere collection of individuals*—a whole greater than the sum of its parts'.[52] Schmemann would have had little use for a concept of priesthood having to do with the relation between an individual and God. Rather, Schmemann holds that is through the eucharist—understood as a communal journey and an ascension in Christ—that we realize our priestly identity most fully. As priests, we bless, receive and offer the world and ourselves to God.

> But we do it *in Christ* and *in remembrance of Him*. We do it in Christ because He has already offered all that is to be offered to God... And we do it *in remembrance of Him* because, as we offer again and again our life and our world to God, we discover each time that there is nothing else to be offered but Christ Himself—the Life of the world, the fullness of all that exists... As the prayer of offering says—"it is He who offers and it is He who is offered."[53]

According to Schmemann, this priestly action transforms both ourselves and the world to become what God intended: a sign of His presence, and a means of communion with God. Thus this *leitourgia*, Schmemann notes, is performed on behalf of the whole. 'The *leitourgia* of ancient Israel was the corporate work of a chosen few to prepare the world for the coming of the Messiah.' So also the church is a *leitourgia*, a calling to act in this world and to bear testimony to Christ and his kingdom.[54] The mission of the church thus begins in this liturgy of ascension. According to Schmemann, it is in and through the liturgy that we both receive our priesthood—by participating in the unique priesthood and offering of Christ—and are enabled to embody this priesthood in the world in the shape of gratitude and sacrificial love.

These contrasting definitions between Mullins and Schmemann might simply highlight the deep difference between Baptist and Orthodox ecclesiologies. A number of Baptist theologians today, however, indicate that Mullin's ecclesiology was in many ways a departure from that of

---

[51] Thompson, 'Re-envisioning Baptist Identity', p. 297.
[52] Alexander Schmemann, *For the Life of the World* (New York: St Vladimir's Press, 1963), p. 25, my emphasis.
[53] Schmemann, *For the Life of the World*, p. 35.
[54] Schmemann, *For the Life of the World*, p. 35.

earlier Baptists as well as the wider (especially British) Baptist community, who were and are far more sacramental.[55] Brian Haymes, for example, following earlier Baptist understandings, states that baptism misunderstood 'as only an expression of commitment to Jesus, a personal act of witness and testimony, reflects an unhelpful christomonism... It is very different when faith is in God as Trinity. The baptismal confession that Jesus Christ is Lord remains a firm center but, through Christ, baptism is into the life and mission of the triune God.'[56] Haymes rightly adds that limiting God's presence and work to the spiritual is reductionistic; the God 'of creation and incarnation does use material means to mediate his saving action'.[57]

Not only is a 'spiritualized' understanding of the church reductionistic, but also a subsequentialist ecclesiology—where the church is secondary to soul competency or the priesthood of the believer—is a relatively short step from not really needing the church at all. Robert Jenson posits the following questions that inevitably result from this view:

> But now a question can no longer be repressed: Why must Christ be embodied for us at all? Why is it not a 'spiritual'—in the vulgar sense—communion enough? That is, why is it not enough privately to think and feel Christ's presence and to know that others in their privacies do the same? Why do I need to live in the assembled church? Or indeed why is it not enough that the bread and cup move me to inward awareness of the risen Christ and to a deeper feeling of communion with him...?[58]

Jenson responds to the questions he poses as follows, a response he gleans from Luther: 'Were Christ's presence in the assembly disembodied, it would be his presence as God but *not* his presence as a human, for as a human he is a risen body.'[59] Luther reacted in horror to a sheer God 'abstracted from his embodied actuality as Jesus'. Our salvation, he rather emphasized, is in God incarnate. Jenson rightly indicates that to deny the necessity of the church is also to deny the humanity of Christ. Both are modes of gnosticism.

---

[55] See especially Cross and Thompson (eds), *Baptist Sacramentalism*; Anthony R. Cross, *Baptism and the Baptists: Theology and Practice in Twentieth-Century Britain* (Studies in Baptist History and Thought, 3; Carlisle: Paternoster Press, 2000); and Stanley K. Fowler, *More Than a Symbol: The British Baptist Recovery of Baptismal Sacramentalism* (Studies in Baptist History and Thought, 2; Carlisle: Paternoster Press, 2002).
[56] Brian Haymes, 'Making Too Little and Too Much of Baptism?', in A.R. Cross (ed.), *Ecumenism and History: Studies in Honour of John H.Y. Briggs* (Carlisle: Paternoster Press, 2002), p. 188.
[57] Haymes, 'Making Too Little', p. 187.
[58] Robert Jenson, *Systematic Theology: Volume II. The Works of God* (New York: Oxford, 1999), pp. 213-14.
[59] Jenson, *Systematic Theology*, II, p. 214.

We are now in a position to say that the modern Baptist understanding of the priesthood of the believer, or of soul competency, inasmuch as it denies the necessity of the church, easily tends toward gnosticism. A compelling example of such can be found in the work Elias Johnson (Baptist theologian in early twentieth century) who claimed that not only is the Holy Spirit 'related to the individual rather than the church, but that to speak of the Holy Spirit operating through physical matter is "unfitting."' He even went so far as to claim that 'to be taught the Good news in full by the indwelling Spirit is better to enjoy than the bodily presence of Jesus'.[60]

If Baptists today, however, are to recover a fuller sense of our priestly identity, then it will have to be tied to a deeper awareness of the incarnational nature of our faith, an awareness enacted in the sacramental worship of the gathered community. As long as the church is secondary to Baptist self-understanding, then the priesthood of the believer will remain a description primarily of the *individual*, and worship will be understood primarily as that which takes places between an individual and God. With the Reformers, however, we must emphasize not unmediated access to God, but rather the sole priesthood of Christ, in which the church as a royal priesthood corporately participates.

For a fuller understanding of the priesthood of Christ, we can fruitfully turn to the idea of *kenosis*. 'God became a human being so that nothing truly human should be deemed alien to God's being, mercy and love.'[61] Such self-emptying applies not only to Christ's birth but includes his ministry, and culminates in his death and resurrection. As Rowan Williams states, 'Our distance from God is itself taken into God, finds place in God; by the Spirit of adoption we enter the relation between Father and Son, the relation of exchange and mutuality.'[62] To call Jesus 'priest' means that we no longer have to live at a distance from God. Rather, through Christ with the Spirit we may enter into the triune life of God. As mediator or priest, Christ is the One through whom we have access in one Spirit to the Father (Eph. 2.18). As stated in Hebrews, earlier priests were prevented by death from continuing in office (Heb. 7.23), but Jesus holds his priesthood 'permanently, because he continues forever'. Thus 'he is able for all time to save those who approach God through him, since he always lives to make intercession for them (Heb. 7.25).

Such a description of the unique priesthood of Christ gives us a deeper understanding of worship as Trinitarian. As indicated by Hebrews, we enter a worship *already* going on in the life of God, where the Son in communion with the Father intercedes on our behalf. Worship is not

---

[60] As quoted by Philip Thompson, 'Re-envisioning Baptist Identity', p. 296.

[61] As quoted from Paul Valliere in Greg Jones, *Embodying Forgiveness* (Grand Rapids, MI: Eerdmans, 1995), p. 120.

[62] As quoted by Jones, *Embodying Forgiveness*, p. 120.

simply our effort, nor something we have to make happen. Rather, 'the Father has given to us the Son and the Spirit to draw us into a life of shared communion...that we might be drawn in love into the very Trinitarian life of God himself'.[63] Further, we do not stand alone before God; rather we enter into the corporate priesthood of the whole church. 'We stand alongside all whom Christ has called as his body—a holy nation of believers that stretches beyond all boundaries of geography and time.'[64]

In worship we discover that we are engrafted into the story of God. It is in worship that we acquire the skills to recognize who we are—sinners.[65] In Trinitarian worship, we also acquire the skills to discover and live our identity as priests, an identity centered in blessing and offering, or receiving and giving. We receive the forgiving and sacrificial love of Christ, and are enabled to extend this to others through intercession and service. Paul Fiddes describes this ecclesial identity well when he states that the church as a *priestly* people has the 'power to serve, to focus the presence of the Spirit and to mediate blessing *only* because it is caught up in the life of the triune God'.[66] To be caught up in the life of God is most certainly a gift of God's grace, one mediated to us through the material Body of Christ. With Schmemann, we need to emphasize that in the church the sum is greater than the parts, not because of human effort but because of the presence of the risen Christ who freely uses 'the created order in the work of redemption, particularly the gathering and building of the church'.[67] The priesthood of all believers is not an internal, spiritual phenomenon, but an ecclesial form of life, sustained by the faithful worship of God. Baptism is not only initiation into the church but also into the priesthood of all believers (Heb. 10.22).

In concluding, we might ask, is not an emphasis on the necessity of the church and an identification of it with sacraments a restriction of the freedom of God?[68] I would say that the liturgical enactment of the deeply

---

[63] Torrance, *Worship*, p. 36.

[64] Andrew Thompson, 'Trinitarian Worship', www.covchurch.org/cov/resources/greenhouse/articles/trinitarianworship.html, my emphasis. In this essay, Thompson compares James Torrance and James McClendon's theology of worship.

[65] I have especially learned this point from Stanley Hauerwas. See, for example, his *The Peaceable Kingdom: A Primer in Christian Ethics* (Notre Dame, IN: University of Notre Dame, 1983), as well as his more recent book, *Performing the Faith: Bonhoeffer and the Practice of Nonviolence* (Grand Rapids, MI: Brazos, 2004).

[66] Fiddes, *Tracks and Traces*, p. 73.

[67] Philip Thompson, 'Toward Baptist Ecclesiology in Pneumatological Perspective' (PhD thesis, Emory University, 1995), p. 61 (forthcoming as *The Freedom of God: Towards Baptist Theology in Pneumatological Perspective* [Studies in Baptist History and Thought, 20; Milton Keynes: Paternoster, 2005]).

[68] Fiddes, *Tracks and Traces*, pp. 172-73.

incarnational nature of our faith actually testifies to the freedom of God to come among us in Christ, an act which frees us to enter into communion with God and to be priests to one another through service and intercession. God's freedom to come amidst us in the material world frees us to worship God more truthfully. We are free to see, as Craig Barnes titled a sermon, that 'It's Not about You'. [69] Offering our praise and thanksgiving to God (as priests) is central to worship 'not because God is insecure and needs lots of affirmation, but because the Bible is concerned that we enjoy the freedom in knowing "it's not about us." If it is always about God, then we are free from the burden of pretending to be gods. Instead, we can return to our mission of witnessing to the grace God is giving us.' [70] As we discover our identity through the faithful worship of the Triune God, we are free to be who God created us to be, not angels or beasts, but priests receiving our lives and the world from God and offering these back to Him in humility and praise. 'As servants of God, [we] live as free people...' (1 Pet. 2.16).

---

[69] This is the title of a sermon by M. Craig Barnes, 'It's Not about You', in Joseph D. Small (ed.), *Fire and Wine: The Holy Spirit in the Church Today* (Louisville, KY: Geneva, 2002), p. 137.
[70] Barnes, 'It's Not about You', p. 137.

CHAPTER 4

The Roots of Baptists in Community, and therefore, Voluntary Membership not Individualism, or, the High-Flying Modernist, Stripped of his Ontological Assumptions, Appears to Hold the Ecclesiology of a Yaho

Mike Broadway

With apologies to John Leland, the title of this essay addresses the seriousness of the task of contemporary churches in western liberal democracies to overcome their obsession with individualistic accounts of the Christian faith.[1] Just as Leland was battling a long tradition of ecclesiastical establishment on the verge of a new era of a waxing free church, now Baptists and many others are battling the hegemonic ideas of modern western thought which have convinced church members and non-members that religion is an individual matter belonging to a private realm such that there is no justification for attending to any pretended external authority. The centrifugal force of modern individualism is such that not only is coercive religious establishment almost universally rejected in such societies (in principle, if not in every detail of practice), but also many, if not most, Christians believe that even the church can have no authority in matters of their religious faith.[2] For some time,

---

[1] My title is based upon the title of a 1791 work by John Leland, 'The Rights of Conscience Inalienable, and Therefore, Religious Opinions Not Cognizable by Law; or, the High-Flying Churchman, Stripped of His Legal Robe, Appears a Yaho', in *The Writings of the Late Elder John Leland, Including Some Events in His Life, Written by Himself, with Additional Sketches, &c.* (compiled and ed. by L.F. Greene; New York: Arno Press and The New York Times, reprint, 1969 [1845]), pp. 179-92.

[2] Cf. T. Stafford, 'The Church: Why Bother?', *Christianity Today* (January, 2005), pp. 42-49, who notes, p. 42, that in the United States there are ten million persons who identify themselves as 'born again Christians' and do not see the church as important to their spiritual lives. This leads to the odd fact that 'born again Christians' make up thirty-five percent of unchurched persons in the United States.

Baptist theologians and historians have celebrated the individualistic possibilities in Baptist theology and practice. However, few have questioned whether this is more a product of modern liberal political thought or of Christian theology. Most assume it to be the pleasant convergence of both. Yet, as churches seem to be fragmenting and disintegrating ever more from this centrifugal individualism, there has been a renewed interest in understanding the communal aspects of Christianity. Baptists have also raised questions of the appropriateness of radical individualism for people who consider themselves participants in the body of Christ. This essay addresses the myth of Baptist individualism and offers resources for a more communal ecclesiology based in the Baptist heritage.

Baptists and Individualism

Four paragraphs into Leon McBeth's extensive history of Baptists, *The Baptist Heritage*, appears the following statement:

> Clearly the Baptists fit the temperament of their times. Conditions were right for the emergence of more individualistic forms of religion, and the spate of new religious groups in England show that they took full advantage of the day. Not only Baptists, but also Levellers, Runners, Ranters, Quakers, Independents, and others rose during this unstable time.[3]

Following the pattern of much Baptist historiography and theology from the twentieth century, McBeth characterizes Baptists as individualistic. It is a claim that rings true in contemporary Baptist life. The corruption of the doctrine of the priesthood of all believers, often renamed as 'the priesthood of the believer', has led to its being interpreted to mean there can be no mediation between Christ and the believer.[4] In vulgar terms, it can be stated 'ain't nobody gonna tell me what to believe'. It is the defiant cry of the Bible reader who says, 'God said it. I believe it. That settles it.' When those three sentences are rearranged, one gets a more accurate depiction of the reader's claim as, 'I believe it. That settles it: God said it.'

McBeth comes by his point of view honestly. His teachers and their teachers before them had been defining individualism as at the heart of Baptist tradition. Influential Southern Baptist writer and pastor from the mid-twentieth century Herschel H. Hobbs's first sentence in *What Baptists Believe* is, 'Basic in the principles of Baptists is the concept of the

---

[3] H.L. McBeth, *The Baptist Heritage: Four Centuries of Baptist Witness* (Nashville, TN: Broadman Press, 1987), p. 20.

[4] Cf. B. Newman, 'The Priesthood of All Believers and the Necessity of the Church' in the present volume.

competency of each individual soul before God.'[5] Here Hobbs is following in the same tradition as Edgar Young Mullins, internationally influential former President of The Southern Baptist Seminary in Louisville, who in his systematic theology states, 'The gospel rests on the infinite worth of individual men.'[6] Winthrop Hudson points out the shape of ecclesiology that such an individualistic theology produces in the work of W.R. McNutt, Professor of Practical Theology at Crozer Theological Seminary in the first half of the twentieth century, commenting that when soul competency and individualism are made 'the cardinal doctrine of Baptists' then it makes 'every man's hat his own church'.[7] McNutt deduced from the primacy of soul competency that the doctrine of the church was a secondary or derivative concept. Christians can freely associate for utilitarian reasons according to the supreme judgment of the individual believers, but they must not concede any of their divinely granted authority to an institution. The examples could be multiplied, but there would be little to gain. Few would be surprised to hear that contemporary Baptists interpret Christian theology with a strong dose of individualism. This interpretation of Baptist theology assumes that the voluntaryism of Baptist ecclesiology is inherently tied to individualist ontology.

A small body of literature has sought to distinguish the terms voluntarism and voluntaryism in Baptist theology. The distinctions are negligible in the broadest meanings of the words. Each can have technical meanings pertaining to philosophical concepts. Voluntarism often describes an ontological claim about the will of the individual, a debate within individualistic ontology, which this essay intends to bypass. The term voluntaryism sometimes refers to a version of the political theory of anarchism, a meaning which goes beyond the scope of this essay. The particular meaning of voluntaryism used in this essay would emphasize the contrast between membership and support of communities on the basis of a governmental, coercive, or natural reasons, and membership and support which requires intentional participation or conversion. The argument which follows will demonstrate that voluntaryism of this sort need not be allied with modern individualism.

---

[5] H. H. Hobbs, *What Baptists Believe* (Nashville, TN: Broadman Press, 1964), p. 7.

[6] E. Y. Mullins, *The Christian Religion in its Doctrinal Expression* (Nashville, TN: The Sunday School Board of the Southern Baptist Convention, 1917), p. 261.

[7] W. Hudson, *Baptists in Transition: Individualism and Christian Responsibility* (Valley Forge, PA: Judson Press, 1979), p. 142.

Is Voluntaryism an Individualistic Concept?

While there is popular justification in the contemporary context for most people to think of voluntaryism as a corollary to individualism, the two are not held together by necessity. Modern individualism makes an ontological claim about the primacy of individual persons in the nature of reality. It can be defined as the theory that knowledge, value, and action find their source in the individual person. Individualism corresponds to a theory of society as articulated by the social contract tradition of Thomas Hobbes, John Locke, Immanuel Kant, and others. This social theory claims that human beings exist first of all as individuals, only later in time and logic entering into society for the sake of some mutual interest. As Hobbes articulated human nature, the unitary principle of natural law comes down to self-preservation. This understanding of human nature was carried forward into capitalist social theory such that self-interest is the assumed motivation of all human beings, who consequently pursue heterogeneous ends. David Hume's moral theories reaffirmed a self-interested hedonism as the true motivation of all human action, even those actions which appear to be altruistic. René Descartes, Hume, and Immanuel Kant in their own ways articulated the epistemology of individualism. Descartes's famous 'I think; therefore, I am' became the asserted foundation for the establishment of all knowledge by means of knowing one's own thoughts. Hume's skeptical questioning of the relationship of perception to reality drew attention to the human subject's assertive role in constructing knowledge. Kant's more complex theory of the structuring of human thought by necessary categories sought to bridge human subjectivity and an elusive objective reality. Kant's ethics rooted all moral goodness in the intention or will of the acting individual. The contemporary ethical proposals of John Rawls, Robert Nozick, and many others continue to remodel the rooms of the Enlightenment's individualistic edifice, adding window dressings to suit twentieth-century sensibilities.[8]

The evolution and devolution of modern individualism has been studied and articulated at great length in the works of such philosophers as Jeffrey Stout, Charles Taylor and Alasdair MacIntyre,[9] and there is no reason to restate their arguments in this essay. However, severing the

---

[8] J. Rawls, *A Theory of Justice* (Cambridge, MA: Belknap Press, rev. edn, 1999); R. Nozick, *Anarchy, State, and Utopia* (New York: Basic Books, 1974).

[9] J. Stout, *The Flight from Authority: Religion, Morality, and the Quest for Autonomy* (Notre Dame, IN: University of Notre Dame, 1981); A. MacIntyre, *After Virtue: A Study in Moral Theory* (Notre Dame, IN: University of Notre Dame, 2nd edn, 1984); C. Taylor, *Sources of the Self: The Making of the Modern Identity* (Cambridge, MA: Harvard University, 1989).

assumed bond between individualism and voluntaryism is a task that must be taken up if Baptists today are to gain a better understanding of their heritage. The anachronistic habit of recent Baptist scholars has been to declare modern individualism to be characteristic of Baptists from their very beginnings. Moreover, Baptists have seldom been willing to stop with Baptist origins, preferring instead to trace modern individualism all the way back to the Bible. Yet there is a growing awareness among scholars of Baptist history and theology that more recent theories of modern individualism should not be attributed to seventeenth- and eighteenth-century Baptists.

Any sort of conversionist understanding of Christian faith entails an aspect of voluntary commitment to Jesus Christ. Baptists and others are quick to point out that Jesus repeatedly approached people and beckoned them to 'Follow me'. They were not coerced into becoming his followers, nor did they follow by fatalistic power beyond their control. There was a voluntary act on their part (enabled by God's grace) to take up the way of Jesus. One would be hard pressed to describe human action as perceived by any number of theoretical understandings of human nature and social existence—whether ancient, medieval or modern—without a concept of voluntary action. While the defining power of personal choice may be overstated by existentialism and other modern anthropological theories, and while the ubiquity of choosing may be overstated in decisionist moral theories, any satisfactory descriptions of human action must make some place for deliberative choice. More classic understandings from Aristotle or Thomas Aquinas help to show that deliberation occurs within the context of one's social formation and training; moreover, they do not assume that all training in traditional moral concepts is a prejudice to be avoided. Thus, acting according to conscience is not so much the immediate and underived knowledge of truth occurring to the mind of the individual, as it is a social formation and habituation toward virtuosity, or viciousness, in behavior. Such voluntary actions entail a person's consent to the reasonability and appropriateness of the best that one can discern in light of one's formation. Such actions appear to be anything but arbitrary or purely individual. This sort of understanding of 'voluntary' is far from the late modern concept of decision in the crisis of the moment, characterized by the sense of isolation and arbitrariness implied in the cliché 'damned if you do; damned if you don't'.

A second aspect of voluntaryism also requires consideration. Theories of modern liberal societies entail a conception of natural societies, such as nation-states and families, and voluntary societies, such as churches, clubs, etc. The nation-state is a collectivity of individuals who define a communal identity articulated in theories of nationalism and mutual self-preservation. Each individual is incorporated into the collectivity through legal obligations imposed by the state in light of an ephemeral or imagined act of consent of the governed. Otherwise, the individuals remain free to associate as they choose. Churches, in turn, become theorized as voluntary associations of individuals. Having originated as independent individuals, persons choose to affiliate according to their religious preferences. When a person leaves an association voluntarily, the converse description applies: one returns to the condition of an individual. It seems perfectly reasonable in modern thought to think of a person as a solitary Christian, apart from the church as articulated by McNutt. Contemporary Christians in the United States maintain a sense of being a 'free agent', comparing various churches with which to affiliate. The practice of comparing preachers, buildings, fellowships, parking lots, and social status of various churches is sometimes called 'church shopping'. Many a church member enters into membership with the assumption that if this church does not work out, there are others to try. While such a theory of religion may seem 'natural' to contemporary readers, it does not represent the only possible interpretation of voluntary church membership. Moreover, this description of churches departs dramatically from the heritage of Christian social thought and ecclesiology.

Analyzing voluntaryism in light of a biblical example need not lead to an individualistic understanding. The disciples who voluntarily followed Jesus went from a community of fishers to a community of Jesus' followers. Another biblical depiction of voluntarily becoming a follower of Jesus would say that a person came out of the world and into the church. There is no need for a theory of an individual status underlying the two social structures, or for a moment of individuality in between membership in two different associations. Again, using biblical language, one may remain a slave to sin or submit to Christ. There is no claim for a neutral position. To be human is to be in relation to one end or another; the untenable concept of being adrift with no end or purpose is rooted in the modern ontology of the isolated individual and not in Christian theology. It is a false consciousness rooted in a misunderstanding of humanity and God. Although Christians in modern times may need to bear witness to people whose consciousness has conceded to individualism, the antidote will not come from a baptized theory of individualism. A contrasting ontology of Christian solidarity as the body of Christ, as a holy nation, as a peculiar people, as a called out community, provides access to a view of humanity informed by Christian theology.

One case from Baptist history can further illustrate a better understanding of voluntaryist ecclesiology. Historians have pointed out that Separate Baptists of the eighteenth-century southern colonies, and later states, practiced a voluntaryist form of ecclesiology. This voluntaryism should not be assumed to mean individualism. The Separate Baptists became known for opposing coercive means of bringing people into the church. Thus, the opposite term for coercive is voluntary. Yet, when persons voluntarily entered into Separate Baptist churches they faced high expectations about their commitment to the community and its mission. To fall short of these expectations consistently would lead to disciplinary consequences. A strong mutual commitment was considered necessary for the church to maintain its identity over against the world. The Separate Baptists believed they were forming the distinct community of God's people.

Baptist theology has clearly been open to individualistic interpretations, yet there is much in the heritage which ought to show that Baptist thought and practice need not revolve around an individualistic axis. The remainder of this essay will examine three aspects of Baptist beginnings to uncover central claims of Baptists which undermine the assumption that Baptist heritage is individualistic to the core. The first is the connection between non-separatist Puritan Independents and the Particular Baptists of England, forerunners of many Baptists in the American colonies. The second is the early seventeenth-century beginnings of General Baptists in England as an outgrowth of Separatist traditions of covenant communities. The third is the eighteenth-century beginnings of Separate Baptists in the North American South as disciplined communities over against the mainstream of society.

Mixed Polity among Non-Separatists and Particular Baptists

Among the many streams of Puritanism, a congregational tradition emerged. This congregational stream of English Christianity accounts for much of the heritage of the Baptist churches. Winthrop Hudson argues that one major strand of Baptist development should locate its early identity in the non-separatist 'Independents' of the Westminster Assembly. He claims that these congregational Dissenters rejected both 'Brownism' (a pejorative term for Separatism) and the hierarchical Presbyterian structure advocated by the Westminster divines. They envisioned a middle way wherein local congregations exercise all the prerogatives of the church, including the selection of their own leaders and excommunication, but these congregations remain responsible to larger associations for advice and maintenance of good order and peace. Such an understanding of the church, with powers distributed both to local congregations and to associations was recorded by the non-Separatists of Westminster in numerous writings. Hudson claims,

This 'middle way'...found its most concise and orderly statement in the Platform of Government appended to the Savoy Declaration and then incorporated by the

Baptists into their London or Philadelphia Confession as their Article on the Church, and was then further explicated in Baptist treatises of church discipline.[10]

The Particular Baptists of seventeenth-century England, such as those in the church led by Henry Jessey, emerged out of this moderate, non-separatist party. They became the larger of the two streams of English Baptist churches of that era, and from among them came many of the early Baptists of the American colonies.

The significance of this argument for Hudson rests especially in its pertinence to a nineteenth-century disagreement among Baptists in the United States. Hudson claims that the powerful wave of individualistic thought in United States' politics eventually affected Baptist understandings of the church. A more individualistic, anarchic understanding of the church led some to propose that all cooperative activity beyond the local congregation be conducted on the 'society' model wherein individual members of many churches unite to pursue a common cause. A robust debate over the proper structure for supra-congregational activity emerged. Hudson points out that the theological resources for a mixed polity of churches and associations had been accepted by the Particular Baptists of England, and their ecclesial descendents carried them forward to North America to be restated by the Philadelphia Association. Its mixed polity with emphasis on con-gergational authority reflected an ecclesiology that did not presuppose the same sort of individualism as the nineteenth-century Baptists were encountering in their social milieu. It is true that Baptists modified the non-separatist Independents' ecclesiology to affirm believers' baptism and a Free Church without aid of the magistrate's sword or purse. Even so, they retained a communal understanding of the church which reached beyond the local congregation to affirm certain types of authority as shared by the churches in association.[11] These associations were made up of churches, not of individuals. It was not the authority of the individual which grounded this sort of ecclesiology. Individuals did not have the authority to speak to or for the church at large, but they spoke as a congregation in their broader ecclesial structures. The ecclesiological

---

[10] Hudson, *Baptists in Transition*, pp. 27-28; the *Savoy Declaration* and its accompanying statement on church order can be found in Williston Walker, *Creeds and Platforms of Congregationalism* (Boston: Pilgrim, reprint edn, 1960), or at 'The Savoy Declaration of Faith and Order, 1658', Center for Reformed Theology and Apologetics, http://www.reformed.org/documents/Savoy_Declaration/index.html, accessed on 11 September 2003; the *Second London Confession* and the *Philadelphia Confession* are available in W.L. Lumpkin, *Baptist Confessions of Faith* (Valley Forge, PA: Judson Press, 1959), or at P. Johnson, 'The Hall of Church History', http://www.gty.org/~phil/creeds.htm, accessed on 11 September 2003.

[11] Hudson, *Baptists in Transition*, pp. 32-33.

significance of the association stands for Hudson as a sign of the non-individualistic heritage of Particular Baptists.

Baptist Covenant Communities

Both Particular and General Baptists in seventeenth-century England participated in the practice of forming covenant communities. This tradition is especially noted in the Separatist movement from which emerged the General Baptist churches. John Smyth's congregation in Gainsborough entered into covenant together to constitute their response to God's calling them out of the worldly Church of England to a common life of mutual admonition toward holiness and diligent study of the scriptures. This joining in covenant was the constitutive act by which they became a church. John Smyth affirmed, in the years before the congregation became Baptist, that their covenant together was the basis of their pilgrimage together.[12] They saw the local congregation as the structure by which discipleship became possible. James Robert Coggins argues that face-to-face, shared accountability and governance followed their understanding of the New Testament pattern by which the saints could together grow to be a holy people. The covenant community could maintain its practices of communal discipline and discernment, of reconciliation and forgiveness, and of a shared interpretation of scripture, only if they also maintained a common life by which members knew one another intimately. After seeking refuge in Holland, the Smyth-Helwys congregation did not join the Ancient Church of fellow English Separatists in part as a way to maintain a size capable of this level of fellowship.[13]

Oddly enough, McBeth never mentions covenants in his introductory section tracing the heritage of Separatist churches which preceded the appearance of the Smyth-Helwys Baptists.[14] Yet it was this very practice of joining together in covenant by which such churches constituted their existence. As he describes the beginnings of first the General Baptist churches and later the Particular Baptist churches, McBeth mentions the existence or composition of covenants mostly in passing. Perhaps this explains his lack of emphasis on the practice of writing and joining in covenant—it may seem to be such an obvious part of the story that it becomes commonplace, an expendable detail. The pervasiveness of covenants to this period of dissenting churches must not, however,

---

[12] J. Smyth, 'Principles and Inferences Concerning the Visible Church (1607)', in *The Works of John Smyth* (ed. W.T. Whitley; 2 vols; Cambridge: Cambridge University Press, 1915), I, p. 252.

[13] J.R. Coggins, *John Smyth's Congregation* (Scottdale, PA: Herald Press, 1991), 41, 151.

[14] McBeth, *Baptist Heritage*, pp. 22-32.

diminish their pivotal role in shaping the believers' church ecclesiology which was in formation. These kinds of covenants represent a substantial element of Congregational, Separatist, and Baptist polity. In churches constituted by their relationship with a ruler or government, or by a hierarchy of priests or presbyters, the discipline and order for congregational life are received from higher authorities. But in a congregational polity, discipline, order, even the very existence of the congregation depends on the mutual commitment of a gathered people to unite in following the Lord Jesus.[15] In contrast to this formative period of covenantal ecclesiology, Hudson points out that the devolution of Baptist ecclesiology in the late nineteenth century came as a result of the hegemony of individualism in the culture of the United States, so that

> Discipline was relaxed, the covenant fell into disuse, the pastoral office was obscured, the deacons were shunted to one side, while boards and committees proliferated. Admission procedures and baptismal practices became lax and indiscriminate; the guarding of the integrity of the Lord's table was forgotten; the covenant meeting was discarded; and the church meeting frayed out in preoccupation with trivialities. The older conception of covenanting with the Lord and with one another to walk together 'in all the ways of obedience which He prescribeth,' which had been partially replaced by the notion of the church as a purely evangelistic center, was now to give way to an understanding of the church which was defined almost completely in instrumental terms.[16]

To enter into covenant with fellow believers is to place oneself under discipline. Not only the General Baptists emerging from Separatism, but also the Particular Baptists practiced covenantal discipleship. Both the *First London Confession* (1644) and the *Second London Confession* (1677) are explicit in their assertion of the ecclesiastical authority of congregations in matters of faith, morality, and order,[17] and in this they exemplify the entire early tradition of Baptist covenantal communities. To enter into covenant is to come out of one body into another, leaving behind the world to enter the church. It is submission to the authority of the church. It is not the same as the later conception of liberal democratic theory by which individuals freely associate and assemble. Covenant communities acknowledged God's gracious calling and joined together as a new people, not a collection of individuals with shared interests. This covenantal heritage stands over against the individualistic ideas of recent history.

---

[15] Coggins, *Smyth's Congregation*, pp. 33-34
[16] Hudson, *Baptists in Transition*, p. 131.
[17] Lumpkin, *Baptist Confessions of Faith*, pp. 168 and 286.

Disciplined Communities

Donald Mathews challenged the conventional wisdom when he suggested that individualism did not correctly describe the churches of the Great Awakening in the South, including the Separate Baptists. In *Religion in the Old South*, he identifies three central characteristics of Separate Baptist belief and practice which provide evidence of the social revolution which their movement represented: the personal religious experience, immersion of adult converts, and submission to the authority of the church. This third characteristic is often ignored by historians and theologians assessing the Baptist tradition. Mathews depicts the movement as communal:

> the gospel preached by [Shubal] Stearns and his itinerant colleagues quite clearly rejected the values that made invidious distinctions between people on the basis of political power, wealth, or family background. The community created by personal experience, baptism and discipline was a reproach to the old order and a promise of a new one.[18]

Mathews goes on to question the dominant thesis of the centrality of individualism in the Evangelical Revival of the eighteenth century. While certain elements of the revival resonate with individualism—intense introspection, illumination of the Holy Spirit, voluntary church membership—these aspects need not be encoded as belonging to the polar opposition between individualism and community. On the contrary, the opposition lay between the church and the world. No solitary Christian stood over against the church; rather, converts accepted the careful oversight and guidance of a distinct community of believers who exercised loving discipline. Rather than privatizing religion, the evangelical revivals led to an elimination of 'private sin'. Any offense was an offense against the community's order and reputation. The fellowship meetings and discipline of the church served to help educate Christians on the way they were to live.[19]

Mathews criticizes the common assumption that the voluntary nature of the evangelical denominations means that they were individualistic. 'Voluntaryism' interpreted as a kind of radical independence of individuals

> does not capture the element of social participation and fellowship which lured people into the Southern Evangelical movement. Nor does the concept incorporate the impact of the networks of discipline and communication which projected social

---

[18] D. Mathews, *Religion in the Old South* (Chicago History of American Religion Series; Chicago: University of Chicago Press, 1977), p. 24.
[19] Mathews, *Religion in the Old South*, pp. 40-45.

relations and obligations beyond the will of the individual into the community, society, and next generation.[20]

Thus, Mathews stresses participation in the life of the community rather than an individualistic interpretation of voluntaryism. Conversion, living within the community and according to its way of life, was required of any Christian. By becoming part of a Separate Baptist church one was not any longer at the mercy of the priesthood and vestry in the old class system inherited from England. Community members shared the governance of the church, admission of members, and discipline. This conversion and voluntary membership describes a movement from one ecclesial and political order to another one.

John Leland was one of the most prolific writers of the Great Awakening in the South. Many have portrayed him as a radical individualist of a more recent sort, and they have done so with good reason. Some of his writings and practices revealed a more thorough individualism than Mathews finds among others of his time. One reason Leland's writings reveal an individualistic voice is because of his extensive reading in modern liberal political thought from such figures as John Locke, Thomas Jefferson, and James Madison. He had learned the language of the secular individualists and found ways to relate it to the evangelical theologies.[21] Yet in many of his writings are signs of a more communal understanding of the church.

When Leland discusses the authority of conscience, he gives no impression that conscience is an innate or native sense that guides one to recognize God's leadership. Rather, the conscience must be rightly informed through training in the life of the community of faith as one studies the scriptures and discerns God's message.[22] Conversion need not be seen in such individualistic terms, as some would have it. Rejecting the established church's pattern of defining church membership did not mean that the Separate Baptists relegated conversion to individuals. Instead, they transferred from the government-supported church to the local church the authority to determine whether a person is qualified to be a member of the church and therefore to be numbered among the regenerate. A believer must confess his faith before the assembly. Particular believers were expected to have a personal conversion in which

---

[20] Mathews, *Religion in the Old South*, p. 57.

[21] J. Leland, 'The Virginia Chronicle', (1790), in *The Writings of the Late Elder John Leland*, p. 108, and 'The Rights of Conscience Inalienable', p. 181; additional evidence of Leland's influence by liberal political thought appears throughout his collected writings, and it has been documented in M. Broadway, 'The Ways of Zion Mourned: A Historicist Critique of Church–State Relations' (PhD thesis, Duke University, 1993), pp. 216-20, 387-92.

[22] Leland, 'Rights of Conscience', in *Leland's Writings*, pp. 180-81.

they found themselves to be under God's grace as defined by the tradition of the Separate Baptists of the Great Awakening, and the gathered church was responsible to determine whether the regeneration was authentic.[23] Thus, in Leland's ecclesiology one finds Mathews's claims spelled out explicitly:

> A church of Christ, according to the Gospel, is a congregation of faithful persons, called out of the world by divine grace, who mutually agree to live together, and execute gospel discipline among them; which government is not national, parochial, or presbyterial, but congregational.[24]

This concern about the separate, disciplined community of faith, over against the world, helps to indicate Leland's argument against establishment as well. Established churches forced everyone under a given civil authority to be members of the church, from birth. Such a church's discipline could not be according to the gospel, which eschews coercion and relies on persuasion.

In a work devoted to the study of Separate Baptist ecclesiology, James Owen Renault argues that after a period of experimentation and indefinite structures, Separate Baptists in the South began to develop a more uniform ecclesiology. While Renault identifies the 'immediate' illumination of the Holy Spirit as an example of individualism, one must wonder if this judgment would apply to the entire history of visions and proclamations going back through the centuries to the New Testament period. If so, it would certainly be a different sort of individualism than modern social thought describes. Renault himself indicates that all such uttered illuminations were subject to the discernment of the church. Nor do ministers escape this communal oversight; Renault points out that Separate Baptist ministers were subject to discipline by the larger associations. If they were judged to be out of order, they could be assigned additional periods of training to gain a better understanding of the teachings of the churches.[25]

Renault criticizes much of the previous work done on Separate Baptist ecclesiology for its lack of analysis of the arguments for and against participation in associations. He points out that in the nature of Separate Baptist practice, these churches seemed inexorably compelled to form associations and meet regularly, while at the same time they feared that associations might usurp local prerogatives. He argues that they arrived at a decentralized form of connectionalism, forming associations for the purposes of mutual encouragement and fellowship, cooperation on

---

[23] Leland, 'Chronicle', in *Leland's Writings*, p. 116.
[24] Leland, 'Chronicle', p. 108.
[25] J.O. Renault, 'The Development of Separate Baptist Ecclesiology in the South, 1755–1976' (PhD thesis, Southern Baptist Theological Seminary, 1978), pp. 115-20.

matters which concerned all of the churches, and providing a clearinghouse for ministerial candidates.[26] This commitment to a mixed polity with some authority resting in associations further undermines the assumption that individualism is the organizing principle for Baptist ecclesiology.

The Separate Baptists' reputation for discipline was recognized early in their development. In 1768, when Separate Baptists were suffering their harshest persecution, the colonial Governor John Blair recommended the release of two imprisoned preachers on the basis of the sect's reputation for communal discipline. He wrote to the county magistrate that Baptists were conscientious not to allow their members to be idle and fail to provide for their families. Their strong moral example had become well known in a short time.[27]

Many matters of communal discipline were discussed at length in weekly meetings of the congregations. Often congregations sent official queries to the associational gatherings in order to seek counsel from the larger Baptist community. In response to one query, churches were advised that a man who marries his wife's sister ought not to be admitted to membership. When answering a query about ordination and local church leadership, the Dover Association in Virginia advised local churches of their particular duty to observe the moral behavior of their ministers.[28] Renault points out that a member's business practices, relationships with others, and treatment of slaves were subject to examination and censure.[29]

Leland emphasized the importance of fellowship and unity of practice in the church. A congregation who shared the zeal of bearing witness to Christ and of mutual concern for one another need not worry much about doctrinal diversity.[30] Semple reports that some churches might allow women to pray in public, even to preach.[31] Such practices were determined by the local congregation. Disciplinary action might be taken against members who failed to participate in the Lord's Supper, business meetings, or other church functions.[32] The extent to which doctrine ought to be a matter of discipline was highly debated. Separate Baptist ministers lacked formal theological training, for the most part, and lay church members most often had even less training. There was a tendency among

---

[26] Renault, 'Ecclesiology', p. 120.
[27] R.B. Semple, *A History of the Rise and Progress of the Baptists in Virginia* (Richmond, VA: John Lynch, 1810), p. 16.
[28] Semple, *History*, pp. 55, 92.
[29] Renault, 'Ecclesiology', p. 111.
[30] Leland, 'Letter of Valediction on Leaving Virginia, in 1791', in *Leland's Writings*, p. 172.
[31] Semple, *History*, 5; Renault, 'Ecclesiology', pp. 114-15.
[32] Renault, 'Ecclesiology', p. 111.

the Separates to avoid confessions of faith or any such theological documents which they feared would usurp the authoritative place of the scriptures within their congregations. To the great displeasure of the older association of Regular Baptists, the Separates did not want to be held to the details of a document written by uninspired human beings. When they grew to have so many churches with so many members that it finally seemed prudent to adopt a confession, the Separates agreed to the *Philadelphia Confession* with some reservations: 'We do not mean that every person is to be bound to the strict observance of every thing therein contained.'[33]

This emphasis on matters of a common life of people 'who mutually agree to live together', as Leland had put it, should turn attention away from individualism toward the communal life of congregations. Separate Baptist communities seem to have paid most attention to the practical piety and fellowship within their congregations. Most of the queries from churches to associations reported by Semple deal with these sorts of matters. They limited their censures concerning doctrinal matters in order to avoid the errors they perceived in established churches focused on coercive imposition of uniformity through a select priestly class. This need not be seen as affirming a kind of individualism that assumes all true knowledge originates in the individual person. Their form of discipline was not tied to the enforcement of a strict legalistic code. The churches hoped to maintain themselves as exemplary communities of mutual concern and righteousness in the midst of a world of unrighteousness and false claims to power. Certain matters deemed to be most fractious, such as some doctrinal disputes, were intentionally placed to the side so that they would not become instruments of division within the called-out community.

Conclusion

One would be hard-pressed to deny that the history of Baptist thought has not found numerous opportunities to turn in individualistic directions. There is little doubt that most denominations in western liberal democratic societies have found ways to incorporate individualism into their self-understanding. Yet to recognize individualistic trends in Baptist history is not the same as showing these trends to be incipient in the origins of Baptists, nor is it the same as showing them to be at the core of Baptist theology.

One can identify numerous causes for the shift in Baptist ecclesiology toward individualism. Already this essay has noted John Leland's example as a Baptist who read and was influenced by Enlightenment

---

[33] Semple, *History*, pp. 68-69.

thinkers. Certainly the ideas of the independent United States of America, its Constitution and Bill of Rights, and its dedication to a free market are concepts which have captured the imaginations of residents of the United States, including church members. As the new world order of democratic revolutions progressed, philosophical and theological ideas raced to make sense of a world in which individuals claimed priority. Mathews cites another reason in the awakenings churches of the South. He argues that the structure of communal discipline began to break down especially over the issues of race and slavery.[34] Mathews examines the attempts of the new churches to bring an end to slavery in the 1780s in light of their understanding that the gospel brings all people—black or white, slave or free—into one family as equals before God. Yet these attempts faltered and failed.[35] Although the Baptists of the awakening held strong moral convictions about family and community life, white Baptists found themselves lacking the will to endorse the family life and marriages of black brothers and sisters in Christ when churches raised this question.[36] Ultimately, they relinquished their authority over the social lives of church members by handing matters of race and slavery over to the government, confessing that these were not matters for the church to decide.[37] This division of authority laid the groundwork for a gradual process of spiritualization and privatization by which the church abdicated authority in social and political realms. By the definitions of liberal political thought, these church members were individuals who have exercised their rights of freedom of assembly to join together in voluntary associations made up of individuals who, in exercising their freedom of religion, have come to similar preferences. Baptists, and others, internalized these ideas to the point that they replaced understandings of humanity and society derived from the scriptures and Christian tradition.

It would be surprising indeed to find that a family of churches as successful as Baptists have been in modern western societies had not adapted themselves to prominent philosophical trends such as individualism. However, Baptists came on the scene as critics of churches who had adapted themselves to the cultural and philosophical mainstream. Having risen in social status and prosperity across the

---

[34] Mathews, *Religion*, p. 76.
[35] Mathews, *Religion*, pp. 68-69, 75.
[36] Semple, *History*, pp. 93-94, 101
[37] The closest that Virginia Baptists came to a public rejection of slavery was a resolution adopted by the General Committee in 1788, which called slavery a 'horrid evil' in contrast to the biblical 'Jubilee'; however, they proposed no church discipline for slaveholding and called on the legislature to proclaim the Jubilee by abolishing slavery, qualifying their statement with the final phrase 'consistent with the principles of good policy', in Semple, *History*, p. 79.

centuries, Baptists have become less likely to offer systemic criticism of the culture and society of the United States. In addition, historical amnesia concerning race and slavery influences white Baptists not to recognize some of the causes of individualistic thought in Baptist theology. Recognizing the preeminence of congregational covenants in the formative period of English Baptists and the social participation and counter-politics of North American Separate Baptists, the evidence seems strong that Baptists should reconsider their self-identification as individualists.

CHAPTER 5

A Good Walk Spoiled?: Revisiting Baptist Soteriology

Mark S. Medley

It is a Wednesday evening prayer meeting service at Listre Baptist Church, the center of official religious activity in the slow and predictable town of Listre, North Carolina. Pastor Crenshaw is to preach a sermon on the temptation narratives in Matthew's Gospel. The occasion for the sermon is Crenshaw's confrontation with and avoidance of temptation to act on his lustful desires for Cheryl Daniels, a voluptuous, nineteen-year-old woman in the church. While he imagines himself making love to Cheryl, the closest he comes to acting on his impulses is a suggestive letter he writes but never sends. Mrs Clark, the church's secretary, finds the seductive letter. However, rather than create a scandal, she merely writes a note to Pastor Crenshaw saying that she would not tell anyone and that she had 'turned it all over to Jesus'.[1] In response to Mrs Clark's note, Pastor Crenshaw confronts his sin and experiences a renewal of faith. Preaching his sermon on the wiles of temptation, he feels 'the power of his redemption, his rededication, his partnership with Jesus'.[2] And Mrs Clark can see Pastor Crenshaw's torment and guilt, confession and repentance. 'He had been through an event that brought Jesus to Listre, and Jesus has saved his life.'[3]

During the sermon six-year-old Stephen Toomey wrestles with the call of Jesus on his heart. Stephen knew 'how you got saved'—that if Jesus called you walked down front and told Pastor Crenshaw that you believed in God and Jesus. After the third stanza of 'Just as I am'

> Stephen felt Jesus' fingers gently touch his heart. The music was touching his cheeks, his whole face. The whole big room was full of Jesus and music. The color of Jesus was a smokey gray. Jesus was there in his head and in his heart, floating around, calling out—Come, come, come. It was happening. He could almost, but not quite, see Jesus. Jesus was whispering into his heart, words that were not words,

---

[1] C. Edgerton, *Where Trouble Sleeps* (Chapel Hill, NC: Algonquin Books, 1997), p. 213.
[2] Edgerton, *Where Trouble Sleeps*, p. 219.
[3] Edgerton, *Where Trouble Sleeps*, p. 223.

words that acted, tugged at him, drawing him down toward the front, down to give his heart to Jesus, down to Preacher Crenshaw, God's man on earth... Mr. Crenshaw said to the congregation, 'Take that first step, take that first step, take that *first step*.'... Stephen stepped into the aisle and Jesus was in him, leading him every step of the way. He was in Jesus. He felt like he was going to cry because he loved Jesus so much. Jesus was saving him.[4]

After Pastor Crenshaw 'counseled' another man, concluding with 'God bless you. Just have a seat. Fill out the form on the clipboard there. God bless you', he turned to Stephen.[5] Asking the young boy if he accepted Jesus as his personal Savior, Stephen, weeping and sobbing, said 'Yes'. At this moment, Stephen's mother, Alease, moved out of the pew and walked down to the front to her son. 'Her main prayer in the world had been answered. Her son *had been* saved... The *final* act had happened. Her son *was* saved.'[6]

What novelist Clyde Edgerton recounts in Stephen's 'walking the aisle' is an aspect of the worship 'experience' common among Baptist congregations of the American South. It reflects the deep conversionist roots of Baptist piety and theology. More specifically, it reflects a narrow understanding of soteriology to a specific 'traumatic event which chronicled the day and the moment from here to eternity'.[7] This practice of salvation expresses the conviction that if one turns from sin, prays 'the sinner's prayer', lets Jesus into one's heart, and believes, one is saved. In other words, this specific experience of regeneration diminishes the journey or story of salvation to a transactional, decisive, voluntary, punctiliar, individual moment which provides immediate salvation, once and for all. The negative effect of such a foreshortening of the drama of salvation for Baptists in the American South has resulted in, first, an overemphasis on justification, understood in almost exclusively forensic terms, and, secondly, an increasing divide between justification and sanctification. Moreover, salvation has been located in the solitary self, whose traumatic conversion experience alone could attest to the efficacy of Christ's work of reconciliation. Thus the soteriological focus is an almost exclusive concern for the gateway to conversion rather than on the way of the Christian life. In other words, Baptists in the American South have 'spoiled' the good walk of the aisle.

Accordingly, one could assess Baptist soteriology as Molly Marshall has: 'As a conversionist denomination, Baptists have a robust understanding of inauguration of salvation but an anemic doctrine of

---

[4] Edgerton, *Where Trouble Sleeps*, pp. 222-23.
[5] Edgerton, *Where Trouble Sleeps*, p. 224.
[6] Edgerton, *Where Trouble Sleeps*, p. 224. Emphasis added.
[7] B.J. Leonard, 'Getting Saved in America: Conversion Event in a Pluralistic Culture', *Review and Expositor* 82.1 (Winter, 1985), p. 111.

sanctification.'[8] Her appraisal of a Baptist focus on justification is accurate. Moreover, her assessment of sanctification is on target, at least regarding contemporary Baptists in the American South. However, one should not take her comment on sanctification to mean that Baptists historically have not had a robust and strong doctrine of sanctification. Such a (mis)perception is the 'myth' this essay seeks to challenge. It will be argued that if a 'way of Baptist theology' is disciplined by the practice of *ressourcement* and returns to seventeenth-century Baptist theology, then one can 'rediscover' and retrieve a Baptist soteriology which emphasizes sanctifying grace and salvation as a journey, a story, or a pilgrimage. Moreover, as Paul Fiddes has recently argued, such a soteriology was not individualistic in character but ecclesially defined, as exemplified in a Baptist theology of covenant.[9]

In order to challenge this 'myth', this essay will first trace the factors that lead to such a 'myth'. Attention will be given to a morphology and theology of conversion influential in American Evangelicalism, and its influence and effect on Baptists in the American South. The essay will then revisit seventeenth-century Baptist soteriology. Following a brief summary of Eric Ohlmann's thesis on Baptists and sanctification, an examination of seventeenth-century Baptist confessions will suggest that Baptists in fact had a refined and robust understanding of sanctification.

Towards a 'Sacrament' of Transaction

Christian life is grounded in the grace of God. It is based on being placed 'in Christ' by the power of the Holy Spirit.[10] Christian life is a dynamic process of transformation of conformity to the image of Christ that is set in motion by the gracious initiative of God. Christian life is patterned after the life, death, and resurrection of Jesus and thus is a continuous dying to an old way of life and a rising to a new one. 'It is both mortification and vivification, both receiving and responding, both passive and active, both gift and task, both being freed and exercising new freedom, both being loved and loving others.'[11] In other words, it is *a*

---

[8] M. Marshall, 'The Doctrine of Salvation: Biblical-Theological Dimensions', *Southwestern Journal of Theology* 35.2 (Spring, 1993), p. 14.

[9] Cf. P.S. Fiddes, *Tracks and Traces: Baptist Identity in Church and Theology*, (Studies in Baptist History and Thought, 13; Carlisle: Paternoster Press, 2003), pp. 1-20; 21-47, 48-64, 65-82, 228-248.

[10] Cf. S.J. Grenz, *The Social God and the Relational Self. A Trinitarian Theology of the Imago Dei* (The Matrix of Christian Theology Series; Louisville, KY: Westminster/John Knox Press, 2001), pp. 323-31.

[11] D.L. Migliore, *Faith Seeking Understanding: An Introduction to Christian Theology* (Grand Rapids, MI: Eerdmans, 1991), p. 175.

process of increasingly learning to be what we have become, participants in God's own life.

Historically, Baptists in the American South, reflecting their pietistic and evangelical heritage, have affirmed that every human being is a sinner, and 'that this alienation from God could be canceled *on the basis of* Christ's redemptive work "for me"...*through* faith that simply trusted Christ, *with the result* being a restoration to God's favor that was (from the sinner's point of view) pure undeserved grace, but that was (on the God's-eye view) purchased at the expense of Christ's sacrificial death'.[12] As James McClendon says, 'this implied Christ's achievement on behalf of each sinner...and a corresponding transaction in the interior life of each one who was brought to salvation'.[13] Thus, Baptists in the American South, especially in the nineteenth and twentieth centuries, have been concerned with the personal experience of conversion, understood as the individual appropriation of justification.[14] They have understood salvation as a mysterious activity of divine grace experienced in the heart of the true believer. Redemption is not found in external works, intellectual assent to creeds or doctrine, or the performance of the sacraments, but by personal encounter with Jesus the Christ.[15] Entrance into the life of Christ and his church is based on a regenerative experience of grace in the heart of every believer.[16]

A particularly helpful essay on how the development of a personal, conscious conversion experience influenced Baptists' ideas of soteriology is Bill Leonard's essay 'Getting Saved in America'. Leonard attempts to answer three questions regarding the relationship between the conversion experience and the American experience: 'how did the theology and morphology of conversion evolve with the growth of the American Republic?'; 'in what ways did the pluralism of American culture influence the diversity of conversion experiences in American churches?'; and 'how has/have such forces as consumerism and mass communications influenced the ways in which American Christians defined conversion?'[17] To answer the first question, Leonard turns to the theology and morphology of conversion as developed by the Puritans in

---

[12] J.W. McClendon, Jr, *Systematic Theology*: Volume 2. *Doctrine* (Nashville, TN: Abingdon Press, 1994), pp. 109-10. Emphasis original.

[13] McClendon, *Doctrine*, p. 110.

[14] Leonard, 'Getting Saved in America', p. 115.

[15] Baptists have not always agreed on when or how a person experiences conversion. For a brief summary of the various Baptist traditions of conversion, see Bill Leonard, 'Southern Baptists and Conversion: An Evangelical Sacramentalism', in G.A. Furr and C.W. Freeman (eds), *Ties That Bind: Life Together in the Baptist Vision* (Macon, GA: Smyth & Helwys, 1994), p. 11.

[16] Leonard, 'Southern Baptists', p. 11.

[17] Leonard, 'Getting Saved in America', p. 112.

the Church of England and New England Puritans in colonial America. Objecting to what they perceived as the objective, sacramental concept of salvation of Catholicism and Anglicanism, the Puritans, like the Pietists, were concerned with an internalized faith which was bestowed on elect individuals through the gracious mercy of a sovereign God.[18] The requirement of a 'conscious conversion' was located within the context of covenant theology where salvation began with God and was accomplished by God.[19]

Puritans understood the conversion to faith as an inner experience, an infusion of 'experimental' grace into the heart by the indwelling of the Holy Spirit. As such, an emphasis on grace as self-involving and the individual appropriation of justification as well as the givenness of God's action in salvation marked a Puritan theology of conversion.[20] Moreover, conversion was not so much a single turning, but a long, slow, difficult process of struggle and preparation for a full conversion.[21] The Puritans increasingly regarded a specific experience of conversion as an essential sign of election.[22] As Leonard notes, citing Perry Miller, for the Puritans 'the arch-exemplar' of the appropriate conversion experience was Paul's 'Damascus Road' experience and Augustine's experience in the garden of Milan. What is important is that such model experiences of conversion, as understood by Puritans, made conversion itself a process, culminating in a decisive salvation event.[23] Still, for many Puritans, a particular

---

[18] Leonard, 'Getting Saved in America', p. 114. Puritans and Pietists shared certain commonalities, such as a form of an *ordo salutis*, reaffirming the importance of a personal conversion experience leading to a sanctified life; a belief of standing in the wake of the Reformers, completing their work; and an ecclesiological concern for the gathered church consisting of visible saints. Yet, they must also be distinguished from each other. Puritans tended to be far more concerned with doctrine and were characterized by a separatist spirit as compared to the Pietists. Pietists tended to give greater accent to orthopraxis and so sanctification than the Puritans. Despite the emphasis on personal conversion, Puritans, reflecting their Calvinistic roots, tended to understand salvation as an objective given. Pietists typically understood salvation in subjective and experiential terms. For assistance on the commonalities and differences between Puritans and Pietists, I am grateful to personal correspondence, 21 June 2004, with Philip E. Thompson.

[19] Although Leonard notes the Puritans' emphasis on the validation of conversions in the visible community of faith, he does not give sufficient accent to the ecclesial location of salvation as emphasized by covenant theology. The notion that salvation occurs within the church was important to early Baptist soteriology. I will return to this point latter in the essay.

[20] Leonard, 'Getting Saved in America', p. 114, cites Jerald Brauer, 'Conversion: From Puritanism to Revivalism', *The Journal of Religions* 58 (1978), p. 234.

[21] McClendon, *Doctrine*, p. 138.

[22] McClendon, *Doctrine*, p. 138.

[23] Despite the delineation of a morphology of conversion, Leonard notes that New England Puritans were divided over how much of the work of preparation was divine and

conversion experience often did not end the question of one's elect status. 'In response to the question, "Who are the elect?", the Puritans [often] responded, "Whoever is truly converted and thereby is demonstrating signs of grace in daily life, that is, is growing in sanctification"... In this manner, the Puritans came to base one's personal sense of election on the believer's own piety.'[24]

The fourth and fifth decades of the eighteenth century witnessed a cross-pollination of Puritanism and Pietism which burst forth in full bloom as the emergence of the Evangelical movement.[25] 'At the heart of this new movement was a concern, inherited from Puritanism but especially from Pietism, for true, heartfelt faith.'[26] As Stanley Grenz and others suggest, John Wesley (and the Wesleyan movement) epitomized the point where Puritanism and Pietism met.[27]

The converging influences of Puritanism and Pietism mediated to eighteenth-century Evangelicalism a concern for, and emphasis on, a personal, conscious experience of the grace of God in conversion.[28] As the revivalistic tendencies of Evangelicalism in Britain and America indicate, interest in the proclamation of the gospel of conversion and new birth and the *experience* of personal regeneration characterized the movement's ethos. Moreover, the advent of Evangelicalism also witnessed a new emphasis on the assurance of salvation. As David Bebbington summarizes: 'Whereas the Puritans had held that assurance is rare, late and the fruit of struggle in the experience of believers, the Evangelicals believed it to be general, normally given at conversion and the result of simple acceptance of the gift of God.'[29] This shift from the Puritan morphology of conversion with its quest for assurance to Evangelicalism's understanding of assurance as part of the believer's 'normal experience' of conversion would be an important move in the narrowing of salvation to a particular moment in an individual's life.

---

how much was human. Cf. Leonard, 'Getting Saved in America', p. 115, citing Perry Miller, *The New England Mind: The Seventeenth Century* (New York: MacMillian, 1939), pp. 3-5.

[24] S.J. Grenz, *Renewing the Center: Evangelical Theology in a Post-Theological Era* (Grand Rapids, MI: Baker Books, 2000), p. 39.

[25] Grenz, *Renewing the Center*, p. 44.

[26] Grenz, *Renewing the Center*, p. 44.

[27] Grenz, *Renewing the Center*, p. 45. Regarding this assertion about Wesley, Grenz identifies the following sources: Scott Kisker, 'John Wesley's Puritan and Pietist Heritage Reexamined', *Wesleyan Theological Journal* 34.2 (Fall, 1999), pp. 266-80; D. Bebbington, *Evangelicalism in Modern Britain: A History from the 1730s to the 1980s* (Grand Rapids, MI: Baker Books, 1992), pp. 34-42.

[28] Grenz, *Renewing the Center*, pp. 46-47.

[29] Bebbington, *Evangelicalism in Modern Britain*, p. 43, quoted in Grenz, *Renewing the Center*, pp. 47-48.

By the nineteenth century, Leonard notes, an Arminian modification of a traditional Calvinistic morphology arose among American Evangelicals, placing a greater stress on the role of human free will and human response in salvation. Such a modification, along with the advent of certain revivalistic techniques aimed at getting people saved, considerably shortened the process of conversion.[30] 'Preparation [integral to the Puritan morphology of conversion] was crowded out by the far more interesting business of discerning genuine conversions amid the revival excitement.'[31] Charles G. Finney's revivalism and his use of methods and techniques to convert unbelieving sinners, such as the 'anxious seat' and the 'prayer of faith', all but reduced salvation to an immediate moment of evangelism itself.[32]

In the end, the morphology of conversion was truncated. No longer understood as an extended period of conviction and preparation, but as an immediately apprehended event, an instantaneous fusion of grace and free will, the conversion experience was reduced to a punctiliar, transactional moment of an individual's life, a moment necessary for salvation. By the late nineteenth and early twentieth centuries, coming forward to the anxious bench or to shake the preacher's hand, was an integral part of being saved in America.[33] Leonard writes, 'It created what might be called the sacrament of walking the aisle, an outward and visible sign of an inward and evangelical grace.'[34] The phrase 'I walked the aisle' became theological shorthand to describe the salvation event itself.

> In many contexts, walking the aisle replaced baptism as public confession of faith. Indeed, many testified that salvation seemed to come in the very act of moving from pew to aisle. With the use of the invitation, evangelicals secured a powerful symbol for dramatizing the need for and possibility of an immediate, conscious conversion event. They needed one more ingredient, a concise way of entering it. They found that in *the prayer*.[35]

Leonard goes on to argue that at some point in the twentieth century—precisely when he does not say—'the invitation to immediate conversion was increasingly associated with a specific prayer for and by

---

[30] Leonard, 'Getting Saved in America', pp. 118-22.
[31] McClendon, *Doctrine*, p. 138.
[32] Leonard, 'Getting Saved in America', pp. 119-22; McClendon, *Doctrine*, p. 139.
[33] Leonard, 'Getting Saved in America', p. 121.
[34] Leonard, 'Getting Saved in America', p. 121. Leonard notes that while Finney may have shortened the process leading to salvation he articulated 'an extensive process of sanctification to reinforce the initial salvific event' (p. 120). However, American Evangelicals accepted Finney's theology of justification without his accompanying theology of sanctification, thus creating theological confusion (p. 120).
[35] Leonard, 'Getting Saved in America', p. 121. Emphasis original.

the sinner which completed the event of salvation'.[36] Thus, by the twentieth century, the lengthy and communally guided conversion experience of Puritan theology had been reduced to an immediate and momentary event of individual experience.

How did such a (foreshortened) process of conversion shape Baptists in America? As a test case, Leonard turns to Baptists of the American South. Heirs to both the Calvinist and the Arminian traditions (and the Puritan and Pietist traditions), Baptists in the American South 'often selected and popularized diverse doctrines of salvation which, when held together, had the potential for serious theological confusion'.[37] They made conversion normative but were divided between conversion as a nurturing process and as a dramatic, immediate event. Consequently, Baptists in the American South have often attempted to have both. Thus, for many Baptists of the American South the rhetoric of Calvinism and the theology of Arminianism come together in 'the transaction of conversionistic individualism'. 'Conversion is less a process of experience with grace than an event which satisfies a salvific requirement.'[38]

Baptists in the American South developed a number of ways of institutionalizing and popularizing a process of conversion in order to evangelize the masses. In so doing, they have created what Leonard identifies as 'a kind of evangelical sacramentalism by which an internal, subjective religious experience might be verified through certain objective criteria. While proclaiming conversion as an intensely personal, individual experience, they also developed elaborate plans, programs, and prayers for fulfilling the necessary salvific transaction.'[39] By making faith punctiliar, Baptists of the American South accelerated 'the probability of doubt since inevitably with time, failing memory, or continued sins, the believer may question motives, context, or even the words utilized in that singularly salvific moment'.[40] A significant negative consequence of such a theology and morphology of conversion is that 'The Christian life is less a life of growth and struggle than a perpetual return to the point of sacramental origins.'[41]

Speaking more generally about Baptists in America, historian Edwin Gaustad contends that the (so-called) 'Isaac Backus–John Leland Baptist tradition' gave priority to the individual person in matters of

---

[36] Leonard, 'Getting Saved in America', p. 122.
[37] Leonard, 'Getting Saved in America', p. 123.
[38] Leonard, 'Getting Saved in America', p. 124.
[39] Leonard, 'Southern Baptists', p. 11.
[40] Leonard, 'Getting Saved in America', p. 124.
[41] Leonard, 'Getting Saved in America', p. 124.

soteriology.[42] The preeminent value of the autonomous individual within this tradition has its roots in the influence of revivalism as well as Enlightenment rationalism.[43] According to Gaustad, Backus understood salvation, effected totally through the power of the divine, as fundamentally a relationship between God and the individual sinner standing 'naked and alone before God'.[44] Persons are called individually; the church is a fact *after* salvation and not an agent of salvation. In other words, 'salvation is not through or with the church, but altogether prior to it'.[45] Thus, the soteriology of the 'Backus–Leland tradition' stressed the decisive moment of individual conversion to faith and personal appropriation of God's justification. Moreover, the church occupied a secondary position soteriologically.[46] Regarding the connection between soteriology and ecclesiology, the 'Backus–Leland tradition' was a regrettable departure from the thought of seventeenth-century Baptists, as will be demonstrated below.

In sum, the soteriology of Baptists in America, particularly the American South, accentuated justification at the expense of similar attention to and concentration upon the ecclesial and the personal 'walk in the newness of life'. As Edgerton exemplifies in six-year old Stephen's conversion experience in the Listre Baptist Church, salvation was reduced to an absolute, punctiliar, voluntary, interior, individual moment of experience characterized by a certain finality. Lutheran theologian Gerhard Forde's comment that sanctification is 'the art of getting used to justification' is arguably applicable to the understanding of soteriology among Baptists in the American South in the eighteenth

---

[42] E.S. Gaustad, 'The Backus–Leland Tradition', in Winthrop S. Hudson (ed.), *Baptists Concepts of the Church* (Philadelphia, PA: Judson Press, 1959), pp. 110 and 113.

[43] On the influence of modernity upon Baptist theology, see two very helpful essays by C.W. Freeman, 'E.Y. Mullins and the Siren Songs of Modernity', *Review and Expositor* 96.1 (Winter, 1999), pp. 23-42, and 'Can Baptist Theology Be Revisioned', *Perspectives in Religious Studies* 24.3 (Fall, 1997), pp.273-302.

[44] L. Leavenworth, 'American Baptists Face Theological Issues', *Foundations* 1 (January, 1958), p. 38, quoted in Gaustad, 'The Backus–Leland Tradition', p. 110.

[45] Gaustad, 'The Backus–Leland Tradition', p. 110.

[46] W.S. Hudson, 'Shifting Patterns of Church Order in the Twentieth Century', in Hudson (ed.), *Baptist Concepts of the Church*, p. 216. Hudson, commenting on the practical effect of E.Y. Mullins' stress on the principle of soul competency, cites the following from W.R. McNutt's *Polity and Practice in Baptist Churches* (Philadelphia, PA: Judson Press, 1959), pp. 21-24: the individual 'has no inescapable need of the church to bring him salvation or to mediate to him divine grace'. The individual stands alone since 'competency reposes authority in religion within the individual'.

through twentieth centuries.[47] Yet, such a view of soteriology has not always been characteristic of Baptist theology.

Revisiting Baptist Soteriology

In attempting to answer the question, 'What is the essence of the Baptists?', Baptist historian Eric Ohlmann lists traditional characteristics of Baptists—biblical authority, soul competency, religious liberty, separation of church and state, autonomy of the local church, evangelisms and missions, baptism by immersion, believer's baptism, the concept of the believers' church—but warns 'the essence of a movement does not necessarily lie in its most distinctive characteristics'.[48] For Ohlmann, the essence of the Baptists lies in their soteriology, especially in the emphasis laid on sanctification. For many Baptist historians and theologians, such an assertion would be contentious. It is not my purpose to argue for or against Ohlmann's thesis. Rather, appeal to his essay is made in support of my thesis since his essay suggests the importance of soteriology, in general, and the attention to sanctification, in particular, for seventeenth-century Baptists.

An early Baptist emphasis on sanctification Ohlmann identifies as a legacy of the Puritan influence on Baptist theology. 'Stress upon obedience and practical religious experience which they inherited from the Puritans in itself surpassed that of their Protestant predecessors.'[49] Like the Anabaptists and Puritans, Baptists, argues Ohlmann, 'conceived of the Christian life as a covenant relationship in which both faith and obedience were indispensable and inseparable'.[50] While wholly affirming the sovereignty of God's grace and justification by faith alone, early Baptists viewed 'good works' not only as 'an expression of gratitude or a consequence of regeneration but increasingly as part and parcel of salvation'.[51] Thus, they strongly emphasized that believers practice 'the

---

[47] G.O. Forde, 'The Lutheran View', in D. Alexander (ed.), *Christian Spirituality. Five Views of Sanctification* (Downers Grove, IL: InterVarsity Press, 1988), p. 13, quoted in M.T. Marshall, 'The Changing Face of Baptist Discipleship', *Review and Expositor* 95.1 (Winter, 1998), p. 63.

[48] E.H. Ohlmann, 'The Essence of the Baptists: A Reexamination', *Perspectives in Religious Studies*, 13.4 (Winter, 1986), p. 99. It must be noted that Ohlmann's focus on sanctification as the distinguishing feature of Baptists betrays a reductionistic tendency to distill a Baptist distinctive or essence rather than uplift the rich and variegated Baptist tradition.

[49] Ohlmann, 'The Essence of the Baptists', p. 99.

[50] Ohlmann, 'The Essence of the Baptists', pp. 99-100.

[51] Ohlmann, 'The Essence of the Baptists', p. 100. While Puritan covenant theology enlarged the function of good works in soteriology, the Puritans, argues Ohlmann, 'did not attribute any salvific value to good works but alleged that regeneration

life of heaven' on earth. According to Ohlmann, Puritan soteriology and covenant theology 'was like the air [the early Baptists] breathed and the food they ate'.[52]

To substantiate his thesis further, Ohlmann turns to a very concise investigation of selected statements from some seventeenth-century Baptist confessions of faith.[53] What follows is not so much a review of his all-too-brief survey of selected seveneteenth-century Baptists confessions of faith, but a lengthier exploration of such documents.

Sanctification in Seventeenth-Century Baptist Confessions

Seventeenth-century Baptist confessions of faith do not develop a detailed *ordo salutis*. An examination of the confessions reveals articles concerned with the soteriological purposes of God, articles on the work of Christ related to salvation, articles on the soteriological mission of the churches, and articles on eschatology that express soteriological concerns, in addition to the classical soteriological themes of justification and sanctification.[54]

Concerning theological matters traditionally taken up in soteriology, the confessions typically emphasize justification as a decision of faith. Such an understanding of the event of justification by faith is well stated in *The Standard Confession* (1660) of the General Baptists:

> That the way set forth by God for men to be justified in, is by faith in Christ...

> That is to say, when men shall assent to the truth of the Gospel, believing with all their hearts, that there is remission of sins, and eternal life to be had in Christ.

> And that Christ therefore is most worthy their constant affections, and subjection to all his Commandements, and therefore resolve with purpose of heart so to subject unto him in all things, and no longer unto themselves...

> And so, shall (with godly sorrow for the sins past) commit themselves to his grace, confidently depending upon him for that which they believe is to be had in him:

---

produced fruits of the spirit which are manifested in outward and observable conduct' (p. 97).

[52] Ohlmann, 'The Essence of the Baptists', p. 98.

[53] Ohlmann looks at *The Faith and Practice of Thirty Congregations*, *The London Confession* of 1644, the *Somerset Confession*, the *Standard Confession*, the *Second London Confession* and the *Orthodox Creed*.

[54] Ohlmann, 'The Essence of the Baptists', p. 101.

such so believing are justified from all their sins, their faith shall be accounted unto them for righteousness...[55]

The confessions affirm that God forgives and frees humanity by a grace that human beings cannot merit. Humanity is justified and hence saved by an act of divine love that comes to humanity as pure gift. Such a divine initiative activates human free will. As the General Baptist *Orthodox Creed* of 1679 states,

> justifying faith is a grace, or habit, wrought in the soul, by the holy ghost, through preaching the word of God, whereby we are enabled to believe...and wholly and only to rest upon Christ...[56]

Yet, contrary to the 'myth' that Baptists have an anemic understanding of sanctification, a good number of seventeenth-century Baptist confessions also emphasize that the grace which frees humanity is also sanctifying grace, which forms in believers a pattern of living that reflects the structure of God's freeing grace. *The Standard Confession* affirms

> That there is one holy Spirit, the pretious gift of God, freely given to such as *obey him*...that thereby they may be throughly sanctified, and made able (without which they are altogether unable) to abide stedfast in the faith, and to honour the Father, and his Son Christ, the Author and finisher of their faith...[57]

As we turn to seventeenth-century Baptist confessions and give attention to their statements on sanctification, one thing can be noted: while justification by faith is largely understood to be an individual matter in which a person stands alone before God and sanctification is viewed as a corporate experience in ecclesial fellowship. Early Baptists perceived these as two aspects of the same process. In other words, as two dimensions of a unified reality of God's love for humanity, justification and sanctification comprise the twofold character of grace that frees and forms humanity. Let us turn to the confessions.

While a non-published, private confession consisting of twenty short articles, it is likely that the *Short Confession of Faith* of 1609 by John Smyth was 'intended to represent the entire party of Smyth's followers'.[58] Following a series of articles on Christology (articles 6-7) and on grace, repentance, and faith (articles 8-9), Smyth addresses justification and sanctification. In article 10, Smyth seems to break down the neat distinction between justification and sanctification. Justification is

---

[55] W.L. Lumpkin, *Baptist Confessions of Faith* (Philadelphia, PA: Judson Press, 1959), pp. 226-27, scripture verses omitted.
[56] Lumpkin, *Baptist Confessions of Faith*, p. 314.
[57] Lumpkin, *Baptist Confessions of Faith*, p. 227, scripture verses omitted.
[58] Lumpkin, *Baptist Confessions of Faith*, p. 99.

not just a legal declaration of being 'in the right' with God and a legal transfer, or 'the imputation' to us 'of the righteousness of Christ apprehended by faith',[59] it is also being made righteous, 'by the operation of the Holy Spirit, which is called regeneration or sanctification'.[60] Thus justification is used in correspondence rather than contrast to sanctification, and vice versa. Echoing the Epistle of James on the relationship between faith and good works (article 11), Smyth further testifies to the positive relationship between justification and sanctification when he professes that one is righteous if he or she does righteousness (article 10). Righteousness is not reduced to a legal pronouncement. In fact, faith, as implied by the confession, involves a change 'in the heart' that issues in changes of behavior, attitude, and practice.

A Short Confession of Faith of 1610, authored by Smyth's group, affirms the sovereignty of God's grace while rejecting Calvinism's notions of election and predestination. After an article on the soteriological purposes of the incarnation (article 8), the confession numerates ten articles on Christology (articles 9-18). Article 11 affirms that Jesus Christ 'hath showed by doctrine and life, the law of Christians, a rule of their life, the path and way of everlasting life'.[61] Article 19 states that the church and the Christian 'graciously enjoy' the benefits of Christ 'through a true, living, working faith'.[62] Again, a neat distinction between justification and sanctification is not drawn. Through faith the Christian is justified by the atoning death of Christ as the righteousness of Christ is legally transferred to us (article 20). Yet, salvation is also understood as an ongoing process or story. To quote article 21 in its entirety:

> Man being thus justified by faith, liveth and worketh by love (which the Holy Ghost sheddeth into the heart) in all good works, in the laws, precepts, ordinances given them by God through Christ; he praiseth and blesseth God, by a holy life, for every benefit, especially of the soul; and so are all such plants of the Lord trees of righteousness, who honor God through good works, and expect a blessed reward.[63]

In this sense, the confession affirms sanctification taking concrete form as Christian believers, participating in the *missio Dei*, are being transformed by the power and presence of the Spirit in the community and in individual lives.

A Declaration of Faith of English People Remaining in Amsterdam of 1611, authored by Thomas Helwys, and considered the first English Baptist confession of faith, acknowledges a connection between

---

[59] Lumpkin, *Baptist Confessions of Faith*, p. 101.
[60] Lumpkin, *Baptist Confessions of Faith*, p. 101.
[61] Lumpkin, *Baptist Confessions of Faith*, p. 105.
[62] Lumpkin, *Baptist Confessions of Faith*, p. 107.
[63] Lumpkin, *Baptist Confessions of Faith*, p. 108.

justification and sanctification. While article 6 affirms humanity's justification through faith by the righteousness of Christ, it concludes rather poignantly by stating that faith without works is dead (Js 2.17). Over against the presumption of the 'security of the believer' without the concomitant exhortations to perseverance, article 7 goes on to affirm the role of transformed living as an expression of authentic salvation. 'But let all men have assurance, that iff they continew vnto the end, they shallbee saved: Let no man then presume; but let all worke out their salvacion with feare and trembling.'[64] Two points can be noted from this rather brief attention to soteriology. First, a processive understanding of salvation is emphasized. Salvation is not complete until the age to come. As did *A Short Confession* of 1610, *A Declaration of Faith* states, secondly, that, in faith, a believer is sanctified by grace. Sanctification involves the believer being set apart to God, by God, for newness of life. This newness of life takes root as one comes to know, in Christ and as a partaker of the Spirit divine, the right way to live righteously as exemplified in works of love and mercy.

The London Confession of 1644 is a moderately Calvinist confession of the seven Particular Baptist churches in London which borrows considerably from the Separatist *A True Confession* of 1596. An emphasis on sanctification can be found in the preamble:

> holding Jesus Christ to be our head and Lord; under whose government wee desire alone to walke, in following the Lambe whersoever he goeth; and wee believe the Lord will daily cause truth more to appeare in the hearts of his Saints, and make them ashamed of their folly in the Land of Nativitie, that so they may with one shoulder, more studie to lift up the Name of the Lord Jesus, and stand for his appointments and Laews...[65]

What is important to note in this quotation is the notion of the community 'walking together'. Indicating the influence of Puritan-Separatist covenant theology, the confession's affirmation of the churches' conviction and commitment to 'walk together' under the authority of Jesus Christ indicates 'a story of salvation which is more complicated and extensive than conversion alone'.[66] Thus, salvation is participation in the renewed human community, the church.

---

[64] Lumpkin, *Baptist Confessions of Faith*, p. 119.
[65] Lumpkin, *Baptist Confessions of Faith*, pp. 155-56.
[66] P.S. Fiddes, 'The Church and Salvation: A Comparison of Orthodox and Baptist Thinking', in A.R. Cross (ed.), *Ecumenism and History: Studies in Honour of John H.Y. Briggs* (Carlisle: Paternoster Press, 2002), p. 142. The notion of the community 'walking together' recalls the practice of baptism as an act of initiation into a social reality prior to the individual's response in faith and as an ingrafting into the body of Christ in order that members of the body may journey together. Cf. also Fiddes' *Tracks and Traces*, p. 233, and '"Walking Together": The Place of Covenant Theology in Baptist

Such a 'deep ontological connection between church and salvation', argues Paul Fiddes, finds expression in Baptist thought in the affirmation that the salvific relation of Christ to the church is conceived as 'the presence and activity of Christ in his household'.[67] Such a notion can be found in the seventeenth-century Baptist appropriation of the Reformation concept of Christ's threefold office of prophet, priest and king applied to the church. Christ's mediatorial activity is not merely between God and the individual sinner, rather, 'Christ is mediator in the sense of being the establisher of a covenant between God and the church', creating a community in which persons repent and come to faith in Christ.[68] Hence, covenant language in the Baptist tradition suggests the salvation of the individual person does not occur somewhere outside of, or apart from, but *within* the church.[69]

Such an ecclesial understanding of salvation is expressed in an almost seamless movement from soteriology to ecclesiology in *The London Confession* (1644). Following a series of articles on the threefold office of Christ (articles 9-21) and the nature of faith (articles 22-26), the doctrine of salvation is addressed, with two initial articles (27-28) on justification. Articles 29-32 address sanctification and the Christian life. Specifically, articles 29 and 30 speak of the community of believers as holy and sanctified. Sanctification 'is a spirituall grace of the new Covenant', and 'peace with God' and 'joy in God' are the benefits of covenantal relationship with God through the atoning work of Jesus.[70] Articles 31-32 confront the costly realities of radical discipleship and call upon Christ to preserve the saints until he comes again in his everlasting Kingdom. These two articles bridge the confession's discussion of salvation as sanctification and ecclesiology. With article 33 comes the first of fifteen articles which address the church as 'a company of visible Saints called & separated from the world, by the word and Spirit of God, to the visible profession of faith of the Gospel...'[71]

Two other Particular Baptist confessions, *The Faith and Practice of Thirty Congregations* of 1651 and the *Somerset Confession* of 1656, make cogent statements which reveal the importance of sanctification for the local body of Christ and for the persons who comprise that body. The former confession states as its first purpose, 'to inform those who have a

---

Life Yesterday and Today', in W.H. Brackney, P.S. Fiddes and J.H.Y. Briggs (eds), *Pilgrim Pathways: Essays in Baptist History in Honour of B.R. White* (Macon, GA: Mercer University Press, 1999), pp. 47-74.

[67] Fiddes, 'The Church and Salvation', p. 126.
[68] Fiddes, 'The Church and Salvation', p. 128.
[69] Fiddes, 'The Church and Salvation', p. 127.
[70] Lumpkin, *Baptist Confessions of Faith*, pp. 164-65.
[71] Lumpkin, *Baptist Confessions of Faith*, p. 165.

desire to know what Religious Duties they hold forth'.[72] In that vein, article 43 states that 'all those that continue stedfastly unto the end of their lives, pressing forward to the mark (Jesus Christ) that is set before them, shall not only have the comfort and joy which is a part of their portion in this life, but they shall also have a Crown of eternal glory in the life to come'.[73] Moreover, article 52, referring to Ephesians 4.15-16, emphasizes

> That the chief or only ends of a people baptised according to the counsel of God, when they meet together as the congregation or fellowship of Christ, are, or ought to be, for *to walk sutably*; or to give up themselves unto a holy conformity to all the Laws and Ordinances of Jesus Christ, answerable to the gifts and graces received, improving them for the glory of God, and the edification of each other in love.[74]

Thus, the confession stresses a processive and ecclesial understanding of salvation with a concomitant call for perseverance through the arduous experience of Christian life. Salvation cannot be reduced to a singular moment of conversion. Rather, it is concrete 'walking', or living the story of Jesus in the present.

In its article on Christology, the *Somerset Confession* affirms that the church, through the powerful teachings of Christ and by the power of the Holy Spirit, ought to grow in Christ and 'be conformed to his will...and sing praises unto his name' because Christ is law-giver, who 'hath given rules unto us, by the which he ruleth over us'.[75] In a unique move vis-à-vis other seventeenth-century Baptist confessions, the document goes on to identify twenty-one specific commandments of Christ, or specific concrete acts of sanctification, by which Christians, who *walk together*, glorify God, and comfort their souls (article 25). In many respects, an identification of such possible actions manifests baptismal identity (article 24).

Such a degree of specificity in identifying acts of grace-filled living suggests that as persons walk together as friends with one another and with Christ, they as well as the ecclesial community grow in and are substantively and materially formed by God's grace. In other words, in faith, God's grace becomes the very essence of individual and ecclesial existence. The specific commandments authorized by the confession suggest so vividly the concrete forming power of sanctifying grace. To know Christ is to live a certain way, to be disciplined into certain patterns of living, to become a person and a community disposed toward certain

---

[72] Lumpkin, *Baptist Confessions of Faith*, p. 174.
[73] Lumpkin, *Baptist Confessions of Faith*, p. 181.
[74] Lumpkin, *Baptist Confessions of Faith*, p. 183. Emphasis added.
[75] Lumpkin, *Baptist Confessions of Faith*, pp. 207-208, scripture verses omitted.

kinds of actions and thoughts. These things that believers do together in response to God's grace are the things that Christians do as their lives are conformed to patterns of holiness.

The *Second London Confession* of 1677, greatly influenced by the *Westminster Confession,* places a strong emphasis on sanctification. In the preface its Baptist authors declare their confession to be a statement of belief 'which with our hearts we most firmly believe, and sincerely indeavour to conform our lives to'.[76] The authors go on to express their hope that

> the only care and contention of all upon whom the name of our blessed Redeemer is called, might for the future be, *to walk humbly with their God,* and in the exercise of all Love and Meekness towards each other, *to perfect holyness* in the fear of the Lord, each one *endeavouring* to have his conversation such as becometh the Gospel; and also, suitable to his place and capacity, *vigorously to promote in others the practice of true Religion and undefiled in the sight of God and our Father.*[77]

The preface closes with a prayerful note that God will pour out the Holy Spirit upon them so 'that the profession of truth may be accompanyed with the sound belief, and *diligent practise of it*'.[78]

Following articles on justification, which reflects a penal substitutionary view of atonement (article 11), and adoption, which affirms the sovereignty of God's grace (article 12), comes an article on sanctification (article 13). This article is one of the lengthiest treatment of sanctification among seventeenth-Baptist confessions. It stresses the interrelationship between justification and sanctification. The first paragraph makes clear that justification is the ground out of which sanctification grows when believers who are united to Christ 'are also farther sanctified'.[79] The second and third paragraphs emphasize the processive character of salvation. Without the practice of holiness, those in union with Christ shall not 'see the Lord,' declares the confession.[80] While life in the present is marked by a struggle of 'Spirit against the Flesh', the saints, empowered by the Spirit, are to 'grow in Grace, perfecting holiness in the fear of God, pressing after an heavenly life, in Evangelical Obedience to all the

---

[76] Lumpkin, *Baptist Confessions of Faith,* p. 246. Cf. Ohlmann, 'The Essence of the Baptists', p. 102.
[77] Lumpkin, *Baptist Confessions of Faith,* pp. 246-47. Emphasis added.
[78] Lumpkin, *Baptist Confessions of Faith,* p. 248. Emphasis added.
[79] Lumpkin, *Baptist Confessions of Faith,* p. 267.
[80] Lumpkin, *Baptist Confessions of Faith,* p. 268. Article 14 addresses good works. According to the confession, works are good only as God's commands, are accomplished completely by the activity and influence of the Holy Spirit upon the person in obedience to God, and are evidence of a true and lively faith.

commands which *Christ* as *Head* and *King*, in his *Word* hath prescribed to them'.[81]

One should notice, first of all, the pneumatological emphasis as compared to earlier Baptist confessions' articulation of sanctification.[82] Once persons are ingrafted into Christ through baptism and the transfiguring work of the Holy Spirit, each person begins to become like Jesus, a saint who 'grows in grace, perfecting holiness'.[83] Thus, the indwelling of the Spirit in the life of Christians (as well as the church) empowers persons (and the church) to manifest the life of Christ. As a processive movement toward likeness of the divine, a person never 'arrives' salvifically in the present, only in the age to come. From here to eternity, the Spirit is the efficient cause of transformation, laboring to help Christians press after a heavenly life.

Second, note the use of such words as 'grow', 'perfecting' and 'pressing after'. Such language not only stresses the processive character of sanctification as well as its ecclesial grounding. It also suggests that sanctification has as one of its central dimensions the identity claim 'you are justified'. Hence, as in earlier Baptist confessions, no neat and clean distinction between justification and sanctification is drawn. In fact, this confession appears to suggest that if sanctification describes the process of 'perfecting holiness' then it also describes the process whereby one comes to know oneself as justified. Sanctification does not merely follow justification; it also precedes it as the distinctly ecclesial condition in which the reality of justification takes hold in a believer's life.

Finally, the second paragraph's statement 'This Sanctification is throughout, in the whole of man, yet imperfect in this life' clearly states that sinless perfection in this life is impossible. However, the claim implies that the perfection of sanctification occurs in eternal life. Such a future perfection of participation in communion with God is understood as glorification.[84]

The final Baptist confession to be considered is the *Orthodox Creed* of 1679. One aspect of this General Baptist confession is its soteriological depth. Following a Christocentric understanding of predestination and election that softens the Calvinism of such doctrines (article 9), the

---

[81] Lumpkin, *Baptist Confessions of Faith*, p. 268. Emphasis original.

[82] As compared to other seventeenth-century Baptist confessions, the *Second London Confession* has a strong pneumatological accent. The one exception to this statement is the *Standard Confession*, which is strongly pneumatological and ecclesiological. I am grateful to Philip E. Thompson for bringing this latter point to my attention (personal correspondence, 21 June 2004).

[83] Lumpkin, *Baptist Confessions of Faith*, p. 268. For the imagery of engrafting through baptism, see article 29 on baptism. Cf. Lumpkin, *Baptist Confessions of Faith*, p. 291.

[84] Lumpkin, *Baptist Confessions of Faith*, p. 268.

confession discusses the new covenant of grace (article 16), Christ as mediator (article 17), the significance of Christ's general atonement (article 18), and repentance and faith (articles 22 and 23). Justification is treated in largely forensic categories, with an emphasis on the justification by faith in Christ as freeing grace (article 24). Reconciliation with God and with other persons and a believer's adoption as co-heir with Christ are regarded as the two principal benefits of justification (article 25).

The confession's article on sanctification gives emphasis to the processive character of salvation as earlier Baptist confessions had. Also implied is the eschatological completion of the present, ongoing personal transformation. Yet, two aspects of the confession's understanding of sanctification stand out. First, the first New Testament reference in the article is Ephesians 4.24.[85] The Christians at Ephesus are urged 'to clothe yourselves with the new self, created according to likeness of God in true righteousness and holiness' (NRSV). This text sets the tone for the entire article. To 'clothe' metaphorically describes the activity by which persons and the church put on behaviors, beliefs, attitudes and dispositions that define who he or she, or the community, is. To adorn oneself with Christ determines not only how others perceive a believer or the community, but also how the believer or the community perceives and embodies an understanding of deepest identity. In other words, when a person or the community of faith 'puts on Christ' certain forms of behavior, beliefs, actions and dispositions are worn that conform the believer or the gathered community to Christ. As a believer or the community responds in gratitude for the grace of the new covenant by Christ 'in Evangelical Obedience', the gifts of grace adorn the Christian as well as the fellowship of pilgrims.

Second, the language of the covenant of grace from and by Christ is present.[86] Paul Fiddes recalls that for seventeenth-century Baptists the term 'covenant' had a threefold meaning.[87] First, it referred to an eternal covenant of grace by which God effects salvation. In a number articles, most notably the one on the new covenant of grace, the *Orthodox Creed* affirms such an understanding of 'covenant'.[88] In light of the first understanding, one can affirm, says Fiddes, a covenant in God's own trinitarian life, between the Father and the Son in the love of the Spirit. The *Orthodox Creed* does speak of an eternal covenant between the

---

[85] The *London Confession* of 1644 also cites Eph. 4.24 in its article on sanctification.

[86] Of the numerous ways baptism is described, the confession refers to this ecclesial practice as 'a sign of our entrance into the covenant of grace'. Lumpkin, *Baptist Confessions of Faith*, p. 317.

[87] Fiddes, *Tracks and Traces*, p. 16.

[88] See, articles 9, 16 and 21 of *The Orthodox Creed.* Cf. Lumpkin, *Baptist Confessions of Faith*, pp. 302-303, 307-308 and 313.

Father and the Son.[89] Third, the term 'covenant', says Fiddes, refers to the act of consent among persons gathered together in a particular locale to be a church. The first two articles on the church in the *Orthodox Creed* express this third meaning.[90] Although he is not very clear on how the eternal covenant decrees of God and the mutual agreement among the ecclesial community interact, Fiddes claims that 'God's making of covenant *with* the church is simultaneous with the making of covenant *by* the church'.[91] To be incorporated into Christ's body, we participate not only in God's covenant with us, but in the inner covenant-making in God.[92] We are thus gifted, by the covenant-making God, with the capacity and responsibility to act as agents in the ecclesial community. Living graced lives, we who belong to God in Christ act both by his power and by our own, for he 'heals and elevates our own capacities'.[93] Thus, in its use of covenant language the *Orthodox Creed*, like other seventeenth-century Baptist confessions, understands 'salvation is about being part of a renewed human community, sharing in the continuing body of Christ on earth'.[94] Sanctification is not only of individual believers, but also of the ecclesial community. And perhaps more than any other seventeenth-century Baptist confession, the *Orthodox Creed* emphasizes salvation as also participating in the communion of the triune God.[95]

Conclusion

As identified above, a convergence of Pietist as well as Puritan heritage, an Arminian modification of a Puritan morphology of conversion and the influence of eighteenth- and nineteenth-century revivalism led Baptists in the American South to view salvation as less a process or journey and more as a transactional, immediate, punctiliar, voluntary, individual moment of conversion. The negative effect of this historical occurrence resulted in a soteriology which overemphasized a forensic and juridical concept of justification at the expense of sanctification. Moreover, salvation has largely been located in the traumatic conversion experience of the individual self, who alone could attest to the efficacy of Christ's work. Such a conversionist soteriology has often mistakenly been

---

[89] See articles 9, 17 and 24 of *The Orthodox Creed*. Cf. Lumpkin, *Baptist Confessions of Faith*, pp. 303, 308 and 314.
[90] See articles 29 and 30 of *The Orthodox Creed*. Cf. Lumpkin, *Baptist Confessions of Faith*, pp. 318-19.
[91] Fiddes, 'The Church and Salvation', p. 147.
[92] Fiddes, *Tracks and Traces*, p. 79.
[93] K. Tanner, *Jesus, Humanity and the Trinity: A Brief Systematic Theology* (Minneapolis, MN: Fortress Press, 2001), p. 58.
[94] Fiddes, 'The Church and Salvation', p. 122.
[95] Cf. Fiddes, 'The Church and Salvation', pp. 122-30.

retrojected onto the earliest Baptists. As this essay has sought to demonstrate, however, such a retrojection is wrong.

The discipline of *ressourcement* can provide Baptists in the American South an opportunity to challenge and correct these deficiencies and liabilities in matters soteriological. Returning to the earliest Baptists and their confessions challenges the exaggerated insistence upon the centrality of justification (and personal conversion) which has engendered a certain abstraction of the work of Jesus Christ from his person, isolating the paschal events from the person who is at their center.[96] In effect, this threatens a drift into a functionalist Christology in which Christ's person is a mere function of his saving activity.[97] Paying heed to the earliest Baptists' emphasis on sanctification can enable Baptists in the American South to resist a theological tendency to allow the motif of justification to become so inflated that it bears the whole weight of Christ's work of reconciliation. Baptist theologians can hopefully integrate justification into

> the wider sweep of the saving economy of God, which stretches from eternity to eternity, and whose centre is...the person and mission of the Son in its entirety—from his submission to the Father's will, through the assumption of flesh, the obedience and humiliation of incarnate existence, the proclamation and enactment of the kingdom of God, the giving of himself to death, the exaltation at resurrection and ascension to glory at the Father's right hand, and the continuing work as prophet, priest and king.[98]

Emphasizing salvation as a journey or a story challenges the propensity to reduce *sola fide* to an absolute moment of experience thereby drastically foreshortening the life of Christian holiness.[99] Baptists of the seventeenth century substantially accented the shaping, determinative work of sanctifying grace in the life of individual believers *and* the believing community. In their confessions, our Baptists forefathers and foremothers testified to the sanctifying process of conforming to Christ as a journey in which one can slowly excel at adorning oneself with the garments appropriate to Christian living. To put on Christ is to adorn oneself with the freedom that Christ gives to become the person and the ecclesial community the triune God intends.

Lastly, a retrieval of a Baptist theology of covenant, as identified in a number of confessions of the seventeenth-century Baptists and suggested by Paul Fiddes, should encourage a renewal of a soteriology ecclesially understood. As Orthodox theologian John Zizioulas claims, 'the goal of

---

[96] J. Webster, *Holiness* (Grand Rapids, MI: Eerdmans, 2003), p. 81.
[97] Webster, *Holiness*, p. 82.
[98] Webster, *Holiness*, p. 82.
[99] Webster, *Holiness*, p. 88.

salvation is that the personal life which is realized in God should also be realized at the level of personal existence'. From this Zizioulas concludes, 'salvation is identified with the realization of personhood'.[100] The process of this realization occurs as humanity participates, through the Spirit, in the glorious relationship between the Son and the Father. To this end, the Spirit unites us as one body in Jesus Christ. Being saved means being 'in Christ' and hence participating in a relational, ecclesial reality. As our Baptist forebears understood, we increasingly learn to be what we have become, participants in God's own life. Salvation is not 'the rescue of isolated souls to fellowship with God', but becoming the holy (*sanctus*) people of God.[101] Hence, becoming complete in our humanity, or to be 'saved', is to participate in the life of God *and* to 'walk together' in the life and worship of the Christian ecclesial community.

---

[100] J. Zizioulas, *Being as Communion: Studies in Personhood and the Church* (Crestwood, NY: St Vladimir's Seminary Press, 1985), pp. 49-50.
[101] Migliore, *Faith Seeking Understanding*, p. 157.

CHAPTER 6

The Myth of the Missing Spirituality: Spirituality among English Baptists in the Early Twentieth Century[1]

Ian M. Randall

In his essay 'The Contemplative Roots of Baptist Spirituality', E. Glenn Hinson argues that John Bunyan's spirituality belongs within the longer Christian tradition of contemplative prayer, a tradition not normally associated with Baptist life.[2] Hinson's stimulating study is one of a series of essays by Baptist authors from North America, each of whom is seeking to recover neglected, and in a number of cases forgotten, aspects of Baptist spirituality. This is part of a wider enterprise on the part of evangelicals to look at what has been traditionally seen as a topic belonging more to the Roman Catholic than to the Protestant Christian tradition. A useful examination of spirituality throughout the history of the church from a contemporary evangelical perspective is to be found in Alister McGrath's *Christian Spirituality* (1999).[3]

What is Christian spirituality? Varied understandings are offered by those writing on the subject. It can be looked at in quite a narrow way, as having to do largely with the life of prayer. Many authors today, however, would see it more broadly and would take the view that there is a theological dimension to spirituality. Philip Sheldrake argues that '(a) theology that is alive is always grounded in spiritual experience'.[4] Another way of looking at this is to see theology as lived out in spiritual

---

[1] Material in this essay is drawn from my larger study, *The English Baptists of the Twentieth Century* (A History of the English Baptists, 4; Didcot: Baptist Historical Society, 2005).

[2] E. Glenn Hinson, 'The Contemplative Roots of Baptist Spirituality', in G.A. Furr and C.W. Freeman (eds), *Ties That Bind: Life Together in the Baptist Vision* (Macon, GA: Smyth & Helwys, 1994), pp. 69-82.

[3] A.E. McGrath, *Christian Spirituality: An Introduction* (Oxford: Blackwell, 1999).

[4] P. Sheldrake, *Spirituality and Theology* (London: Darton, Longman and Todd, 1998), p. 3.

expressions.[5] In a study of Lutheran spirituality, Bengt Hoffman proposed the expression *sapientia experimentalis*, a term Martin Luther used and which may be translated 'knowledge by experience', to convey the inner aspect of Christian faith.[6] Using a framework proposed by Philip Sheldrake in *Spirituality and History* (1991), reproduced in *Exploring Christian Spirituality* (2000), spirituality may be seen as concerned with the conjunction of theology, communion with God and practical Christianity.[7]

This essay seeks to explore a number of different approaches to spiritual experience that were present among English Baptists in the first two decades of the twentieth century. The impression is sometimes given that in the first half of the twentieth century Baptists had relatively little involvement in areas of spiritual renewal. Michael Walker, in what is an insightful study of movements such as liturgical renewal and charismatic renewal—both features of English Baptist life in the second half of the twentieth century—refers to the emergence of these movements in the 'setting of a weakened concept of the Lord's Supper and preaching grown powerless to stem the ebbing tide'.[8] By 'ebbing tide' Michael Walker had in view primarily numerical decline in church membership and attendance in the early decades of the twentieth century, but it is significant that he also sees that period as one of spiritual ineffectiveness and he devotes little attention to it in his essay.

I wish to argue that the idea—to the extent that it exists at least as an assumption—of a missing spirituality in early twentieth-century English Baptist life is a myth. In *Evangelical Experiences* (1999), I examined a number of movements of evangelical spirituality in the 1920s and 1930s (the inter-war years) and sought to show in one of the chapters that despite the tensions within evangelicalism there was considerable Baptist vitality in that period, within the context of wider Free Church developments.[9] H. Wheeler Robinson, for example, the Principal of Regent's Park College, was pressing home the priority of spiritual renewal in the 1920s. In 1925 he expressed his conviction that, as he put it, issues

---

[5] W. Principe, 'Towards Defining Spirituality', in K.J. Collins (ed.), *Exploring Christian Spirituality* (Grand Rapids, MI: Baker Books, 2000), pp. 48-49.

[6] B. Hoffman, 'Lutheran Spirituality', in Collins (ed.), *Exploring Christian Spirituality*, p. 124.

[7] P. Sheldrake, *Spirituality and History* (London: SPCK, 1991), p. 52, and 'What is Spirituality?', in Collins (ed.), *Exploring Christian Spirituality*, p. 40.

[8] M.J. Walker, 'Baptist Worship in the Twentieth Century', in K.W. Clements (ed.), *Baptists in the Twentieth Century* (London: Baptist Historical Society, 1983), p. 23.

[9] I.M. Randall, *Evangelical Experiences: A Study in the Spirituality of English Evangelicalism, 1918–1939* (Studies in Evangelical History and Thought; Carlisle: Paternoster Press, 1999), chs 6 and 7. Ch. 6 contains material on Strict Baptists.

of Christian experience had been gathering force since the sixteenth-century Reformation and that, furthermore, it was in experiencing the reality of the Spirit of God that the more theological thinker and the 'ordinary' Christian were brought together and stood side by side.[10] Robinson encouraged a Free Church Retreat movement which gave opportunity for the reality of his own commitment to spirituality to be spread.[11]

Here I will focus on the first two decades of the twentieth century and will investigate the journeys made by some Baptists in their desire for spiritual renewal. The study will look only at churches and individuals in the Baptist Union and will concentrate on the religious currents of the time rather than the socio-political context. Significant elements that can be found in Baptist spirituality in this period were the desire for an experience of God in corporate worship; the hope of revival in the Baptist denomination; the awareness of the call to personal surrender to God and teaching about the concept of sanctification by faith; the desire to listen to God; the search for an experience of the baptism of the Spirit; and the attraction of the retreat movement with its call to 'come apart'. Many of these features are present in other eras in Baptist life, although not necessarily in quite the same form. This study simply takes one period and uses it as an example of currents of spiritual life to be found in the Baptist story.

Spirituality and Corporate Worship

A common way to seek to bring about and foster spiritual vitality in Baptist life has been through preaching. Walker speaks of preaching as becoming 'the dominant hall-mark' of Baptist worship in the nineteenth century and he instances examples of fine preaching in the early twentieth century.[12] The nature and function of this preaching in the post-Victorian period has, however, sometimes been misunderstood. Horton Davies, in volume five of his *Worship and Theology in England*, which deals with 1900–1965, is positive about some of the liturgical developments among Baptists at the end of this period, especially in the 1960s. He describes *Orders and Prayers for Church Worship*, produced in 1960 by Ernest Payne and Stephen Winward, as 'a most courageous publication'.[13] But Davies shows no similar enthusiasm for Baptist

---

[10] *The Baptist Times* 17 April 1925, p. 251.
[11] *The British Weekly* 19 November 1925, p. 178; *The Baptist Times* 18 November 1926, p. 832.
[12] Walker, 'Baptist Worship in the Twentieth Century', pp. 21-22.
[13] H. Davies, *Worship and Theology in England. Volume 5: The Ecumenical Century, 1900–1965* (Princeton, NJ: Princeton University Press, 1965), pp. 380-81. See

preaching during the decades he is considering. He talks about the 'New Theology' preached by R.J. Campbell, at the Congregational City Temple, London, and by other Free Church preachers in the early years of the twentieth century and he links with the controversial Campbell 'the doughty John Clifford, Baptist divine of London'. For Davies, the theological emphasis to be found among these preachers on the immanence of God and on ethical action meant that 'adoration of God lost its primacy and holiness its ultimacy'.[14]

This is neatly put, but does it convey a fair picture of Baptist worship?[15] At Westbourne Park Baptist Church, London, where John Clifford was minister, congregations certainly heard highly intellectual sermons. A visitor in 1907 noted that the Bible reading was from the recent Weymouth translation of the Bible and that a telegram was read about the progress of the Hague Peace Conference. The ethical stress was clearly present. Yet the climax of the sermon was an evangelistic appeal to people to come to Christ. Indeed, Clifford had to abandon the last hymn because he was carried away by his theme.[16] Another London Baptist church, the Shoreditch Tabernacle, which had a congregation of over 1,000, was perhaps more typical of large Baptist churches of the period. It could not be said that the concept of holiness was absent. 'Under my ministry here, of over thirty years', stated William Cuff, the minister, 'all that is holy, sacred and blessed has become a real experience to [the people]'. Cuff described meetings characterized by the preaching of the word of God, prayer and praise. In 1903, however, the famous survey by Charles Booth, *Life and Labour of the People of London*, said that the Shoreditch Tabernacle was 'perfect in its way, but its way is not that of being a house of God. No feeling of sacredness attaches to it'. William Cuff was understandably amazed at what he called this 'wild' statement. [17] Although Baptist worship was markedly different from High Anglican approaches, this does not mean that genuine spirituality was absent.

Corporate Baptist spirituality not only had preaching as a focus; it was also expressed in singing. Here again, Horton Davies is somewhat dismissive, referring to the way in which the Free Churches in the twentieth century had to overcome 'Victorian customs, in which heartiness rather than discrimination was characteristic of congregational singing'.[18] What this fails to appreciate is that it is possible to combine an

---

E.A. Payne and S.F. Winward, *Orders and Prayers for Church Worship: A Manual for Ministers* (London: Carey Kingsgate Press, 1960).
[14] Davies, *Worship and Theology in England*, pp. 131-33.
[15] For a fine overview of Baptist worship see C.J. Ellis, *Gathering: A Theology and Spirituality of Worship in Free Church Tradition* (London: SCM Press, 2004).
[16] *The Christian World*, 22 August 1907, p. 5.
[17] *The British Weekly* 16 April 1903, p. 4.
[18] Davies, *Worship and Theology in England*, p. 105.

appetite for hearty singing of congregational hymns with an appreciation of high standards of praise. While Davies notes that among Baptist ministers F.B. Meyer, at Christ Church, Lambeth, was interested in liturgy (he describes Meyer as one of the 'rebels' against the 'school of spontaneity'), the fact is that Meyer wanted to—and did—incorporate in public worship both liturgical forms and free expressions of praise. In 1903 Meyer was able, after much discussion with his church leaders at Christ Church, to fulfil his aim of introducing non-liturgical, evangelistic evening services, and in 1905 he wanted to make them more powerful, with better preaching and a 'real Salvation Army Choir'.[19] The Christ Church organist, Mr Griffiths, disliked the modern 'Sankey' hymns which Meyer enjoyed. However, on one occasion Meyer collapsed during a communion service and Mr Griffiths, obviously moved, broke into 'Safe in the arms of Jesus'.[20]

This was a period when a number of changes were taking place in aspects of Baptist worship. A *New Baptist Church Hymnal* was produced in conjunction with the Psalms and Hymns Trust in 1900. This book, which introduced new hymns and also chants, attracted both criticism and praise.[21] There was a recognition by some that development was inevitable. *The Baptist Times* suggested in 1901 that the kind of music which might be heard and enjoyed in a Baptist chapel a hundred years in the future would split the churches in 1901 if it was even considered.[22] It was a perceptive statement that anticipated later, often acrimonious splits which would take place over music, and was in the context of a debate beginning to emerge at that time. Perhaps, it was suggested, timidity was frightening Baptist congregations into 'dull mediocrity' in worship.[23] Yet this analysis did not do justice to the full picture. Creativity was to be found. At the well-known Woolwich Tabernacle in London, for example, a full orchestra was playing at the Sunday services.[24]

Another change was the increasing use at Baptist communion services of single glass cups instead of a common cup. This change had begun in Congregationalism in the 1890s and it was suggested in the *Baptist Times* in 1901 that people were staying away from Baptist communion services

---

[19] Minutes of Christ Church elders' meeting, 1 May 1903; *The British Weekly* 7 September 1905, p. 509; Davies, *Worship and Theology in England*, p. 380.

[20] *The Baptist Times* 13 October 1905, p. v; interview with John Lake, former member of Christ Church, 10 March 1989.

[21] For an overview, see A.E. Peaston, *The Prayer Book Tradition in the Free Churches* (London: James Clarke, 1964).

[22] *The Baptist Times* 8 March 1901, p. 157.

[23] *The Baptist Times* 8 March 1901, p. 157.

[24] J.E.B. Munson, *The Nonconformists: In Search of a Lost Culture* (London: SPCK, 1991), p. 48.

because they were not happy with the common cup.[25] From a temperance standpoint, it was argued that churches should use non-alcoholic wine at communion. By 1904 this was the practice in over 2,000 Baptist churches. But the single cup was seen as unhygienic when non-alcoholic wine was used. Linked with the temperance issue, therefore, was the late Victorian concern for hygiene.[26] One theme that was taken up by those arguing for the common cup was that this expressed unity in a way that was not true of individual cups. In September 1901, the Baptists at London Road, Lowestoft, suggested that they had found a way to overcome this problem. All the members now drank from individual cups simultaneously.[27] Over the next year many Baptist churches were adopting a new liturgy: passing round individual cups on a tray, with the idea of the members 'drinking together'.[28] While this overcame some problems, individual cups enhanced the idea of spiritual experience at communion as individualistic. Writing in 1960, Neville Clark, although not mentioning individual cups, bemoaned the presence in Baptist worship of 'a sub-Christian individualistic temper and outlook which, however fiercely it may be repudiated on the conscious level, still governs the basic assumptions that mould our liturgical practice'.[29] The response might have been that both personal and corporate experience was important for Baptists.

The Hope of Revival

The hope of many Baptists in the early years of the new century was for a spiritual revival which would have individual and communal dimensions; which would be personal and would also affect the churches and influence society. It seemed that this was happening with the Welsh Revival of 1904–05. Evan Roberts, the young revival leader, was seen by some as rather an enigma, but several Baptist leaders visited Wales to seek an understanding of the movement and to draw from it. Thomas Phillips, the minister of Bloomsbury Central Baptist Church, London, himself Welsh, was one. 'There is no doubt', he reported, 'that the Revival is a very real thing.' Speaking of the emotion of the meetings, he said, 'I would welcome such ecstasy, just for a change, at some of our Nonconformist assemblies.' The need in England, he suggested, was not

---

[25] *The Baptist Times* 16 August 1901, p. 552.
[26] I. Sellers (ed.), *Our Heritage: The Baptists of Yorkshire, Lancashire and Cheshire, 1647–1987* (Leeds: Yorkshire Baptist Association and Lancashire and Cheshire Baptist Association, 1987), p. 81.
[27] *The Baptist Times* 6 September 1901, p. 606 (report by J. Edgar Ennals)
[28] *The Baptist Times* 13 June 1902, p. 441.
[29] N. Clark, *Call to Worship* (Studies in Ministry and Worship; London: SCM Press, 1960), p. 12.

the Welsh Revival but the Holy Spirit—the power which brought revival.[30] J.W. Ewing, later the London Baptist Area (Metropolitan) Superintendent, said in 1905, after visiting Wales, 'I seemed to be searched through and through by the white light of the Spirit of Holiness.' Ewing spoke of being personally deeply stirred by his visit.[31]

But Baptist spiritual experience influenced the pre-history of the Welsh Revival, as well as being influenced by the revival movement as it developed. In 1903 some young Welsh ministers came to 'a pitch near desperation' in their anxiety to receive personal revival. One of them, Owen Owen, who had trained for Baptist ministry at Spurgeon's College (then called the Pastors' College), London, and who would later have ministries in Liverpool, Birkenhead and Exeter, wrote to Meyer on behalf of the rest of the group asking for help. Meyer advised the group to attend a convention to be held in August in Llandrindod Wells.[32] Meyer's impact at the convention was considerable. When he gave opportunity for expressions of surrender and dedication it seemed as if everyone wanted to receive 'the fullness of blessing'. Meyer was cautious about Welsh emotionalism, but it was clear that something significant was happening. Young Baptist and Forward Movement ministers had been devastated by Meyer's insistence on the Holy Spirit's total authority and some, such as R.B. Jones, one of the Baptist ministers, had private interviews with Meyer.[33] Jones and others returned from the convention 'altogether changed' and became leaders in missions which played a part in initiating and furthering the Welsh Revival.[34]

The influence of the Welsh Revival on Baptist life in England as well as in Wales was significant. Four Welsh students at the Pastors' College were invited by the Principal, Archibald McCaig, to talk about their experiences. This led to mission services at the Metropolitan Tabernacle.[35] Baptist Union membership increased to an all-time high in 1906, although decline followed. F.B. Meyer was among those who was not satisfied that the churches had fully incorporated the spiritual revitalization offered. One practical solution, which attempted to address the apparently short-lived revival, was an 'experiment' in which the

---

[30] *The British Weekly* 22 December 1904, p. 315.
[31] *The Baptist Times* 6 January 1905, p. 5.
[32] R.B. Jones, *Rent Heavens: The Revival of 1904* (London: n.p., 1931), pp. 27-28; *The Spiritual History of Keswick in Wales 1903–1983* (Cwmbran, Gwent: Christian Literature Press, 1989), pp. 7-8; and *The King's Champions* (Cwmbran, Gwent: Christian Literature Press, 1968), p. 48.
[33] *The Life of Faith* 12 August 1903, p. 572; 26 August 1903, p. 595; Jones, *Keswick in Wales*, p. 11, and *King's Champions*, p. 86.
[34] Jones, *Rent Heavens*, p. 28. Another important revivalist was Seth Joshua, who travelled to London to talk to Meyer in 1904.
[35] Jones, *King's Champions*, pp. 66-67.

spiritual 'laws' of the Revival would be put into operation in other meetings. These laws included the use of the 'empty chat' (i.e., no human chairman) and a 'prayer-force' rather than a choir. At meetings in 1908 in Leicester—where Meyer had been minister at Victoria Road Church and Melbourne Hall—Meyer was part of such an experiment, although he took the role of chairman. His platform colleagues were Jessie Penn-Lewis and R.B. Jones, both formidable characters. Penn-Lewis and Jones enlisted Evan Roberts, who had been the foremost figure at the height of the Welsh Revival and who was present at the Leicester meetings, to act as a catalyst. From then on the meetings enjoyed what was termed an 'indescribable' mixture of sweet singing, testimonies and sharing of biblical texts. The same formula was tried elsewhere but there was considerable unease about what was perceived to be human efforts to produce revival.[36]

An important stream of revivalist spirituality that flowed in part from the Welsh Revival was Pentecostalism, with its teaching that Christians should seek the baptism of the Spirit and the gift of speaking in tongues. Grant Wacker has vividly set out the hostility expressed towards Pentecostalism by many evangelicals on both sides of the Atlantic especially in the first decade of Pentecostal growth, from 1906.[37] One Baptist minister in England who expressed opposition to Pentecostalism was W. Graham Scroggie, who wrote three articles on subjects related to Pentecostalism in 1912 for the magazine of the Baptist church of which he was then minister, Bethesda Free Church, Sunderland. He looked at seven words associated with the ministry of the Spirit—baptism, indwelling, gift, sealing, earnest, anointing and fulness—and argued in favour of the need for continuous filling of the Spirit in the life of the Christian.[38] In this period Sunderland was, through conferences convened by Alexander and Mary Boddy at All Saints' Church, Monkwearmouth, something of a Pentecostal centre for many evangelicals.[39] In the light of this, what Scroggie had to say was particularly pertinent. After considering texts relating to the baptism of the Spirit, Scroggie made 1 Corinthians 12.13 his focus. Every person who believed in Christ, he argued, was according to this text baptized into the body of Christ. 'Incorporation into the Body of Christ', he insisted, 'is by the Baptism of the Spirit, so that, if one has not received this Baptism he is not of the

---

[36] *The Life of Faith* 25 November 1908, p. 1263; 25 November 1908, p. 1265; 16 December 1908, p. 1431; 10 February 1909, p. 141.
[37] G. Wacker, 'Travail of a Broken Family: Evangelical Responses to Pentecostalism in America, 1906–1916', *Journal of Ecclesiastical History* 47.3 (1996), pp. 505-28.
[38] *Bethesda Record*, July 1912, p. 113.
[39] I.M. Randall, 'Old Time Power: Relationships between Pentecostalism and Evangelical Spirituality in England', *Pneuma* 19.1 (1997), pp. 53-80.

Body, that is he is not a Christian at all.'[40] Although Scroggie disagreed with Pentecostalism, especially over its claim that speaking in tongues was an evidence of Spirit-baptism, he affirmed what he saw as genuine spiritual experience.

Other Baptist ministers took a different view of Pentecostal phenomena. In 1915 the Pentecostally-orientated preaching of Albert Saxby, the minister of Duckett Road Baptist Church, Harringay, London, caused severe tensions in the church. A 'church defence league was formed' and when this did not dampen the pastor's revivalistic practices the organist, an uncompromising Scot, and most of the choir resigned. However, Saxby's advocacy of the baptism of the Spirit attracted new people, such as Donald Gee, who was later to become one of the most prominent leaders in the largest Pentecostal denomination, the Assemblies of God. With the withdrawal of the Duckett Road organist from the church, Gee, who was a gifted young musician, stepped into the breach. He formed what was in effect a Pentecostal choir. Saxby was delighted with the note of praise to be found in the Pentecostal-type meetings. The 'bondage of custom' in traditional services was compared in harsh terms with Pentecostal glory in worship. Discussions took place between Saxby and officers of the London Baptist Association about how to cope with the changes at Duckett Road, and it was suggested that Saxby limit his Pentecostal services at Duckett Road to one per week. Instead, Saxby decided to resign from the pastorate. Gee followed him into Pentecostalism, later enunciating the view that revival required new bottles—Pentecostal churches—to hold the new wine.[41] Baptists and Pentecostals were to go their separate ways for the next half-century, but in Britain and elsewhere much Pentecostal spirituality, with its strong revivalist ethos, was first nurtured in Baptist settings.[42]

Sanctification by Faith

Another stream of spirituality in which Baptists played a part in the early years of the twentieth century, and which stood in contrast to Pentecostalism, was the Keswick Convention movement. The first Keswick Convention was held in 1875 in the Lake District town of that name and three decades later over 5,000 evangelicals were gathering each year for

---

[40] *Bethesda Record*, July 1912, p. 118.

[41] *Things New and Old*, April 1922, p. 7; *Redemption Tidings*, October 1932, p. 2; D. Gee, *These Men I Knew* (Nottingham: Assemblies of God, 1980), pp. 80-81; R. Massey, *Another Springtime* (Guildford: Highland, 1992) p. 23.

[42] See I.M. Randall, '"Days of Pentecostal Overflowing": Baptists and the Shaping of Pentecostalism', in D.W. Bebbington (ed.), *The Gospel in the World: International Baptist Studies* (Studies in Baptist History and Thought, 1; Carlisle: Paternoster Press, 2002), pp. 80-104.

the week-long convention, with its emphasis on full surrender to God. The formative Keswick message was that sanctification, like justification, was to be received by faith.[43] By the early 1900s, with Keswick having become fairly central to evangelicalism, there were worries that the original Keswick message about power to live a holy life might be diluted. F.B. Meyer, who spoke initially at Keswick in 1887 and became the Convention's most prominent Free Church speaker, expressed concern in 1902 that Keswick was becoming a platform for the delivery of brilliant addresses rather than a place where people met God.[44] In 1903, perhaps to remedy this, Meyer urged his Tuesday evening Keswick listeners to address things which were wrong in their lives. If they needed to make financial restitution to someone they should immediately write a cheque for the amount, with interest. Similarly, letters of apology to those wronged in any way should, Meyer insisted, be written immediately. Following this, spiritual blessing would come. On the Wednesday evening of the Convention Meyer was able to report that people had responded and had told him about it. Marriage relationships were being put right. By the Thursday evening Meyer was revealing that engagements to be married 'which ought never to have been made' had been broken off.[45] Keswick spirituality was being worked out in practice.

To what extent did Keswick spirituality affect Baptists? The largest denominational group at Keswick, on the platform and in the audience, was Anglican. Estimates in the 1920s and 1930s suggested that at least 60% of those attending Keswick were Church of England and that this proportion had been fairly constant since the beginning.[46] Although a number of Baptist leaders were wary of Keswick, seeing it as purveying an inward-directed piety that drew people away from social involvement, nevertheless it is likely that Baptists were the next largest denominational group at the Convention. W.Y. Fullerton, who was well known in the Baptist denomination as an evangelist, a pastor (at Melbourne Hall, Leicester) and then more widely as Home Secretary of the Baptist Missionary Society from 1912, delivered a Keswick address for the first time in 1913, having been deeply affected by the Keswick message about 'the abiding Presence of Christ'.[47] He became part of Keswick's inner circle. Speaking at the Convention in 1918 he referred to the Anglican Thomas Dundas Harford-Battersby, who had been the first chairman of Keswick, as 'the sainted founder'. It was Harford-Battersby's experience

---

[43] D.W. Bebbington, *Evangelicalism in Modern Britain: A History from the 1730s to the 1980s* (London: Routledge, 1995), ch. 5.
[44] *The Keswick Week*, 1902, p. 149.
[45] *The Keswick Week*, 1903, p. 66; 1903, pp. 97-98; 1903, p. 146.
[46] *The Life of Faith* 10 February 1926, p. 14; *The Baptist Times* 21 July 1932, p. 513.
[47] W.Y. Fullerton, *At the Sixtieth Milestone* (London: Marshall, [1917]), p. 89.

of entering into 'resting faith' which was often quoted as an example of how the message of Keswick effected profound change in Christian experience. At Keswick, Fullerton became friendly with well-known Anglican speakers such as Handley Moule, who, as Bishop of Durham, was the leading Anglican ecclesiastic at Keswick.[48] Both Meyer and Fullerton continued to be influential Keswick figures in the 1920s. By that time Keswick spirituality had spread much more widely among Baptists.

In some cases Baptists were drawn to Keswick not because they were seeking for a deeper spiritual experience but because they had already had such an experience and so found the atmosphere of Keswick congenial. Graham Scroggie was an example of this process.[49] His first ministry, in Leytonstone in Essex, came to a premature end after two years. Scroggie described a decisive period of inner conflict he had known at that point when he felt personally broken. This paved the way for a new experience in which—as he was to say in different ways and on several occasions to hearers at Keswick—the Bible and Christ came alive to him.[50] He felt that he had to give up his first pastorate and start afresh since, as he put it, he had been 'a middleman between his books and his people but not of the Book... I was spiritually bankrupt, and I well nigh became a spiritual casualty.'[51] Scroggie spoke for the first time at Keswick before the First World War, and in subsequent years he emerged as the Convention's most penetrating thinker. By 1950 he could be referred to as indisputably the foremost living Keswick teacher.[52] Scroggie took the Convention's morning daily Bible Readings on twelve different occasions, and it was at these Readings that his views, especially on the necessity of accepting Christ as Lord as well as Saviour—views which he wished to see accepted as mainstream evangelical spirituality—were most clearly set out. Scroggie's approach to spirituality shifted some of the focus of Keswick. Jean Rees, a popular evangelical writer, noted that Scroggie opposed the idea of 'Let go—and let God' and that he argued for victory coming through 'fighting and striving to make true in experience what is true for us positionally'.[53]

---

[48] *The Life of Faith* 24 July 1918, p. 682; 31 July 1918, p. 711; 14 August 1918, p. 758.
[49] I.M. Randall, 'Graham Scroggie and Evangelical Spirituality', *Scottish Bulletin of Evangelical Theology* 18.1 (2000), pp. 71-86.
[50] *The Keswick Week*, 1921, p. 168; 1927, pp. 144-5; *The Keswick Convention* (London: The Life of Faith, 1930), pp. 128-29.
[51] W. Whyte, *Revival in Rose Street: A History of Charlotte Baptist Chapel, Edinburgh* (Edinburgh: Charlotte Chapel, n.d.), p. 44.
[52] *The Keswick Week*, 1950, p. 43.
[53] *The Life of Faith* 11 July 1951, p. 479.

Although, as we have seen, Scroggie was often negative about Pentecostal spirituality, he did not want to limit the work of the Holy Spirit. Scroggie did not deny, for instance, the possibility of speaking in tongues in the contemporary church. He saw the gifts of 1 Corinthians 12 as standing or falling together and he had no doubt that they remained available.[54] But it was the quieter spirituality of Keswick that appealed to Scroggie. When he moved to Charlotte Chapel, Edinburgh, in 1916, he told the Chapel congregation that he was looking to them for 'spiritual inspiration', but he soon found the shouts of 'Hallelujah! Amen! Glory! Praise the Lord!', which were a feature of this large Baptist congregation, to be disturbing and unhelpful.[55] Scroggie stressed biblical exposition, and he was determined that expositions should be received thoughtfully. At the same time, Scroggie insisted that evangelicals should be open to new experiences and encounters with God. It was because of this conviction that he often told the story of his own journey. In 1942 he recalled at Keswick how four decades before he had indicated to his wife during a period of spiritual anguish that he would abandon ministry. 'I have no message', he had agonized, 'I have no power; I have no joy, and it will kill me.' But it was in the midst of this despair that he 'met with God'. He was grateful, he said on another occasion, that he had learned many things at Spurgeon's College during his training there, but he stated that he had not learned at that time how to live the Christian life victoriously.[56] It was this message of the possibility of spiritual victory, by faith in Christ and through submission to him as Lord, which was accepted by many Baptists.

Listening to God

It was in part the Keswick movement that spawned another stream of renewal that had links with and affected a considerable number of Baptists—what became widely known in the 1930s as the Oxford Group and later as Moral Re-Armament. Probably the most important formative Baptist influence on the Oxford Group was Meyer, whom Frank Buchman, the founder of the Group, heard at D.L. Moody's influential Northfield Student Conferences in Massachusetts, USA. Meyer's friendship with D.L. Moody dated from his pastorate at Priory Street Baptist Church in York, where, in 1873, he had hosted Moody's first evangelistic meetings in Britain. As a result of these meetings Meyer's own vision for evangelism grew stronger.[57] Through the friendship with

---

[54] *Bethesda Record*, July 1912, p. 118.
[55] Whyte, *Revival in Rose Street*, p. 44.
[56] *The Keswick Week*, 1942, pp. 70-71; 1950, p. 192; 1954, pp. 5-6.
[57] See I.M. Randall, 'Mere Denominationalism: F.B. Meyer and Baptist Life', *Baptist Quarterly* 35.1 (January, 1993), pp. 19-34.

Moody, Meyer became a highly popular speaker in the 1890s at Northfield and in other parts of North America. It was while Frank Buchman was at a Lutheran theological seminary in Mount Airy, Pennsylvania, that he attended the Northfield Conference. Buchman reported that the visit, including Meyer's teaching, 'completely changed' his life, and from this point, in 1901, he dedicated himself to winning people for Christ—what he called 'life-changing'. A year later Buchman started a new Lutheran congregation in one of Philadelphia's suburbs and until 1907 ran a hostel for young men in a poor part of the city. From 1909 he held posts at Pennsylvania State College (as YMCA Secretary) and Hartford Theological Seminary, but he was increasingly drawn to international itinerant ministry.[58]

As Meyer travelled and spoke at meetings connected with the call to deeper spiritual life, he was always on the look-out for those with potential as spiritual leaders, and while at Northfield Meyer had given Frank Buchman an inscribed copy of his book about his own mission endeavours in London, *Reveries and Realities*.[59] In the summer of 1908 Buchman visited the Keswick Convention, hoping to encounter Meyer again, but he found that Meyer was not present. Feeling acutely disappointed, Buchman attended a local Primitive Methodist chapel where he listened to Jessie Penn-Lewis, who had been deeply affected by the Welsh Revival, addressing a congregation of seventeen people on the subject of the cross of Christ. Buchman had what he described as 'a poignant vision of the Crucified' and he left the chapel determined to share his experience and to ask forgiveness from people he had wronged.[60] Buchman went on to take up the idea of four 'absolutes' to express the relationship between inward surrender and its practical demonstration. God's call, as he explained it, was to absolute honesty, purity, unselfishness and love. The idea of the absolutes came from another Northfield speaker and missionary statesman, Robert Speer.[61] Buchman's ability to use ideas to challenge people to a life of spiritual effectiveness was to prove appealing to many Baptists.

Links between Meyer and Buchman continued. In 1912 Meyer was speaking at Pennsylvania State College—he was then minister of Regent's Park Chapel, London, but was travelling widely—and during his visit he advised the activist Buchman that he should set aside an hour a day to listen to God. Meyer also suggested to Buchman that he should make personal conversations with individuals the focus of his evangelism. The

---

[58] G. Lean, *Frank Buchman: A Life* (London: Collins, 1985), chs 3–9.
[59] F.B. Meyer, *Reveries and Realities: Or Life and Work in London* (London: Morgan & Scott, 1896).
[60] T. Spoerri, *Dynamic out of Silence* (London: Grosvenor, 1976), pp. 24-25.
[61] R.E. Speer, *The Principles of Jesus* (New York: Fleming H. Revell, 1902), pp. 34-36.

story of how Meyer found Buchman so busy that he was using two telephones was often retold. Meyer's point was that hearing the voice of God was more important than listening to human voices on two telephones.[62] Buchman's view was that in his 'personal work' (i.e., witness to individuals) he was a 'flat failure' before meeting Meyer.[63] As a result of Meyer's influence, according to Buchman, people became a priority, and in addition he 'decided to devote and hour, from 5 a.m. to 6 a.m....in a daily time of quiet'.[64] This procedure reflected standard evangelical devotion, common in Baptist circles, which normally consisted of daily prayer and Bible study—the 'quiet time'. The distinctive practice of the Group was to write down specific points of guidance which had arisen out of this exercise of listening to God. In his *Five 'Musts' of the Christian Life*, Meyer exhorted his readers to obey exactly what God said. 'Listen to that still small voice—the voice of the Spirit of God.' This is the message which Buchman was conveying.[65] Meyer also helped to shape the Group's commitment to 'confession'—open sharing of personal problems and failures. Frederick C. Spurr, who followed Meyer as minister of Regent's Park Chapel, London, in 1914, having been a Baptist Union missioner and a minister in Australia, recalled how Meyer had opened his heart in confession to fellow-ministers. This had been a great help to Spurr and others.[66] Baptists were engaging with fresh approaches to spirituality.

Although the major impact of the Group on Baptists in England was to be found in the 1920s and 1930s—it was from 1921 that Buchman began direct evangelistic work in Britain, initially in Cambridge and soon centred in Oxford, and it was in the early 1920s that he attended the Keswick Convention—Buchman's connections with Baptists who were part of English Baptist life were significant in the first two decades of the twentieth century.[67] Meyer was his closest contact, but T.R. Glover, a notable Baptist of a more liberal evangelical theological hue and Public Orator of Cambridge University, first met Buchman in 1914 and thereafter followed his activities with interest. Buchman's relatively undogmatic approach to theology was appealing to Glover. Despite his own broader views and his considerable involvement with the

---

[62] M. Guldseth, *Streams* (Alaska: Moral Re-Armament, 1982), pp. 98-99; K.D. Belden, *Reflections on Moral Re-armament* (London: Grosvenor, 1983), p. 38.
[63] Draft biography, ch. 2, Morris Martin Files, Moral Re-Armament Archives, Library of Congress, Washington DC.
[64] Spoerri, *Dynamic*, p. 30.
[65] F.B. Meyer, *Five 'Musts' of the Christian Life* (London: Morgan & Scott, [1928]), p. 107.
[66] *The Baptist Times* 14 February 1935, pp. 134-37.
[67] I.M. Randall, '"Arresting People for Christ": Baptists and the Oxford Group in the 1930s', *Baptist Quarterly* 38.1 (January, 1999), pp. 3-18.

theologically diverse Student Christian Movement, Glover felt some affinity with the conservative evangelical students in the Cambridge Inter-Collegiate Christian Union, defending their adherence to the message: 'You must be born anew'.[68] Glover saw himself as an apologist for the Christian faith, yet when comparing himself with Buchman's spiritual impact Glover expressed the wish that he had more gift for 'arresting people for Christ'.[69] Another significant Baptist whom Buchman appreciated was Oswald Chambers, who died from peritonitis while at the height of his creative powers as a thinker and speaker. Chambers became most famous after his death through the widely-used book of daily readings, *My Utmost for his Highest*. This book became a manual for the Oxford Group. In 1923 Buchman was struck by Chambers' view that God was not being heard 'because we are so full of noisy, introspective thoughts'.[70]

In the 1930s many younger Baptists, including younger Baptist ministers, testified to spiritual renewal through the Group. Tensions, however, also emerged. In some cases Group involvement resulted in people leaving denominational life. G.H. Boobyer, who had trained at Bristol College and had a DTh from Heidelburg University, was one young and promising Baptist minister who resigned and devoted himself to Group activities.[71] It is likely that Boobyer felt guided to do this, but this kind of Group guidance was coming under critical scrutiny. J.B. Middlebrook, who studied at Rawdon College, Leeds University and Mansfield College, Oxford, before becoming minister of New North Road Baptist Church, Huddersfield, in 1923, declined to join the Group despite being told by Group members whom he knew that all their 'guidance' pointed to the rightness of his joining. A wealthy Group member offered him total financial backing if he worked for the Group. Middlebrook was worried by what he heard from Regent's Park College about students who were Groupers 'playing fast and loose with preaching engagements in the churches at the behest of the Spirit', and about several 'first class men' being lost to the Baptist denomination.[72] These disappointments

---

[68] D. Johnson, *Contending for the Faith: A History of the Evangelical Movement in the Universities and Colleges* (Leicester: Inter-Varsity Press, 1979), p. 154.

[69] T.R. Glover to F. Buchman, 3 August 1928, Box 35, Moral Re-Armament Archives, Library of Congress. On Glover and Buchman, see also H.G. Wood, *Terrot Reaveley Glover: A Biography* (Cambridge: Cambridge University Press, 1953), pp. 178, 182-84.

[70] D. McCasland, *Oswald Chambers: Abandoned to God* (Grand Rapids, Mich.: Discovery House Publishers, 1993), chapter 13. F. Buchman to Mary Borden, 6 October 1923, Box 14, Moral Re-Armament Archives.

[71] E.A. Payne, *The Baptists of Berkshire: Through Three Centuries* (London: Carey Kingsgate Press, 1951), p. 130.

[72] Personal Memoir by J.B. Middlebrook, Angus Archive, Oxford.

contributed to a lessening of Group influence among Baptists. Nonetheless, the Group contributed to the deepening of spiritual life in sections of the Baptist denomination.

The Baptism of the Spirit

Some Baptists who were not attracted by Pentecostal revivalism, were not involved in Keswick and did not warm to the undogmatic spirituality purveyed by Buchman, nevertheless sought a powerful experience of the Holy Spirit. At the Baptist Union's Assembly in spring 1900, William Cuff, minister of the large Shoreditch Tabernacle, London, spoke about the importance of being 'saturated with the Holy Ghost'. In his view such an experience of the power of the Holy Spirit was crucial for every Christian.[73] F.B. Meyer, throughout the period we are looking at, was one of the most prominent Baptists stressing this theme. He grounded his thinking about the Spirit in the experience of Jesus, who, he argued, did not attempt his public ministry until he was 'filled with the Holy Ghost'.[74] This took place at his baptism. Since Jesus had to be 'anointed with the Holy Ghost', Meyer saw it as foolish for Christians to plunge into service until they had received power through their own anointing.[75] The apostles, Meyer asserted, were regenerate before Pentecost, but they had to 'wait within closed doors until they were endued with power'.[76] A two-stage work of the Spirit, both in Jesus and in believers, was at variance with much evangelical teaching, but Meyer was convinced that many believers were on the wrong side of Pentecost experientially.[77]

One Baptist figure who was convinced by what Meyer said and who made spiritual reality a priority was Oswald Chambers. In 1897, when he was on the staff of a small Bible College in Dunoon, Scotland, Chambers, whose father was a Baptist minister, heard Meyer speak about the Holy Spirit. Chambers recalled: 'I determined to have all that was going and went to my room and asked God simply and definitely for the baptism of the Holy Spirit, whatever that meant. From that day on for four years nothing but the overruling grace of God and the kindness of friends kept me out of an asylum.' Contrary to all his expectations of spiritual blessing, Chambers had, he asserted, no conscious communion with God

---

[73] *The Baptist Times* 27 April 1900, supplement, p. v.
[74] F.B. Meyer, *From Calvary to Pentecost* (London: The Keswick Library, [1894]), p. 110.
[75] *Regions Beyond* 45 (1924), p. 81.
[76] F.B. Meyer, *David: Shepherd, Psalmist, King* (London: Morgan & Scott, 1895), p. 18.
[77] *The Life of Faith* 8 February 1893, p. 113; F.B. Meyer, 'The Outpouring of the Holy Spirit', in A.G. Brown, *et al.*, *The Glorious Person and Work of the Holy Spirit* (London: Elliot Stock, [1896]), p. 46.

for those four years. Although outwardly he continued as a popular evangelical teacher, he considered this period—a 'dark night of the soul'—to have been inner hell on earth.[78] It was through an interdenominational organization called the Pentecostal League of Prayer that Oswald Chambers found spiritual freedom. He testified in November 1901, following a Pentecostal League of Prayer event, that '[b]y an entire consecration and acceptance of sanctification at the Lord's hands, I was baptized with the Holy Ghost'.[79]

The Pentecostal League of Prayer (the word 'Pentecostal', the League was to insist, did not mean it had any association with the Pentecostal 'tongues' movement) was founded in 1891 as an organization explicitly dedicated to praying for the Pentecostal filling of the Holy Spirit for all believers, for revival in the churches and for the spread of holiness. The founder, Richard Reader Harris, an Anglican, was a barrister—a Queen's Counsel—but his deepest passion was for spiritual revival. From 1889, when he and his wife Mary claimed sanctification through the influence of two North Americans, F.D. Sandford and G.D. Watson (who brought with them Wesleyan ideas of entire sanctification), Harris had a vision for spreading his new convictions. By the end of the century the emphases of Harris and the League were promoted by almost 150 networked local prayer groups throughout Britain, with a total of 17,000 members. When Harris died in 1909 leadership passed to his wife, although considerable support was also being offered to the League by Chambers, who had been baptized at Rye Lane Baptist Chapel, Peckham, London, and was also associated with Eltham Park Baptist Church, London. Some Baptist networks were affected by this spiritual impetus.[80]

One important aspect of the contribution of the League was the significant opportunities for ministry it offered to women as well as men. This was a period when Baptists were giving more attention to the spiritual contribution of women in leadership. Violet Hedger, who trained for the ministry at Regent's Park College, had come to the conclusion by 1925 that there was a growing need for women ministers. The ideal, she suggested, might be churches with a male and female pastor.[81] Hedger was not the first woman Baptist minister in England. Edith Gates began as pastor at Little Tew and Cleveley, Oxfordshire, in 1918, qualifying as a

---

[78] B. Chambers, *Oswald Chambers: His Life and Work* (London: Simpkin Marshall, 1933), p. 78; D.W. Lambert, *Oswald Chambers* (London: Christian Literature Crusade, n.d.), p. 23.

[79] G.H. Chambers, *Oswald Chambers: His Life and Work* (London: Simpkin Marshall, 1933), pp. 28, 79.

[80] M.R. Hooker, *Adventures of an Agnostic* (London: Marshall, Morgan & Scott 1959), p. 112; McCasland, *Oswald Chambers*, ch. 13.

[81] *The Baptist Times* 16 January 1925, pp. 35-36.

probationer in 1922.[82] The important role of the Order of Deaconesses in Baptist life—they were active in London and elsewhere—was highlighted by Hettie Rowntree Clifford, from West Ham Central Mission.[83] In 1897, in a book *Pentecost in the Churches*, Reader Harris had argued from his pan-denominational perspective in favour of women preachers. He considered that when Paul told women to keep silent (e.g., 1 Cor. 14.33b-35) the reference was to chattering in services. His conclusion was that the scriptures 'plainly teach that women are called to preach the Gospel'. Biddy Chambers, the wife of Oswald, was a League of Prayer speaker, as was Mary Hooker, daughter of Reader and Mary Harris, who became head of Ridgelands Bible College, London. Joan Hooker, Mary's daughter, married Graham Scroggie.[84]

Oswald Chambers' first public address following his experience of the power of the Spirit in 1901 resulted in forty people coming to the front in consecration. From November 1906, Chambers found himself, for almost a year, engaged in constant travel. He taught for six months at God's Bible School in Cincinnati, USA, a school which identified with Wesleyan holiness teaching, and then travelled to Japan, conducting holiness meetings with Juji Nakada, who in 1917 became the first bishop of the Japan Holiness Church. Fresh from these experiences, Chambers threw himself into League of Prayer gatherings throughout Britain. In the years 1907–10, when the League was convening over 13,000 interdenominational services every year, Chambers, with his brilliantly imaginative presentation of the message of holiness, was the League's most effective speaker. He also set up a Bible Training College in London in 1911, which trained 106 men and women students, forty of whom became missionaries.[85] The League believed that Keswick teaching was not strong enough in the area of holiness, although the League's leaders also opposed the Pentecostal emphasis on speaking in tongues. The impact of Chambers was cut short by his death in 1917 at the age of forty-three—he was in Egypt doing YMCA work during the First World War—but the stress on the Spirit that he and others represented had made

---

[82] Minutes of Baptist Union Ministerial Recognition Committee, 7 November 1922.

[83] *The Baptist Times* 8 May 1925, p. 323. See F. Bowers, *A Bold Experiment: The Story of Bloomsbury Chapel and Bloomsbury Central Baptist Church, 1848–1999* (London: Bloomsbury Baptist Church, 1999), pp. 266-71.

[84] R. Harris, *Pentecost in the Churches* (London: S.W. Partridge, 1897); *Spiritual Life*, December 1924, p. 2. Scroggie's first wife died and he married Joan Hooker in 1941.

[85] *God's Revivalist* 6 December 1900, p. 9; Chambers, *Oswald Chambers*, pp. 79, 171-74; McCasland, *Abandoned to God*, pp. 84-86, 171-74, ch. 15.

an impact on Baptist life and would surface again in the 1960s with the emergence of charismatic spirituality.[86]

'Come ye apart'

Of equal significance for Baptist spirituality, especially in the longer term, was the Retreat movement. In two articles in *The Baptist Times*, the first entitled 'Come ye apart', F.C. Spurr reflected on the way in which retreats had been a means of spiritual renewal for him and for the congregations of which he had been pastor in the early twentieth century. He argued that although the word 'Retreat' had a Roman Catholic or Anglo-Catholic sound for many Baptists (and was therefore regarded with suspicion), the idea was in line with the words of Christ, 'Come ye yourselves apart and rest awhile' (Mk 6.31). Spurr had put into practice the concept of retreat in creative ways. From his own experience he advocated about twenty or thirty people going away for three or four days to spend the time on ordered thought and prayer. The format he suggested was one in which each day began with the Lord's Supper. There were no expository sermons, but rather addresses on certain themes connected with God's desire for people to know deeper spiritual life. These addresses were followed by periods of silent meditation. Discussion was, Spurr stressed, not permitted. Spurr commended retreats to ministers as a way to obtain 'a new accession of spiritual power' and he saw retreats for congregations as a means by which 'to recover the faded vision and the lost power'.[87]

Spurr did not expect that all his *Baptist Times* readers would agree with his views. However, he was in tune with a growing movement. Contact with those outside their own circles was broadening the thinking of Baptists. The Free Church Fellowship, which began when about a dozen friends gathered at Mansfield College, Oxford, at Easter 1911, attracted many future Free Church leaders, and by 1913 it had 250 members.[88] There was a heart-felt desire among these younger Free Church men and women to appropriate 'the experience of all the saints concerning the practice of the Presence of God' and a hope for 'a Free Church so steeped in the spirit and traditions of the entire Church Catholic as to be ready in due time for the reunion of Christendom'.[89] Among Baptists who joined in the early period were M.E. Aubrey, who was minister of St Andrew's Street Baptist Church, Cambridge, and who from 1925 would

---

[86] For this, see D. McBain, *Fire over the Waters: Renewal among Baptists and Others from the 1960s to the 1990s* (London: Darton, Longman and Todd, 1997).

[87] *The Baptist Times* 26 September 1935, p. 700; 10 October 1935, p. 734.

[88] Free Church Fellowship Occasional Paper No. 1, October 1911, p. 4; Occasional Paper No 4, October 1912, pp. 19-20, 22.

[89] *The Grounds of our Fellowship* (Oxford: n.p., [1911]), p. 7.

follow J.H. Shakespeare as the Secretary of the Baptist Union. In 1916, at the annual Free Church Fellowship Swanwick conference, at 'The Hayes' conference centre, the atonement was the subject and meditations from Julian of Norwich and Thomas à Kempis were utilized.[90] Baptists who were influential within the Union were exploring broader spirituality.

In 1914 J.H. Shakespeare paid tribute to Newton Marshall, who had grown up under John Clifford's ministry at Westbourne Park Baptist Church, Paddington, London, and had been minister at Heath Street Baptist Church, Hampstead. Marshall's early death in 1914 deprived the Baptist denomination of one of its finest theological thinkers. Shakespeare reported that the last words that Marshall—who had been the chairman of the Baptist Union's Spiritual Welfare Committee—had said to him concerned the need for a 'Retreat movement' for ministers, concentrating on prayer and penitence. 'Alas!', observed Shakespeare, 'We have no room in our bustling life for Retreats.' It was perhaps a comment on Shakespeare's own hectic life. The activist Shakespeare did call, however, for what he termed the 'mystical way' to be taken.[91] It is possible that these comments of Shakespeare's were of encouragement to F.C. Spurr. Two years later, during the Second World War when congregations were suffering considerable losses through young men being killed on the Front, Spurr was among those advocating an advance in spiritual welfare in the denomination. Echoing Marshall, he suggested congregational retreats for spiritual renewal. At this stage Spurr linked these events to deeper fellowship in church meetings, service to the community and the need for every Christian to be involved in witness.[92]

One increasingly significant Baptist who was seeking in his writings to relate theology and spirituality was H. Wheeler Robinson, who from 1906 until 1920 was a tutor at Rawdon College, Leeds. Robinson was especially interested in two areas of theological enquiry: the theology of baptism and the theology of the Holy Spirit, subjects on which he would write significant material. He argued in 1914 that thinking about water baptism among Baptists placed too much emphasis on the personal act of faith and not enough on 'the spiritual energies which that act of faith mediates'. Robinson argued for a close association between the gift of the Spirit and baptism.[93] Later, when Principal of Regent's Park College, Robinson began a weekly communion service, which became the heart of College life. His talks on these occasions showed 'catholicity and

---

[90] *Free Church Fellowship Notes*, No. 16, September 1916, p. 3.
[91] *The Baptist Times* 20 March 1914, p. 243.
[92] *The Baptist Times* 3 November 1916, p. 671.
[93] *The Baptist Times* 24 July 1914, p. 601; cf. A.R. Cross, 'The Pneumatological Key to H. Wheeler Robinson's Baptismal Sacramentalism', in A.R. Cross and P.E. Thompson (eds), *Baptist Sacramentalism* (Studies in Baptist History and Thought, 5; Carlisle: Paternoster Press, 2003), pp. 151-76.

depth'.[94] Robinson's book *The Christian Experience of the Holy Spirit* (1928) owes a great deal to his own experiences in prayer. He had become increasingly fascinated by the thinking of John Henry Newman, had attended retreats at the High Church Mirfield community led by W.H. Frere, and led ministerial retreats in which time was given to quiet worship.[95] Here was a further resource for Baptist spirituality.

Conclusion

The threads of theology, communion with God and Christian practice as key elements of Christian spirituality have been themes in this study. As has been true throughout Baptist history, Baptists in the first two decades of the twentieth century drew significant spiritual help from corporate worship. This was, however, a time of fresh theological thinking and that had its impact on experience and practice. In the main free prayer, for example, was defended as against set prayers, but there were those like F.B. Meyer who used liturgy, and by the 1930s Baptist ministers looking for fresh liturgical approaches would be able to use Tait Patterson's *Call to Worship*, with its prayers deliberately drawn from the catholic treasury of prayers. At Highams Park Baptist Church, in East London, under the innovative ministry of Stephen Winward, liturgy was encouraged. Weekly communion became the established pattern and was an integral part of the service.[96] The impact of revival movements and of Keswick spirituality continued to be felt among Baptists in the inter-war years. Although the Oxford Group was later to change direction and become a more general religious movement when it took 'moral re-armament' as its focus, nonetheless it was a powerful source of renewal among Baptists and others for at least two decades. It would have its counterpart in the later charismatic movement.[97] Desire for a baptism of the Spirit—however that was defined—continued in the inter-war years. In 1936 Henry Townsend, President of Manchester College, speaking as incoming President of the Baptist Union, said that he was yearning that 'the Church we love may be baptised of the Holy Spirit'.[98] Finally, the interest in retreats which began before the First World War, continued to feature in some sectors of Baptist

---

[94] E.A. Payne, *Henry Wheeler Robinson: A Memoir* (London: Nisbet, 1946), p. 71.

[95] Payne, *Henry Wheeler Robinson*, pp. 59-60.

[96] Walker, 'Baptist Worship in the Twentieth Century', pp. 23-24. For an overview of these developments, see Norman Wallwork, 'Developments in Liturgy and Worship in Twentieth-Century Protestant Nonconformity', in A.P.F. Sell and A.R. Cross (eds), *Protestant Nonconformity in the Twentieth Century* (Carlisle: Paternoster Press, 2002), pp. 118-24.

[97] Bebbington, *Evangelicalism in Modern Britain*, ch. 7.

[98] *The Baptist Times* 16 April 1936, p. 294.

life. A Baptist Union Discipleship Group meeting in 1935 stressed the value of retreats. J.B. Middlebrook and M.E. Aubrey were asked to pursue this further in order to encourage spiritual leadership by lay people in the churches.[99] To imagine that the period we have been examining was one in which forms of vibrant spirituality were not to be found in Baptist life is to subscribe to a myth.

---

[99] Minutes of the Baptist Union Discipleship Committee, 12 September 1935.

CHAPTER 7

The Myth of English Baptist Anti-Sacramentalism

Anthony R. Cross

Introduction

To many the juxtaposition of the words 'baptismal sacramentalism' and 'Baptists' is unthinkable. It is widely believed that Baptists are non- or even anti–sacramental. Baptism is understood to be an ordinance—the personal profession of faith of the baptismal candidate, a witness or testimony to the faith in the crucified and risen Christ which they have come to as a response to the gospel—and little more. Some examples will illustrate this point.

In his impressive survey of world Baptists, Albert W. Wardin summarizes Baptist identity as including belief that baptism represents *'symbolically* the rising of the believer from the watery grave to walk a new life with Christ'.[1] Similar views reverberate throughout much Baptist writing on baptism and grass-roots Baptist belief. For example, a recent correspondent in *The Baptist Times* responded with surprise to the opening of a report beneath the photograph of a baptism in Kathmandu which read 'Washing their sins away': he asked, 'Surely we don't believe that, do we?' He continued expressing his confidence 'that the washing away of the candidate's sin was gloriously granted first by their prior saving faith in Christ, and was a pre-requisite to their witnessing in baptism—not dependent on it'.[2] Such a symbolic understanding of baptism pervades much Baptist thought. This despite Acts 22.16, where Ananias tells Saul to 'Get up, be baptised and was your sins away, calling on his name', and Titus 3.5's 'He saved us through the washing of rebirth and renewal by the Holy Spirit.'[3]

---

[1] A.W. Wardin, *Baptists Around the World: A Comprehensive Handbook* (Nashville, TN: Broadman & Holman, 1995), p. 2. As a summary and inclusive statement of Baptist belief this is certainly representative of the Baptist position.

[2] See the original photo and brief report, 'Believers baptised in a bath', *Baptist Times* 25 March 1999, p. 4, and R. Foster, 'Baptism', *Baptist Times* 15 April 1999, p. 6.

[3] That Tit. 3.5, however it is interpreted, refers to baptism, see, e.g., I.H. Marshall and P.H. Towner, *The Pastoral Epistles* (International Critical Commentary;

In England, many Baptists associated with the Baptist Union of Great Britain (and Ireland) (f.1813/32) have perpetuated a non-sacramental interpretation of baptism. Indeed the majority of Baptists have held to a solely symbolic understanding of baptism. Charles Williams, one of the foremost Baptist ministers of his time, denied that baptism was either a condition of salvation or a sacrament. For Baptists 'baptism is not part of the gospel which Christ has commanded to be preached...but an ordinance intended only for those who repent of sin and believe the gospel'. 'They cannot, without doing violence to their own principles, ascribe to baptism any cleansing efficacy or regenerating influence or saving grace': it is 'a profession of discipleship and a test of loyalty to the Lord Jesus Christ'.[4] The Baptist historian W.T. Whitley condemned both sacerdotalism and sacramentalism as 'twin errors: believe one, and the other must follow; destroy either, and the other must die'.[5] On Acts 2.38 he commented that 'To suppose that Peter meant baptism was now an extra condition before sins were remitted, is to represent him as making salvation harder than [the prophets, John the Baptist or Christ] had done.'[6] Another historian, A.S. Langley, declared, 'The ordinances are not sacraments. They do not convey saving grace. They are symbols observed, and preserved by the churches. They are of value to those who observe them only as their meaning is observed.'[7] For example, the Baptist layman, F.F. Whitby, entitled a whole chapter 'The Ordinance of Baptism Symbolical of our Faith'.[8] Four ministers who made up the Radlett Fellowship discussed the meaning of the ordinance solely in terms

---

London: T&T Clark, 1999), pp. 13-22; and Lars Hartman, *'Into the Name of the Lord Jesus': Baptism in the Early Church* (Studies of the New Testament and Its World: Edinburgh: T&T Clark, 1997), pp. 108-13.

[4] C. Williams, *The Principles and Practices of the Baptists, to which is added a Baptist Directory* (London: Kingsgate Press, 2nd edn, 1903), pp. 16-17, 20 and 22 respectively.

[5] W.T. Whitley, *Church, Ministry and the Sacraments in the New Testament* (London: Kingsgate Press, 1903), p. 244. On p. 271 he submitted that sacerdotalists appended the Bible to tradition. See also his epilogue 'Sacerdotalism and Sacramentarianism', pp. 276-81.

[6] Whitley, *Church*, p. 120.

[7] A.S. Langley, *The Faith, Heritage and Mission of the Baptists* (London: Kingsgate Press, 1931), p. 8. For him baptism represents a death, burial and resurrection, and symbolizes complete cleansing from sin, complete consecration and surrender to Christ. Cf. also L.A. Read, 'The Ordinances', *The Fraternal* 67 (January, 1948), pp. 8-10.

[8] F.F. Whitby, *Baptist Principles from a Layman's Point of View* (London: Kingsgate Press, n.d. [1908]), pp. 58-73. Cf. also W.G. Channon, *Much Water and Believers Only* (London: Victory Press, 1950), *passim*.

of a proclamation of the gospel, a witness to conversion and an act of discipleship.[9]

Among the Grace/Strict Baptists, who are more explicitly Reformed in their views than the descendents of the Particular Baptists who remain with the Baptist Union, there is the unequivocal rejection of anything suggestive of sacramentalism. On Romans 6, Eric Lane declares that 'It is almost always the case in the epistles that "baptism" means Spirit-baptism being used pictorially.' He continues: 'while the direct reference of this passage is to Spirit-baptism, the terms in which it is described make some reference to water-baptism.' He then makes the stark assertion that 'Paul never speaks explicitly about baptism in his epistles', but he does not believe that this in any way undervalues baptism or that it should be neglected for, with the Lord's Supper 'they are used as *illustrations* of salvation'.[10]

Similarly, Erroll Hulse maintains that 'For Baptists the ordinance of baptism is not a sacrament in which grace is infused into the believer in any way, but rather the ordinance is a testimony of what God has done in regeneration and is a testimony by the believer of repentance and faith. It is a testimony of one who can give a credible testimony of God's grace in bringing him into a union with Christ, a union symbolised in burial and rising again to newness of life, as well as a symbol of discipleship.'[11]

According to Jack Hoad, an Independent Baptist minister, 'the ordinances are acts of obedience which set forth the central truths of the gospel, particularly the death and resurrection of Christ. The ordinances are therefore symbolic declarations of the Gospel and not in themselves channels of special grace to the obedient.' He then acknowledges that in this Baptists share Zwingli's view rather than Luther's.[12] He further makes the statement that 'Baptists understand the pentecostal scripture of Acts 2:38 not to imply that baptism procures the forgiveness of sins but that it is *the sign* of that remission, indeed the visual declaration of the means of it, namely, the death, burial and resurrection of Jesus Christ.'[13]

---

[9] P.J. Goodland, P.J. Hetherington, J.L. Pretlove and D.J. Warner, *Faith and Life: Practical Lessons in Christian Living* (Radlett: Radlett Fellowship, 1966), n.p..

[10] E. Lane, *I Want to be Baptised* (London: Grace Publications, 1986), pp. 93-96, italics added.

[11] E. Hulse, 'The 1689 Confession—Its History and Role Today', in P. Clarke *et al*, *Our Baptist Heritage* (Leeds: Reformation Today Trust, 1993), p. 18. For a more detailed account of Hulse's views, see his *The Testimony of Baptism* (Haywards Heath: Carey Publications, 1982).

[12] J. Hoad, *The Baptist: An Historical and Theological Study of the Baptist Identity* (London: Grace Publications, 1986), p. 237.

[13] Hoad, *The Baptist*, pp. 249-50, italics added. On pp. 244-45 (italics added) he writes that 'baptism *signifies* the previous entrance of a believer into communion with his Lord and Saviour... It declares that regeneration has taken place through union with

The Articles of the Gospel Standard Baptists declare that 'Baptism and the Lord's Supper are ordinances of Christ' and 'reject as blasphemous the doctrine of Baptismal Regeneration; that is, that the person baptized is or can be regenerated in, by, or through baptism...'.[14] The commentary to these Articles states that 'Believers' Baptism...possesses no inherent virtue—not in the slightest degree does it contribute to salvation or influence regeneration.'[15]

In discussions of Baptist theology one of several possible classifications draws the distinction between evangelicals and sacramentalists, the view on baptism being the determinative factor.[16] While this is a popular, tenacious and widespread opinion, it is too simplistic a dividing line, for there have been a significant number of Baptists who have held a sacramental interpretation of baptism from the earliest times, and many of the leading Baptist sacramentalists today are evangelicals, as mention of the names of George Beasley-Murray, R.E.O. White and, more recently, John Colwell demonstrates.[17] The purpose of this paper, then, is twofold: first, to show that from the beginning of the Baptist movement in the seventeenth century a significant number of Baptists have held a sacramental understanding of baptism;[18] and second, to make more widely known

---

Christ' and that it is a *symbol* of four things: the death and resurrection of Christ (Rom. 6.3); the purpose of that death, i.e. atonement for sin (Rom. 6.4, 11); accomplishment of the work of grace in the baptized (Gal. 3.27); and union with Christ and all believers in Christ (Eph. 4.5; 1 Cor. 12.13).

[14] Being Articles 15 and 18, see J.H. Gosden (for many years editor of the *Gospel Standard* magazine), *What Gospel Standard Baptists Believe: A Commentary on the Gospel Standard Articles of Faith* (Chippenham: Gospel Standard Societies, 1993), pp. 77-78. For commentary on these Articles see pp. 77-95. On the origins and date of these Articles, see pp. v-vii.

[15] Gosden, *What Gospel Standard Baptists Believe*, p. 85.

[16] E.g., H.L. McBeth, *The Baptist Heritage: Four Centuries of Baptist Witness* (Nashville, TN: Broadman, 1987), p. 511.

[17] See H. Wheeler Robinson, *The Life and Faith of the Baptists* (London: Kingsgate Press, rev. edn, 1946), p. 16, who claims that 'The baptism of believers by immersion has not only emphasized conscious faith as essential to the Church, but it has also, by its symbolism, constantly recalled men to the foundation of the Gospel in history, the death and resurrection of Jesus Christ, which, as Paul argued, are represented in the act of believer's immersion and his rising from the waters of baptism. That act, constantly repeated before the eyes of Baptists, has taken the place of any formal creed, and *helped to keep them an evangelical Church*, without any authoritative confession of faith.'

[18] This understanding of Baptist history has recently been accepted by B.J. Leonard, *Baptist Ways: A History* (Valley Forge, PA: Judson Press, 2003), pp. 375-76.

some of the significant research covering this subject which has been produced in recent years.[19]

Seventeenth-Century Baptismal Sacramentalism

In the last few years two North American scholars have studied seventeenth-century English Baptist theology and shown that, contrary to popular, widespread and oft-repeated opinion, a significant number of Baptists maintained a sacramental understanding of baptism.

Stanley K. Fowler draws a line of continuity between twentieth-century Baptist sacramentalists and their Baptist forebears, a significant number of whom also advocated a sacramental understanding of baptism. He demonstrates that the oft-repeated assumption that Baptists have traditionally held to a Zwinglian interpretation of baptism as an ordinance and that a Baptist sacramentalism is a relatively modern innovation, is simply in error. He shows quite clearly that some of the earliest seventeenth-century English Baptists spoke of the efficacy of baptism in sacramental terms.

Philip E. Thompson also sets out to expose the 'serious misrepresentation of early Baptists by their modern descendents [which refers] to the early Baptists as non– or anti–sacramental'.[20] In his paper delivered to the National Association of Baptist Professors of Religion in Wisconsin, June 1999, Thompson dispels the deeply entrenched and oft-repeated assumption 'that Baptist theology has remained fairly constant throughout the four centuries of Baptist existence', and his focus is specifically on a 'punctiliar, voluntarist, individualist, conversionist soteriology bequeathed to Baptists by revivalism in the late eighteenth and nineteenth centuries', and it is this which has often been 'retrojected onto the earliest Baptists'.[21] A second concern of Thompson's is to challenge the individualism which dominates Baptist thought.[22]

---

[19] See S.K. Fowler, *More Than a Symbol: The British Baptist Recovery of Baptismal Sacramentalism* (Studies in Baptist History and Thought, 2; Carlisle: Paternoster Press, 2002); P.E. Thompson, 'A New Question in Baptist History: Seeking a Catholic Spirit Among Early Baptists', *Pro Ecclesia* 8.1 (Winter, 1999), pp. 51-72, and 'Practicing the Freedom of God: Formation in Early Baptist Life', in D.M. Hammond (ed.), *Theology and Lived Christianity* (The Annual Publication of the College Theology Society, 45; Mystic, CT: Twenty-Third Publications, 2000), pp. 119-38; A.R. Cross, *Baptism and the Baptists: Theology and Practice in Twentieth-Century Britain* (Studies in Christian History and Thought, 3; Carlisle: Paternoster Press, 2000), and 'Dispelling the Myth of English Baptist Sacramentalism', *Baptist Quarterly* 38.8 (October, 2000), pp. 367-91 (this being a shorter version of the research on which this chapter is based).

[20] Thompson, 'A New Question', p. 66, italics his

[21] Thompson, 'Practicing the Freedom of God', p. 119. At this point Thompson's work ties in with one dimension of my own work on Baptist baptismal theology and

While writing within and to the context of North American Baptists, Fowler's and Thompson's criticism of Baptist misreadings of their past is equally applicable to the English situation. They note that many twentieth-century Baptists reject a sacramental understanding of baptism as being unfaithful to their heritage, but both scholars show that such a position is historically indefensible.

Thompson's first paper, 'A New Question in Baptist History: Seeking a Catholic Spirit Among Early Baptists', shows that early Baptists had a greater sense of being a part of the universal church than is usually acknowledged. For example, Article 29 of the Midland General Baptists' *Orthodox Creed* of 1678 confessed that

> There is one holy catholick church, consisting of, or made up of the whole number of the elect, that have been, are, or shall be gathered, in one body under Christ, the only head thereof...[23]

He traces this catholicity as it is clearly revealed in the acceptance of the ancient creeds, the episcopacy and the sacraments of baptism and the Lord's Supper, and argues that 'This connection to the church through the ages provided the early Baptists a context within which they could affirm the importance of the church's tradition.'[24] In short, they were not predisposed, as so many of their nineteenth- and twentieth-century descendents have been, to reject *a priori* a sacramental understanding of baptism simply because of its prevalence within paedobaptist traditions.

Fowler begins his work by setting the early Baptists within their historical context at the beginning of the seventeenth century in which 'almost all English Christians were formally committed to the understanding of baptism expressed in the Thirty-Nine Articles of the

---

practice in the twentieth century, namely the widely held assumption that Baptists' baptismal theology has always been the same. One of the conclusions of my own research is that baptismal theology has developed over the years. See Cross, *Baptism*, e.g., pp. 456-60. See also Thompson's chapter in the present volume, '"As It Was in the Beginning?": The Myth of Changelessness in Baptist Life and Belief'. This conclusion is further supported by the work of Stan Fowler.

[22] Thompson, 'Practicing the Freedom of God', pp. 119-20.

[23] *An Orthodox Creed, or A Protestant Confession of Faith, being an Essay to Unite and Confirm all True Protestants in the Fundamental Articles of the Christian Religion, Against the Errors and Heresies of Rome* (London: 1679), Article XXIX, in W.L. Lumpkin, *Baptist Confessions of Faith* (Valley Forge: Judson Press, 2nd edn, 1969), p. 318. Thompson, 'A New Question', p. 63 n. 64, notes that the 'General Baptists held to an even stronger institutional catholicity than did their Calvinist cousins'.

[24] Thompson, 'A New Question', pp. 58-69, quotation from p. 63.

Church of England'.[25] Here the 'Sacraments ordained of Christ' are understood to be 'not only badges or tokens' but also 'certain sure witnesses and effectual signs of grace and God's good will towards us, by the which he does work invisibly in us and does not only quicken, but also strengthen and confirm our faith in him' (Art. 25). Baptism is seen as 'a sign of regeneration or new birth, whereby as by an instrument, they that receive baptism rightly are grafted into the church; the promises of the forgiveness of sin and of our adoption to be the sons of God, by the Holy Ghost, are visibly signed and sealed; and grace is increased by virtue of prayer unto God' (Art. 27).[26] Both Anglicans and Puritans agreed that 'the sacraments both commemorate the work of Christ and communicate grace to those who receive them in faith'.[27] It was into this situation that the earliest Baptist leaders were born, only later, while in exile in Holland (between 1608–12), were they exposed to a non-sacramental theology through their contact with the Mennonites which may have modified their views. 'At the very least, this contact gave them another option to consider as they began to formulate their own baptismal theology.' Fowler then adds the following caution: 'However, it would be a mistake to conclude that since Baptists shared the Mennonite rejection of infant baptism, they therefore shared their non–sacramental interpretation of the efficacy of baptism', noting, for example, that Baptists rejected the Mennonites' pacifism and formulated their own distinctive doctrine of baptism.[28] Fowler's conclusion, which we will go on to illustrate, is that

> Early Baptist authors consistently argued against any kind of sacramentalism which posits an automatic bestowal of grace through baptism, but they did not deny that baptism has an instrumental function in the application of redemption. It is crucial to note that Baptist refutations of baptismal regeneration were almost always stated in reference to *infant baptism*. The point which they insisted on is that regeneration is always connected to active faith in the recipient, so that it is meaningless to speak of the regeneration of passive infants by baptism or any other means. Therefore, Baptist protests against baptismal regeneration did not necessarily deny that baptism is instrumental in some way in the experience of spiritual rebirth by confessing believers.
>
> Some early Baptists spoke more strongly than others, but there was among them a recurring affirmation that the reception of the benefits of Christ is in some way

---

[25] This paragraph summarizes Fowler, *More Than a Symbol*, pp. 10-11, quote from p. 10.
[26] 'The Thirty-Nine Articles', in M.A. Noll (ed.), *Confessions and Catechisms of the Reformation* (Leicester: Apollos, 1991), pp. 221-22.
[27] Fowler, *More Than a Symbol*, p. 10. See H. Davies, *Worship and Theology in England: From Cranmer to Baxter and Fox, 1534–1690* (Grand Rapids, MI: Eerdmans, combined edn, 1996), I, pp. 62-64.
[28] Fowler, *More Than a Symbol*, p. 11.

mediated through baptism. Their theology of baptism may not have been absolutely uniform, but they consistently asserted that God, by his Spirit, bestows spiritual benefit through baptism. Christian baptism was for them a human response to the gospel, but this human act of obedience did not exhaust the content of the event. This Baptist sacramentalism was somewhat unelaborated due to the demands of controversy about baptismal subjects and mode, but it was undeniably present.[29]

Fowler first notes the presence of this sacramental language in several confessions of faith.[30] For example, the 1654 London General Baptist confession, *The True Gospel-Faith Declared*, contended 'That God *gives* his Spirit to believers dipped [immersed] through the prayer of faith and laying on of hands.'[31] While the possible presence of sacramental theology in the Particular Baptist *Second London Confession* of 1677 is usually rejected,[32] Fowler hesitates from this conclusion on the basis that 'some of the signatories of the confession had thought about that efficacy of baptism' and that because there 'was...no developed consensus about the right kind of "sacramental" language, and it comes as no surprise that a debate largely absent from the Baptist literature of the time would be absent from this confession', the intention of which was to be a 'consensus of a large number of churches and pastors'.[33] The *Baptist Catechism*, written by Benjamin Keach and William Collins, was prepared to accompany, interpret and apply the *Second London Confession*, and took the form of question and answers. 'Q.93. What are the outward Means whereby Christ communicates to us the benefits of Redemption? A. The outward and ordinary Means whereby Christ communicates to us the benefits of redemption, are his Ordinances, especially the Word, Baptism, the Lord's Supper, and Prayer; all which

---

[29] Fowler, *More Than a Symbol*, pp. 31-32. Earlier Fowler, p. 10, notes that 'imprecision regarding what exactly happens in baptism is characteristic of much Baptist literature of the 17th century, because the writers were in most cases concerned primarily about the question of paedobaptism, secondarily about the mode of baptism, and only to a limited degree about the sacramental issue'.

[30] For more detailed discussion of baptism in the various confessions of faith, see Fowler, *More Than a Symbol*, pp. 11-20.

[31] *The True Gospel-Faith Declared According to the Scriptures, 1654*, Article XII, citing Acts 8.15; 8.17; 5.32; and Eph. 1.13-14, in Lumpkin, *Baptist Confessions*, p. 193, italics added.

[32] E.g. by J.M. Ross, 'The Theology of Baptism in Baptist History', *Baptist Quarterly* 15.3 (July, 1953), p. 101.

[33] Fowler, *More Than a Symbol*, p. 18, see pp. 17-18. Those signatories who 'had thought about the efficacy of baptism' included Benjamin Keach and William Collins. See Fowler's discussion on pp. 18-19, and below. For a list of the signatories, see Lumpkin, *Baptist Confessions*, p. 239.

Means are made effectual to the Elect, through faith, for Salvation.'[34] Similarly, Keach's catechism of 1702 asked, 'What are those gospel Ordinances called Sacraments, which do confirm us in this Faith?'[35] The *Orthodox Creed* spoke of the 'two sacraments' of baptism and the Lord's Supper as 'ordinances of positive, sovereign, and holy institution'. It also stated that 'as [Israel] had the manna to nourish them in the wilderness to Canaan; so have we the sacraments, to nourish us in the church, and in our wilderness-condition, till we come to heaven'.[36]

Taking up the theme of means of grace, Philip Thompson observes that for Baptists at this time, 'The Church was...the principal locus of God's freedom for using the things of creation as means of grace', but the church should not presume that it possessed salvation simply by possessing the means—for that was God's prerogative.[37] According to the General Baptist, Thomas Grantham, within the church was to be found the *'few solemn Rites by command from Heaven, to commemorate the Love of God in the Gift of his Son; and for Christians to express their Unity and Communion in the Mystery of the Gospel'*.[38] The early Baptists called these means of grace 'ordinances', by which was meant more than is meant today, for they recognized seven, each of which was to be found within the context of the church's corporate worship. They were worship; preaching; private devotional reading; the office of pastor; prayer, both private and corporate; and baptism and the Lord's Supper. 'The early Baptists were careful in their terminology... [T]hey numbered several ordinances of ecclesial life by which God works for salvation. Two of these were sacraments.'[39]

As already mentioned, Benjamin Keach, one-time General Baptist who became a Particular Baptist, adopted a clear sacramentalism in his *Catechism*, but it is also present in a 1689 work of his in which, on the basis of Acts 2.38 and Titus 3.5, he referred to 'the Baptism of

---

[34] B. Keach and W. Collins, *The Baptist Catechism: Commonly Called Keach's Catechism* (Philadelphia, PA: American Baptist Publication Society, 1851 [1793]), p. 23, cited by Fowler, *More Than a Symbol*, p. 18. Fowler, *More Than a Symbol*, p. 19, comments that 'The fact that [baptism] is parallel to the Word and prayer indicates that it somehow leads to the benefits signified by it, rather than simply testifying to a prior possession of those benefits. Furthermore, it was indicated here that it is Christ himself who communicates the benefits of his saving work through the ordinances, which is to say that baptism is a means of grace as well as an act of personal confession.'

[35] B. Keach, *The Child's Delight: Or Instructions for Children and Youth* (London, 1702), p. 38, cited by Thompson, 'Practicing the Freedom of God', p. 128.

[36] *Orthodox Creed*, Articles XXVII and XIX, in Lumpkin, *Baptist Confessions*, pp. 317 and 311-12 respectively.

[37] Thompson, 'Practicing the Freedom of God', p. 124.

[38] T. Grantham, *Christianismus Primitivus: or, The Ancient Christian Religion* (London, 1678), I.13, italics original.

[39] Thompson, 'Practicing the Freedom of God', p. 128.

Repentance for the Remission of Sins' and 'the Washing of Regeneration.' Later he urged,

> Consider the great Promises made to those who are obedient to it, amongst other things, *Lo, I am with you always, even to the end of the World*. And again, *He that believeth, and is baptized, shall be saved*. If a Prince shall offer a Rebel his Life in doing two things, would he neglect one of them, and say this I will do, but the other is a trivial thing, I'll not do that? Surely no, he would not run the hazard of his Life so foolishly.
>
> And then in Act. 2.38. *Repent, and be baptized every one of you for Remission of Sin, and ye shall receive the Gift of the Holy Spirit*: See what great Promises are made to Believers in *Baptism*.[40]

Keach also discussed the role of baptism as an instrument of the Spirit in the regeneration of believers:

> ...outward Water cannot convey inward Life. How can Water, an external thing, work upon the Soul in a physical manner? Neither can it be proved, that ever the Spirit of God is ty'd by any Promise, to apply himself to the Soul in a gracious Operation, when Water is applyed to the Body... Baptism is a means of conveying this Grace, when the Spirit is pleased to operate with it; but it doth not work a physical Cause upon the Soul as a Purge doth upon the Humours of the Body: for 'tis the Sacrament of Regeneration, as the Lord's Supper is of Nourishment. As a Man cannot be said to be nourished without Faith, so he cannot be said to be a new Creature without Faith... Faith only is the Principle of spiritual Life, and the Principle which draws Nourishment from the Means of God's Appointment.[41]

Grantham believed that only as baptism was 'the Sacrament or washing of Regeneration' which 'belongs to those who are born from above' could it be 'the Sacrament of initiation'.[42] Thompson observes that '[t]he two aspects could be distinguished, but not separated',[43] because for Grantham, following Calvin, baptism involved, first, mortification, that is dying with Christ and, second, vivification, that is rising to new life in Christ. Grantham explained: *'that first is called burial with Christ; the second, a rising with Christ; the Sacrament of both of these is Baptism, in which we are overwhelmed or buryed, and after that do come forth and*

---

[40] B. Keach, *Gold Refin'd; or Baptism in its Primitive Purity* (London, 1689), p. 173, italics original.

[41] Keach, *Gold Refin'd*, pp. 128-29.

[42] T. Grantham, *The Loyal Baptist: or An Apology for the Baptized Believers* (London, 1684), see *The Second Part of the Apology for the Baptized Believers*, p. 15. Thompson, 'A New Question', p. 60 n. 48, rightly notes that this volume by Grantham comprises two separate works in one volume, the latter of which is a sermon against the paedobaptist, views of the Anglican Nathaniel Taylor.

[43] Thompson, 'A New Question', p. 67.

rise again; It may be said indeed, but Sacramentally, of all that are Baptized, that they are buried with Christ, and raised with him, yet really only of such as have true Faith, mark that!'[44] Elsewhere Grantham developed this:

> Baptism in the ordinary way of God's communicating the grace of the Gospel is antecedent to the reception thereof, & is propounded as a means wherein not only the Remission of our sins shall be granted to us, but as a condition whereupon we shall receive the gift of the Holy Ghost... [It] was fore-ordained to signifie and sacramentally to confer the grace of the pardon of sin, and the inward washing of the Conscience by Faith in the Bloud of Jesus Christ.[45]

In one place Grantham speaks of what baptism does, rather than does not do:

> And thus was our Lord himself the chief founder of the Gospel in the Heavenly Doctrine of *Faith, Repentance,* ann [sic.] *Baptism for the remission of Sins...* Now the necessity of this Sacred Ordinance to a true Church-State, is further evident from the Institution or first delivery of it.

A few lines later he continues:

> This Baptism is joyned with this Gospel repentance, that as repentance being now necessary to the admission of Sinners into the Church of Christ, even so Baptism being joyned thereto, by the will of God, is necessary to the same end.[46]

For Grantham the water, bread and wine were sanctified by the Word and Spirit and set forth Christ in the church,[47] the sacraments thereby functioning as 'the two Seals' of the covenant.[48] Baptism is the locus of the Word's action on the baptized.[49] Thompson remarks, 'Earlier Baptists did not understand the sacraments in terms of the symbolic minimalism that so characterizes contemporary accounts. Rather, there was definite and saving effect in the rites by the presence of the Lord held forth in

---

[44] Grantham, *Christianismus Primitivus*, II/2.ii.4, italics original. Cf. John Calvin, *Institutes of the Christian Religion* (1559), 4.15.5.
[45] T. Grantham, *A Sigh for Peace: or The Cause of the Division Discovered* (London, 1671), pp. 87-88, cited by Thompson, 'A New Question', p. 67.
[46] Grantham, *Christianismus Primitivus*, II.i.5, italics original.
[47] See Grantham, *Christianismus Primitivus*, II/2.i.8 and II/2.vii.6 respectively for baptism and the Lord's supper.
[48] Grantham, *The Second Part of the Apology for the Baptized Believers*, pp. 19-20.
[49] Grantham, *The Second Part of the Apology for the Baptized Believers*, p. 12: 'the Word of God must act upon the Soul in true Baptism'.

each.'[50] 'Baptism, by the working of the Holy Spirit, holds forth Christ who acts, saving through pardon of sin and granting of eternal life.'[51]

As well as Keach and Grantham who are discussed in the present paper, Fowler also examines the sacramentalism in the work of the Particular Baptists Robert Garner, Henry Lawrence and William Mitchell, but enough has been discussed to show the presence of baptismal sacramentalism in the thought of some of the earliest Baptists.[52]

Eighteenth-Century Baptismal Sacramentalism

Fowler begins his discussion of the eighteenth century noting that at this time Baptists were 'in many cases preoccupied with concerns other than baptismal theology, concerns which were often much more foundational than any baptismal issues'.[53] Many General Baptists had gone over to Unitarianism and this led the remaining trinitarians to form the New Connexion of General Baptists, while the Particular Baptists were dominated by high-Calvinism.[54] Given the General Baptists' drift into heterodoxy and their numerical decline, there is little from this period which deals with baptism. The Particular Baptists, however, focused on the defence of believer's immersion, though the efficacy of baptism was occasionally addressed.[55]

Leading Particular Baptists, such as John Gill and Abraham Booth, were non–, even anti–sacramental, but there are traces of sacramentalism

---

[50] Thompson, 'A New Question', pp. 66-67.

[51] Thompson, 'A New Question', p. 67, who goes on, in n. 97, to cite Grantham's *St. Paul's Catechism* (London, 1687), pp. 35-36: '[I]t is Christ who is held forth in Baptism, which saveth...', quoting 1 Pet. 3.21. The Holy Spirit was also seen to act redemptively in baptism in Benjamin Beddome's hymn which says, 'Eternal Spirit, heavenly Dove,/ On these baptismal waters move;/ That we thro' energy divine,/ May have the substance with the sign', in J. Rippon (ed.), *A Selection of Hymns from the best authors, Intended to be An Appendix to Dr. Watts' Psalms and Hymns* (London, 1787), number 460, cited by Thompson, 'Practicing the Freedom of God', p. 129, who, in n. 49 on p. 137, also refers to hymn numbers 443, 449, 450, 453 and 468.

[52] See the whole of Fowler's section in *More Than a Symbol*, pp. 20-31, which discusses not only Grantham and Keach, but also Robert Garner, *A Treatise of Baptism* (London, 1645), Henry Lawrence, *Of Baptism* (London, 1659), and William Mitchell's posthumously published (by David Crosley) *Jachin and Boaz* (London, 1707), reprinted in *Transactions of the Baptist Historical Society* 3 (1912–1913), pp. 65-88 and 154-75.

[53] See Fowler's section on this period, *More Than a Symbol*, pp. 32-57, quotation from p. 32.

[54] On these movements, see A.C. Underwood, *A History of English Baptists* (London: Kingsgate Press, 1947), pp. 116-200; R. Brown, *The English Baptists of the Eighteenth Century* (A History of the English Baptists, 2; London: Baptist Historical Society, 1986); McBeth, *Baptist Heritage*, pp. 153-78.

[55] Fowler, *More Than a Symbol*, pp. 32-33.

in the work of the pamphleteer Anne Dutton, and, in a very subued and ambivalent form, in Andrew Fuller and John Ryland, Jr, at the turn of the nineteenth century.

In one of her many pamphlets, Anne Dutton identified the threefold purpose of baptism as: to represent; to seal or assure; and to initiate.[56] Reflecting her Calvinist background, Dutton's understanding of baptism as a seal indicated the way in which God works in baptism. In the same way that immersion is a pictorial representation of the facts of redemption, so 'the finish'd Work of Redemption, and the Whole of our Salvation thereby, is seal'd up, and *made sure* to Believers in their Baptism'.[57] As baptism is performed in the name of the Trinity, so the Trinity works in baptism at the subjective but also the objective level.

> All the three Persons in GOD, do, as it were, solemnly engage to make good all the great Things represented therein, to a baptized Believer. They hereby set their Seal...to all that Salvation represented in Baptism, and give the highest Assurance thereof to baptized Believers. This the Lord always gives to the *Persons* of Believers, in the due Administration of the Ordinance; and very frequently He gives this Assurance to their *Spirits* in their Submission to it. As God the Father honoured his Son, with Testimonies of his infinite Favour, upon his baptism. And as the Eunuch, after he was baptized, went on his Way rejoicing. And as the Jaylor and his House, after their Baptism, believing in God, rejoiced.—But when this is not experienced by Believers upon their Baptism, they are not to think it null and void, because, as we said, the Lord gives them a solemn Assurance in the very Ordinance of all the great Things represented therein, as it is his Appointment, and done by his Authority.[58]

Baptism is also initiatory 'into a true Gospel Profession of Christ'. On the basis of Galatians 3.27 and the language of putting on Christ, Dutton shows that the subject of baptism becomes a Christian through this ordinance:

> He hereby professeth himself to be a lost Sinner, that he believes Christ to be the only Saviour, that he looks to Him as his Saviour, and that all his Hope of Salvation stands alone in the CHRIST of GOD. He likewise hereby professeth to take Christ in all his offices, as his Prophet, Priest and King; and to give up himself to Him, to be His for ever, to follow the LAMB, even whithersoever He goeth.'[59]

Fowler acknowledges that Dutton's language here 'is fundamentally about the *human* act of confessing faith in Christ, but it is the human side

---

[56] A. Dutton, *Brief Hints Concerning Baptism: of the Subject, Mode, and End of this Solemn Ordinance* (London, 1746), p. 12. All references to Dutton's work come from Fowler, *More Than a Symbol*, pp. 46-48.
[57] Dutton, *Brief Hints*, p. 20, italics added.
[58] Dutton, *Brief Hints*, p. 21.
[59] Dutton, *Brief Hints*, p. 22.

of the initial entrance into union with Christ, not (as for Gill) some kind of second-stage entrance into a deeper communion with Christ'.[60]

Andrew Fuller was one of the founders of the Baptist Missionary Society and the father of the evangelical Calvinism which for many Particular Baptists superseded the high-Calvinism associated with John Gill and John Brine. In an association circular letter he explored the influence of baptism, concluding its principal purpose to be '*A solemn and practical profession of the Christian religion*'.[61] In his discussion of Galatians 3.27's imagery of the believer putting of Christ, Fuller spoke of baptism as the believer's oath of allegiance (Latin *sacramentum*), but he left the issue of the divine aspect of baptism unclear.[62] But later, when examining the relationship of baptism to the remission of sins, he reflects what Fowler calls 'a common Baptist ambivalence' in that he recognized 'that Scripture points to some kind of instrumental function of baptism', but he felt the need to significantly qualify this:[63]

> baptism in the name of Christ is said to be *for the remission of sins*. Not that there is any such virtue in the element, whatever be the quantity; nor in the ceremony, though of Divine appointment: but it contains a *sign* of the way in which we must be saved. Sin is washed away in baptism in the same sense as Christ's flesh is eaten, and his blood drank, in the Lord's supper: the sign, when rightly used, leads to the thing signified. Remission of sins is ascribed by Peter not properly to baptism, but to the *name* in which the parties were to be baptized. Thus also Saul was directed to WASH AWAY HIS SINS, *calling on* THE NAME OF THE LORD.[64]

Fowler notes Fuller's language: that while the remission of sins is 'properly' ascribed to Christ, they clearly 'in some sense' come through baptism, otherwise there would be nothing to clarify by the word 'properly'. 'Fuller's statements indicate that there is some instrumental value in baptism, some way in which baptism leads to reception of the benefits of Christ, but the evidence is minimal and undeveloped.'[65] A similar position is evident in the thought of John Ryland, Jr, President of

---

[60] Fowler, *More Than a Symbol*, p. 50. For a detailed study of Gill's understanding of baptism, see S.K. Fowler, 'John Gill's Doctrine of Believer Baptism', in M.A.G. Haykin (ed.), *The Life and Thought of John Gill (1697–1771): A Tercentenary Appreciation* (Leiden: Brill, 1997), pp. 69-91.

[61] A. Fuller, 'The Practical Uses of Christian Baptism (1802)', in J. Belcher (ed.), *The Complete Works of the Rev. Andrew Fuller: with a memoir of his life by Andrew Gunton Fuller* (3 vols; Harrisonburg, VA: Sprinkle Publications, 1988 [1845]), III, p. 339, italics original.

[62] Fuller, 'Practical Uses', pp. 339-40.

[63] Fowler, *More Than a Symbol*, p. 49.

[64] Fuller, 'Practical Uses', p. 341, italics his.

[65] Fowler, *More Than a Symbol*, p. 50.

the Bristol Baptist College.⁶⁶ Fowler notes that 'The same kind of dialectic which has been seen in other Baptists was present in Ryland, i.e., although the persons admitted to baptism must make a credible confession of repentance and faith, and are thus evidently in a state of grace, the benefits of salvation are being sought via baptism.' This paradox he attributes to the Particular Baptists' Calvinism which affirmed that regeneration is a divine work which, logically but not temporally, precedes and empowers faith; that faith is a means by which salvation which is invisible becomes both visible and experiential; and 'that baptism is the divinely-ordained event in which the initial confession of faith occurs, so that the effects of baptism are the effects of faith'.⁶⁷

Most significant of all are Fowler's summary and analysis of the eighteenth-century situation. He offers four characteristics of baptismal theology in this period.⁶⁸ First, that the term 'sacrament' was only used occasionally for baptism, 'ordinance' becoming established as the norm. Second, baptism was called a 'sign' but only rarely a 'seal' partly due to the term's use by Calvinistic Paedobaptists.⁶⁹ Third, Baptists were generally preoccupied with the subjects and mode of baptism, with little attention given to the meaning of the rite. The human side was focused on, but little was said of the divine side of baptism. Fourth, whenever the effects of baptism were discussed, little was said of the divine side, and passages which spoke of the efficacy of baptism (such as Acts 2.38; 22.16; 1 Pet. 3.21; Mk 16.16) were 'interpreted in a modest and defensive way'.

Fowler's analysis of the differences between seventeenth- and eighteenth-century Baptist thought is of especial value. He begins by observing that eighteenth-century writers rarely quoted or interacted with their Baptist predecessors, and this makes the reasons for the evident conceptual shift unclear. However, he offers two reasons for this. First, he appeals to the common assumption among Baptists that each Christian has direct access to God's Word and its meaning without need of mediation. Second, is the polemical nature of much Baptist literature

---

⁶⁶ J. Ryland, Jr, *A Candid Statement of the Reasons Which Induce the Baptists to Differ In Opinion and Practice from So Many of Their Christian Brethren* (London: W. Button, 1814), discussed by Fowler, *More Than a Symbol*, pp. 51-52, who believes that this oft-repeated sermon represents Ryland's theology at the end of the eighteenth century.

⁶⁷ Fowler, *More Than a Symbol*, p. 52.

⁶⁸ Fowler, *More Than a Symbol*, p. 53.

⁶⁹ Fowler, *More Than a Symbol*, p. 50, makes this point of the Reformed use of 'seal' for infant baptism, adding that another reason why it was dropped from Baptist vocabulary was because of its perceived absence from scripture.

which sought to convince Paedobaptists of the rightness of the Baptist position. To this end, appeal to earlier Baptist work was out of place.[70]

Fowler concludes this section of his work suggesting five theological factors involved in the development of baptismal thought.[71] First is to notice that undue emphasis on the disuse of the word *sacrament* should be avoided, as the words ordinance and sacrament were never mutually exclusive—the former was the broader term, the latter the more focused. Fowler admits that the reasons why ordinance became the standard term for Particular Baptists 'are not entirely clear'. Two possible explanations are suggested: that while ordinance conveyed the sense of a command of the Lord, sacrament had more ecclesiastical overtones; and Baptists wanted to avoid the constant clarification of the meaning of sacrament due to its various uses amongst other traditions. But while eighteenth-century writers did not use the term sacrament, neither did they reject it.

Second, is the decline of the use of the term *seal* already noted, though it was used by some, like Anne Dutton. Third, the retreat from a sacramental understanding was due more to neglect than positive rejection of it. The focus on the subjects and mode of baptism continued well into the twentieth century. Fowler rightly observes, 'It was increasingly true that Baptists knew more about what did not happen in the sprinkling of infants than they did about what does happen in the immersion of believers.'[72] Fourth, the influence of high-Calvinism had disastrous consequences for the theology of baptism in that it minimized the significance of human acts. Fifth are what Fowler describes as uncompelling reasons: Baptists wanted to avoid *ex opere operato* views associated with Catholicism; that the more people talked of the necessity of baptism the more they were inclined towards paedobaptism and rantism, i.e. baptism by sprinkling; and that they minimized the efficacy of baptism in order to refute the charge they made too much of it.

Nineteenth-Century Baptismal Sacramentalism[73]

David Thompson notes that 'One of the most striking differences in the life of the British Churches between the last quarter of the eighteenth century...and the last quarter of the twentieth...must surely be the changed attitude to the sacraments.' A sacramental revival has taken place in the Church of England, Church of Scotland and in some parts of

---

[70] Fowler, *More Than a Symbol*, pp. 53-54.
[71] Fowler, *More Than a Symbol*, pp. 54-57.
[72] Fowler, *More Than a Symbol*, p. 56.
[73] A more detailed discussion of this section is to be found in Cross, *Baptism*, pp. 6-17.

Nonconformity within the modern period.[74] He comments that the General and Particular Baptists' rejection of infant baptism was 'only one aspect of a more broadly based radical religious position; and the touchstone for developments in sacramental theology in the Reformation was the Lord's Supper'. By the early eighteenth century this radical upsurge had become a spent force; Baptists and Quakers had become more defensive and introspective, threats to religious orthodoxy coming from within in the form of Unitarianism and Socinianism, and in Deism and scepticism from without. The Evangelical Revival, however, changed this, old issues re-emerging and new ones appearing. Its emphasis on personal religious experience

> brought out the tension between individual and social religion, placing the debate between infant and believer's baptism in a new light. The emphasis on the Bible brought a new interest in biblical patterns for church life and a re-examination of the biblical evidence for infant baptism. The contrast drawn between vital and formal religion brought a new questioning of sacramental theology. All these issues crystallized around the emphasis on conversion. If conversion was necessary to the Christian life, what was the significance and meaning of baptism? Did baptism, particularly the baptism of infants, effect anything?[75]

Thompson has convincingly argued that from 1800 to 1830 three sets of issues concerning baptism came to dominate, the Evangelical Revival having significantly affected the way in which they were expressed and discussed. First, there was the issue of the proper subjects of baptism which was most keenly debated in Scotland. Second, was the terms of communion—whether communion was only for those baptized as believers or whether baptism was necessary for communion, or, by extension, for membership. Third was the matter of baptismal regeneration, which preoccupied mainly the Church of England.[76]

---

[74] D.M. Thompson, 'Baptism, Church and Society in Britain since 1800' (unpublished Hulsean Lectures, 1983–84), p. 1 (this will shortly be published with an additional chapter as *Baptism, Church and Society in Britain from the Evangelical Revival to Baptism, Eucharist and Ministry* [Milton Keynes: Paternoster, 2005]). See also his 'The Theology of Adult Initiation in the Nineteenth and Twentieth Centuries', in D.A. Withey (ed.), *Adult Initiation* (Alcuin/GROW Liturgical Study 10 [Grove Liturgical Study 58]; Nottingham: Grove Books, 1989), pp. 6-23.
[75] Thompson, 'Baptism, Church and Society', p. 3.
[76] Thompson, 'Baptism, Church and Society', p. 4. He discusses each of these issues on pp. 5-10, 10-12 and 12-17 respectively. J.H.Y. Briggs, *The English Baptists of the Nineteenth Century* (A History of the English Baptists, 3; Didcot: Baptist Historical Society, 1994), p. 43, agrees with this classification of the issues, and discusses them on pp. 43-44, 44-45 and 45-50 respectively. J.R.C. Perkin, 'Baptism in Non-Conformist Theology, 1820–1920, with special reference to the Baptists' (DPhil thesis, Oxford University, 1955), p. 6, similarly identified this period, but especially

For roughly the first half of the century the baptismal debate focused primarily on the mode of baptism and more specifically on the meaning of the Greek verbs βάπτω and βαπτίζω, leading Jim Perkin to the hyperbolic statement that, 'No other single word had so much written about it in the last century as this one.'[77] As the baptismal controversy wore on, the tendency was to give more importance to the subjects of baptism and on the conception of the church which underlies it.[78] More than anything else, it was the concept of the church made up of believers which determined the Baptist attitude to infant baptism. In fact, the nineteenth century proves that the 'distinguishing feature of Baptists is not their doctrine of baptism, but their doctrine of the Church'.[79] Though this was seldom made explicit in the period from 1820–1920, the whole baptismal controversy cannot be understood unless it is realized that it was this difference in ecclesiology which caused the clash.[80]

Perkin contends that the decade ending 1864 saw little of the controversy, especially when compared to 1830–40. Questions other than the philological ones had taken on a new importance and in general the books written became shorter and kinder in tone.[81] By 1870 it had become clear that the question of baptism had entered a new stage in its

---

1820–30, as marked by an increased interest in baptism. Thompson, 'Baptism, Church and Society', p. 4, shows that baptism was, at this time, a significant and widespread issue by 'the fact that books, pamphlets and tracts are being written on baptism in the early nineteenth century, whereas thirty years before they were not. But publication was a response to the fact that the issues were being debated among Christians; and some indication of this is seen in the growth of the Baptists during the period, and also in the divisions that produced new Baptist congregations.'

[77] Perkin, 'Baptism', p. 25.
[78] So Perkin, 'Baptism', pp. 211, 217-18.
[79] Perkin, 'Baptism', pp. 10-11. This is true even if it is acknowledged that Baptist ecclesiology was not all it should have been. See Briggs' discussion, e.g., of 'John Clifford's Diminished Ecclesiology', *English Baptists*, pp. 22-27, which is set within a larger discussion of the nineteenth-century Baptist theology of the church, pp. 15-30.
[80] Perkin, 'Baptism', p. 11. The implications of the primacy of ecclesiology for baptismal theology can best be shown in recognition of the fact that Baptists maintain that baptism is solely for *believers*, those already converted. This is why Baptists used to be called (and more accurately called, as Paedobaptist traditions do practice the baptism of believers who were not baptized as infants) Antipaedobaptists.
[81] Perkin, 'Baptism', pp. 335-36. This changed when, in 1864, C.H. Spurgeon launched his vitriolic attack on evangelical Anglicans through his famous sermon condemning baptismal regeneration, 'Baptismal Regeneration', *Metropolitan Tabernacle Pulpit* 10 (Pasadena, TX: Pilgrim Publications, 1981 [1885]), pp. 313-28. See M. Nicholls, *C.H. Spurgeon: The Pastor Evangelist* (Didcot: Baptist Historical Society, 1992), pp. 122-29; Briggs, *English Baptists*, pp. 48-50; and Fowler, *More Than a Symbol*, pp. 79-83.

history, a stage which was the prelude to the twentieth-century debate. The latter part of the nineteenth century saw the virtual passing away of the pamphleteer, the writer of theological doggerel and the preacher of unkindly, eclectic sermons:

> Men were trying to use the Bible as a basis and guide for their theology, not a hunting ground for proof-texts; sermons took on a new note of practical application of the gospel and denominational rivalry began to change into toleration. In the womb of the nineteenth century the twentieth was already being formed.[82]

Thompson agrees that baptism receded from the forefront of theological debate from the early 1860s, offering four reasons for this.[83] First, the Gorham judgment of 1850 resulted in a stalemate as far as baptismal doctrine in the Anglican communion was concerned, though it had established the legitimacy of an Evangelical reading of the *Book of Common Prayer*.[84] Second, controversy over the eucharist became more widespread in the 1850s with the development of the ritualist movement.[85] Third, the transformation of Calvinistic Dissent into an evangelical

---

[82] Perkin, 'Baptism', p. 337.
[83] Thompson, 'Baptism, Church and Society', p. 72. See Michael Walker's discussion of Spurgeon's and Clifford's theologies of communion, M.J. Walker, *Baptists at the Table: The Theology of the Lord's Supper amongst English Baptists in the Nineteenth Century* (Didcot: Baptist Historical Society, 1992), pp. 164-96, both preachers having more to say on communion than baptism. According to Nicholls, *Spurgeon*, p. 158, the 1899 index to the *Metropolitan Tabernacle Pulpit* lists only four sermons by Spurgeon on baptism.
[84] On the Gorham case, see Thompson, 'Baptism, Church and Society', pp. 30-33; O. Chadwick, *The Victorian Church: Part I: 1829–1859* (London: SCM Press, 3rd edn, 1971), pp. 250-71; K. Hylson-Smith, *Evangelicals in the Church of England 1734–1984* (Edinburgh: T&T Clark, 19989), pp. 123-25, 156 and 161; G. Carter, *Anglican Evangelicals: Protestant Secessions from the Via Media, c.1800–1850* (Oxford Theological Monographs; Oxford: Oxford University Press, 2001), pp. 312-55, which focuses on B.W. Noel (see below) and the Gorham case; J.C. Whisenant, *A Fragile Unity: Anti-Ritualism and the Division of Anglican Evangelicalism in the Nineteenth Century* (Studies in Evangelical History and Thought; Carlisle: Paternoster Press, 2003), pp. 20-23; and, in the broader context of the discussion of the sacraments, also M. Wellings, *Evangelicals Embattled: Responses of Evangelicals in the Church of England to Ritualism, Darwinism and Theological Liberalism 1890–1930* (Studies in Evangelical History and Thought; Carlisle: Paternoster Press, 2003), pp. 27-40.
[85] Thompson, 'Baptism, Church and Society', p. 72, comments that, 'In so far as the baptismal controversy in the first half of the century had been one between catholic and Calvinist sacramental theology, this division received much sharper focus in the second half of the century over Holy Communion. Antipathy to the Mass, transubstantiation, the real presence etc., was more easily mobilised than suspicion of baptismal regeneration.'

theology attached relatively little importance to the sacraments. The 1860 Norwich Chapel Case effectively settled the Baptist communion controversy which had flared up in the second decade of the century around the two figures of the Rev. Robert Hall of Leicester and the Rev. Joseph Kinghorn of Norwich.[86] From this time, the practice of open communion began to spread, to the point that, by mid-century, it had become the norm amongst Baptists.[87] Fourth, the development of biblical criticism and historical scholarship began to undermine the simpler defences of existing baptismal practice, forcing a reassessment of the basis of baptismal theology within the churches.[88]

'The context for the [baptism] debate soon became that heightened sacramentalism within the established church which mid-Victorian Baptists perceived to be the fruit of the Oxford Movement.'[89] Baptist

---

[86] The most recent discussions of this controversy are to be found in Walker, *Baptists at the Table*, pp. 32-83, and Briggs, *English Baptists*, pp. 61-68. Briggs, *English Baptists*, p. 65, writes: 'The close communionists defended a higher view of the sacraments than that to which Hall by default was driven. As relations across denominational boundaries opened up, so the pressures for open communion—and later open membership—developed. In such a context it was all too easy for the low view of the sacraments Hall had come to support to become widely pervasive, especially as it accorded with evangelical antipathy to a revived catholicism, which made Baptists far too negative and reactive in their thinking about the sacraments, now more frequently referred to as ordinances, although all too often conceived in such minimalist terms as even Zwingli would not own.'

[87] Thompson, 'Baptism, Church and Society', p. 68. Those churches which retained closed communion, generally left the Baptist Union to form the Strict and Particular Baptist churches. However, the Baptist Evangelical Society was formed in order to defend strict-communionist principles, whose work was not seen as antagonistic to that of the Baptist Union, see G.R. Breed, *The Baptist Evangelical Society—An Early Victorian Episode* (Dunstable: Fauconberg Press, 1987) and *Particular Baptists in Victorian England and their Strict Communion Organizations* (Didcot: Baptist Historical Society, 2003). That the majority of Baptist Union churches by 1996 were open membership is shown by C.J. Ellis, *Baptist Worship Today* (Didcot: Doctrine and Worship Committee of the Baptist Union of Great Britain, 1996), pp. 22-23.

[88] Thompson, 'Baptism, Church and Society', p. 72, believes that in the long term this was the most significant development.

[89] Briggs, *English Baptists*, p. 46. R. Hayden, *English Baptist History and Heritage* (Christian Training Programme, G3; London: Baptist Union of Great Britain, 1990), p. 100, overstates the case when he writes, 'It is almost impossible to exaggerate the impact of the Anglo–Catholic Tractarian Movement in Nonconformist churches. The word "sacrament" now became totally unacceptable in Baptist circles... Baptists, in this period, tended to give a higher priority to what the individual believer did than to God's action in baptism. Baptists regarded this ordinance as primarily a testimony to personal faith in Christ and a disciplined following of the example of Jesus.' That this is hyperbole is shown below in the discussion of the, admittedly few, Baptists who maintained a form of baptismal sacramentalism.

antipathy to the theory of baptismal regeneration was a major factor in the 'down grading' of baptismal theology. It also resulted in perhaps the majority of Baptist literature on the subject being reactionary in tone and content.[90] 'The vehemence of the rejection of baptismal regeneration, particularly by Baptists, led to the reduction of the rite to a mere sign in many quarters.'[91] But other factors were also involved. In his detailed study of the Baptist theology of the Lord's Supper, Michael Walker shows that the majority of Baptists were influenced in their eucharistic theology by both Zwinglianism and Calvinism, while others had inherited more from the radical Anabaptists with their separation of spirit and matter and their suspicion of anything approximating to ritualism.[92] These influences equally affected Baptist baptismal theology, as none of these 'controlling' influences predisposed Baptists to think 'sacramentally' about baptism. The Catholic Revival of the 1830s–40s received a very negative reaction from Baptists, so much so that anything which could be construed as in any way 'Catholic' was vehemently repudiated. For instance, in a sermon on 'Baptismal Regeneration' delivered on 7 May 1882, the Rev. George Duncan of Oakes Baptist Chapel, Lindley, near Huddersfield declared that 'Regeneration does not come through baptism. We are regenerated by the Spirit, and baptism is the profession of our discipleship.'[93]

While some Baptists allowed their Zwinglianism to lead them into an extreme subjectivism, others were discontented with the memorialist position imposed by the denominational norm.[94] Contrary to the prevailing closed-communion stance of the majority of the denomination, Robert Hall contended that Paedobaptists should be welcomed to the Lord's Table, rejecting bare memorialism in favour of the Supper as a participation in the sacrifice offered by Christ.[95] Careful to ensure that his views were incapable of being interpreted as speaking of the presence of Christ in the eucharist, Hall maintained that it was the Holy Spirit's

---

[90] Cf. the similar conclusion of Fowler, *More Than a Symbol*, p. 88.
[91] Perkin, 'Baptism', pp. 160-61.
[92] Walker, *Baptists at the Table*, p. 3.
[93] G. Duncan, *Baptism and the Baptists* (London: Baptist Tract and Book Society, 1882), p. 74. The sermon is mistakenly recorded as being on Tit. 4.8, but should be Tit. 3.5. Fowler, *More Than a Symbol*, p. 58, sees the main context of nineteenth-century baptismal theology as the controversy over baptism as a means of grace. One of the weaknesses of Perkins' work is the scant attention he pays to the Oxford Movement, while it is one of Walker's strengths.
[94] Walker, *Baptists at the Table*, pp. 8-9.
[95] R. Hall, *On Terms of Communion*, in O. Gregory (ed.), *The Entire Works of the Rev. Robert Hall, A.M., with A brief Memoir of his Life, and a Critical Estimate of his Character and Writings* (6 vols; London: Holdsworth and Ball, 1831–32), II, pp. 63-64, where Hall referred to holy communion as a 'federal rite'.

presence in communion who raised the believer into Christ's presence where they could feed upon him by sharing in his risen and glorified life, thereby enabling him to speak of a 'spiritual participation' in the body and blood of Christ.[96] Walker points out the irony that Hall's belief in the value of the Lord's Supper eventually led others to value both it and baptism less highly than he did. Hall argued that a rite which had such implications for the Christian life should not be kept from fellow Christians on the grounds of baptismal 'irregularity', believing that admission to the Lord's Table was more important than whether the communicant was a Baptist or Paedobaptist. This eventually led him to relegate baptism to the status of merely the 'ceremonial', a view which later Baptists also assigned to the Lord's Supper.[97] In his discussion of the Baptist understanding of faith, baptism and the church, John Briggs comments that 'All too many Baptist apologists were at once too protestant, too rational, too didactic and too individualistic. Sacraments smacked of magic; by contrast, post-Enlightenment Baptists saw believer's baptism as the mental response to the revelation of truth, undertaken with free volition by rational men and women.'[98]

A concomitant of an impoverished theology of baptism was a discomfort with the relationship of the Holy Spirit to the rite. Perkin observed that Baptists 'did not feel happy about the doctrine of the Holy Spirit, whether in conjunction with baptism or not. This constitutes a serious lacuna in the theology of the period'.[99] A reason for this was, he suggests, that at this time 'Baptist theology...was essentially empirical and practical rather than theoretical. Obedience, faith, the church, dying, rising—all these were concrete ideas, readily interpreted and understood. But the gift of the Spirit belongs to a realm of experience and theology only spoken of by the very learned and the very ignorant.'[100] Briggs, however, notes that this inhibition did not extend to Baptist hymn-writers. For example, Maria Saffery's hymn ''Tis the great Father we adore'

---

[96] Hall, *On Terms of Communion*, p. 64.
[97] Walker, *Baptists at the Table*, pp. 9-10. Fowler, *More Than a Symbol*, pp. 59-60, detects an 'enormous amount of ambivalence in Hall's references to the efficacy of baptism', on the one hand minimizing its place as a means of grace, and on the other interpreting it as possessing great significance and momentous effects. He concludes that there is no obvious resolution to the tension. Fowler, pp. 65-72, also finds similar tensions in the writings of Charles Stovel, *The Baptismal Regeneration Controversy Considered* (London: Houlston & Stoneman, and Dyer, 1843), pp. 72-80.
[98] Briggs, *English Baptists*, p. 52.
[99] Perkin, 'Baptism', pp. 13-14.
[100] Perkin, 'Baptism', p. 261.

(1818), includes verse 4: 'Blest Spirit! with intense desire,/ Solicitous we bow;/ Baptize us in renewing fire,/ And ratify the vow.'[101]

Both Perkin and Walker stand within the Baptist tradition which is seeking to re-establish the sacramental nature of baptism, and both highlight those nineteenth-century Baptists who recognized in baptism the nature of a sacrament. Perkin, for example, comments that, 'A large part of the dearth of sacramental theology among Baptists must be laid at the door of the Victorians. On the other hand, there was throughout the whole period a "minority movement" within the Baptist denomination which stood for a sacramental view over against the *nuda signa* doctrine of its contemporaries.'[102] For most nineteenth-century Baptists, baptism was a sign that indicated something previously done through faith at conversion. Its necessity lay in it being an imitation of Jesus' example, not because it did anything for the candidate. Even Nonconformist Paedobaptists tended to regard baptism merely as a sign rather than a sacrament. But for the minority of Baptists, only a sacramental interpretation of baptism could adequately accord with New Testament teaching.

Many of these sacramentalists were those who became Baptists later on in their lives. The best known of these was the former Anglican, Baptist Noel, who commented on Acts 2.38: 'Since, then, baptism is thus necessary to remission of sins, and is so closely connected with it... Repentance and baptism are declared in the text to secure the gift of the Holy Ghost.'[103] But a number of 'life-long' Baptists also used sacramental language of baptism. The Rev. William Hawkins interpreted baptism as a Roman soldier's *sacramentum*, 'a sovereign oath...to our Sovereign Prince, in which we swear allegiance to him...', a use which was

---

[101] Briggs, *English Baptists*, pp. 54-55. See Maria Saffery, in *Psalms and Hymns and Supplement* (London: Psalms and Hymns Trust, 1891 [1st edn, 1858]), no. 707; cf. B.W. Noel, 'Lord, Thou has promised to baptize' (1853), *Psalms and Hymns*, no. 713.

[102] Perkin, 'Baptism', p. 11. Cf. p. 244, 'It must be regarded that the majority of Baptists did not regard baptism as a sacrament at all; at best it was a sign of something already accomplished.'

[103] B.W. Noel, *Essay on Christian Baptism* (London: James Nisbet, 1849), p. 99. Cf. the former Independent Isaac Orchard's sermon, *Christian Baptism* (London: Wightman & Cramp, 1829), p. 11, 'Baptism is an appointed means for obtaining a greater outpouring of the Holy Spirit', cited by Perkin, 'Baptism', p. 197. On Noel (and his *Essay on Christian Baptism*), see Perkin, 'Baptism', pp. 322-34; D.W. Bebbington, 'The Life of Baptist Noel: Its Setting and Significance', *Baptist Quarterly* 24.8 (October, 1972), p. 398; Briggs, *English Baptists*, pp. 46-47, 49-50, 54, and *passim*; and Fowler, *More Than a Symbol*, pp. 72-75.

followed by the anonymous author of six articles in the *Baptist Magazine* in 1857.[104]

There were, then, three distinct phases of the baptismal debate in the nineteenth century running from approximately 1800 to 1840, 1840 to 1864, and from 1864 to the end of the century, and four major factors can be identified as having influenced Baptist baptismal theology at this time. The first factor was individualism. The second was the catholic revival which began in the 1830s,[105] at the centre of which was the doctrine of baptismal generation.[106] Third, there was the impact of increased population mobility which caused Baptists, among others, to think carefully as to who they could share fellowship with. This is seen first in the terms of communion controversy, and in the debates over the terms of membership.[107] Fourth, there were the beginnings of movement towards ecumenism. Walker called this 'the age of initiative' when 'Christians were not so much drawn together as thrown together' in, for instance, missionary endeavour and philanthropic work. 'For Baptists, these changes called for a reappraisal of their doctrinal position', for their ecclesiology 'drew a clear line of demarcation between the church and a world in whose life and welfare they were increasingly engaged. Their doctrine of baptism, especially when accompanied by the corollary of closed communion, separated them from Christians with whom they

---

[104] W. Hawkins, *A Sermon on Baptism* (London: Wightman and Cramp, 1827), p. 22, cited by Briggs, *English Baptists*, pp. 51-52; and, e.g., Anonymous, 'Sacramental Meditations', *Baptist Magazine* 49 (January, 1857), pp. 22-23.

[105] Walker, *Baptists at the Table*, p. 131.

[106] See Thompson, 'Baptism, Church and Society', pp. 18-35. Briggs, *English Baptists*, pp. 45-53 and 223-27, discusses the whole issue of baptismal regeneration and the threat of Tractarianism as they affected Baptist thought, as does Walker, *Baptists at the Table*, pp. 84-120. Broader studies of anti–Catholicism are to be found in P. Toon, *Evangelical Theology 1833–1856: A Response to Tractarianism* (Marshalls Theological Library; London: Marshall, Morgan & Scott, 1979), and J. Wolffe, *The Protestant Crusade in Great Britain, 1829–1860* (Oxford Historical Monographs; Oxford: Clarendon Press, 1991).

[107] Differences over the terms of communion led many churches which wished to remain closed in membership and communion to separate from the Baptist Union churches, forming the Strict Baptists, on which see E.A. Payne, *The Baptist Union: A Short History* (London: Baptist Union of Great Britain and Ireland, 1959), pp. 40-41 and 86-87, and K. Dix, *Strict and Particular: English Strict and Particular Baptists in the Nineteenth Century* (Didcot: Baptist Historical Society/Strict Baptist Historical Society, 2001). Many of the remaining churches opened up first access to the Lord's Supper to those not baptized as believers and later to the practice of open membership where those from Paedobaptist traditions were allowed into membership on profession of faith not believer's baptism.

increasingly worked in common cause.'[108] John Briggs offers the following summary:

> The history of Baptists in the nineteenth century is very largely a reactive and responsive one: consciously to the Catholic Revival, which must be held partly responsible for the development of low views of church-manship, ministry and the sacraments; and unconsciously to the many secular pressures which also shaped the pattern of church life... Baptists particularly faced difficulties as Christians became more tolerant of one another, because their restrictive baptismal practice, that is their distinction in confining baptism to believers only, necessarily challenged any easy accommodation even to other recognizably evangelical groupings; the consequences of that are to be seen in the debates about open communion and open membership, and the long-running dispute with the Bible Society on the legitimacy of translating βαπτιζω by words signifying immersion.[109]

By the close of the nineteenth century, then, baptism was, with a few exceptions, described as an ordinance, the subjective, personal testimony of a believer's faith in Christ and not an objective means of conveying the grace of God and the benefits of redemption through Christ to those who believe. We can agree with Fowler's identification of six factors which effected this shift, though he avoids the danger of seeing these as all the factors.[110] First, was the neglect of discussion of the meaning of baptism due to their controversy with Paedobaptists and preoccupation with the subjects and mode of baptism. In all this sacramentalism came to be identified with infant baptism and rejected along with it. Second, emphasizing the confessional aspect of baptism focused Baptists on what precedes baptism. Third, a sacramental understanding was perceived to be a threat to the doctrine of justification by faith alone. Fourth, the influence of high-Calvinism on Particular Baptists led to the undermining of the human side of faith. Fifth, the Evangelical Revival, which originated within the Church of England, seemed to have demonstrated that God's saving work was not tied to baptism and seemed to confirm the point already made on justification *sola fide*. Sixth, most Baptist works on baptism were attempts to correct the errors of Paedobaptists who seemed to overemphasize the efficacy of baptism to the point of its operation *ex opere operato* and, in the process, went to the opposite extreme. Baptists were clearer on what baptism was not, than on what it was. This all said, however, there were a not insignificant number of Baptists who advocated baptismal sacramentalism.

---

[108] Walker, *Baptists at the Table*, pp. 42-43.
[109] Briggs, *English Baptists*, pp. 11-12.
[110] Fowler, *More Than a Symbol*, pp. 86-88.

Twentieth-Century Baptismal Sacramentalism[111]

The development of baptismal theology in the twentieth century can be divided into three periods: 1900–1937, 1938–1966 and 1967–1999.[112] The theological debate throughout the first period was conducted largely around the twin poles of the mode and subjects of baptism, with only the beginnings of the realization that it was the theology of baptism which would provide the most profitable way forward in the discussion of the baptismal issue from both the Baptists' and also Paedobaptists' point of view.[113] The beginning of the second period coincides with the seminal work by the Swiss theologian, Emil Brunner, which was quickly followed by the better known work of Karl Barth, and together these works set the theological agenda as far as baptism was concerned for the next three decades.[114] Baptists were late to join this debate, which they did so predominantly from the mid-1950s to the mid-1960s, the latter providing the close of the second period. The third period, examines the developments which have taken place from 1967 to 1999, which witnessed unprecedented developments within the domestic ecumenical scene.

While there have continued to be many who maintain a non– and even anti–sacramental understanding of baptism,[115] the number who have come to recognize baptism as a sacrament, a means of conveying God's grace, has grown significantly, and the major influence in this has been the ecumenical movement.[116] The sheer volume of sources available to demonstrate the development of baptismal sacramentalism in the twentieth century means that selection is essential. To this end, therefore, three sets of sources have been selected: a number of statements either endorsed or released by the Baptist Union; the evidence of ministers' manuals; and the most recent work of a number of prominent Baptist scholars.

First, while twentieth-century Baptists have not produced anything comparable to the confessions of faith of the seventeenth century, the Baptist Union has nevertheless, from time to time, published 'official' statements of the Baptist position. Many of these reflect growing

---

[111] Detailed discussion of this period is to be found in Cross, *Baptism*, and 'Baptists and Baptism—A British Perspective', *Baptist History and Heritage* 35.1 (Winter, 2000), pp. 104-21; and Fowler, *More Than a Symbol*, pp. 89-155.

[112] So Cross, *Baptism*, pp. 2-4.

[113] This was also recognized by Ross, 'Theology of Baptism', pp. 100-112.

[114] E. Brunner, *Wahrheit als Begegnung* (Zürich: Zwingli-Verlag, 1938)/*The Divine Human Encounter* (London: SCM Press, 1944); K. Barth, *Die Kirchliche Lehre von der Taufe* (Theologische Studien, 14; Zürich: Evangelischer Verlag A.G. Zollikon, 1943)/*The Teaching of the Church Regarding Baptism* (London: SCM Press, 1948).

[115] See Cross, *Baptism*, e.g. pp. 98-108 and 210-43.

[116] See Cross, *Baptism*, pp. 341-48.

acceptance of forms of baptismal sacramentalism and it is significant that all the reports and statements considered here were written in the context of and as responses to ecumenical developments.

Under J.H. Shakespeare's guidance (General Secretary of the Baptist Union at the time),[117] in 1918 the Baptist Union Assembly accepted the doctrinal basis of the Federal Council of the Evangelical Free Churches of England (f. 1919), even though the actual wording was not penned by Baptists. The declaratory statement recognized that 'The Sacraments—Baptism and the Lord's Supper', as 'instituted by Christ', are 'signs and seals of His Gospel not to be separated therefrom'. It continues, noting that they 'confirm the promises and gifts of salvation, and, when rightly used by believers with faith and prayer, are, through the operation of the Holy Spirit, true means of grace',[118] even though it must be recognized that 'means of grace' was then, as it still is, capable of a variety of explanations. Similarly, the 1926 *Reply of the Churches in Membership with the Baptist Union* to the 1920 Lambeth Appeal, accepted baptism as a sacrament in terms of a 'means of grace to all who receive [it] in faith', but criticized the Appeal's over-emphasis of the sacraments,[119] a point taken up by others who, for example, criticized its 'manifest sacramentalism' and 'undisguised sympathy with sacerdotalism'.[120] The 1934 response to the report of the 1927 Lausanne Faith and Order Conference guardedly accepted the term 'sacrament', but preferred 'ordinance', and emphasized 'again our insistence on faith in the recipient as a condition of the effectiveness of the Sacraments'.[121] In 1937, the Baptist Union's Special Committee looking into possible union with the Congregationalists and Presbyterians—a committee comprised of those representing the full breadth of Baptist opinion—rejected baptismal

---

[117] The most detailed study of Shakespeare is P. Shepherd, *The Making of a Modern Denomination: John Howard Shakespeare and the English Baptists 1898–1924* (Studies in Baptist History and Thought, 4; Carlisle: Paternoster Press, 2001).

[118] 'Declaratory Statement of Common Faith and Practice, adopted on 26th March 1917 as the Doctrinal basis of the projected Federal Council of the Evangelical Free Churches of England; approved by the Baptist Union Assembly, April 1918; accepted as the Doctrinal basis of the Free Church Federal Council, September 1940', in Payne, *The Baptist Union*, pp. 275-78, quotation from Section V, p. 276. For a detailed discussion of this and the other 'statements', see Cross, *Baptism, passim*.

[119] *Reply of the Churches in Membership with the Baptist Union to the 'Appeal to all Christian People' issued by the Lambeth Conference of 1920*, in Payne, *The Baptist Union*, pp. 279-82, quotation from p. 280.

[120] E.g., J.D. Freeman, a Canadian by birth and minister in Leicester, 'The Lambeth Appeal', *The Fraternal* os 13 (March, 1922), p. 8.

[121] 'Baptist Union of Great Britain and Ireland', in L. Hodgson (ed.), *Convictions: A Selection from the Responses of the Churches to the Report of the World Conference on Faith and Order, held at Lausanne in 1927* (London: SCM Press, 1934), pp. 61-64, quotation from p. 63.

regeneration, but included those who accepted the use of 'sacrament' and saw baptism and the Lord's Supper as 'not merely symbolical, but...appointed instruments and vehicles of grace for those who come to them with a right disposition... [A] sacrament...is primarily the Word and the Act of God, conveying the grace of God to men.' Shortly after they added, 'We hardly need to point out that such a view does not mean either that the bestowal of grace is limited to the sacraments or that any priestly mediation is necessary.' They continued: 'Upon this view baptism is more than a mere symbol and also more than a mere confession of faith. This view treats baptism as a vehicle for the conveyance of grace, but it does not involve the assertion that baptism is an essential condition of regeneration or of salvation and it implies the necessity of a moral response on the part of the baptized person.'[122]

It is clear that by mid-century the term 'sacrament' had become firmly re-established and accepted within Baptist parlance, though this is not to suggest that there were and still are many who reject it. At the time of the creation of the World Council of Churches in 1948, the Baptist Union produced its statement on 'The Baptist Doctrine of the Church', in which the two sacraments are said to be '"means of grace" to those who receive them in faith' and that baptism is 'a means of grace to the believer and to the church'. It acknowledged that in the New Testament there is clear indication of 'a connection of the gift of the Holy Spirit with the experience of baptism', but qualified this when it continued that 'without making the rite the necessary or inevitable channel of that gift, yet makes it the appropriate occasion of a new and deeper reception of it'.[123]

The 1967 report, *Baptists and Unity*, which frequently employs 'sacrament', includes the note that 'The word sacrament is here understood as a symbol through which the grace of God becomes operative where faith is present.'[124] This is made all the more explicit in the 1996 discussion document, *Believing and Being Baptized*, which affirms 'that the grace of God as well as a human response in faith is active in believers' baptism', these two elements being inseparable 'since

---

[122] *Report of the Special Committee appointed by the Council on the Question of Union between Baptists, Congregationalists and Presbyterians* (London: Baptist Union, n.d. [1937]), pp. 28-29. Interestingly, the *Report* also made this admission: 'we are all convinced that today...the witness which is given to the Baptist doctrine of baptism is often inadequate and in some instances grievously inadequate', p. 35. Cf. the similar comment on p. 38.

[123] 'The Baptist Doctrine of the Church: A Statement approved by the Council of the Baptist Union of Great Britain and Ireland, March 1948', in Payne, *The Baptist Union*, pp. 283-91, quotation from pp. 288-89.

[124] *Baptists and Unity* (London: Baptist Union of Great Britain and Ireland, 1967), p. 43 n. *.

it is the grace of God that enables us to respond to him in faith at all'. It continues:

> Candidates for believers' baptism will have first professed repentance towards God and *faith* in the Lord Jesus Christ... Thus the act of baptism is a powerful witness to the effect of the gospel of Christ and an opportunity for the candidate to testify to his or her faith... But the act is much more than an occasion for a profession of faith and obedience... As a person comes in faith to the baptismal pool, the triune God meets him or her with a gracious presence which transforms his or her life. Of course, a relationship between the believer and God has already begun before the moment of baptism, but this is now deepened in a special moment of encounter... In this particular meeting place ordained by Christ, there is such a rich focus of life-giving that we can, with New Testament writers, apply to it the images of new birth or regeneration (John 3:5, Titus 3:5), forgiveness of sins and cleansing from sin (Acts 2:38, 1 Cor 6:11, Hebrews 10:22), baptism in Spirit (1 Cor 12:13, Acts 2:38, 10:47 cf Mark 1:9-11), deliverance from evil powers (Col 1:13), union with Christ (Gal 3:27), adoption as children of God (Gal 3:26) and membership in the Body of Christ (1 Cor 12:13, Gal 3:27-28). Baptism is thus administered in the name of the triune God who opens to us the eternal life that is shared among Father, Son and Spirit.[125]

Second, the three most recent and widely used minister's manuals all reflect a strong baptismal sacramentalism, and all of them have been influenced indirectly by the ecumenical movement and directly by the liturgical movement. Each in their own way, the three manuals have sought to bring baptism back into the worship-life of the church.[126]

In 1960 Ernest Payne and Stephen Winward produced their *Orders and Prayers for Church Worship* in which they tried to encourage the pattern of worship of baptism–Lord's Supper (–and reception into membership when appropriate), including the laying on of hands either as part of or following the baptismal service.[127] The meaning of baptism is explicated in the minister's declarations which follow the reading of scripture verses. The rubric suggested the words: 'Let us now set forth the great benefits which we are to receive from the Lord, according to his word and promise, in this holy sacrament.' These benefits include union with Christ through faith; the washing of the body signifying the cleansing of the soul from sin through the sacrifice of Christ; the gift of the Holy Spirit who 'is given and sealed to us in this sacrament of grace';

---

[125] *Believing and Being Baptized: Baptism, So-called Re-baptism, and Children in the Church* (Didcot: Baptist Union of Great Britain, 1996), pp. 9-10, italics original.

[126] For an overview of this subject, see M.J. Walker, 'Baptist Worship in the Twentieth Century', in K.W. Clements (ed.), *Baptists in the Twentieth Century* (London: Baptist Historical Society, 1983), pp. 21-30.

[127] E.A. Payne and S.F. Winward, *Orders and Prayers for Church Worship* (London: Carey Kingsgate Press, 1960), pp. 127-43.

and that 'By this same Holy Spirit, we are baptized into one body and made members of the holy catholic and apostolic Church'. 'These great benefits are promised and pledged to those who profess repentance toward God and faith in our Lord Jesus Christ.' The prayer following the questioning of the candidates and preceding the immersion included the invocation that the baptized may 'receive according to thy promise the forgiveness of their sins, and the gift of the Holy Spirit'.[128]

Praise God diverged from previous manuals in its adoption of the phrase 'Christian Initiation' which, like Payne and Winward, sought to bring together baptism, possibly with the laying on of hands, reception into membership and admission to communion.[129] The 'Statement' prior to the questioning of the candidate opens, 'Let us now recall what we understand concerning the benefits promised by our Lord to those who receive believers' baptism and become members of his church. In baptism we become one with Christ through faith, sharing with him in his death and resurrection...'.[130] The most recent manual offers several patterns of service: that of baptism, reception into membership and the Lord's Supper, and a service of just baptism, which includes the laying on of hands.[131] Here too baptism is seen as part of 'initiation into the Body of Christ'.[132] One of the suggested introductory statements states that the candidate's 'baptism marks an ending and a beginning in life: they are washed free of sin to begin a new life in the power and joy of the Spirit'. This is followed by a prayer which includes the invocation, 'Send your Holy Spirit that this baptism may be for your servants a union with Christ in his death and resurrection that, as Christ was raised from death through the glory of the Father, *they* also might live new *lives*.' An alternative prayer contains the request that 'this important step on *their lives' journeys* wash away the fears and sins of the past'.[133]

Third, it is not without significance that some of the most influential Baptists who have written on baptism have been involved in the ecumenical movement in its various forms: the Free Church movement, the British Council of Churches and its successor body the Council of Churches for Britain and Ireland (later renamed Churches Together in Britain and Ireland), the Faith and Order Movement and the World

---

[128] Payne and Winward, *Orders and Prayers*, pp. 131-33.
[129] A. Gilmore, E. Smalley and M.J. Walker, *Praise God: A Collection of Resource Material for Christian Worship* (London: Baptist Union, 1980), pp. 137-40.
[130] Gilmore, Smalley and Walker, *Praise God*, p. 139.
[131] *Patterns and Prayers for Christian Worship: A Guidebook for Worship Leaders* (Oxford: Oxford University Press/Baptist Union of Great Britain, 1991), pp. 93-107.
[132] *Patterns and Prayer*, p. 93. For discussion of the development of baptismal debate in the twentieth century to that of the wider discussion of Christian initiation, see Cross, *Baptism*, pp. 320-34.
[133] *Patterns and Prayers*, pp. 98-100, italics original.

Council of Churches—among them, H. Wheeler Robinson, Ernest A. Payne, Neville Clark, Morris West, George Beasley-Murray, and to a lesser extent, J.H. Rushbrooke, Keith Jones and David Coffey.[134] While the ecumenical context has been unquestionably the most significant influence on the development of baptismal sacramentalism, this is closely followed by biblical study,[135] the importance of which is shown when it is remembered that Wheeler Robinson was one of the leading British Old Testament scholars of his time, and both George Beasley-Murray and R.E.O. White were New Testament scholars.[136] However, it is appropriate to conclude this survey of baptismal sacramentalism by briefly sketching two of the contributors to *Reflections on the Water* (1996).

Christopher J. Ellis believes that while in part due to a reaction against Tractarianism, Baptist antipathy to the term 'sacrament' is predominantly a response to the Roman Catholic and Reformed Churches' institutional commitment to a comprehensive state church.[137] To counter this, he seeks 'to give meaning to a Baptist use of the word "sacrament" with regard to

---

[134] See A.R. Cross, 'Service to the Ecumenical Movement: The Contribution of British Baptists', *Baptist Quarterly* 38.3 (July, 1999), pp. 107-22.

[135] The centrality of scripture in Baptist thought is discussed, e.g., by W.M.S. West, *Baptist Principles* (London: Baptist Union of Great Britain and Ireland, 3rd edn, 1975), pp. 5-11; and Hayden, *English Baptist History and Heritage*, pp. 65-67.

[136] Amongst their many works see, e.g., H.W. Robinson, *The Christian Experience of the Holy Spirit* (The Library of Constructive Theology; London: Nisbet, 1928), *Baptist Principles* (London: Carey Kingsgate Press, 3rd edn, 1938), and *Life and Faith of the Baptists* (on which see A.R. Cross, 'The Pneumatological Key to H. Wheeler Robinson's Baptismal Sacramentalism', in A.R. Cross and P.E. Thompson, *Baptist Sacramentalism* [Studies in Baptist History and Thought, 5; Carlisle: Paternoster Press, 2003], pp. 151-76); R.E.O. White, *The Biblical Doctrine of Initiation* (London: Hodder & Stoughton, 1960), and *Invitation to Baptism: A Manual for Inquirers* (London: Baptist Union of Great Britain and Ireland, 1962); G.R. Beasley-Murray, *Baptism in the New Testament* (Exeter: Paternoster Press, 1972 [1962]), and *Baptism Today and Tomorrow* (London: Macmillan, 1966) (on which see A.R. Cross, 'Faith-Baptism: The Key to an Evangelical Baptismal Sacramentalism', *Journal of European Baptist Studies* 4.3 [May, 2004], pp. 5-21). The importance of these three scholars along with A.C. Underwood (see, e.g., his *Conversion: Christian and Non-Christian: A Comparative and Psychological Study* [London: George Allen & Unwin, 1925], and 'Conversion and Baptism', in J.H. Rushbrooke *et al*, *The Faith of the Baptists* [London: Kingsgate Press, n.d. (1926)], pp. 21-35), is highlighted by Cross, *Baptism*, e.g. p. 454; and Fowler, *More Than a Symbol*, pp. 89-155. Both Cross and Fowler supplement this list.

[137] C.J. Ellis, 'Baptism and the Sacramental Freedom of God', in P.S. Fiddes (ed.), *Reflections on the Water: Understanding God and the World through the Baptism of Believers* (Regent's Study Guides, 4; Macon, GA: Smyth & Helwys/Oxford: Regent's Park College, 1996), pp. 29-30. He maintains that within such state church systems, *ex opere operato* theologies objectify God's activity 'within the institutional processes of liturgical activity, thus enabling church and state to control the dispensing of salvation'. For a discussion of the volume as a whole, see Cross, *Baptism*, pp. 344-48 and 381-84.

The Myth of English Baptist Anti-Sacramentalism 159

baptism',[138] 'defining' it as suggesting 'the power of symbols to link us to the depths of reality, and points us to the use by God of material means to mediate His saving action'.[139] On the relationship between grace and faith, Ellis believes that '[t]he issue for Baptists is not whether grace has priority, but the kind of action of grace within baptism itself.'[140] Baptists are free of this precisely because they understand baptism to be a divine–human encounter.[141] The faith they see as essential to the rite 'is the recognition that faith involves trust and reliance upon the grace of God. Therefore, if faith becomes the key pivot of divine activity, that very faith looks to God's graciousness and offers not an anthropocentric but theocentric understanding of what happens in baptism'. Ellis adds, 'Christians must acknowledge that faith itself is a gift and the human response is a part of the divine action.'[142] As believers' baptism assumes the faith of the one being baptized prior to baptism, there can be no distinction between saving faith and any other kind of faith. Further, the prior reality of faith encourages the view of salvation as a process in which baptism plays a significant part.[143] Ellis counters those Baptists who reject the sacramental dimension of baptism because they believe it threatens the sovereign freedom of God, by recounting the variations of conversion experience noted in the book of Acts and various historical texts, concluding that

> A constant theme is that God is not restricted by the sacraments as the only means whereby He may graciously work in the lives of men and women. Any theology that is developed concerning baptism as a means of grace must make room for this inconvenient, yet gloriously inspired, belief in the freedom of God.[144]

---

[138] Ellis, 'Baptism', p. 24.
[139] Ellis, 'Baptism', p. 36. On the use of material means by God to act as vehicles of grace see J.E. Colwell, *Living the Christian Story* (Edinburgh: T&T Clark, 2001), esp. ch. 8 'The Indwelling of the Story', pp. 149-65, and *Promise and Presence: An Exploration of Sacramental Theology* (Milton Keynes: Paternoster, 2005), ch. 5 'The Sacrament of Baptism'; and A.R. Cross, 'Being Open to God's Sacramental Work: A Study in Baptism', in S.E. Porter and A.R. Cross (eds), *Semper Reformandum: Studies in Honour of Clark H. Pinnock* (Carlisle: Paternoster, 2003), pp. 355-77.
[140] Ellis, 'Baptism', p. 29.
[141] Ellis, 'Baptism', p. 38. This term is taken from Emil Brunner's work, see n. 114 above.
[142] Ellis, 'Baptism', pp. 30 and 38.
[143] Ellis, 'Baptism', pp. 30-31.
[144] Ellis, 'Baptism', pp. 24 and 33-35, quotation from p. 35. See also his 'A Vew from the Pool: Baptists, Sacraments and the Basis of Unity', *Baptist Quarterly* 39.3 (July, 2001), pp. 107-20. Ellis has most recently discussed sacramentalism in terms of means of grace in his *Gathering: A Theology and Spirituality of Worship in Free Church Tradition* (London: SCM Press, 2004), see e.g., pp. 75-89 in general and specifically on

Building on Ellis's idea of sacraments, Paul Fiddes identifies and explores five biblical motifs connected with water: birth, cleansing, conflict, refreshment and journey. For him,

> the event of believers' baptism opens up an expansion of meaning about salvation as it evokes experiences connected with these motifs in everyday life. Thus the baptism of believers does not merely *picture* these central experiences of being in the world; it actually *enables* participation in the creative-redemptive activity of God that is taking place in both the natural world and human community.[145]

He stresses that sacraments are pieces of matter which God takes and uses as places of encounter with himself, grace transforming nature, grace being nothing less than God's gracious coming to his people and his world. Generally Baptists have shied away from the 'stuff' of creation, despite the inherent potential of total immersion and the involvement of the person and the community at every level of what he describes as this 'multimedia drama'.[146]

When the drama of baptism is properly arranged, he suggests that 'the contact with the element of water should arouse a range of experiences in the person baptized and in the community that shares in the act', evoking a sense of descent into the womb, a washing away of what is unclean, encounter with a hostile force, a passing through a boundary marker and reinvigoration. Water, thereby, becomes a place in the material world that can be a rendezvous with the crucified and risen Christ. Anticipating the accusation that such a kaleidoscope of natural motifs would suggest that baptism means anything and everything and therefore nothing in particular, Fiddes emphasizes that the controlling event is the death and resurrection of Jesus.[147] The symbolism of water resonates on both the levels of creation and redemption, concerning both natural phenomena and human history.[148] When the baptismal candidate, or the witnessing

---

baptism pp. 200-21, though it must be noted that sacramentalism is not the primary focus of attention in this book.

[145] P.S. Fiddes, 'Introduction', in Fiddes (ed.), *Reflections*, p. 3.

[146] Fiddes, 'Baptism and Creation', pp. 47-48. This chapter also appears in his *Tracks and Traces: Baptist Identity in Church and Theology* (Studies in Baptist History and Thought, 13; Carlisle: Paternoster Press, 2003), pp. 107-24. See pp. 107-108 for this section.

[147] Fiddes, 'Baptism and Creation', pp. 57-58/*Tracks*, p. 117.

[148] Fiddes, 'Baptism and Creation', p. 59/*Tracks*, p. 119. He continues, 'There is no merely random collection of images here; they refer to the activity and self-disclosure of the God who relates Himself to every dimension of the life of His universe. Baptism into the body of Christ means a new depth of relationship between the believer and Christ; it must also involve a new relationship between the believer and the whole community of those who are consciously in covenant partnership with God in Christ (the church—1 Cor 12:13). But further still, in the light of the commitment of the triune God to the body of

community, encounters God anew through this particular water 'they will be the more aware of the presence of God in other situations where water is involved in birth, conflict, cleansing, journey, or refreshment'.[149]

Grace is not a supernatural substance but the gracious coming of God as supremely personal into relationship with his creatures. If salvation is understood not as a momentary event but a journey of growth, then baptism provides a point within the process when 'God draws near to transform persons in a special way. Salvation cannot be isolated within the act of baptism...but it can be "focused" there in the moment when the Christian believer is made a part of the covenant community of Christ's disciples. Using an element of His creation, water, God offers an opportunity in baptism for a gracious encounter which is rich in experience and associations.'[150]

Fiddes maintains that too often the church has narrowed the meaning of baptism, different traditions over-emphasizing one of the five motifs over the others. The Roman Catholic Church has majored on the imagery of cleansing, infant baptism being the washing away of original sin and original guilt, thus enabling a theology in which infants are seen as the 'proper' subjects of baptism. Baptists, on the other hand, have tended to stress baptism as a boundary marker for believers, stressing it as the moment of separation from past life and commitment to new kingdom values. Despite the rich potential of meaning, they have sometimes narrowed it to 'following Christ through the waters of baptism', a mere phase on a pilgrim journey. Baptists like Fiddes, however, can argue that 'only the baptism of believers at a responsible age can adequately draw upon the whole range of water-symbolism and enable the baptismal pool to be the focus for God's creative-redemptive process'. Baptists, he notes, should be more alert to the width of the range of significance. Reflection on the birth motif with its strong element of initiation, should lead Baptists more consistently to practise the sequence followed by other churches of baptism followed by the eucharist.[151]

---

the cosmos, baptism means a new relation of believers to as yet unredeemed humanity and to our whole natural environment.'

[149] Fiddes, 'Baptism and Creation', p. 59/*Tracks*, p. 119.
[150] Fiddes, 'Baptism and Creation', pp. 60-61/*Tracks*, p. 120.
[151] Fiddes, 'Baptism and Creation', pp. 61-62 (cf. the slightly different parallel passage to this in *Tracks*, pp. 121-22. On p. 63 (cf. *Tracks*, pp. 122-23), Fiddes argues that believers' baptism underlines a final allegiance to Christ alone which is not worked out as a private individual but within the whole human community. It is the entrance to church membership which carries with it the responsibilities of active discipleship under the Lordship of Christ.

Conclusion

This survey has shown that, contrary to widespread academic and popular belief, there has been a continuous sacramental understanding of baptism in English Baptist thought from the movement's origins in the early years of the seventeenth century down to the present day. While a great many contemporary Baptists have come to accept the use of sacramental terminology for baptism,[152] and while they have become happier to ascribe it some measure of efficacy (often contenting themselves to use biblical language and imagery),[153] this has not, however, been accompanied by anything that can be called a truly Baptist sacramental theology of baptism, though *Reflections on the Water* marks a step in this direction. Further, these developments have had little effect on the practice of baptism,[154] which is still largely seen as a person's testimony of their conversion, an evangelistic opportunity, and continues to be separated from conversion,[155] and often still from entrance into church membership and communion. Two challenges for Baptists to take up, then, are to explore further baptismal sacramentalism and to translate it into baptismal practice.

---

[152] See Cross, *Baptism*, pp. 344-45, especially n. 97 for a list of those who, in the last thirty years or so, have *only* employed the word 'ordinance'. One of the problems of this is, of course, that most Baptists are not writers—the word ordinance is still widely held, but the point is that it is not frequently found in written sources.

[153] A notable exception to this general rule are the contributors to *Reflections on the Water*, in addition to Ellis and Fiddes discussed above, Roger Hayden, Brian Haymes, Richard Kidd and Hazel Sherman, with 'A Response: Anglican Reflections' from Prof. Christopher Rowland, a Church of England priest who describes himself, p. 117, as 'an erstwhile crypto-Baptist'.

[154] For a detailed discussion of the practice of baptism in the twentieth century, see Cross, *Baptism*, pp. 386-453.

[155] I have recently argued for a return to the practice of the New Testament period, namely conversion-initiation, which includes seeing baptism as part of the conversion-process and the administration of the rite as soon as possible, see my '"One Baptism" (Ephesians 4.5): A Challenge to the Church', in S.E. Porter and A.R. Cross (eds), *Baptism, the New Testament and the Church: Historical and Contemporary Studies in Honour of R.E.O. White* (Journal for the Study of the New Testament Supplement, 171; Sheffield: Sheffield Academic Press, 1999), pp. 173-209, and '"One Baptism" and Christian Initiation in the Ecumenical Age', published on the 'Baptists Doing Theology in Context: A Continuing Consultation' website: http://www.rpc.ox.ac.uk/theology-in-context/papershtml/cross-a2001.htm; and 'Spirit- and Water-Baptism in 1 Corinthians 12.13', in S.E. Porter and A.R. Cross (eds), *Dimensions of Baptism: Biblical and Theological Studies* (Journal for the Study of the New Testament Supplement, 234; Sheffield: Sheffield Academic Press, 2002), pp. 120-48.

CHAPTER 8

Forgotten Sisters: The Contributions of Some Notable but Un-noted British Baptist Women

Karen E. Smith

In 1902, when a list of 'Memorable Names among Baptists' was printed in *The Baptist Handbook*, the name of only one woman, the eighteenth-century hymn writer, Anne Steele (1717–78), appeared.[1] The impression given was that while the denomination had been reliant on the work of men, Baptist women had made little contribution to church life. This was patently false. In fact, the opposite was true. Although, W.T. Whitley later printed a longer 'Index to Notable Baptists' which included the names of several other women, the contribution of women to Baptist life has often been underestimated.[2]

The omission of women may be due to the fact that many of the written accounts of the history of Baptists have concentrated on institutional life and public leadership roles which have been dominated by men.[3] It is also true that, on the whole, women often seemed content to focus on the work for Christ rather than highlighting the contributions of any one personality. In her account of service in India as a missionary, for example, Lilian Edwards stressed that 'the work is what counts... As for me I have done nothing. I am only a tool in the Master's hand. Let us forget the tool.'[4]

While women in Baptist life have often served 'behind the scenes' in ways that appeared to be traditionally and culturally acceptable, the

---

[1] 'Memorable Names Among Baptists', in *Baptist Handbook* (London: Baptist Union of Great Britain and Ireland, 1902), pp. 223-26.

[2] W.T. Whitley, 'Index to Notable Baptists', *Transactions of the Baptist Historical Society* 7 (1920–1921), pp. 182-239. J.H.Y. Briggs began to address this imbalance with his article, 'She-Preachers, Widows and Other Women: The Feminine Dimension in Baptist Life since 1600', *Baptist Quarterly* 31.7 (July, 1986), pp. 337-52.

[3] See my article 'Beyond Public and Private Spheres: Another Look at Women in Baptist History and Historiography', *Baptist Quarterly* 34.4 (April, 1991), pp. 79-87.

[4] Lilian M. Edwards, *A Welsh Woman's Work in India* (Edinburgh: B. McCall Barbour, 1940), p. 98. Lilian Edwards was the daughter of William Edwards, the Principal of the Baptist College in Pontypool and later Cardiff from 1880–1925. Her step-mother, Sarah, was outspoken religious and civic leader.

participation of women in Baptist life has enabled the development of covenant life, nurtured spiritual growth and shaped expressions of mission and outreach into local communities and the world. This article will explore the contribution of women in these three areas and suggest that while often forgotten, the work of these sisters played an important role in shaping Baptist identity.

The Development of Covenant Life

The earliest Baptist confessions and covenants included statements that reflected their belief that women, as well as men, were called into relationship with Christ and should play a part in the life and leadership of the church. John Smyth wrote a *Short Confession of Faith in XX Articles* in 1609 in which he stated 'that the ministers of the church are, not only bishops ("Episcopos"), to whom the power is given of dispensing word and the sacraments, but also deacons, men and widows, who attend the affairs of the poor and sick brethren'.[5] The next year, Smyth and a group of followers published *A Short Confession of Faith*, which stated that that 'every believer is a member of the body of Christ' and at least sixteen of those who signed the confession were women.[6] Likewise, when Thomas Helwys published *A Declaration of Faith of English People remaining at Amsterdam in Holland* (1611), Article 10 of which stressed 'that the Church off CHRIST is a compony off faithful people...separated from the world by the word & Spirit off GOD'.[7] Significantly, in Article 20, mention is made of 'Deacons Men, and Women who by their office releave the necessities off the poor and impotent brethr[en] concerning their bodies'.[8]

Helwys and his congregation returned to London in 1611/12 and formed the first identifiable Baptist church on English soil at Spitalfields in London. In that year, he published *A Short Declaration of the Mystery of Iniquity*. Addressing his plea to the King, he wrote:

> For men's religion to God is between God and themselves. The king shall not answer for it. Neither may the king be judge between God and man. Let them be

---

[5] *Short Confession of Faith in XX Articles by John Smith* (1609), Article 16, in W.L. Lumpkin, *Baptist Confessions of Faith* (Valley Forge, PA: Judson Press, rev. edn, 1969), p. 101.
[6] *A Short Confession of Faith* (1610), Article 24, in Lumpkin, *Baptist Confessions*, pp. 108-109 and 113.
[7] *A Declaration of Faith of English People* (1611), Article 10, in Lumpkin, *Baptist Confessions*, p. 119.
[8] *A Declaration of Faith of English People*, Article 20, pp. 121-22.

heretics, Turks, Jews or whatsoever, it appertains not to earthly power to punish them in the least measure. This is made evident...by the Scriptures.[9]

While this is often seen as a statement of toleration for Baptists within seventeenth-century English society as a whole, it may also be seen as a broad declaration on the freedom of all people—men and women—to participate in the body of Christ.

Helwys and the London congregation were General Baptists, but it appears that as early as 1639 Calvinistic Baptist congregations were emerging out of Puritan-Separatist congregations. By 1644, a group of Calvinistic churches attended a meeting in London and published a confession of faith.[10] While the document was signed by fifteen men on behalf of seven churches in London, it was obviously assumed and expected that women as well as men were members of the church which was identified as 'a company of visible Saints, called & separated from the world, by the Word and Spirit of God, to the visible profession of the faith of the Gospel, being baptized into that faith, and joyned to the Lord, and each other, by mutuall agreement, in the practical injoyment of the Ordinances, commanded by Christ their head and King'.[11] No mention is made in this confession of women serving as pastors or deacons, but emphasis is given to participation of the whole fellowship in the decisions of the church:

> every Church has power given them from Christ for their better well-being, to choose to themselves meet persons into the office of Pastors, Teachers, Elders, Deacons, being qualified according to the Word, as those which Christ has appointed in his Testament, for the feeding, governing, serving, and building up of his Church...[12]

It also claimed that power had been given to the whole church to discipline members, 'not one particular person, either member or Officer, but the whole'.[13]

Clearly local covenant life in which men and women participated together was very important to early Baptists. When local churches formed, women as well as men signed or made their mark on the covenant documents. For instance, in June 1655 when a group of Calvinistic Baptists met at Porton in Wiltshire 'brethren and sisters' from

---

[9] T. Helwys, *A Short Declaration of the Mystery of Iniquity* (ed. Richard Groves; Macon, GA: Mercer University Press, 1998), p. 53.
[10] See B.R. White, 'The Organisation of the Particular Baptists, 1644–1660', *Journal of Ecclesiastical History* 17.2 (October, 1966), p. 226.
[11] *The London Confession* (1644), Article 33, in Lumpkin, *Baptist Confessions*, p. 165.
[12] *The London Confession* (1644), Article 36, p. 166.
[13] *The London Confession* (1644), Article 42, p. 168.

surrounding villages met to declare their desire to 'walk as becometh saints'.[14] Likewise, membership within the churches was based on a testimony or confession of faith and, until the mid-nineteenth century, in many churches women as well as men were expected to give a public testimony of their experience of grace before baptism.

By the early nineteenth century, however, some congregations began to raise questions about the way in which persons should come into membership. In response to a query over the scriptural method for receiving members into a church, especially with regard to females, an article in the *Baptist Magazine* in 1810, listed three ways in which 'a church as a collective body can obtain satisfaction respecting the piety of candidates for communion': first, personal address to the church when collected together or a reply to questions posed; secondly, written confession; and, thirdly, the church appointing representatives to engage in free conversation with individuals and afterwards report.[15] Since the main purpose of this article was to emphasize the scriptural injunction that 'women should keep silence in the churches', while affirming that the first and second ways were definitely practised by churches, the writer, known simply as 'Probus', wrote that the third, that of an 'extended interview', was best. For while the first—that of a personal interview—was, according to him, 'long practiced', it was not satisfactory with regard to females since it was not only against scripture (1 Corinthians 14.34-35; 1 Timothy 2.11-12), but 'such is the perturbation and confusion into which they are thrown, that they nearly if not entirely lose the powers of memory and reflection'.[16] Similarly, his objection to written confessions was simply that 'few women could do it'.[17]

While some congregations began to allow a private testimony of faith, others appear to have still practised the method of requiring a person to give a testimony of faith to the congregation. For instance, the Romsey church in Hampshire wrote in their 'rules for government' that 'we admit none into communion unless they give a faithful relation of the dealings of God with their souls and that before the church assembled and if they are unanimous in their approbation that person shall be admitted as members of the church to enjoy all the privileges connected therewith'.[18]

After being received into membership, church records indicate that women as well as men were expected to attend church meetings, though

---

[14] The *Broughton Church Book (1653–1689)*, Angus Library, Regent's Park College, Oxford.
[15] *Baptist Magazine* 2 (1810), p. 388
[16] *Baptist Magazine* 2, p. 388.
[17] *Baptist Magazine* 2, p. 388.
[18] 'Rules for the Government of the Church' (1807) in *The Church Book belonging to the Particular meeting at Romsey commencing 1 January 1802*, Romsey Baptist Church, Romsey, Hampshire.

how much women were allowed to say in the meetings is debatable. In 1656, for example, Baptists in Somerset published a confession that stressed 'THAT it is the duty of every man and woman, that have repented from dead works, and have faith towards God, to be baptized...'[19]. It also insisted that the visible church was a company of men and women separated out of the world by the preaching of the gospel to walk together in communion in all the commandments of God.[20] Among the commandments listed, however, was the statement that 'THE women of the church to learn in silence, and in all subjection'.[21] The insistence that women should keep silence was a biblical injunction which must be kept was found in most church books, though at times it was with a proviso that women could speak when asked a question![22]

In theory, it appears that early Baptists upheld the belief that the church was a covenant community made up of women as well as men. In their confessions and covenants Baptists spoke easily of the need 'to preach the Gospel to sons and daughters of men' and to share together in covenant life. However, in practice, it appears that at times there was not an equal sharing in their life together as women were sometimes discouraged from speaking out in church meetings. In fact, although women usually outnumbered men in all dissenting congregations, for the most part, it appears that among early Baptists, it was mainly men and not women who were called out to preach and to serve as pastors and deacons.[23]

In the nineteenth century it appears that while women and men were sometimes segregated for prayer meetings, nevertheless the women took part in the spiritual life of the congregation. For example, in 1835 a letter to the editor of the *Baptist Magazine* told how women as well as men had gathered for prayer at 5 a.m. and 'many females retired into the vestry to hold a prayer meeting'.[24]

There were, of course, exceptions to this exclusion and in the nineteenth century women began to push against the strongholds of all-male leadership. By the early twentieth century and certainly during the Great War, women began to assume leadership roles in the church which they would not relinquish. Frank Buffard describes the important leadership roles held by women in Heath Street Baptist Church in

---

[19] *The Somerset Confession* (1656), Article 24, in Lumpkin, *Baptist Confessions*, p. 209.
[20] *The Somerset Confession*, Article 24, p. 209.
[21] *The Somerset Confession*, Article 25.15, p. 210.
[22] *Lockerley Church Book 1808-1945 (with transactions from a former book, 1752)*, Lockerley Baptist Church, Lockerley, Hampshire.
[23] Michael R. Watts, *The Dissenters: Volume 1. From the Reformation to the French Revolution* (Oxford: Clarendon Press, 1978), pp. 319-320.
[24] *Baptist Magazine* 28 (January, 1836), pp. 5-9.

Hampstead. Miss Clara Southwell, for example, was one of a small group of women elected to serve as deacons in 1918. Devoted to the Baptist Missionary Society, she gave generously to the work and, with the exception of The Congo, visited all the BMS mission-fields at the time. Her work in the church and especially during the war days was lauded.[25] The church at Heath Street produced other very fine women leaders, especially from among the Angus and Pearce Gould families. Miss K.M. Pearce Gould not only served as a deacon, but exercised a deep influence in the church. Likewise, Miss Amelia Gurney Angus was described as 'a pillar of strength to countless people young and old'.[26] The work of women in churches like Heath Street point to the fact that although women were sometimes told to keep silent in the church they found ways to speak and to serve. While men were often in publicly visible roles of leadership and service, women, too, helped to nurture the spiritual growth of congregations.

Nurturing Spiritual Growth: Hymns, Poems and Printed Testimony

It appears that with only a few exceptions Baptist women did not seek or expect, nor were they given opportunities, to preach in local congregations. There is, of course, some evidence of women serving in leadership in churches. In the church at Broadmead in Bristol, for example, women appear to have taken an active part in the church in the seventeenth century, including the church's appointment of a deaconess in 1662.[27] However, for the most part, women had to find different ways for their voices to be heard. Although many would not have had the formal education which would allow them to enter into theological debate, there are a few examples of some women who wrote tracts on various subjects, like Anne Dutton of Great Gransden, Huntingdonshire.[28] However, while she claimed to be 'one who has tasted that the Lord is gracious', she has often been depicted as censorious and tetchy in her dealings with others.[29] Her contribution to theological insight is debatable,

---

[25] F. Buffard, *Heath Street 1861–1961* (London: n.p., 1961), p. 39.

[26] Buffard, *Heath Street*, p. 39.

[27] Roger Hayden (ed.), The Records of a Church of Christ in Bristol, 1640–1682 (Bristol Record Society's Publication, 27; Bristol: Bristol Record Society, 1974), pp. 12, 13, 16, 18, 19, 85, 87-91, 97, 131 and 154.

[28] E.g., W.T. Whitley, *Baptist Bibliography* (2 vols; London: Kingsgate Press, 1916–22), I, p. 88, notes that Katherine Sutton wrote *A Christian Woman's Experiences of the Glorious Working of God's Free Grace* (1633). Anne [Williams] Dutton born in 1692 in Northamptonshire, was married to Benjamin Dutton, pastor of Great Gransden Baptist Church, Huntingdonshire

[29] Joann Ford Watson (ed.), *Anne Dutton, Eighteenth-Century, British Baptist, Woman Theologian: Volume 1. Letters* (Macon, GA: Mercer University Press, 2003), and

though it is notable that she wrote to evangelical leaders in the eighteenth century including Philip Doddridge, as well as revivalists Howell Harris, George Whitefield and John Wesley.[30] In addition to tracts on baptism, free grace, justification, the nature of God and a host of other doctrinal subjects, Dutton also wrote verse. While Anne Dutton's hymns did not enjoy the wide acceptance of the work of Anne Steele, the hymn writer from Broughton in Hampshire, the work of both women represents the way they used the printed word to encourage and nurture the spiritual lives of believers.[31] Anne Steele's work, in particular, was valued by Baptist ministers, some of whom she corresponded with and her hymns were included by John Ash and Caleb Evans of Bristol in the hymn book, *A Collection of Hymns Adapted to Public Worship*, which they published in 1769.[32]

In addition to hymns and poetry, in the nineteenth century Baptist women also wrote and distributed penny tracts and short stories which became a popular means of spreading the gospel, stimulating the work of Sunday schools and encouraging support for the growing missionary movement. Significantly, it was not only that women found a voice in writing stories which were published and read by men and women, but also the fact that as they were read, the stories encouraged other women to speak up and step out in service to Christ. The tracts written about mission work led many young women to offer themselves as missionaries. Lilian Edwards, of Cardiff, claimed that not only had she been encouraged to think of mission work as she listened to her father speak to 'his ministerial friends', but she was also challenged by reading the *Junior Missionary Herald* and Miss Carmichael's book, *Things As They Are*.[33]

In addition to evangelical and missionary tracts, another source of evangelical witness was the printed deathbed testimony. While stories of 'a happy death' had been told for many years as a means of encouraging men and women and even children to think about their eternal destiny, among evangelicals in the nineteenth century the printed deathbed

---

Volume 2. *Discourses, Poetry, Hymns, Memoir* (Macon, GA: Mercer University Press, 2004).

[30] Joann Ford Watson does not include any of the correspondence between Dutton and Doddridge, but these are noted in G.F. Nuttall (ed.), *Calendar of Correspondence of Philip Doddridge, 1702–1751* (London: Her Majesty's Stationary Office, Historical Manuscripts Commission, 1979), pp. 192, 309, 313.

[31] Anne Steele (1717–78) was born in Broughton, Hampshire, to William and Anne [Froud] Steele. Writing as Theodosia, her first volume of poetry, *Poems on Subjects Chiefly Devotional*, was published in 1760. See the Correspondence of Anne Steele, Steele Family Papers, Angus Library, Regent's Park College, Oxford.

[32] Others who wrote hymns are noted by Briggs in 'She Preachers, Widows and Other Women', p. 342.

[33] Edwards, *A Welsh Woman's Work*, p. 2.

testimony became an important evangelistic tool.[34] Not only were they used as a means by which an individual could witness to a personal experience of Christ, but also they came to be used as a means for evangelization as people were warned of the dangers of hell and charmed by the delightful visions of the prospect of heaven. Deathbed sagas even found their way into the literature for Sunday schools. For women, printed deathbed testimonies became a means of public proclamation, indeed, the deathbed was their pulpit.

The practice of visiting the bedside of the dying was not unique to nineteenth-century evangelicals. Attendance at deathbeds and emphasis on 'holy dying' had been significant to Puritan devotion.[35] However, while it has been suggested that attendance at the bedside of a believer by members of the congregation may have indicated something of the Puritan's understanding of the 'priestly nature of the whole society', by the nineteenth century, as Doreen Rosman has pointed, deathbeds had almost a 'sacramental function' in the evangelical experience as it provided an opportunity to speak of personal union with Christ.[36] Gathering around the bed of the dying, the questions of the on-lookers were carefully designed to prompt testimonies that would enable the believer to speak with confidence of the assurance of faith and personal communion with Christ. These testimonies were written down and printed in order to demonstrate the relevance of religion and to encourage readers to deeper commitment. The deathbed of Mary Elyett, a member of the Salisbury congregation for nearly fifty-five years before she died in 1810, for example, was described as a sort of 'privileged station' by those who visited her and questioned her about her faith.[37] Asked about the meaning and significance of religion in the face of death, she reportedly answered, 'the same I have long thought, that there is one thing needful'. Questioned about the fear of death she replied, 'I am not afraid to die, for I can say, Thanks be to God, who giveth me the victory; but it is all through Christ.'[38] On the lips of Esther Horsey, wife of Joseph

---

[34] P. Sangster discusses the way death-beds were used as a way to teach children in *Pity My Simplicity: The Evangelical Revival and the Religious Education of Children, 1738–1800* (London: Epworth, 1963), p. 151.

[35] For an informative introduction to the Puritan attitude toward death see, D.E. Stannard, *The Puritan Way of Death: A Study in Religion, Culture, and Social Change* (New York: Oxford University Press, 1977), and G. Wakefield, *Puritan Devotion* (London: Epworth Press, 1957), p. 146

[36] Doreen Rosman, *Evangelicals and Culture* (London: Croom Helm, 1984), p. 103. Linda Wilson notes some of the problems with using obituaries in *Constrained by Zeal: Female Spirituality amongst Nonconformists, 1825–1875* (Studies in Evangelical History and Thought; Carlisle: Paternoster Press, 2000), pp. 24-27.

[37] *Baptist Magazine* 3 (1811), p. 73

[38] *Baptist Magazine* 3 (1811), p. 73.

Horsey, of Portsea, were lines to a well known hymn which were often quoted on deathbeds in the nineteenth century, when she reportedly said 'Everybody thinks that I lie uneasy but they are mistaken; no, Jesus can make a dying bed feel soft as downy pillows are.'[39]

While it may be argued that many of the printed deathbed testimonies follow a similar stylistic pattern, this does not mean that the experience of all the women was the same. Indeed, closer examination of the testimonies provides information not only about their faith in Christ, but the expression of that faith in family life and in the wider community.

It is evident that the printed deathbed testimonies not only provided a place for the voice of women to be heard, but at the same time, they provided a means for presenting what was considered to be an acceptable view of 'Christian womanhood'. Naturally, for the most part they seem keen to reinforce the culturally accepted view that women belonged in the home. Indeed, most of the printed testimonies of women draw a picture of women who were submissive to and supportive of their husbands, and looked after their children. In the *Bunhill Memorials*, for example, J.A. Jones included the dying testimony of his wife Ann and claimed that she was a person with an even temper and a cheerful disposition, loving and kind to the children and who was always ready to 'share in my bitters, as well as my sweets'.[40] While this kind of printed testimony may be viewed as a means of keeping women in cultural captivity, it is also clear from the details given about the lives of these women that they often made a significant contribution to the spiritual development of others.

In fact, even in the nineteenth century it was noted that the contribution of women, though far-reaching, was largely unnoticed. In the *Baptist Magazine* in 1812, 'A Memoir of Miss Ann Price who died in London on 16th June 1812' by Joseph Ivimey was commended to the readers with the note that while in heaven there may be well-known leaders, like David Brainerd and William Carey, yet 'in the midst of every company...we shall find a large proportion of unassuming characters, many of them the younger female branches of pious families, little known, seldom heard of, little noticed... [T]he influence of such characters spreads like leaven unobserved.'[41]

Nurturing Spiritual Growth: Family Life and Education

Like the Puritans before them, family devotions were a very important part of spirituality in Baptist life. The entire household was regarded as a religious community and all were expected to gather daily for reading

---

[39] *Baptist Magazine* 11 (1819), p. 148.
[40] J.A. Jones (ed.), *Bunhill Memorials* (London: James Paul, 1849), p. 385.
[41] 'Brief Memoir of Miss Ann Price, who died in London June 16th, 1812 in the 21st year of her age by Joseph Ivimey', *Baptist Magazine* 4 (1812), pp. 523-24.

and prayer.[42] Spiritual journals, which were sometimes kept as a means of examining progress in the Christian life, give evidence of the tone and tenor of these gatherings. And women often took a lead in organizing these home meetings.

Christian nurture was not, however, confined to the home. In the nineteenth century, as the Sunday school movement developed, women expanded their role as teachers and leaders in Christian education within the church. By the late nineteenth century, the role of women as Sunday school teachers in the church was accepted and much appreciated.

Along with Sunday schools, in the nineteenth century as churches began to expand their outreach and witness, women again took a leading role and formed groups to assist in mission and outreach. To give one example, it was reported in 1911 that a church in Hemel Hempstead had eight other groups including the young people's society of Christian Endeavour, Band of Hope, Baptist Missionary Auxiliary, Zenana Mission Fund, Tract Society, Benevolent Society, Maternal Society, and Dorcas Society, all led by women.[43] In all of these women were contributing as leaders and officers. Women were not at this time, however, serving as deacons because mention was made of: the 'valuable and instinted service rendered to the Church' by wives of deacons.[44] 'This band of *Mothers in Israel* fulfil tasks for which they are especially qualified with disinterested and unfailing zeal. Made expert by experience, and perfect by practice, they are ever willing, when occasion calls, which is frequently, to promote the common good.'[45]

In spite of their notable contribution within the local church, many believed that women should be given more opportunities to use their talents in the wider life of the church. Just as society was beginning to recognize the contribution of women, so it was claimed the church should allow women a greater voice in the public sphere.

Significantly, in 1918 J.H. Shakespeare, the General Secretary of the Baptist Union of Great Britain and Ireland, included in his work *The Church at the Cross-Roads*[46] an appeal to include women in leadership roles within the church. He wrote:

> The only other outstanding fact with which I shall deal at this point, as deeply concerning the Church, is the new place of women in the social order. In the mediaeval period she had great public power and authority in the religious orders.

---

[42] Wakefield, *Puritan Devotion*, p. 55.
[43] W.W. Robinson, *Jubilee Annals of the Marlowes Baptist Church Hemel Hempstead* (Hemel Hempstead: Weston Brothers, 1911), pp. 6-7.
[44] Robinson, *Jubilee Annals*, p. 42
[45] Robinson, *Jubilee Annals*, p. 43.
[46] This work was dedicated to his friend Isabel Riley James and her father A.F. Riley.

Forgotten Sisters 173

We must confess, however, that she has had but little help from the Church of our day in gaining her altered position. Yet it would be a profound mistake to suppose that the cause has owed little place to Christianity. At the very heart of our religion lie ideas and forces, which, though often obscured and slumbering, have protected women and emancipated her. In Christ Jesus there is and can be no distinction. The whole place of woman in our western civilization is due to the nobler conceptions which the Gospel has brought in its train. The question now, however, has been taken out of the merely speculative and academic. With an amazing swiftness, the position has changed. Political power has been given to six million women voters. Many doors which are at present closed against women will certainly be thrown open. I regard the liberation of woman from the bonds of prejudice, the growth of the power to serve at the call of new responsibilities, and the gift of her intellect, intuition and moral earnestness as the most helpful features of our time. Only at its peril can the Church make itself the last ditch of prejudice in this respect or forget that its problems will be best solved by men and women working together.

I do not propose to discuss the exact ecclesiastical functions or positions which women may claim in the coming days. No door in the State will be permanently closed to them. The learned professions are opening up to them one by one, though it may be reluctantly. They will be in Parliament, and there is no reason to doubt that sooner or later they will be in the Government. Go where you will today, you find them cool and clever administrators, organizing armies of women workers or raising large funds. It has been my business to interview some of them, and I have been impressed by the air of quiet confidence and mastery of detail. I have seen them surrounded by masses of correspondence, with duties and calls thronging upon them from every side. But they are not flurried, and they speak with that aspect of leisure to attend the thing in hand which is always the mark of a capable administrator. Does anyone think that women of this order can be permanently excluded from the highest service of the Church? The danger is lest they should lose patience with the Church as an institution and live their lives elsewhere. It is distressing to attend gatherings of women leaders and workers in social, educational and political spheres, and to find that many have already done so. Of course, no one by a stroke of the pen can efface the differences between men and women. I contend that they can take precisely the same place or render the same service. At any rate, in the new world, women will enter upon hitherto untried paths, they will assume added responsibilities and will advance in power, efficiency and self-confidence; prejudice will disappear and the Church will be compelled to accept the principle that sex in itself can be no bar to position and service.[47]

While members of the denomination as a whole were slow to heed these words, Shakespeare certainly did his best to encourage women to take part not only in British Baptist life but also to participate in meetings of the Baptist World Alliance.[48]

---

[47] J.H. Shakespeare, *The Churches at the Cross-Roads: A Study in Church Unity* (London: Williams and Norgate, 1918), pp. 9-11.
[48] See my article, 'British Women and the Baptist World Alliance: Honoured Partners and Fellows Workers?', *Baptist Quarterly* 41.1 (January, 2005), pp. 25-46.

Outreach and World Mission

In addition to their contribution to the leadership of groups for nurture and spiritual formation within the local church, it is perhaps not surprising that women also took a strong lead in world mission. Although the story of the history of the Baptist Missionary Society (BMS) is often told from an almost exclusively male perspective, early on women were doing their part to assist the mission work. For example, not only were William Carey, William Ward and Joshua Marshman actively engaged in work in India from 1790s, but alongside the 'Serampore Trio' as they became known, were women who contributed in many different areas, including translation, printing, agriculture and education.[49] Of course, even though Carey claimed as early as 1796 that women were needed in order to 'communicate the Gospel...in a situation where superstition secludes all women of respectability from hearing the word unless from their own sex',[50] yet he and the other men still maintained that the call for European women to learn the language in order to be 'instrumental in promoting the salvation of millions of native women applied mainly to women who were married and had accompanied their husbands to the mission field. Indeed, the brethren at Serampore, unlike American Baptists, did not approve of sending unmarried females to serve in the Mission. This was likewise the view of the Mission Society at home. For there are numerous examples of women accompanying their husbands to the mission field, but the men alone were ordained and, indeed, considered to be the real missionaries. Women, not being ordained, were likewise not paid. While some women had been allowed to go as teachers, generally speaking women were not appointed and the wives of missionaries were not viewed as missionaries in their own right! In spite of this, there is overwhelming evidence that women worked alongside the men and, in many cases, in addition to schools for the local population, they likewise established boarding schools for European and Anglo–Indian children which provided an income for many of the mission outposts.[51] Hence, while they were not considered to be equal partners, their contribution was of inestimable value.[52]

---

[49] See my article, 'The Role of Women in Early Baptist Missions', *Review and Expositor* 89.1 (Winter, 1992), pp. 35-48.

[50] *Periodical Accounts Relative to the Baptist Missionary Society* (1792–1799), I, p. 347: Carey to BMS, 'Houghly River', 28 December, 1796 as cited by E.D. Potts, *British Baptists in India, 1793–1837: The History of Serampore and its Mission* (Cambridge: Cambridge University Press, 1967), p. 18.

[51] See my 'The Role of Women in Early Baptist Missions', p. 39.

[52] Discussion of some of the issues confronting women in the nineteenth century are explained in M.T. Huber and N.C. Lutkehaus (eds), *Genedered Missions, Women and Men in Missionary Discourse and Practice* (Ann Arbor, MI: University of Michigan Press, 1999).

Forgotten Sisters 175

In writing the *History of The Baptist Missionary Society, 1792-1992*, Brian Stanley noted that, '[a]lthough missionary wives had been essentially involved to varying degrees in the work of the BMS from the beginning, their contribution was rarely acknowledged and hence has left little historical record.'[53] Yet, he claims, 'women played an indispensable role as missionary collectors and organizers'. Still, women had no representation on the Society's committees and no voice in its public meetings despite the fact that they probably formed the majority of the audience.[54]

In the late-nineteenth, a group was established by women in the denomination which would give women a greater voice in supporting and encouraging mission work. In 1866, the Ladies Association for the Support of Zenana Work and Bible Women in India, in connection with the Baptist Missionary Society (later known as The Baptist Zenana Mission [BZM] in 1897), was formed. The zenanas were those parts of high caste Hindu dwellings from which all males outside the immediate family were excluded.[55] Because women were kept isolated from the outside world, even women who had accompanied their husbands to the mission field found it difficult to make contact with the zenana women. Although the formation of The Baptist Zenana Mission was approved by the Baptist Missionary Society, with E.B. Underhill presiding over the first meeting of twenty-five ladies, the idea for the movement came from the wives of missionaries. As early as 1854 Elizabeth Sale had been allowed in to a zenana in Jessore, but the formation of the BZM was a response to a pamphlet, entitled '*A Plea for Zenanas*', written by Marianne Lewis in 1866.

Portrayed by Lewis as those who were held captive in their homes, the Zenana Mission was formed in order to educate and reach out with the gospel to these women. However, it is also true that the women who were sent out by the Zenana Mission were finding and giving expression to their belief in the rights of women. In fact, it may be argued that the British women who were sent as missionaries had themselves been captive to their own culture and in their work as missionaries they would find a new freedom and opportunity for the expression of their gifts.

Up until the formation of the Zenana Mission it had not been the practice of the Baptist Missionary Society to appoint women as missionaries. Although the need for women on the mission field had been recognized, in the main only men were officially appointed by the Society. The Zenana Mission thus became an important organization, supported and directed totally by women, they sent many women to work

---
[53] B. Stanley, *The History of the Baptist Missionary Society 1792–1992* (Edinburgh: T&T Clark, 1992), pp. 227-28.
[54] Stanley, *History*, p. 228.
[55] Stanley, *History*, p. 228 n. 90.

with women in India and China. They worked as doctors, nurses, teachers and 'Bible women' who made regular visits into the zenanas. One example is the work of Ellen Farrer, whose work twice earned her the award of honours from the Indian imperial government for distinguished public service.[56]

The Zenana Mission insisted that women should learn the languages and many of the women were very able linguists. For instance, Sarah Ann Raine was first appointed by the BZM to the Kurku and Indian Hill Mission in 1891.[57] After three years she married John Drake of the same mission and it was reported that much of their time was given to 'pioneer touring, on foot and on horse-back, in the jungles of that region and to the acquisition of the Kurku language'. Together they translated the Gospel according to Mark in Kurku and later a grammar in Kurku.[58] She was also a naturalist and sent specimens as a regular honorary collector to the British museum.[59]

Outreach in the Local and National Sphere

As the involvement of women in mission endeavours increased it seems that there was a growing awareness of the work of women in the denomination. Although the first female delegate to the Baptist Union Assembly appears to have been a Mrs Stockford,[60] who was sent by the Moss Side church in Manchester in 1894, in 1889 women took the platform of the Assembly to speak on 'Young Women's Guilds' and 'Women's Work in the Church'.[61] In 1891, Dr Ellen Farrer and Miss

---

[56] Ellen Margaret Farrer, the daughter of William Farrer, was born at Hampstead on 20 September 1865. Originally a member of Grenville Congregational Church, she was baptised on 10 June 1891 at Heath Street Baptist Church, Hampstead. Educated at South Hampstead High School for girls and Bedford College, London, she then trained at the London School of Medicine for Women and the Royal Free Hospital. She became the first woman doctor for the Baptist Zenana mission. She died at Rickmansworth on 14 October 1959 at the age of ninety-four. See *The Baptist Handbook 1961* (London: Carey Kingsgate Press, n.d.), p. 347

[57] 'Death of Mrs John (Annie) Drake', in *Monthly News Letter* 41 (November, 1929), BMS miscellaneous papers, Angus Library, p. 2.

[58] 'Death of Mrs John (Annie) Drake', p. 4.

[59] 'Death of Mrs John (Annie) Drake', p. 4.

[60] The Council considered whether women were eligible to be delegates and an affirmative vote was given. E.A. Payne, *The Baptist Union: A Short History* (London: Baptist Union of Great Britain and Ireland, 1959), pp. 150-51.

[61] Mrs Edward Medley spoke on 'Young Women's Guilds' at the spring assembly, 1889. She was identified as the daughter of the Revd C.M. Birrell and wife of the Revd Edward Medley, who served a number of different churches in England and was a tutor at Regent's Park College from 1896–99. Mrs Dawson Burns, spoke on 'Women's Work in the Church'. She was the wife of the Revd Dawson Burns, who was very active in the

Edith Angus[62] both spoke to the Assembly on work among the needy and ill.[63]

Among women there was a growing awareness that much could be done at home to promote the work of Christ through the denomination. The Deaconess Order, which was organized in 1890, was growing and developing with sisters taking an active part in social ministry.[64] In 1908, the Baptist Women's Home Auxiliary, which in 1910 became the Baptist Women's League (BWL), was formed.[65] The formation of the ladies auxiliary was proposed to the Baptist Union by C.S. Rose as a way of encouraging more help on behalf of the Home Work Fund.[66] On 23 April 1908 a constitution for the Ladies auxiliary was submitted to the Baptist Union. The object of which was 'the development of the home work fund of the Baptist Union through the agency of Baptist women by the raising of funds to render church aid and promote evangelisation and colportage and also to welcome church members passing from one district to another and by assisting Baptist girls seeking situations'.[67]

While it was C.S. Rose who provided the public voice in favour of the auxiliary, his wife was one of the leaders within the organization. Moreover, although it was her husband who was appointed by the Baptist Union to engage in a caravan mission in 1908, latterly, when the report of the caravan mission was made to the Baptist Union, it was Doris Rose who was singled out for her good work.[68]

---

temperance movement. *The Baptist Handbook* (London: Baptist Union of Great Britain and Ireland Publications Department, 1910), pp. 476-78. J.H.Y. Briggs, *The English Baptists of the Nineteenth Century* (A History of the English Baptists, 3; Didcot: Baptist Historical Society, 1994), pp. 286, 334-337.

[62] Edith Angus was the daughter of Amelia Gurney Angus and Dr Joseph Angus. A member of Heath Street Church, Hampstead, she was the leader of the Women's Meeting at Drummond Street Mission and served on the committees of the Baptist Missionary Society since 1894. See Buffard, *Heath Street*, p. 35.

[63] 'The Training of Women for Christian Work' papers were read at the autumn Assembly of the Baptist Union held in Manchester on Thursday, 8 October 1891. 'Women's Work Among the Sick Poor' by Dr Ellen Farrer, and 'Women's Work in Connection With the Social Condition of the Poor' by Miss Edith A. Angus.

[64] D.M. Rose, *Baptist Deaconesses* (London: Carey Kingsgate Press, 1954)

[65] See *Fifty Years' Achievement: The Baptist Women's League, 1908-1958* (n.p.: n.p., [1958]). See also Ian M. Randall, *The English Baptists of the Twentieth Century* (A History of English Baptists, 4; Didcot: Baptist Historical Society, 2005), *passim*; and Ruth M.B. Gouldbourne, *Reinventing the Wheel: Women and Ministry in English Baptist Life* (The Whitley Lecture, 1997-1998; Oxford: Regent's Park College, Whitley Publications), p. 24.

[66] *BU Minute book, 1906-1909*, Angus Library, Regent's Park College, Oxford.

[67] *BU Minute book, 1906-1909*, Angus Library, Regent's Park College, Oxford.

[68] C.S. Rose reported on the work of the caravan mission during 1909. Caravans operate in Bedfordshire and a considerable part of Cambridgeshire. Eighteen places are

One of the key leaders among women in England in the early part of the twentieth century was Isabel Riley James (d.1957) who, like her father before her, was a close friend of J.H. Shakespeare. At the encouragement of Shakespeare, the first meeting of the BWL met in Isabel James' home. This group became in the words of Ernest Payne, 'an important and valued adjunct to the work of the union'. Actually, it became much more than that—the women's group became the primary organization for fund raising within the denomination. Women, in fact, gave much support to the sustentation fund for ministers in 1911.[69] They also supported a hostel for women in London, which opened in June 1912 and the work of the Training College for Baptist deaconesses.[70] In all of these activities Isabel James was a driving force. She appears to have been active in the Liberal Party and aware of the changing roles of women in society. In an address given by her to women meeting at the Baptist World Alliance in Philadelphia in 1911, it is clear that she was concerned that women were not always given the same opportunities as men in Baptist life and claimed that involvement in the BWL had opened many women to 'new spheres of labour adequate to the measure of their capacity and will' and it had been 'the means of spiritual and social good among the churches' in Britain.[71] She also argued that it was 'high time that the enormous reserve force of energy, the varied gifts and talents' of women in the churches should be utilized. In fact, she insisted, 'the future of our denomination greatly depends upon the loyalty and faithful work of our Baptist women'. The truth of Isabel James' claims is borne out by church records. Indeed, the dependence of Baptist churches on women was blatantly obvious: for example, the Heath Street church published a booklet in 1911 which listed twenty-eight different organizations in the church and eighteen of those were served by women.[72]

Social Concern: Reaching Out with the Word

In addition to missionary work within the local church and in the denomination, some Baptist women became involved in social action in

---

mentioned. 'Home Work Fund Report, 14 February 1910', *BU Council Report*, Angus Library, Regent's Park College, Oxford.

[69] *BU Council Report*, year ending 1911, p. 42, Angus Library, Regent's Park College, Oxford.

[70] On the founding of the Training College in particular and the office of deaconesses in general, see Randall, *The English Baptists of the Twentieth Century*, passim. See also Rose, *Baptist Deaconesses*.

[71] Mrs Russell [Isabel] James, 'The British Baptist Women's League', in *The Baptist World Alliance: Second Congress, Philadelphia, June 19-25, 1911: Record of Proceedings* (Philadelphia, PA: Harper & Brother, 1911), p. 167.

[72] *Heath Street Church 1861–1911 Jubilee Souvenir* (n.p.: n.p.), 1911, pp. 38-39.

their communities. Their social concern included work in orphanages, establishing homes for unwed mothers, and shelters for the poor and support for the temperance movement. This kind of involvement may be seen clearly in the work of Sarah Anne Edwards who was married to William Edwards, the Principal of the Baptist College in Cardiff.[73]

As with many other women, Sarah Anne Edwards' (often referred to as Mrs Principal or Mrs Dr Edwards!) contributions to Baptist life seemed to have been overshadowed by the achievements of her husband.[74] A member of Tredegarville Baptist Church, Cardiff, she gave her support to women's groups locally, in Wales, and as part of the Baptist Union of Great Britain, too. In 1906 she was the first President of the Baptist Women's Missionary Association in Wales and remained in office until her death in 1947. In 1907 she was elected a member of Baptist Missionary Society committee and in 1927 she was made a life member of the national executive of the BMS. She was for many years the honorary organizing secretary for Wales for the BWL. When she was President of the BWL of Great Britain in 1916–17, she helped to raise £15,000 in Wales alone for the work of Protestant churches who had suffered in France during the Great War. She was also one of the

---

[73] Edwards served the College which was located in Pontypool and later moved to Cardiff from 1880 to 1925. His work as an educator and Baptist leader are well documented. Educated at the Baptist College in Pontypool and then at Regent's Park College before returning to Pontypool as the classical tutor in 1872. He was then invited to be Principal of the Baptist College in 1880 and was responsible for moving the College to Cardiff in 1893 when the University College of South Wales and Monmouthshire was established in Cardiff. Establishing himself as an able administrator and scholar he wrote a number of works in Welsh and English, but is probably best known for his translation of the New Testament into Welsh and his translation of many hymns. He served as President of both the Baptist Union of Wales and the Baptist Union of Great Britain and founded the Welsh and English Baptist Sunday School Unions in Wales. He had degrees conferred on him by William Jewel College and Bucknell University in America and the LLD by the University of Wales. See T.W. Chance (ed.), *The Life of Principal William Edwards* (Cardiff: Priory Press, 1934), and D.M. Himbury, *The South Wales Baptist College (1807–1957)* (Cardiff: South Wales Baptist College, 1957), *passim*.

[74] Sarah Ann Evans (1865–1947) was born 1865 in Pontlottyn in the Rhymney Valley where she attended Zoar Baptist Church. She trained as a vocalist at the royal academy of music. In 1891 she married William Edwards, just after he had taken over as Principal of the College in Pontypool. This was his second marriage, as his first wife had died in 1880 after giving birth to their third child. Sarah and William had four children. The marriage to Sallie, as her husband called her, was a happy one. Their children noted that in her he found his real counterpart one to whom he always submitted his projects and problems and whose helpful criticism he relied upon.

founders of the Girls' Hostel which was established in London by the BWL.[75]

Locally, she was involved in social ministry. In 1904, in the height of the revival, she established a 'Midnight Mission' which had as its aim 'the reclaiming of fallen womanhood'.[76] This Mission met at Tabernacle Welsh Baptist Church, the Hayes, Cardiff. With a group of enthusiastic workers, Mrs Edwards would 'scour the city, gently and persuasively leading women and girls of the streets to the chapel vestry' where it was said that a 'bright fire, warm refreshment, music and fellowship helped in the work of regeneration'.[77] She was also instrumental in establishing a Rescue Home in Cardiff which could accommodate twenty-five girls.[78] It was also reported that she opened the rooms of the College to 'scores of the lonely, dejected, depressed, and poor people of Cardiff... Meals were prepared for them day and night, and each one was welcomed and ministered unto by Mrs. (Dr.) Edwards herself'.[79]

She was President of the Cardiff and South Wales sisterhood on three occasions 1918–20, 1926 and 1938. This was a gathering of women's groups from all the Free Churches and it is claimed that largely under her leadership the membership grew to 20.000 members. Among their practical activities they endowed fourteen beds at Cardiff Royal Infirmary.[80] Since Edwards was also a member of the board of management for the Royal Infirmary this would have been a concern close to her heart.

While acknowledging her work in the denomination, it should also be noted that her influence as a Baptist leader extended beyond denominational bounds and into civic life. In 1926 she was named as a magistrate of the city of Cardiff.[81] She also served as an official visitor appointed by the Home Office to the women at Cardiff prison.

She devoted a great deal of time to the British Women's Temperance Association and was for many years President of the Cardiff and District Union of the British Women's Temperance Association. She was also President of the Glamorgan Union of the British Women's Temperance Association and representative for Wales on the National Executive of the British Women's Temperance Association. However, she was not just a committee person but went out to the centre of Cardiff at midnight appealing to women on the street to abstain from the use of alcohol.

---

[75] Irene Myrddin Davies (ed.), *Memory an Inspiration* (Cardiff: Priory Press, 1957), p. 30.
[76] Davies (ed.), *Memory an Inspiration*, p. 25.
[77] Davies (ed.), *Memory an Inspiration*, p. 26.
[78] Davies (ed.), *Memory an Inspiration*, p. 26.
[79] Davies (ed.), *Memory an Inspiration*, p. 21.
[80] *The Cardiff Year Book* (Glamorgan Record Office, 1927), p. 276.
[81] *The Cardiff Year Book* (Glamorgan Record Office, 1926), p. 24.

Her temperance work brought her into contact with other women's groups which were agitating for equal voting rights for women. She attended meetings of the Cardiff Women Citizen's Association when they were demanding equal franchise for women and was a member of the last deputation to go to the government prior to the granting of the franchise to women. She also served as leader of a deputation to Lord Asquith as Prime Minister to ask for legislation condemning drinking clubs.

Politically involved, she was vice president for several years of the Women's Liberal Association in Cardiff and, in addition to being a member of the board of management for the Royal Infirmary, she served as a member of the visiting committee to the Institution for the Mentally Defective, a member of the local National Insurance Committee (the first woman to be appointed), government representative on the unemployment tribunal's board for Cardiff and the Rhondda Valley and a Referee under the old age pensions act. She was also an honorary member of the Gorsedd of the National Eisteddfod of Wales.[82]

Sarah Edwards was apparently much in demand as an engaging, forceful public speaker. It is said that she spoke eloquently and without notes, as one person put it, 'in a personal way as a friend to friend'. Obviously all were not so enamoured with Mrs Edwards. On one occasion a friend recalled that a male deacon in one of the churches came up and said to her and Mrs Edwards, 'If you two ladies continue to speak on public platforms, let me warn you, you will lose your femininity and charm.' When he was 'out of earshot' the woman said that she and Mrs Edwards turned to one another and 'laughingly agreed that they would risk it!'[83]

Judging from all her activities, Sarah Edwards was quite a remarkable Baptist leader. Indeed, while her work has gone un-noted, as one friend commented, had Principal Edwards been less remarkable himself, he would have been simply known as the husband of Mrs Edwards of Cardiff.[84] It appears, however, that William Edwards realized his wife's gifts. In 1926 he gave an address entitled 'Our Inspirations' to the Triennial Conference of the Three English Baptist Associations in South Wales and Monmouthshire, at Swansea, 18 June 1925. Here he spoke of growth and development of the service of 'consecrated womanhood'. One can imagine that he had his wife Sallie in mind as he spoke of women whose 'zeal and energy know no bound'. He claimed:

> Woman, like man was a special creation of God, capable of rendering great service in the sphere in which she should be placed; yet her place in public life is a great evolution. Although loved and revered as she should be, yet throughout the ages she

---

[82] Davies (ed.), *Memory an Inspiration*, p. 13.
[83] Davies (ed.), *Memory an Inspiration*, p. 23.
[84] Davies (ed.), *Memory an Inspiration*, p. 23.

was unaccountably ignored, and here many gifts were not called into requisition; but even confining ourselves to the last sixty or seventy years, what transformation has taken place! Mere man has been obstinate in giving her rightful position but she has fairly won it, and we maintain she will take care to keep it... They have covered the land with a network of agency and as British women—their zeal, energy and spirit of self-sacrifice know no bound.[85]

Indeed, Edwards seems to have realized the vital contribution women had already made to local churches when he commented that during the Great War 'many a little Bethel would have been closed; but amid their anxiety and their tears with unperishable (sic) devotion they kept them open'.

While there were men like William Edwards and J.H. Shakespeare who tried to encourage the work of women within the denomination and society, many others continued to insist that women should continue to find their primary place of service in the home. In spite of this, however, Baptist women continued to speak and to shape the witness to Christ in their homes, communities and in the wider world.

Throughout the twentieth century the role of women in the church continued to grow. While they often found it difficult to be heard within the denomination, especially in the years after the World Wars, it became obvious that life in the churches had changed and women would continue to play an active part in leadership. However, some still felt that more should be done to encourage women. In a series of studies entitled, *Everywoman's Chance,* published by the Young Women's Committee, Baptist women were urged to change the approach to their BWL meetings.[86] In a lesson entitled 'Serving the Church' it was claimed:

> The great majority of women's meetings are devoted entirely to the cultivation of the devotional life. Out talks range between Martha and Mary and we may be in danger of forgetting that many women have the wider interests and intellectual powers that fit them for the more virile and strenuous activities which men once regarded as male prerogatives. Even when exclusively masculine deacons' boards plan the work of the church, their imagination so far as women's work is concerned, seldom takes them beyond social evenings and tea parties and sewing meetings. The war time revelations of women's capacity may revolutionize our whole conception of 'women in action' within the church.[87]

---

[85] W. Edwards, 'Our Inspirations', An Address delivered at the Triennial Conference at Swansea of the Three English Baptist Associations in South Wales and Monmouthshire, 18 June 1925, p. 7.

[86] Violet Hedger (ed.), *Everywoman's Chance* (Younger Women's Commission Baptist Women's League; Walthamstow: Walthamstow Press, n.d.). According to this leaflet, The Young Women's Committee was set up by the BWL to consider the challenge and opportunity to-day in women's work.

[87] Hedger (ed.), *Everywoman's Chance,* p.17.

Urging women to take on board the changing role of women in society and to address problems of sociology and economics, of sex and marriage, the study continued:

> Increasing numbers of women earn their own livelihood, we must adapt our work to meet the doubts and questions they face... [T]he old mother's meetings where people remained in blissful ignorance are gone... [W]e must take a growing share in the more virile and challenging work of the Church, in its administration and in its activities. Many new opportunities for leadership will come to women in the post-war years. In clubs, institutions, in social service, in propaganda campaigns, planning Church work, in teaching and preaching women will carry a growing responsibility.[88]

Women now serve as pastors, teachers in the Baptist colleges, and leaders in the denomination, as well as continuing to share in leadership within local churches. While there are still those who claim that women should 'keep silent' in the church, there can be little doubt that women have made a valuable contribution to Baptist life. Indeed, without the contribution of notable but often un-noted sisters, the doors of many Baptist churches would have closed long ago.

---

[88] Hedger (ed.), *Everywoman's Chance*, p.18.

CHAPTER 9

'As It Was in the Beginning'(?): The Myth of Changelessness in Baptist Life and Belief

Philip E. Thompson

'He proposes to speak to them things old and new; and what is old and familiar is still unknown, for it can never be brought to remembrance.' Karl Barth[1]

My intent is not to demonstrate the existence of a myth among Baptists in America claiming Baptist doctrine and the life it enables have been unchanging over the course of Baptist existence.[2] Baptists often assume some sort of changelessness in their particular expression of Christian faith, so such claims are commonplace. R. Stan Norman has noted that writings seeking to catalogue 'Baptist distinctives' often rest their claims on appeals to this changelessness in order to establish unassailable precedent. 'This is the practice of using statements like "Baptists have always believed this" or "this [particular doctrine] has always been a part of the distinctive Baptist identity".'[3] While Norman lists no concrete examples, that his statement is accurate. Neither will I demonstrate that such claims are mistaken, since it is not hard to show that Baptist beliefs have changed in form and content over their history.[4] While there are

---

[1] K. Barth, *The Epistle to the Romans* (trans. Edwyn C. Hoskins; London: Oxford University Press, 1968), p. 34.
[2] My reference is to the largest segments of the Baptist family in America, found in the Southern Baptist Convention and American Baptist Churches in the USA, and those bodies that preceded them and that have emerged from them. The influence from this large grouping has extended through many other conventions, associations, unions, and conferences of Baptists.
[3] R.S. Norman, *More Than Just a Name: Preserving Our Baptist Identity* (Foreword by R.A. Mohler, Jr; Nashville, TN: Broadman & Holman Publishers, 2001), p. 4.
[4] E.g. P.E. Thompson, 'Re-envisioning Baptist Identity: Historical, Liturgical, and Theological Analysis', *Perspectives in Religious Studies* 27.3 (Fall, 2000), pp. 287-302; and P. Thompson, 'Sacraments and Religious Liberty: From Critical Practice to Rejected Infringement', in A.R. Cross and P.E. Thompson (eds.), *Baptist Sacramentalism* (Studies in Baptist History and Thought, 5; Carlisle: Paternoster Press, 2003), pp. 36-54.

various interpretations of what gave rise to these changes, the bare fact of change is not difficult to see.

We can gain better understanding of this part of the Christian family, however, when we scrutinize this feature. It is not a simple historical oversight or factual error, for it is too frequent to be merely a mistake. Norman suggests that the situation arises from ignorance of Baptist history or personal agendas on the part of writers that lead to a distortion of Baptist characteristics. His suggestion has merit, for these have contributed to the myth's perpetuation. Yet this interpretation ultimately proves too facile. Across the spectrum of debate over Baptist identity, the claim surfaces among persons too well trained to be ignorant and, hopefully, aware enough not to be so thoroughly agenda-driven. Thus I propose to explore the function of this myth in Baptist life, and the effect it has had. This will lead me to offer a meditation on the condition of Baptist theology, which I would describe as 'wounded'. I contend that the poor health of much Baptist theology is not congenital, but results from a wound of memory; wounded by a partial, unhealed excision of tradition.

'We Have *Never* Put the Future Under the Bond of the Past': The Ambiguity of Tradition in Baptist Theology

It is an understatement to say that Baptists in America are of two minds concerning tradition; though only one is a conscious mind. Mark S. Medley, in summarizing Baptist literature on this matter, concludes that 'Baptist theologians often do not reflect on tradition as a theological category'.[5] Medley very properly describes the state of affairs not as an

---

[5] M.S. Medley, 'Catholics, Baptists, and the Normativity of Tradition', *Perspectives in Religious Studies* 28.2 (Summer, 2001), pp. 119-21, especially n. 2 in which he summarizes the place given to tradition in several major Baptist theologians in America over the last two centuries. The two Baptist theologians Medley presents as exceptions to this tendency, James Wm McClendon, Jr, and Stanley J. Grenz, have written for wider audiences, and more from 'baptist' and 'evangelical' perspectives, rather than those best designated as 'Baptist' per se. Medley notes further, p. 121, that his doctoral seminar in theological method at a Baptist seminary did not specifically address tradition as a theological category.

This situation is, happily, changing with some speed. In addition to Medley's own essay, three other works have appeared since. In the United States there are E.G. Hinson, 'The Authority of Tradition: A Baptist View', in D.H. Williams (ed.), *The Free Church and the Early Church: Bridging the Historical and Theological Divide* (Grand Rapids, MI: Eerdmans, 2002), pp.141-61; and the excellent piece by S.R. Harmon, 'The Authority of the Community (of All the Saints): Toward a Postmodern Baptist Hermeneutic of Tradition', *Review and Expositor* 100.4 (Fall, 2003), pp. 587-621. Despite the American focus of this essay, I would add the most sustained Baptist theological reflection on tradition to date by English theologian S.R. Holmes, *Listening to the Past: The Place of Tradition in Theology* (Carlisle/Grand Rapids, MI: Paternoster/Baker Academic, 2002).

absence of tradition, but a lack of reflection on it. This lack makes itself readily apparent, for tradition is both esteemed and yet ironically denigrated in Baptist theology, invoked solemnly at times and sanctimoniously dismissed at others. E. Glenn Hinson has spoken perceptively of this ambiguity:

> In the main, Baptists have tended more toward the 'Scripture alone' end of the spectrum and have disclaimed the authority of tradition. However there has not been thorough consistency on this view.... The fact is, Baptists have not really given serious overt attention to the authority of tradition, even their own tradition. Tradition, therefore, exerts usually an undefined and possibly even unadmitted influence on the interpretation of Scripture, in shaping theological views, or in forming or conserving ecclesiastical observances.[6]

Hinson concludes that this lack of reflection renders lengthy study of Baptist views on tradition unprofitable. I do not believe this to be the case, however, for it can yield valuable insight into Baptist thought not otherwise apparent.

Hinson is broadly accurate in his observation. I would add, however, that while there is a general ambiguity, many Baptists in America make implicit distinctions among traditions. They tend to value 'Baptist tradition', notwithstanding the problems that attend articulating the content of this tradition. More often, the tradition that is denigrated is what we might call 'catholic tradition'. Yet because this distinction is not explicit, these Baptists sound as though they are rejecting tradition *qua* tradition. In its turn, this of course renders yet more problematic the blind invocations of a Baptist tradition of any sort.[7]

Hinson's and Harmon's essays are written from a consciously Baptist perspective. Holmes' is more broadly evangelical. While the situation is changing, and these works are encouraging, they are still not representative of the mainstream of Baptist writers.

Also worthy of note are the attention devoted to tradition by the National Association of Baptist Professors of Religion, Region at Large, with sessions of their annual meetings in 2002 and 2004 devoted in part or in whole to the topic of tradition; and Steven R. Harmon's forthcoming *Toward Baptist Catholicity: Essays on Tradition and the Baptist Vision* (Studies in Baptist History and Thought, 27; Milton Keynes: Paternoster, 2006).

[6] Hinson, 'The Authority of Tradition', pp. 141-42. Cf. Harmon, 'The Authority of the Community', pp. 590-93.

[7] I am speaking, admittedly, in a very general way. One can find statements that appear contrary to what I am claiming here. For example, G. Thomas Halbrooks, 'Why I Am A Baptist', in Alan Neely (ed.), *Being Baptist Means Freedom* (Charlotte, NC: Southern Baptist Alliance, 1988), pp. 1-2, notes early in his essay on Baptist identity that part of his Baptist commitment is an awareness of the church catholic. He appreciatively notes the recitation of the Apostles' Creed as the first act of the Baptist World Alliance in 1905.

Turning now to our examination of this ambiguity, tradition and the conditions that are necessary for tradition have, on one hand, been dismissed in Baptist writings for the past two centuries. This dismissal has often been conveyed in populist rhetoric, revealing an Enlightenment rationalism that asserts a 'right' of each individual to interpret the Bible for her/himself.[8] Paradigmatic is Francis Wayland's influential *Notes on the Principles and Practices of Baptist Churches*. He declared in the mid-nineteenth century that God speaks in the Bible to every individual 'as much as though that individual was the only being whom it addressed'.[9] For Baptists, then, 'all appeals to the Fathers, or to antiquity, or to general practice in they early centuries... are irrelevant and frivolous'.[10] Indeed, he asserted, Baptists have arrived at a clearer knowledge of the truth precisely because they have had no profound philosophers, learned philologists, or acute logicians. Their 'whole power is in the people'.[11] In the same vein, Frederick Anderson could later maintain that Baptists are 'natural enemies of ecclesiasticism and churchianity'.[12] W.T. Conner

---

[8] These find expression in Baptist writings throughout the nineteenth and twentieth centuries. Cf. for representative examples across the years: W.B. Johnson, *The Gospel Developed Through the Government and Order of the Churches of Jesus Christ* (Richmond, VA: H.K. Ellyson, 1846), p.16; W.C. Duncan, *A Brief History of the Baptists and Their Distinctive Principles and Practices From the 'Beginning of the Gospel' to the Present Time* (New York: Edward H. Fletcher, 1855), p. xix; T.H. Pritchard, 'The Difference Between A Baptist Church and All Other Churches', in C.A. Jenkins (ed.), *Baptist Doctrines: Being and Exposition, In a Series of Essays by Representative Baptist Ministers, of the Distinctive Points of Baptist Faith and Practice* (St Louis, MO: Chancy R. Barnes, 1884), pp. 270-74; E.T. Hiscox, *The New Directory for Baptist Churches* (Philadelphia, PA: Judson Press, 1953 [1894]), the late reprint shows the endurance of influence of these ideas; F.H. Kerfoot, 'Why the Baptist Doctrine?', in J.M. Frost (ed.), *Baptist Why and Why Not* (Nashville, TN: Sunday School Board of the Southern Baptist Convention, 1900), pp.355-55; E.Y. Mullins, *The Axioms of Religion: A New Interpretation of the Baptist Faith* (Philadelphia, PA: Judson Press, 1908), gives the classical statement of this in his principle of soul competency; Mullins's view has been continued in basically the same form ever since. Recent expressions of the idea include W.B. Shurden, *The Baptist Identity: Four Fragile Freedoms* (Macon, GA: Smyth & Helwys, 1996), pp. 23-32 *et passim*; H.L. McBeth, 'God Gives Soul Competency and Priesthood to All Believers', in C.W. Deweese (ed.), *Defining Baptist Convictions: Guidelines for the Twenty-First Century* (Franklin, TN: Providence House, 1996), pp. 62-70; and G.C. Cothen and J.M. Dunn, *Soul Freedom: Baptist Battle Cry* (Macon, GA: Smyth & Helwys Publishers, 2000).

[9] Francis Wayland, *Notes on the Principles and Practices of Baptist Churches* (New York: Sheldon, Blakeman, 1857), pp. 123-24.

[10] Wayland, *Notes*, p. 86.

[11] Wayland, *Notes*, p. 38. Cf also. p. 123.

[12] F.L. Anderson, 'Historical Baptist Principles', in *Baptist Fundamentals: Being Addresses Delivered at the Pre-Convention Conference at Buffalo June 21 and 22, 1920* (Philadelphia, PA: Judson Press, 1920), p. 18.

remarked that 'The authority of the church is repressive and oppressive in its nature.... Man's mind and conscience are enslaved.'[13] The Bible, in which alone Baptists find their authority, is a different sort of authority than the church, and so does not depend upon or even require the church.

The very conditions of tradition have been in one sense or another cast off through a radicalized *sola scriptura* principle.[14] Historian Henry Vedder reasoned since the church is a regenerate, spiritual body, it takes its rise anew with each generation. The only real succession is that of successive persons having faith in Christ.[15] Such a situation would make tradition unnecessary, especially if the truths that guide and inform Baptists are so self-evident. These truths, some have argued, are indeed self-evident. For example, Charles A. Jenkins observed that 'Though [Baptist] churches are entirely separate and independent, they nevertheless harmonize in doctrine, because the Scriptures constitute their bond of union.'[16] Wayland believed Baptist principles to be so clearly evident in scripture, he could write comfortably on them even though he pretended 'no learning in ecclesiastical history'.[17]

This attitude toward tradition is not a uniquely Baptist propensity, but one that Baptists in America have shared with other American churches and American culture broadly. Baptists in America gained considerable strength during the period following the Revolution and through the first half of the nineteenth century. This was in large part because they so fully accommodated the democratic principles that animated the 'American experiment'.[18] It was a time, reports Michael G. Kammen, in which tradition was eclipsed by the ideas of nature and progress.[19] The cultural and ecclesial ethos of the time is reflected in Emerson's declaration that 'The divine gift is not the old but the new', and the

---

[13] W.T. Conner, *Revelation and God: An Introduction to Christian Doctrine* (Nashville, TN: Broadman Press, 1951), p. 97.

[14] Cf. Harmon, 'The Authority of the Community', p. 592.

[15] H.C. Vedder, *A Short History of the Baptists* (Philadelphia, PA: American Baptist Publication Society, 1891), pp. 44 and 212.

[16] C.A. Jenkins, 'Introduction', in Jenkins (ed.), *Baptist Doctrines*, p.20.

[17] Wayland, *Notes*, p. 16.

[18] The seminal study of this dynamic in American Christianity generally remains N. Hatch, *The Democratization of American Christianity* (New Haven, CT: Yale University Press, 1989). Cf. N.O. Hatch and M. Noll (eds), *The Bible in America: Essays in Cultural History* (New York: Oxford University Press, 1992); and B.A. Harvey, *Another City: An Ecclesiological Primer for a Post-Christian World* (Christian Mission and Modern Culture; Harrisburg, PA: Trinity Press International, 1999). Curtis W. Freeman, 'Can Baptist Theology be Revisioned?', *Perspectives in Religious Studies* 24.3 (Fall, 1997), pp. 273-302, examines particular effects of this on Baptist theology.

[19] M.G. Kammen, *Mystic Chords of Memory: The Transformation of Tradition in American Culture* (New York: Alfred A. Knopf, 1991), pp. 40-51.

earlier admonition of Baptist Isaac Backus, 'Be intreated no longer to take Things by Tradition'.[20] Kammen notes that evangelical churches in America were more interested in destiny than in history. Thus tradition was accorded little significance.[21] Baptist Walter Rauschenbusch thus argued for free inquiry by pastors and teachers of theology because Baptists 'have never put the future under the bond of the past'.[22] Kammen continues that the most pertinent consequence of this 'liberation' from tradition has been superficial collective self-knowledge. 'Identity was more commonly assumed or invented than inherited; and when it was knowingly inherited the process occurred mindlessly, without critical inquiry, without curiosity, without qualms.'[23] Kammen could have been writing of Baptists alone. Indeed, Baptists have come to be a typically modern religious phenomenon in many ways.[24]

Voices, some Baptist, have recently been raised critiquing this state of affairs. Baptists, among others, have utterly lost touch with tradition, they say. Baptist patristics scholar, D.H. Williams, has so indicted Baptists and other 'free church evangelicals': 'If one word could sum up the current theological situation, it would be *amnesia*.'[25] To a degree this is true. Various segments of the church in America, not simply Baptists, do indeed, for diverse reasons, show a lamentable forgetfulness of large portions of the church's catholic tradition.[26] I would not wish to deny the needed insights and timely admonition Williams and others bring. I would, however, encourage us to seek perhaps a more precise diagnosis. I have come to believe that the phenomenon we see among our Baptists is not amnesia.[27] Amnesia, the inability to remember, brings a concomitant

---

[20] Kammen, *Mystic Chords*, pp. 43 and 42.
[21] Kammen, *Mystic Chords*, pp. 50-51.
[22] D.R. Sharpe, *Walter Rauschenbusch* (New York: McMillan, 1942), p.106, quoted in L. Moore, 'Academic Freedom: A Chapter in the History of Colgate Rochester Divinity School', *Foundations* 10.1 (January–March, 1967), p. 67. Note the ironic invocation of tradition in this statement.
[23] Sharpe, *Walter Rauschenbusch*, p. 52.
[24] Cf. Harvey, *Another City*, *passim*; and H. Bloom, *The American Religion: The Emergence of the Post-Christian Nation* (New York: Simon and Schuster, 1992), *passim*; and the essays in the present volume by Mike Broadway and Beth Newman.
[25] D.H. Williams, *Retrieving the Tradition and Renewing Evangelicalism: A Primer for Suspicious Protestants* (Grand Rapids: Eerdmans, 1999), p. 9. Italics original.
[26] The work of R.L. Wilken stands out as an effort to address this on a more ecumenical scope. Cf. the collection of his outstanding essays, *Remembering the Christian Past* (Grand Rapids: Eerdmans, 1995). This diagnosis reflects again the way in which the church reflects the culture around it. Kammen, *Mystic Chords*, p.701, notes of America, 'the penchant for amnesia is greater here'.
[27] I will focus on Baptists in this essay. I believe that this sort of analysis needs to be extended to American evangelicalism more generally.

loss of identity. Were *precisely amnesia* the problem, one would expect there to be as well a corresponding loss of ability to sense threat to or change in identity.

While perhaps not sensing actual change, Baptists do manifest a sense of threat of change in what they regard to be their identity. Both aspects of this are important.[28] Writings have recently appeared in fair number declaring that 'Baptist' is 'more than just a name', that Baptists have 'principles worth protecting', because their identity is bound up in something 'fragile' and in need of the rally of a 'Baptist battle cry'.[29] At least with regard to being Baptist, a sense of identity remains intact enough to give this awareness of actual or threatened loss. If this is so, then memory and tradition remain in some way operative, as Hinson's observation indicates. I would argue, though, that this sense is not strong enough to allow full awareness of the nature of the change. Eric Ohlmann has stated the matter with clarity, 'Not knowing what rightfully belongs to our heritage, we are inadvertently and recklessly discarding some priceless heirlooms'.[30] Ironically, the discarding often takes place in the very name of upholding tradition.

Three questions now confront us: first, do we in fact find tradition operating in Baptist thought? Secondly, if so, how does it function; and, thirdly, if the problem in Baptist thought is not precisely amnesia, what is it and what are the implications?

Turning to the first question, we do indeed find tradition working in Baptist thought. As frequently as the authority of tradition was cast out the front door by Baptists of the last century and a half that same authority has, so to speak, slipped quietly in again through the back door. Dismissals of tradition notwithstanding, invocations of tradition, most often implicit, have been numerous in Baptists' last century and a half in America. None other than Wayland, even while dismissing the bearers of tradition and his own 'qualification' to be such a bearer, stated forcefully that 'Baptists have *ever* believed in the entire and absolute independence of the churches'.[31] 'Are not', asked William Cecil Duncan, 'the views...of

---

[28] I will not address the question of whether the Baptists I am considering have a sense of loss of catholic identity. While this is a very important question, my focus is on an explicitly Baptist identity. I contend that this narrower sense of identity that I am discussing affects the broader, perhaps more important, sense of identity.

[29] For titles on Baptist identity including these words, cf. Norman, *More Than Just a Name*; G. Parker, *Principles Worth Protecting* (Macon, GA: Smyth & Helwys, 1993); Shurden, *The Baptist Identity*; and Cothen and Dunn, *Soul Freedom*.

[30] E.H. Ohlmann, 'The Essence of the Baptists: A Reexamination', *Perspectives in Religious Studies* 13.1 (Winter, 1983), p. 83.

[31] Wayland, *Notes*, p.177. Italics mine. I note this not for the specific belief, but for the certainty with which one who 'pretends to no learning in ecclesiastical history' (p.16).

those known among Christians as Baptists, substantially, and in all essential points, identical with the doctrines...of Christianity during this Apostolic period'?[32] Even as he offered a 'new interpretation' of Baptist life and faith, E.Y. Mullins invoked soul competency as 'the historical significance of Baptists', and the significance to which he attributed this was great indeed.[33] Rauschenbusch noted that Baptists have *'never* put the future under bond to the past'.[34] Anderson lauded Baptist rejection of tradition as one of their 'historical principles'.[35] Robert P. Jones has found no contradiction in arguing against tradition's normativity precisely because he believes, 'Baptists have *always* understood this [anti-creedalism and principal of confessional revisionism] in part'.[36] Indeed, Baptist tradition's content has been depicted as so clear, it seems to take on a life of its own: '[A] certain genius has permeated Baptist development, has sustained Baptists through thick and thin, has enabled Baptists to make major contributions to human civilization, and will guarantee the Baptist future.'[37] All of these are important claims on behalf of tradition.

We come then to our second question: what is the function of tradition in Baptist life? We may answer this best perhaps by asking how tradition functions in modern religion generally.

No Belief Without Tradition, No Tradition Without Memory

Baptists seem to lack the ability either to dismiss tradition completely or make good sense of it, despite their rhetoric and perhaps despite their

---

[32] Duncan, *A Brief History*, pp. 71-72.
[33] Mullins, *Axioms of Religion*, pp. 45-58.
[34] Quoted in Moore, 'Academic Freedom', p. 67.
[35] Anderson, 'Historical Baptist Principles', *passim*.
[36] R.P. Jones, 'Revision-ing (sic) Baptist Identity from a Theocentric Perspective', *Perspectives in Religious Studies* 26.1 (Spring, 1999), pp. 37, 46. Italics mine.
[37] C.W. Deweese, 'Ten Traits of the Baptist Genius', *The Baptist Studies Bulletin: A Monthly Emagazine Bridging Baptists Yesterday and Today* 3.1 (January, 2004): http://www.mercer.edu/baptiststudies/jan04.htm

Deweese has frequently invoked this language. Cf. his 'The Resiliency of Historic Baptist Principles', *The Baptist Studies Bulletin: A Monthly Emagazine Bridging Baptists Yesterday and Today* 3.2 (February, 2004): http://www.mercer.edu/baptiststudies/feb04.htm. 'Century after century, Baptist principles have survived mild tampering and deliberate manipulation in a no-compromise fashion. *Their* force and character have risen victoriously during times of persecution. *They* have hung tough when misguided leaders attempted to revise them for personal or institutional advantage. *Their* integrity and usefulness have persisted even when well-intentioned Baptists have neglected them.' Italics mine. Note that even the title of this electronic publication rests upon Baptist tradition.

intentions. We must ask why this is the case. Are Baptists simply inconsistent, their thinking not as precise as it ought to be? Or is it the case that tradition is somehow inescapable, despite modern pretenses that would elevate individual experience and/or individual interpretation of the canonical texts? I would argue that it is the latter. Nicholas Wolterstorff is correct to observe that it is incoherent to take a position beyond all tradition.[38] This may be true especially for those communions that, like Baptists, have been profoundly influenced by Enlightenment categories. Indeed, the testimony of theology, philosophy, and the social sciences lend support to the claim that tradition is inescapable, and refusal to give it serious consideration carries detrimental consequences.

There is a profound ambiguity concerning tradition in late modernity, such as we have seen in Baptists. It has been explored in recent work by French sociologist Danielle Hervieu-Léger. She has concluded that while tradition is indeed necessary to religious life, it is called into question by modernity. We live in a 'post traditional' age, an age in which tradition is dismissed but does not withdraw, rather it remains even as it is influenced by modern individualism.[39] For the purposes of this essay, a brief survey must suffice in order that we might turn to consider the bearing of this on the question of amnesia.

Hervieu-Léger has inquired into the failure of the once regnant secularization theory to forecast the end of religion and religious institutions even as she acknowledges that modernity has altered religious belief. While modernity has called into radical question traditional systems of belief, belief itself has not been forsaken. Believing plays a crucial role in modernity, for in spite of the demystification of the world through science and technology, these 'clearly have not obliterated the need for *assurance* which is at the source of the search to make the experience of life intelligible and which constantly evokes the question why'.[40] Belief, she contends, is a conscious or unconscious surrender of the self to an order that imposes itself from the outside.

Her inquiry has thus led her to define religion principally in terms of the invocation of tradition to provide this order and so to support belief.[41] Religion is a 'chain of memory' that cannot do without tradition if it is to have any communal embodiment. Though this might seem contradictory,

---

[38] N. Wolterstorff, *John Locke and the Ethics of Belief* (Cambridge: Cambridge University Press, 1996), p. 246, quoted in T. Tilley, *Inventing Catholic Tradition* (Maryknoll, NY: Orbis, 2000), p. 19. Cf. Harmon, 'The Authority of the Community', pp. 591-92.
[39] D. Hervieu-Léger, *Religion as a Chain of Memory* (trans. Simon Lee; New Brunswick, NJ: Rutgers University Press, 2000).
[40] Hervieu-Léger, *Chain of Memory*, pp. 72-73. Italics original.
[41] Hervieu-Léger, *Chain of Memory*, pp. 72-76.

she concludes that modernity does indeed produce what is in essence contrary to itself.[42]

That ordering of life that exalts the self as a private project ironically gropes for tradition to give it content beyond the self. In the process, claims Hervieu-Léger, it comes to be 'perpetually haunted by its opposite'.[43] 'In order for meaning to have an effect, there must be at a given point the collective effect of meaning shared; meaning that is individually constructed must be attested by others, it must be given social confirmation.'[44] Thus while modern individuals seek out 'affinity groups' in which to share meaning, this social confirmation comes through reference to something beyond the desire of individuals; a common lineage—a tradition. Voluntary groups are able to endure through reference to the continuity and authority of a shared past. She concludes, therefore, that the ultimate form of individualism is collective.[45]

Certainly in modernity, 'all syncretisms are possible'; all combinations of belief forms are imaginable. Yet in all but the most individualistic religiosity, belief is accompanied by the invocation of the authority of a tradition that ensures that the meaning of present actions is located within a transcendent realm.[46] There must be, Hervieu-Léger argues, some sort of perceived continuity with the past, the expression of a lineage to which a believer lays claim and which confers membership in a spiritual community that gathers past, present, and future members together.[47]

---

[42] Harvey, *Another City*, pp. 123-24, gives an excellent example of the way in which, in the name of individual sufficiency, such basic tasks as rearing children is ceded over to a legion of technicians.
[43] Hervieu-Léger, *Chain of Memory*, p.93.
[44] Hervieu-Léger, *Chain of Memory*, p. 94.
[45] Hervieu-Léger, *Chain of Memory*, pp. 94-96. The contours sketched by Hervieu-Léger are striking in the accuracy with which Wayland described the Baptist understanding of the church. The church for Wayland, *Notes*, pp.179-80, is comprised of 'Men who, by such an examination of the New Testament, arrive at the same conclusions respecting its requirements unite together.... In doing this, however, they neither assume on the one hand, nor concede on the other, any power of original legislation over each other.' We must remember Wayland's presumption of a common Baptist lineage and tradition.
[46] Hervieu-Léger, *Chain of Memory*, pp. 72-76. The fact of this hyper-individualism, what R. Bellah, et al. call 'Sheilaism', and accompanying abandoning of religious institutions, or consumerization of 'religious goods', should not be underestimated. Our focus, however, is upon those communities of belief that still exist in and negotiate modernity and still preserve a sense of collective identity. Cf. R. Bellah, et al. *Habits of the Heart: Individualism and Commitment in American Life* (New York, NY: Harper & Row, Publishers, 1985), pp. 220-221.
[47] Hervieu-Léger, *Chain of Memory*, pp. 81-86.

The distinctive mark of tradition, then, is that it at least claims to actualize the past in the present, and so to locate human lives within the ongoing memory of some essential core reality that enables human life to make sense.[48] McClendon recognizes this as well. 'Unquestionably in every church, indeed in every human community, there is a strong tendency...to hold fast to the ways of the recent past.'[49] James Booth has likewise noted that political and religious communities require for their very being a tie between past, present and future. This tie is rooted in a narrative that can be prefaced by the pronoun 'our'. Absence of this shared narrative of lineage results in communities turning into 'leaves scattered by the wind'.[50] The theological task in light of this reality, according to McClendon, is to recognize and honor this conservative tendency, for 'without it, human life together would hardly be possible, since we could never in any circumstance know what to expect from others'.[51]

Among the Baptists I have been examining, invocations of tradition have been precisely in order to show continuity, and to legitimate particular configurations of Baptist life. They have occasionally reached to the earliest Christian community for this. We saw earlier Duncan rhetorically ask whether Baptists' views are not identical with those of the apostolic period. He continued, Baptists are not 'like' the early Christians. 'It is the *same* Church'.[52] More frequent have been connections of Baptists to 'principles' of the Reformation, foremost the idea of *sola scriptura* and the supposed Reformation dismissal of tradition.[53] Anderson claimed that the early Protestants 'had no further use for popes, bishops, creeds, or external authority', and that Baptists 'have tried to carry Protestant principles through to their legitimate

---

[48] Hervieu-Léger, *Chain of Memory*, p. 88.

[49] J.W. McClendon, Jr, *Systematic Theology: Doctrine* (Nashville, TN: Abingdon Press, 1994), p.470. I would take exception only to the word 'recent'. Our Baptist examples have demonstrated most often claims to a well-established and venerable tradition. Cf. Holmes, *Listening to the Past*, p. 6, who notes that some sense of historical location is unavoidable.

[50] W.J. Booth, 'Communities of Memory: On Identity, Memory, and Debt', *American Political Science Review* 93.2 (June, 1999), pp. 249-60. I would question a too easy distinction between 'political' and 'religious' communities. We will see that tradition is itself a political phenomenon. Cf. Kammen, *Mystic Chords*, p. 5.

[51] McClendon, *Doctrine*, p. 470.

[52] Duncan, *A Brief History of the Baptists*, pp. 71-72. Italics original.

[53] Cf. Harmon, 'The Authority of the Community', pp. 592-93. The very notion of *sola scriptura* and its Reformation pedigree are examined in Williams, *Retrieving the Tradition*, pp.173-204 and 229-234; C.E. Braaten and R.W. Jenson (eds.), *The Catholicity of the Reformation* (Grand Rapids, MI: Eerdmans, 1996); and Holmes, *Listening to the Past*, p. 7. *Sola scriptura* claims are often placed in tandem with the aforementioned claim for a right of individual interpretation.

conclusions.'[54] Thus '[t]hey are Protestants of Protestants'.[55] Cecil Sherman concludes that the Reformation meant that 'The old material that had been authority for hundreds of years had to go'.[56] This revolution in authority was brought to completion in the Baptists. 'So, with the Bible in hand, these first Baptists changed everything. Authority had rested in bishops, councils, and traditions. Now authority would be in the Bible.'[57]

Also prevalent has been an invocation of tradition in a more distinctively American-republican cast. This is an aspect of making reference to Baptist tradition precisely in order to give credence to the very ideas of destiny and progress that Kammen explains displaced tradition among Americans. Landmark Baptist leader J.R. Graves noted that it was the Baptists who bequeathed 'Republicanism and republican institutions' to the world. It was from Baptists that these ideas came even to Thomas Jefferson.[58] Jenkins interpreted Baptist ideals coming to America as analogous to Israel crossing the Red Sea.[59] Mullins waxed eloquent in his vision for the triumph of liberal democracy. Such triumph meant, he believed, that the world was approaching a 'Baptist age'.[60] In this we get a strong sense indeed of the emergence and development of what Nathan Hatch has called 'republican eschatology' in which America was assigned a principal role in providential history.[61] In the Baptist version of this, it was America, with its inheritance of Baptist ideals that had been divinely reserved for the noble end of realization of religious liberty.[62] The content of Baptist tradition was thus for Mullins to some degree an eschatological datum.

Quite obviously, some of these appeals have at the very least problematic connections with historical fact, while others may be contested as apt readings of history. This strange state of affairs in which Baptists have appealed to tradition in articulating normative positions,

---

[54] Anderson, 'Historical Baptist Principles', pp. 15-16.
[55] Anderson, 'Historical Baptist Principles', pp. 15-16.
[56] C.E. Sherman, 'The Bible is the Sole Written Authority for Baptist Faith and Practice', in Deweese (ed.), *Defining Baptist Convictions*, p. 55.
[57] Sherman, 'The Bible', p. 55. Cf. McClendon, *Doctrine*, pp. 468-72, discusses tradition as a challenge to biblical authority. He rightly includes among such challenges, however, biblical criticism and inerrancy. Cf. too Kammen, *Mystic Chords*, p. 7.
[58] J.R. Graves, 'Introduction', in G.H. Orchard, *A Concise History of Foreign Baptists* (Nashville, TN: Graves, Marks, & Rutland, 1855), pp. xviii-xix.
[59] F.L. Anderson, 'Introduction', in *Baptist Fundamentals*, pp. 27-28.
[60] Mullins, *Axioms*, pp. 66-67 and 275.
[61] N.O. Hatch, *The Sacred Cause of Liberty: Republican Thought and the Millennium in Revolutionary New England* (New Haven, CT: Yale University Press, 1977), pp. 145-48 and 170-71.
[62] Anderson, 'Introduction', p. 27.

even as they have denied 'tradition' per se a normative role, has left them unable to make good sense of their own situation. Norman provides a recent clear example in his own articulation of Baptist theological identity. He rightly interprets recent arguments within the Southern Baptist Convention and those groups that have come to be positioned at the margins of Southern Baptist life as a debate over a normative interpretation of Baptist history, even if he does not use that precise term. He then identifies two major interpretive traditions which he designates 'Reformation' and 'Enlightenment' and offers an analysis of writings on Baptist principles from both standpoints. Interestingly, authorities for theology in these traditions are, respectively, the Bible and experience. There is no place in either for tradition as a source of understanding.[63] Indeed, he joins those who would reject tradition on the basis of an assumed Reformation principle of *sola scriptura*.[64] Yet, in spelling out his position, he tacitly employs an argument from tradition. 'The Reformation tradition of Baptist distinctives contains the most historical continuity and theological stability.'[65] Notably, he does not explain the reference point that enables him to name this continuity and stability and so in the end articulates a vision of Baptist identity not fully consonant with the earliest Baptists.

This is, however, significant. The invocations of tradition do not require faithfulness to the past, pretensions to replicate it almost exactly notwithstanding. Kammen quotes Moses Finley's bold claim that historical reliability is irrelevant 'so long as the tradition is accepted, it works, and must work if the society is not to fall apart'.[66] Indeed, the function of tradition is not to preserve the past, but to supply cohesion on the basis of lineage, regardless of the degree of (re-)construction of that lineage involved. The ambiguity of tradition in modernity, certainly including Baptist life, is that it is at once necessary for religious communities to exist and function, and yet it is not necessarily associated with accurate recall and interpretation of the past.

Hervieu-Léger's analysis includes this ambiguity. The future of religion, she contends, is associated with the problem of collective memory. Lineage involves mention of the past, memories that are consciously shared and passed on. These are 'authorized' memories that are passed on in various ways.[67] We might say they are 'authoritative' memories, for the core of religious power is constituted by recognized

---

[63] Norman, *More Than Just a Name*, pp. 2-18. Certainly his methodological choice of using narrow dichotomies to contrast the two approaches limits him tremendously.

[64] Norman, *More Than Just a Name*, p. 41.

[65] Norman, *More Than Just a Name*, p. 43.

[66] Kammen, *Mystic Chords*, p. 7. Cf. Hervieu-Léger, *Chain of Memory*, p. 96.

[67] Hervieu-Léger, *Chain of Memory*, pp. 123-26.

ability to expound the true memory of the group.[68] At the same time, a chief characteristic of modern societies is that they are no longer societies of memory; that is, ordered with a view toward reproducing that which is inherited. There is a profound loss of continuity in modern collective memory. There is rather 'anomic memory', memory as simply some of the pieces of information with which persons in modern society are inundated and from which they are expected and to make their own identities and order their own lives.[69]

Kammen notes that people who live in vacuums concoct memories.[70] Yet because no vacuum is total, the utterly novel concoction is rare. This is true in the case of Baptists. Because religious communities continue in modernity, there is not a total loss of collective memory as a functional phenomenon. Yet the memory itself, its nature, contents, and implications, becomes a question before us.

Because of the breakdown in continuity in memory and tradition, their construction and articulation becomes a matter of an entrepreneurial competition of goods peddled to persons living in the midst of modernity. Helpful here is Anne Swidler's theory of the dynamics of social action and identity construction in settled and unsettled times.[71] Swidler postulates that culture provides a 'tool kit' or 'repertoire' from which strategies of action and identities are constructed, sets of skills and habits yielding images of the world.[72] In settled times, culture is integrated with action. The images of the world, including communal identity within it and corresponding strategies of action, have the authority of common sense. These ways of existence are passed down through the generations, preserving and perpetuating collective memory through tradition.

Large-scale breakdown in legitimation of the 'common sense' ways of ordering and speaking of life brings a society into an unsettled time. In such times, there is competition to establish new images of the world and with them strategies and patterns of social action. There are '[b]ursts of ideological activism', Swidler notes, 'in periods when competing ways of organizing action are developing and contending for dominance'.[73]

---

[68] Hervieu-Léger, *Chain of Memory*, p. 126. Thus we see a nearly constant competition in Baptist life to expound the authoritative memory of what it means to be Baptist, whether it is between an educated elite and 'the common person' as in Wayland, or representatives of opposing theological viewpoints in the recent Southern Baptist Convention.

[69] Hervieu-Léger, *Chain of Memory*, pp. 128-132.

[70] Kammen, *Mystic Chords*, p. 656.

[71] A. Swidler, 'Culture in Action: Symbols and Strategies', *American Sociological Review* 51.2 (April, 1986), pp. 273-86. While no period in a culture is entirely settled or entirely unsettled, we may make relative distinctions.

[72] Swidler, 'Culture in Action', pp. 276-77.

[73] Swidler, 'Culture in Action', pp. 278-79.

Doubtless, the successive revolutions of modernity, intellectual and otherwise, have made it a time in which unsettledness has become a near normal state. How then does tradition function?

Hervieu-Léger notes three modern constructions of traditionalism identified by George Balandier. These constitute the field within which the claims and realities of the modern functioning of tradition unfold, and provide helpful insight into Baptist employment of tradition.[74] The first is 'fundamental traditionalism'. Here the most deeply rooted values and models of social and cultural practice are maintained against the claims and conventions of modernity. Fundamental traditionalism serves to maintain 'a state of permanence' amid modernity, an enclave maintaining settled ways in the midst of unsettledness.

'Formal traditionalism' upholds the forms of the socio-cultural practices within modernity, yet changes the substance in some degree of accommodation to modernity. It gives the appearance of continuity, and indeed preserves a link with the past while serving new designs and new demands upon the community.

Finally, 'pseudo-traditionalism' occurs most notably in periods of most acutely perceived accelerated change, and provides a reassuring familiarity in the midst of great disruption. Here, however, tradition provides a stock of symbols and images that enable a new construction of ways of understanding and living while conforming to modern categories and conventions.[75]

In light of the foregoing, I would urge that we expand the theological task to which McClendon referred. Tradition's intent may indeed be conservative of identity, yet the conservative impulse of tradition may be apparent only. In reality it may be far from conservative. As a profoundly complex reality in and through which a community's identity and way of life is negotiated, argued, and constructed, tradition is, as Kammen notes, a political phenomenon.[76] This renders ambiguous the memory that is borne by tradition. The content and media of memory thus become matters for theological reflection. This raises again our third question; that of amnesia.

(Par)amnesia

The examples drawn here from Baptist writings appear to intend a 'fundamental' or perhaps 'formal' traditionalism, even though they would just as certainly eschew either term. In the first case, we would locate the less sophisticated argument that Baptists now are precisely what

---

[74] Hervieu-Léger, *Chain of Memory*, pp. 88-89.
[75] G. Balandier, *Le Désordre. Élogue du mouvement* (Paris: Fayard, 1988), pp. 37-38, quoted in Hervieu-Léger, *Chain of Memory*, pp. 88-89.
[76] Kammen, *Mystic Chords*, p. 5.

they have always been; in the second, those claims that traditional Baptist principles enable Baptists to meet the challenges of the contemporary situation in creative and prophetic ways.

Yet the degree of change that is evident throughout the course of Baptist existence leads me to conclude that our Baptists throughout the nineteenth century manifested characteristics of 'pseudo-traditionalism', emerging as it has during unsettled times in the context of the American republic and becoming so accommodated to the American republican version of liberal democracy. During the twentieth century, however, Baptist tradition has taken on the characteristics more of a formal traditionalism, with the substantive connection to the past having been fundamentally redefined in the previous century.[77] This process has caused a fundamental, though not total, alteration and, one could argue, loss of the content of Baptist memory even if the forms of its expression have remained.[78] The memory to which tradition is joined is of more recent vintage. Baptists appear in their employment of tradition thus to suffer what Kammen terms a shallow remembering and deeper forgetting.[79]

A better diagnosis than amnesia, I have come to conclude, is one described more properly as *paramnesia*. Where amnesia is the absence of memory and a concomitant loss of identity, Edward S. Casey has defined paramnesia as *remembering the wrong thing*.[80] The concomitant in this case is altered identity in accord with a faulty memory. Casey contends that this is a threat in its own right, apart from amnesia. The ramifications are indeed grim.

Hervieu-Léger cautions that a 'draining of memory' threatens the survival of religion.[81] Political scientist James Booth observes that we are

---

[77] Hervieu-Léger, *Chain of Memory*, p. 141, notes that accelerated change paradoxically gives rise to appeals to memory. We can see that in the last century, such appeals to Baptist tradition have come precisely at unsettled times such as the fundamentalist–modernist controversy, the aftermath of Landmark agitation, and the shift to a more theologically and socially conservative stance in the Southern Baptist Convention.

[78] Cf., as an example, my essay in *Baptist Sacramentalism* in which I demonstrate how the Baptist tradition of religious liberty has been formally retained, and yet the application has been expanded to matters of church practice. While this is something that early Baptists did not say, they are now remembered as saying precisely that—'*always*'.

[79] Kammen, *Mystic Chords*, p. 656. This would serve to explain the oft-bemoaned pattern in Baptist studies among many within branch Baptist family in the American South that, when speaking of 'early Baptists', what is intended is Baptists from around 1845, the year in which the Southern Baptist Convention was founded.

[80] E.S. Casey, *Remembering: A Phenomenological Study* (Studies in Phenomenology and Existential Philosophy, Studies in Continental Thought; Bloomington, IN: Indiana University Press, 1987), pp. 280-84.

[81] Hervieu-Léger, *Chain of Memory*, p. 141.

not at liberty simply to pick and choose our traditions though we are to decide what future to fashion out of that which has been received. Paramnesia causes communities to lose sight of fashioning and construction under the illusion of continuity, and so to lose sight of the moral presence of the past, thus effectively breaking with the past in a strong sense. It is paramnesia, I believe, that has come in many instances to guide Baptist reflection on what it is to be Baptist at all.

Theological Implications of Paramnesia

What are the theological implications of this paramnesiac state? My reflection to this end has been informed by the recent work of Episcopal theologians Ephraim Radner and R.R. Reno. Both engage in sustained examination of and theological reflection on the church in its divided state. Their work speaks to paramnesia, though they do not develop their theses in explicitly memorial terms. I will seek to make this connection clearer, because their work contributes what I take to be a necessary feature to their analysis and suggests a task for Baptist theology.

I will focus here on Reno, who draws on Radner's work, and argues that theology is confused, disordered, and obscured by the divided state of Christianity. Theology has too often come to be focused not on the central convictions of the Christian faith, but on peripheral matters that divide the churches.[82] Drawn from the center of first-order language and practice, theology would be Christ-formed in logic, shape, and content. This, of course, is the intent of the church catholic's 'great tradition'. Frequently, however, it goes about shoring up the periphery of Christian thought and practice where divisions are most evident and revolve around contested issues. The 'priorities of the periphery' have come to overwhelm those of the center.[83]

Reno argues that there are three broad strategies in the western church by which, over many years, Roman Catholics and Protestants each argued for the truth of their churches and the falsity of their rivals in a situation of division. He terms these strategies of 'supersessionism'. Two of them are more prominent in the history of theology. Catholics have utilized a 'juridical supersessionism', maintaining that the unity of the true church is found in the structures of the church subject to the pope.[84] Protestants,

---

[82] R.R. Reno, 'Theology in the Ruins of the Church', *Pro Ecclesia* 12.1 (Winter 2003), pp. 15-36.
[83] Reno, 'Theology in the Ruins', p. 30.
[84] Reno, 'Theology in the Ruins', pp. 21-26.

for their part, have asserted a 'doctrinal supersessionism' in which the criterion of unity is found in fidelity to a correct confessional stance.[85]

Baptists have certainly shared from their inception the doctrinal supersession characteristic of all Protestants.[86] In American, they have also manifested at least a version of juridical supersession in the movement known as Landmarkism. Reno names as well a less prominent, third form of supersessionism that has existed alongside and within many expressions of Baptist thought in America over the last two centuries. This is 'conceptual supersessionism' that privileges some theory apart from first-order Christian language and practice as the source of cogency, vigor, and cognitive potency of the faith.[87] He locates this primarily in the programs of individual theologians; Rahner's transcendental anthropology for example.

We find this analogously among Baptists in E.Y. Mullins' doctrine of soul competency. Mullins defined Christianity in terms of six axioms embodied, if not explicitly stated, in the New Testament. The distinctive of Baptists was that they alone had most consistently held to a mother principle from which these axioms themselves emerge, that of the soul's competency in religion. This clearly demonstrates Reno's assertion that scripture itself must be displaced in order to make the case for any strategy of supersessionism.[88]

Mullins is surely a linchpin in Baptist thought. The refrains of his articulation of Baptist tradition and identity have resounded in Baptist voices ever since.[89] The concept that sets Baptists apart *is* thus Baptist

---

[85] Reno, 'Theology in the Ruins', pp. 26-30. Of course, these strategies have had the effect of dividing the Roman Catholic Church from both the Orthodox and Protestant churches as well as splintering Protestant churches still further along confessional lines.

[86] Examples of this throughout Baptist literature over the entire scope of their existence are so abundant that even a representative list is not possible here. I would only note here that E. Radner notes the way in which the doctrine of Christ's presence in the Eucharist has been a chief locus for this doctrinal claim. Cf. his *The End of the Church: A Pneumatology of Christian Division in the West* (Grand Rapids, MI: Eerdmans, 1998), pp. 199-275, et *passim*. We find clear examples of this in the Particular Baptists' *Second London Confession*, article XXX and the General Baptists' *An Orthodox Creed*, XXXIII, see W.L. Lumpkin, *Baptist Confessions of Faith* (Valley Forge, PA: Judson Press, 1969), pp. 291-293 and 321-322. Each of these Baptist pieces speaks of the true nature of Christ's presence in the Supper and rejects 'popish' teachings on the same.

[87] Reno, 'Theology in the Ruins', p. 25. Reno gives examples of this only from the Catholic side.

[88] Mullins, *The Axioms of Religion*. Cf. Reno, 'Theology in the Ruins', pp. 28-30.

[89] H. Bloom, *The American Religion: The Emergence of the Post-Christian Nation* (New York: Simon & Schuster, 1992), p. 199, notes that Mullins 'was the not the founder of the Southern Baptists but their re-founder, the definer of their creedless faith'. I would note, though, that we may also find in other nineteenth century Baptist writers in

tradition, drawn together in Mullins's articulation of soul competency, the contents of which are a misremembering of the Baptist past and lead to a severe truncation of the memory of vital aspects of the Christian past. The effect is the same throughout. Baptists are set apart from others as either the only true Christians or, more commonly, as the most true Christians. Mullins stated that fidelity to soul competency, which is the mother principle from which the very axioms of religion itself emerged in the New Testament, is that *'which separates [Baptists] from all other Christian bodies'*.[90]

In much recent Baptist thought, indeed, much Baptist thought over the last two hundred years of their existence, the widely-shared features of Christian life and practice are bypassed in order to give primacy of place to that which divides.[91] Baptists, then, are in no wise unique, but are bound together with other communions in that ironic unity of seeking distinctiveness. We are likewise bound in the effects of that dismal unity.

Reno's concern is with a weakened theology as an element of this unity. Theology, to be truthful, must be Christ-formed in logic, structure, and content. Since theology is born of the life of the church, this 'christoformation' must emanate from that communion which, by the power of the Holy Spirit, is constituted as the very body of Christ.[92] Further, the power to conform the logic, structure, and content to Christ is in the church, for it is 'equipped with the pneumatic instruments—Word and sacrament'.[93] These are the very means of Christian memory. Yet the varieties of supersessionism threaten to remove theology, and in particular the first-order theology of prayer and worship, from this 'animating core', and so from faithful memory.[94]

America, albeit without the fullness of development in Mullins, more inchoate expressions of what became in Mullins the doctrine of soul competency.

[90] Mullins, *Axioms of Religion*, p. 50. Emphasis mine. On the division wrought by this Baptist conceptual supersessionism, cf. Mullins, *Axioms of Religion*, pp. 59-65, in which he censured Roman Catholicism for its sacramental and priestly system of mediation presuming the soul's incompetence; and the various Protestant bodies judged as being in varying degrees inconsistent, in one way or another too beclouded by 'tradition', to discover the mother principle upon which pure religion rests. Mullins felt certain, however, that eventually all other Christian bodies, indeed all persons of good faith, would embrace this Baptist position in the coming 'Baptist age of the world'.

[91] Reno, 'Theology in the Ruins', p. 27, notes that conceptual supersessionism in particular yields a generally unpersuasive theology that is difficult to understand. I would note anecdotally that non-Baptist readers of my article, 'A New Question in Baptist History: Seeking a Catholic Spirit Among Early Baptists', *Pro Ecclesia* 8.1 (Winter, 1999) pp. 51-72, have expressed difficulty with the very alien concept of soul competency.

[92] Reno, 'Theology in the Ruins', pp. 17-19.
[93] Reno, 'Theology in the Ruins', p. 19.
[94] Reno, 'Theology in the Ruins', p. 30.

What happens when theology is not simply displaced from the core, but the very core itself has been displaced? What then becomes of the life and practices of the community? In portions of Baptist life and thought, the displacement of which Reno speaks has been particularly alarming. For Baptists, in many cases, the core itself has been remade in the cast of Enlightenment individualism.[95] *This* becomes the content of memory. The erstwhile 'pneumatic instruments', therefore, cannot then but produce paramnesia.[96] The formation wrought by memory and tradition proceeds under the constitution of paramnesia. Baptist identity thus falls prey to being constituted by and constitutive of another reality than that of Christ.[97]

I must allow a representative case to suffice to show the way in which a particular instrument of memory, baptism, has undergone striking alteration over the course of Baptist history.[98] For the first two hundred years of their existence, Baptists displayed awareness of formation in the memory of Christ even while lamenting division among Christians, as does Reno. This formation was ecclesial and it was sacramental, for in church and sacrament was what Thomas Grantham called 'the form of Godliness', neglect of which would quickly cause true religion to vanish 'or become unknown conceit, every man being at liberty to follow (what he supposes to be) the motions of the Spirit of God, in which there is so great a probability of being mistaken as in nothing more...'.[99] He defined true religion in terms of Titus 2.11-14, which speaks of the formation of

---

[95] We may certainly see this displacement in the dust jacket of a recent book, R.W. Stacy (ed.), *A Baptist's Theology* (Macon, GA: Smyth & Helwys, 1999), the back cover of which notes that the book is '[c]omposed from the distinctive Baptist perspective that no one Baptist can speak with authority for another in matters of faith.'

[96] I trace this broadly in 'Re-envisioning Baptist Identity', and with particular reference to the sacraments in 'Sacraments and Religious Liberty'.

[97] I do not mean in any way to imply that this is true in every case. Without doubt, scripture and the church's tradition inform us that God can bring about what God intends quite apart from the best or worst degrees of human faithfulness to God's decrees. Still, that does not give us excuse to ignore these matters.

[98] See, also, my earlier discussion of this, 'Memorial Dimensions of Baptism', in S.E. Porter and A.R. Cross (eds), *Dimensions of Baptism: Biblcal and Theological Studies* (*Journal for the Study of the New Testament Supplement Series*, 234; Sheffield: Sheffield Academic Press, 2002), pp. 304-24.

[99] T. Grantham, *Christianismus Primitivus: or The Ancient Christian Religion* (London: n.p. 1678), II/2.i.1. I would note that a residue of this remained even once the formal distancing from tradition had commenced. A striking example would be the evening hymn by John Leland, 'The Day is Past and Gone', which employs the ancient liturgical analogy of sleep and death: 'The day is past and gone, The evening shade appears; O may we all remember well The night of death is near.' J. Leland, 'Evening Hymn', in L.F. Greene (ed.), *The Writings of the Late Elder John Leland* (New York: Arno Press and *The New York Times*, 1969 [1845]), p. 322.

a people. In this context, Grantham plainly affirmed the mediation of grace in baptism for the sake of conformity to Christ.[100] Grantham, an Arminian, was not alone in holding this view of the initiatory rite. Evangelical Calvinist Andrew Fuller noted roughly a century later that 'Sin is washed away in baptism in the same sense as Christ's flesh is eaten, and his blood drunk in the Lord's Supper: the sign...leads to the thing signified'.[101]

Yet our Baptists have undergone a marked shift over the past two hundred years. Another memory has emerged. The language by which they come to speak of baptism reveals if anything a more clearly memorial quality. Baptism is now a dramatic representation of the experience of conversion and faith. According to the *Baptist Faith and Message* (1963), it is 'an act of obedience *symbolizing the believer's faith in a crucified, buried, and risen Saviour...*'.[102] As such it is, in the words of one Baptist writer, 'a post-conversion dramatization of conversion'.[103]

Formation in a certain memory continues through this rite that in part constitutes Baptist tradition. Whether this is 'christoformation' is another matter. This initiatory rite either displaces memory of the gospel of Christ by asserting memory of individual appropriation of it, or else it reduces the gospel to individual appropriation of saving knowledge. In either case, individual believers and their belief have come to occupy the center of memory and so of tradition. Thus we are not surprised to find Stewart Newman assert that baptism's meaning is largely the meaning given to it by the person baptized.[104] Even though a type of baptismal interrogation is included in a recent Baptist ministers' manual, the focus is once again

---

[100] T. Grantham, *A Sigh for Peace: or The Cause of Division Discovered* (London: Printed for the Author, 1671), pp. 87-88: '...Baptism in the ordinary way of communicating the grace of the Gospel is antecedent to the reception thereof, & is propounded as a means wherein not only the Remission of our sins shall be granted to us, but as a condition whereupon we shall receive the grace of the Holy Ghost... [It] was foreordained to signifie and sacramentally to confer the grace of the pardon of sin, and the inward washing of the Conscience by Faith in the Bloud of Jesus Christ.'

[101] A. Fuller, 'Circular Letters', in *The Complete Works of the Rev. Andrew Fuller With a Memoir of His Life by Andrew Gunton Fuller* (2 vols; Boston, MA: Lincoln, Edmans, & Co., 1833), II, p. 469.

[102] H.H. Hobbs, *The Baptist Faith and Message* (Nashville, TN: Convention Press, 1971), p. 83. Emphasis mine. This definition is also given in the 1925 predecessor confession as well as the 2000 successor.

[103] C.W. Gaddy, *The Gift of Worship* (Nashville, TN: Broadman Press, 1992), pp. 141-42. Cf. J.M. Frost, *The Moral Dignity of Baptism* (Nashville, TN: Sunday School Board of the Southern Baptist Convention, 1939), p. 45: 'The very power of the ordinance lies in its *declarative* character. It declares in the plainest way what *we* believe, what *we* have experienced...'. Emphasis original.

[104] S.A. Newman, *A Free Church Perspective: A Study in Ecclesiology* (Wake Forest, NC: Stevens Book Press, 1986), p. 79.

on the individual. Rather than the traditional interrogation along the contours of the Apostles' Creed, the candidate is led by the minister to declare, '*I* take God as *my* Father, Jesus as *my* Savior...'.[105] No longer is the triune life of God the object of memory, nor participation in that life a declared intent. Modern Baptist baptism is a declaration of personal choice and meaning in the vehicle of a traditional rite. This is paramnesia.

Concluding (For Now, But Not Final) Words

With apologies to Carl Jung, bidden or unbidden, tradition is present in the theology and life of Baptists, and it functions. Addressing this fact and the situation as I have here depicted it will require much work. I would offer at this point only a sketch of the shape I think such an address should take.

A pressing need is to recast the way in which the authority of tradition is regarded and engaged. We have seen that Baptists tend to contest, at least formally, the idea of tradition's authority. For Baptists, notes Robert Jones in a clear example, 'tradition has no inherent authority *qua* tradition'.[106] This may well be true if authority is conceived as coercive power. Yet this is a deficient understanding of authority. I would suggest that we think of authority in terms of a moral claim. Were this the case, Jones' statement would be quite false. The past cannot but place a moral claim on the present. The dead place a moral claim on the living.[107] With regard to the earliest Baptists, this does not mean that we are to be slaves to their thought and practices. Indeed, their own claim becomes relativized by the authority of scripture and the tradition of the church catholic under which we and they alike stood and stand. Rather, I believe that this moral claim, whatever else it may mean, means that we have an obligation to listen to our past and seek to receive the testimony of those who have gone before us as accurately as possible.[108]

This is no simple claim or task. We find a profound meditation on this in Jacques Derrida's reflection on the task of speaking in memory of departed friends. Derrida acknowledges that in speaking of the dead we face dangers inherent in what appears to be a simple act of fidelity. We

---

[105] P.W. Powell, *The New Ministers Manual* (np: Annuity Board of the Southern Baptist Convention, 1996), p. 74. Emphasis mine.

[106] R.P. Jones, 'Revision-ing Baptist Identity', p. 37.

[107] I readily acknowledge that this recasting demands further work on my part, and what I offer here does not wrestle with the complexities of which I am aware. Still, I believe that this idea does hold potential aid in addressing the questions of tradition and its authority.

[108] This has been explored seminally by E. Wyschogrod, *An Ethics of Remembering: History, Heterology, and the Nameless Others* (Chicago, IL: University of Chicago Press, 1998).

find ourselves at a loss in attempting to speak of and in a sense for an 'other' who is no longer living. Yet 'this being at a loss also has to do with a duty: to let a friend speak, to turn speech over to him, his speech, and especially not to take it from him, not to take it in his place—no offense seems worse at the death of a friend'.[109]

This raises second, similar point, regarding the work of the Holy Spirit in the church through the media of memory. In *The End of the Church: A Pneumatology of Christian Division in the West*, Radner notes that in a time in which the practices of the church are diminished, the life of the Holy Spirit in it is reduced to mortal repentance.[110] That is to say that the memorial media, which ought to be signs of the unity of the church through their mediation of formation in Christ, are points of contention and division. Certainly Baptist practices by which memory and tradition are perpetuated in altered form are what Radner would describe as an 'insensible shell of ecclesial mortality'. As such, they may yet be 'by grace, a vehicle of inspired penance'.[111]

This names well the attitude in which we ought to undertake this work of engaging tradition. As we strive for faithful memory of the displaced core, we are aware that the displacement that has occurred. Thus it may well be memory that is more sorrowful than triumphalist. Yet this is appropriate, at least, perhaps, for the time being. Casey notes that mourning is etymologically implicit and so implicated in memory. Etymologically related to memory are 'care, solicitude, sorrow, and anxiety'. Memory and the tradition bound with it are in a sense sorrowful burdens; burdens because of the tenuous connection of memory to that which is remembered, yet borne as a demonstration of the worthiness to be remembered of that which is remembered. To remember is thus to care for that which is remembered.[112] In this way, by the grace alone of the one who Jesus said would lead us into remembrance (Jn 14.26), despite our collective wandering from our past and from the Christian past, even while purporting to preserve and celebrate them, we may be given to know ourselves more truly as we know God in Christ more truly.

---

[109] J. Derrida, *The Work of Mourning* (ed. and trans. P.–A. Brault and M. Naas; Chicago, IL: University of Chicago Press, 2001), pp. 5-6 and 29.

[110] Radner, *The End of the Church*, pp. 20-32 and 319. Cf. J. LeGoff, *History and Memory* (trans. S. Rendall and E. Claman; European Perspectives: A Series in Social Philosophy and Cultural Criticism; New York: Columbia University Press, 1992), p. 87.

[111] Radner, *End of the Church*, p. 1.

[112] Casey, *Remembering*, pp. 273-74.

CHAPTER 10

1653 or 1656: When did Oxford Baptists Join the Abingdon Association?

Larry J. Kreitzer

In 2003 New Road Baptist Church, Oxford, officially celebrated its 350th anniversary, and, as part of the various activities associated with the event, the fellowship commissioned a celebratory volume of essays exploring the life and history of the church. The resultant volume is edited by Rosie Chadwick and is entitled *A Protestant Catholic Church of Christ: Essays on the History and Life of New Road Baptist Church, Oxford*. The book was published by the church in April 2003 with an official book launch in the Town Hall in Oxford, followed by the opening of a special exhibition in the nearby Museum of Oxford entitled 'Dissenting Voices: The Story of Baptists in Oxford 1653-2003'. One of the articles published within the volume is on the seventeenth-century roots of the Baptists in Oxford.[1] Considering that the chapter deals with the beginnings of Baptist witness in Oxford, the matter of the dating of such beginnings is crucial within a volume dedicated to exploring the history and heritage of New Road Baptist Church. Unfortunately, there is an internal inconsistency regarding the date of the first confirmed evidence of the existence of the Baptist church in Oxford within the article. Roger Hayden presents two dates in this regard: 1653 and 1656. This inconsistency is confusing and needs clarification. I propose to attempt to address the matter under three headings.

First, the inconsistency of dates that are presented will be demonstrated. Then I will move on to offer a possible explanation as to how and why the two alternative year dates have arisen, and offer a suggestion as to how the historical question can be resolved. This will involve a careful examination of the two primary seventeenth-century

---

[1] Roger Hayden, '"Through grace they are preserved": Oxford Baptists, 1640-1715', in Rosie Chadwick (ed.), *A Protestant Catholic Church of Christ: Essays on the History and Life of New Road Baptist Church, Oxford* (Oxford: New Road Baptist Church, Oxford), pp. 9-33.

manuscripts that serve as their basis; each of these documents will be treated in turn.

1653 or 1656?

It is generally agreed that the official 'beginning' of Baptists in Oxford is to be associated with the date at which they were first welcomed into what became the Abingdon Association at a meeting which took place at the village of Tetsworth, south of Oxford on the road to London. The only real question is: when did this take place? Inexplicably, Hayden gives conflicting statements in this regard. For example, he states on page 9 that the date for this welcome into the life of the Abingdon Association was 17 March 1653:

> 'the first date for which there is indisputable evidence' of a Baptist church is 17 March 1653, when Oxford sent messengers to a meeting at Tetsworth of what was to become the Abingdon, or Berkshire, Association.[2]

The 1653 date is then again mentioned in passing four pages later of the article:

> There is evidence of Oxford people with Baptist views well before 1653.[3]

However, a few pages later Hayden twice asserts the date of 1656 in connection with Oxford Baptists joining the Abingdon Association:

> in 1656, Oxford sent messengers to meetings with fellow Baptists at Tetsworth, providing indisputable evidence of a Baptist church.

and

> It was into this Association that the Oxford church was received in 1656, and the Association records give a picture of the Oxford church and the issues which concerned it.[4]

---

[2] Hayden, '"Through grace they are preserved"', p. 9. The unacknowledged quote within the statement is from Walter Stevens, 'The Pioneers and their Successors', in Walter Stevens and Walter W. Bottoms, *The Baptists of New Road, Oxford* (Oxford: Alden Press, 1948), p. 3. Geographically, to describe the meeting as the 'Berkshire Association' is a bit of a misnomer, and it is more properly designated as the 'Abingdon Association'. See B.R. White (ed.), *Association Records of the Particular Baptists of England, Wales and Ireland. Part 3: The Abingdon Association* (London: Baptist Historical Society, 1974), p. 206, on this point.
[3] Hayden, '"Through grace they are preserved"', p. 13.
[4] Hayden, '"Through grace they are preserved"', p. 16.

How could such a confusion of dates arise? Ultimately, I suggest, the answer is to be found in an uncritical use of secondary sources, for most of his discussion of the Oxford Baptists in the article is wholly derivative and second-hand in nature,[5] relying heavily on the work of six main authors, each of which is cited repeatedly within the article.[6] It looks as if Hayden is caught here between the opinions of two of the major secondary sources upon which he draws: Walter Stevens (who argues for 1653), and B.R. White (who argues for 1656). As it stands, we are left with two conflicting dates. It is this dependence upon secondary sources that lies at the heart of the confusion over 1653 and 1656 as foundational dates within the congregational life of Baptists in Oxford.

What are we to make of this discrepancy over dates? The reason for the two dates is complex, and its resolution involves a careful consideration of several key documents within the Angus Library at Regent's Park College, Oxford. These include *The Longworth Churchbook* (Longworth 1/1), a nineteenth-century volume known as *The Gould Manuscript* (D/GOU 1),[7] and *The Abingdon Association Records Book* (D/AA 1). Let us examine this matter in more detail.

---

[5] A number of other errors are made in dating key events within the article, including several which fail to take into account the fact that in many of the seventeenth-century documents the year was said to begin on 26 March. This means that March was reckoned as the first month of the year, a matter which becomes especially important in the dating of the Abingdon Association records. For a detailed critique of Hayden's study, see my 'Recycling History or Researching History?: Baptist Beginnings in Oxford according to Roger Hayden—An Assessment' (unpublished twenty-eight page article deposited in the Angus Library, June 2003, designated 'Oxford New Road 67').

[6] The six authors and their works are: Andrew Clark (ed.), *The Life and Times of Anthony Wood, antiquary, of Oxford, 1632-95, described by Himself* (Oxford: Clarendon Press, 1891), volume 1; M.G. Hobson, *Oxford Council Acts 1626-1665* (Oxford: Clarendon Press, 1933); *Oxford City Council Acts 1665-1701* (Oxford: Clarendon Press, 1939); Walter Stevens, 'The Pioneers and their Successors', in Walter Stevens and Walter W. Bottoms, *The Baptists of New Road, Oxford* (Oxford: Alden Press, 1948), pp. 3-9, and 'Oxford's Attitudes to Dissenters', *Baptist Quarterly* 13.1 (January, 1949), pp. 4-17; B.R. White, 'The Baptists of Reading, 1652-1715', *Baptist Quarterly* 22.5 (January, 1968), pp. 249-70, 'John Pendarves, the Calvinistic Baptists and the Fifth Monarchy', *Baptist Quarterly* 25.6 (April, 1974), pp. 251-71, *The English Baptists of the Seventeenth Century* (ed. J.F.V. Nicholson; London: Baptist Historical Society, 2nd edn, 1996), and White (ed.), *Association Records. Part 3: The Abingdon Association*; Christina Colvin, 'Protestant Nonconformity and Other Christian Bodies', C.R. Elrington (ed.), *The Victoria History of the Counties of England* (Oxford: Oxford University Press, 1979), IV, pp. 415-24; Philip Hayden, 'The Baptists in Oxford 1656-1819,' *Baptist Quarterly* 29.3 (1981), pp. 127-36.

[7] B.R. White, 'Who Really Wrote the "Kiffin Manuscript"?', *Baptist History and Heritage* 1.1 (October, 1966), pp. 3-10, 14, offers a suggestion about the relationship between the *Gould Manuscript* and the so-called *Stinton Repository* (D/STI 1) within the Angus Library. For more on the so-called *Stinton Repository*, see Champlin Burrage, 'A

The Proposed Date of 1653: *The Longworth Churchbook*

The earliest reference I have found to 1653 as the foundation date for a Baptist church in Oxford is in an article from 1910–11 by W.T. Whitley, and his date is adopted by other Baptist historians, including Walter Stevens, Ernest Payne and Roger Hayden who follow his lead.[8] Whitley's comment about Oxford Baptists is part of a general survey of the beginnings of churches prior to 1660; it is arranged by counties and has eight entries for churches within Oxfordshire. The comment about Oxford simply reads:

> Oxford. 1653 joined the Berkshire Association.

Unfortunately, no details as to the historical basis for the statement are given; no primary source documents are cited, no evidence offered in support. So where did Whitley get his information? It looks as if he was basing the date of 1653 on either the *Longworth Churchbook* or, more likely, on the transcription of it commonly known as *The Gould Manuscript*. As it now stands *The Gould Manuscript* is a hand-written copy of documents illustrating the origins and growth of Baptists which (apparently) were first gathered together by the Baptist pastor and reliquary Benjamin Stinton (1676–1719). It appears that this copy of Stinton's work was gathered together by the Rev. George Gould of Norwich sometime before 1880 (hence the name *The Gould Manuscript*). This folio, consisting of some 190 handwritten pages, was passed down to his son, the Revd George Pearce Gould, then the Principal of Regent's Park College, Oxford, and through him it became part of the Angus Library. The latter part of *The Gould Manuscript* consists of thirty-four pages of text and is entitled 'Records of the Barkshire Association'. It is

---

Brief Examination of the Gould Manuscript', *Baptist Review and Expositor* 2.4 (October, 1905), pp. 445-71, and *The Early English Dissenters in the Light of Recent Research (1550-1641)* (2 vols; Cambridge: Cambridge University Press, 1912), I, pp. 336-56, II, pp. 292-308; and John Stanley, *The Church in the Hop Garden* (London: Kingsgate Press, 1935), pp. 63-71. Unfortunately, Stanley perpetuates some of the transcription errors contained in *The Gould Manuscript*, notably a misreading of the date on p. 23 of the censure of John Moulden, a wayward member of the church—he gives the date as 1648 rather than 1658. Much of Stanley's hypothetical reconstruction of the earliest years of the churches at Coat-Longworth and their relationship to the mother church in Abingdon is built upon this simple misreading of a *4* for a *5* by the anonymous scribe of *The Gould Manuscript* (see folio 186 recto).

[8] So W.T. Whitley, 'Baptist Churches till 1660', *Transactions of the Baptist Historical Society* 2 (1910-11), p. 251; Walter Stevens, 'The Pioneers and their Successors', in Stevens and Bottoms, *The Baptists of New Road, Oxford*, p. 3; Ernest A. Payne, *The Baptists of Berkshire Through Three Centuries* (London: Carey Kingsgate Press, 1951), p. 149.

within this section of *The Gould Manuscript* (pp. 156-89) that we find reference to the Oxford Baptists participating in Association life as early as March of 1653.[9] Thus, we read:

> The messengers being mett at Tetsworth the 17th day of ye first month 1652/3, signed ye agreement following in the name & by the Consent of all the said Churches respectively.
>
> The Agreement of Certaine Churches, vizt. of Abingdon, Reading, Henly, Kensworth, Evershalte, Wantage, Kingstone, Pirton, Woatlingeon, Hadnam, Oxford, Honinsteed.[10]

The date of 17 March 1653 in *The Gould Manuscript* is almost certainly based upon the so-called *Longworth Churchbook*, although how and under what circumstances the document was transcribed into *The Gould Manuscript* is now impossible to determine with certainty. *The Longworth Churchbook* contains twenty-three pages of minutes and includes an account of *eight* meetings of messengers from various Baptist churches in the seventeenth century on its first seven pages, and minutes for *one* subsequent meeting on the verso of p. 21. The first of these meetings took place in Wormsley on 8 October 1652, and the last recorded is the one that is found on p. 21 and is dated 27 November 1657.[11] Explicit mention of the church in Oxford is made within these minutes at three points. The first explicit mention of messengers from Oxford occurs in connection with the *third* of the nine meetings. The opening paragraphs of this minute read:

> The messengers being mett at Tetsworth the 17th day of ye first month 1652/3, signed ye agreement following in the name & by the Consent of all the said Churches respectively.

---

[9] There is a twentieth-century copy of *The Gould Manuscript* in the Angus Library at Regent's Park College which has recently been found by Jennifer Thorp, the college Archivist. This document (which has been given the catalogue designation D/GOU 2) was in a box of unsorted papers belonging to W.T. Whitley. The copy was made by William Keymer, master of Grey Friars Priory School, in the spring of 1905. The 'Records of the Barkshire Association' are contained on pp. 167-201, but the copying work is incomplete and there are many gaps in the material found in *The Gould Manuscript* (D/GOU 1).

[10] *The Gould Manuscript*, p. 158. This paragraph is also found in D/GOU 2, p. 169.

[11] The manuscript goes on to record the minutes of three subsequent meetings which took place on 17 September 1707, 8 April 1708 and 3 September 1708; the church in Oxford is not listed among those who participated in these later meetings. The scribe for these latter minutes is probably Thomas Barfoot, a messenger from the church in Witney, near Oxford.

> The agreement of Certaine Churches, vizt. Of Abingdon, Reading, Henly, Kensworth, Evershalte, Wantage, Kingstone, Pirton, Woatlingeon, Hadnam, Oxford, Hempstead.[12]

Specific mention of messengers from the church in Oxford is also contained in the minutes for the meeting held on 13 March 1656. This is found on p. 5 of the manuscript, where an opening paragraph introduces ten separate proposals for discussion and agreement amongst the churches in the subsequent meetings of the Association. This opening paragraph reads:

> At a meeting of chosen messengers of the Churches, vizt. Abingdon, Reading, Henly, Kensworth, Evershalte, Wantage, Kingston, Hadnam, Watlington, Pirton, Oxford, Hempstead at Tetsworth were these ten proposalls subscribed by the messengers the 13th day of the first month 1656, as followeth:[13]

The third time that the church of Oxford is mentioned occurs in the minutes for the meeting held on 27 November 1657. As noted, this is found on p. 21 verso of the manuscript, where the opening paragraphs reads:

> At a meeting of the Churches of Longworth with several messengers from the churches of Abingdon, Wantage and Oxford at Barcourt the 27 day of the 9th monthe 1657 it was unanimously agreed as followeth that it would most tend to the glory of god:

> That those members neare Faringdon doe stand upp as a distinct Church of Jesus Christ. And that our Brother Coombe bee a member with them, to be with them to help on the worke of the lord two first dayes in three and to stand as an helpe to ye Church of Longworth to be with them one first day in three.[14]

Unfortunately, the names of the messengers from the Oxford church are not recorded at any point within the manuscript, although the names of some of the messengers from some of the other churches are given at various points. To obtain information about the persons involved we need to turn to another seventeenth-century manuscript held within the Angus Library, namely *The Abingdon Association Records Book*, where such additional details are often provided. A careful comparison of the *Abingdon Association Records Book* with the *Longworth Churchbook* reveals some interesting differences of detail, including the proposed date

---

[12] *The Longworth Churchbook*, p. 4.
[13] This paragraph is contained in both D/GOU 1, folio 160 recto and D/GOU 2, p. 171.
[14] These paragraphs are contained in D/GOU 1, folio 189 recto. Interestingly they are *not* found on the comparable page in D/GOU 2, p. 200.

as to when Oxford Baptists were welcomed into the Abingdon Association.

The Proposed Date of 1656: *The Abingdon Association Records Book*

The *Abingdon Association Records Book* manuscript contains forty-seven foliated pages and records the minutes of twenty-three meetings of messengers from various Baptist churches from December of 1652 to June of 1660.[15] Crucially, the minutes of the Abingdon Association clearly show that the Oxford church was welcomed into the Association during the meetings held on 11-14 March 1656.[16] Interestingly, this manuscript goes on to name the two Oxford representatives as Thomas Tisdale[17] and Richard Tidmarch (see Figure 1). This is the earliest reference that we have of the names of members of the Baptist church in Oxford. More to the point, in the *Abingdon Association Records Book* we are presented with something of a difficulty as to the date when Baptists in Oxford first began to participate in Association life. The *Abingdon Association Records Book* suggests 1656, in contrast to 1653 as stated in the *Longworth Churchbook*. Is there a way to resolve this tension?

One possible way is to accept the account given in the *Longworth Churchbook* and take it that the messengers from Oxford attended the earlier meeting in 1653, but were not welcomed into the Abingdon Association as such at that time. Perhaps the Oxford messengers were there as mere observers, or were serving out some sort of preliminary phase of full membership. The problem with this as a solution is that there is no indication of other churches having to undergo such a procedure.

A better solution is to be found by a careful examination of the *Longworth Churchbook* manuscript as a whole, and recognize that it exhibits signs of editorial revision over time. If we accept the explicit date of 11-14 March 1656 given in the *Abingdon Association Records Book* as historically correct, then the *Longworth Churchbook* could be said to

---

[15] The *Abingdon Association Records Book* was purchased by Dr Ernest A. Payne, then General Secretary of the Baptist Union of Great Britain and Ireland, from Guntrips Bookshops Ltd, of 115, Week Street, Maidstone, Kent, in June 1954 for £5 5s 0d.

[16] The reference is *The Abingdon Association Records Book* (D/AA 1), folio 13 verso. See White (ed.), *Association Records: Part 3. The Abingdon Association*, p. 145.

[17] Thus, Thomas Tisdale, who represented the Baptist church in Abingdon at the fifth meeting of the Abingdon Association in 1653, also represented the Baptist church in Oxford in the thirteenth meeting of that same Abingdon Association in 1656. See B.R. White, 'The Organization of the Particular Baptists, 1644–1660', *Journal of Ecclesiastical History* 17.2 (October, 1966), p. 218; *Association Records: Part 3. The Abingdon Association*, pp. 131, 145, 210.

offer us something of a revisionist history in light of these subsequent events. I would like to propose that the anonymous recorder of the seventeenth-century minutes inserted the name of the Oxford church back into the minutes of the meeting held on 17 March 1653, even though Oxford was not to be welcomed into association until the meetings held three years later on 11-14 March 1656. Several unusual features of the relevant paragraphs support this suggestion: the first is the fact that the first explicit reference to the Oxford church within the *Longworth Churchbook* (the reference appearing on p. 4) appears to be written by another pen and in a darker ink. A second is the fact that this insertion is squeezed between two lines of the text and interrupts the regular pattern and spacing of the paragraph as a whole (see Figure 1). Yet another concerns the way in which 'Oxford' is included among the list of places sending messengers to the Association. This feature requires further explanation.

The standard formula for listing the churches of the Association, which is used in the opening paragraphs of the various meetings, exhibits some variation. Thus, for the meeting on 8 October 1652 the churches listed are 'Henly, Reading, and Abingdon'; for the meeting held on 3 November 1652 the list runs 'Abingdon, Reading, Henly, Kingsworth, Evershalt'; for the meeting held on 27 December 1654 the list runs 'Abingdon, Reading, Henly, Evershalt & Kensworth'; for the meeting on 20 June 1655 the list runs 'Abingdon, Reading, Henly, Kensworth, Evershalt & other churches'; and a meeting concluded on 13 March 1656 the list runs 'Abingdon, Reading, Henly, Kensworth & Evershalt'. It is interesting to note that this last listing of churches follows a fairly standard pattern, probably indicating that this formula is in deference to these five churches as the founding members of the Abingdon Association. As time goes on the names of other churches are added, and it looks as if the *first* reference to the Baptist church in Oxford (in the paragraph at the top of p. 5) fits this pattern quite well. This is the meeting for 17 March 1653 and there are twelve churches listed in this paragraph, with the church in Oxford being one of seven places (Wantage, Kingston, Pirton, Watlington, Hadnam, Oxford, Hampsteed) that sends messengers to join the traditional five (Abingdon, Reading, Henly, Kensworth, and Evershalt) which were listed at the top of the page in connection with meetings held earlier in the year on 3 November 1652. It is these additional seven names that are squeezed into the space between lines on p. 4, breaking the meter and spacing of the paragraph as a whole.

In fact, the *second* mention of Oxford in the *Longworth Churchbook*, which is found on p. 5 and describes the Association meetings that took place on 13-17 March 1656, accords precisely with the *Abingdon Association Records Book* (folio 13 verso), where it is stated that it was at this particular meeting that Oxford and Hempsteed were formally welcomed into the Abingdon Association. In addition, on p. 5 of *The Longworth Churchbook* the paragraph immediately following the opening declaration (which, as we noted, is the second reference to the Baptist church in Oxford within the document) is an after-the-fact report about an earlier meeting held on 27 December 1653. In effect, the anonymous writer copies from the minutes of that earlier meeting, inserting an introductory paragraph from the 1653 minutes before going on to list the first four of the ten proposals dealt with in the Association meetings (mentioned above). Thus, the second paragraph on p. 5 reads:

At a meeting of chosen messengers of the Churches at Tetsworth the 27th day of the 10th month 1653 they agreed to the foure first as followeth:

This paragraph (see Figure 2) has all the hallmarks of being an anachronistic backdating of history, at least insofar as implicating the church in Oxford with Association business dating to 1653 is concerned. In other words, because the paragraph *immediately preceding* mentions Oxford in connection with the meetings held in March of 1656 (an appropriate inclusion since Oxford Baptists had joined the Abingdon Association during those meetings), the paragraph following which deals with meetings held on 27 December 1653 ('the 27th of the 10th month 1653') was incorrectly assumed to include Oxford as well. Once the unfortunate juxtaposition of the two paragraphs on p. 5 of *The Abingdon Association Records Book* is recognized, then the 17 March 1653 date for the official welcome of the Baptists into the Abingdon Association on p. 4 of the manuscript can be put down to a (later?) copyist's unwarranted inference about precisely when it was that Oxford Baptists joined the Association. In short, a later copyist, writing with a different ink, draws an incorrect inference about the place of the Oxford church within Association life from p. 5 of the manuscript, and inserts that on p. 4 of the same document, inadvertently creating an historical 'problem' in the process. This explanation allows for a consistency of detail between the records of *The Longworth Churchbook* and *The Abingdon Association Records Book* to be historically reconstructed and re-asserted—Oxford Baptists were welcomed into the Abingdon Association in March of 1656.

In short, it appears that the date of 1653 (which serves as the official anniversary date) has erroneously slipped into New Road Baptist Church documents and historiography. This is due to Walter Stevens's uncritical acceptance of W.T. Whitley's use of the so-called *Gould Manuscript*, which in turn offers a transcription of a copyist's insertion in *The Longworth Churchbook*, one that is at variance with the records of *The*

Abingdon Association Records Book.[18] All of which means that any suggestion of 17 March 1653 as the date when Baptists in Oxford were welcomed into the Abingdon Association is the perpetuation of an error which is third-hand, or even fourth-hand, at best. The inclusion of two contradictory dates in Hayden's article is probably due, as I have suggested, to an uncritical reliance upon secondary sources which were not checked against the available seventeenth-century documents.

---

[18] Whitley apparently did not know of the existence of the *Abingdon Association Records Book*, which clearly gives the later date of 11-14 March 1656, for he never discusses the latter date as an alternative.

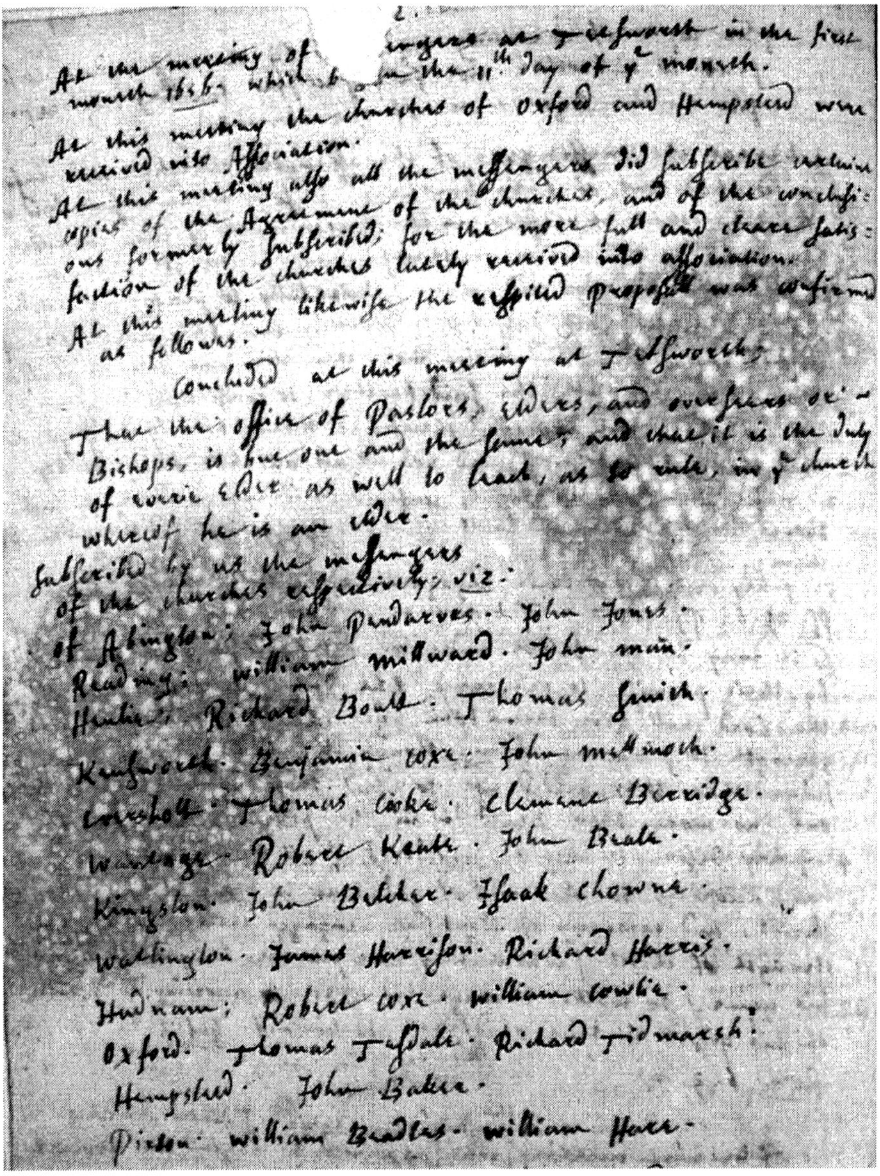

Figure 1: *The Abingdon Association Records Book*, folio 13 verso.

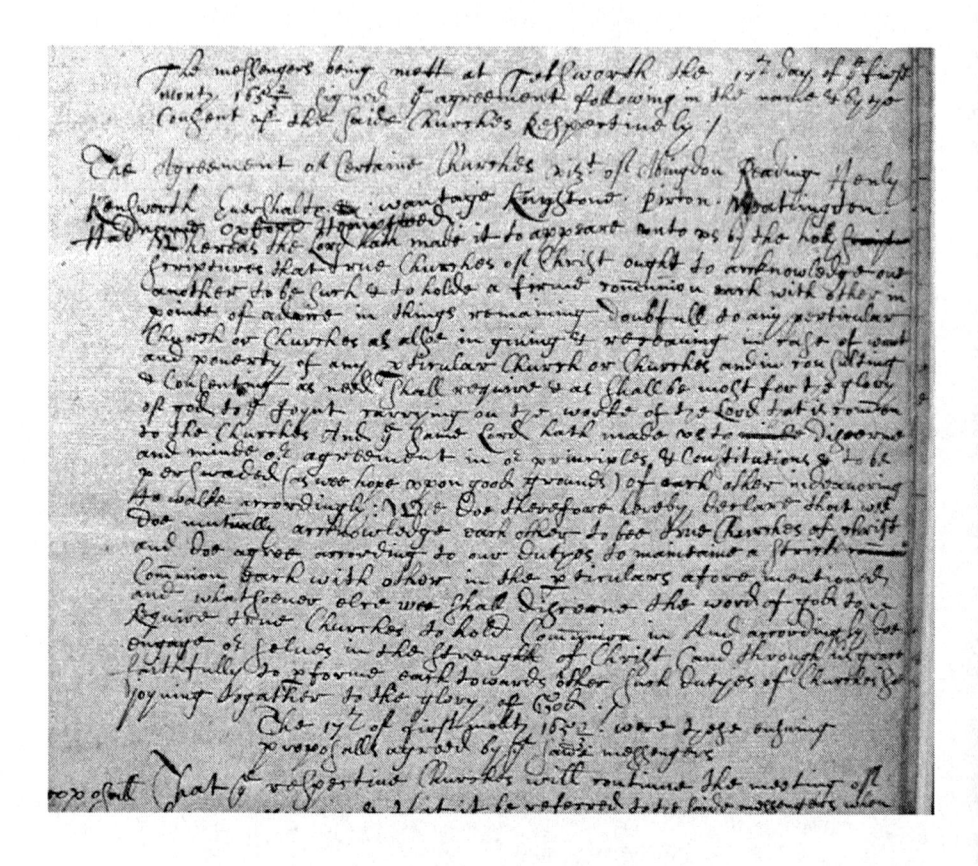

Figure 2: *The Longworth Churchbook*, p. 4.

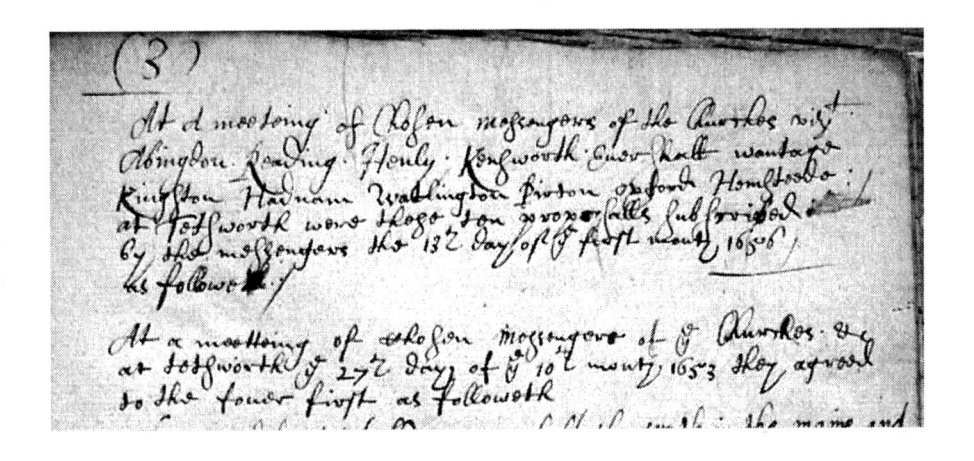

Figure 3: *The Longworth Churchbook*, p. 5.

CHAPTER 11

The Fifth Monarchist John Pendarves (d.1656): A Victim of 'Studious Bastard Consumption'?*

Larry J. Kreitzer

There has always been a certain degree of mystery about the circumstances of the death in September of 1656 of the controversial Baptist leader and Fifth Monarchist John Pendarves. The comment on Pendarves made by Anthony Wood in his *Athenae Oxonienses* (1692) offers the best-known discussion on the matter and remains the starting point for most discussion. Wood writes,

> At length after a short life spent in continual agitation, he [Pendarves] surrendered up his last breath at *London* about the beginning of *September* in sixteen hundred fifty and six. Whose body thereupon being embowelled and wrap'd up in Sear-cloth by the care of the Brethren, and afterwards Preparations made for his Funeral, the body was some weeks after conveyed by water to *Abendon* in *Berks*.[1]

The two most important documents which give details of the transportation of his body from London to Abingdon and his burial are written from opposite sides of the religious divide between Conformity and Nonconformity. The Baptists produced *The Complaining Testimony of Some...of Sions Children* (London, 1656), which was a response to the clash between mourners and government troops at the funeral service on 2 October 1656.[2] Unfortunately it tells us nothing about the death of

---

* This study was first published in the *American Baptist Quarterly* 23.3 (September, 2004), pp. 281-89.
[1] *Athenae Oxonienses: An Exact History of all the Writers and Bishops who have had their education in the most ancient and famous University of Oxford* (London, 1692), pp. 127-28.
[2] The abuse of Baptist mourners by government troops is also mentioned in an anonymous tract entitled *A Witnes to the saints in England and Wales* (London, 1657), pp. 95-96: '[W]e are sent out amongst Wolves, Bears and other cruel beakes of Prey, as appeareth by experience that they had at *Abingdon*, in doing that office of love to our late deceased Brother *John Pendarves*, being beaten, reproached and hindred, both in the

Pendarves or the bringing of his body to Abingdon and concentrates on events surrounding the funeral service itself. Certainly there is no indication within this tract about the cause or circumstances of Pendarves' death earlier in London. The second document, representing the perspective of the religious establishment of Anglicanism, offers a little more information about the transportation of Pendarves' body from the capital. This is William Hughes's *Munster and Abingdon* (Oxford, 1657), which records a rather more hostile version of events. This is no doubt influenced by the fact that Hughes and Pendarves had publicly crossed swords in the past. Hughes writes:

> Mr *Pendarves*, late pastour to the Adversaries of Infant-Baptisme in that *Towne*, having yeelded up the Ghost some weeks before at London, and changed his many quarrels here for everlasting *peace* (I am so persuaded from that intimacy some years agoe betwixt us) in our fathers kingdome; after some hot debates twixt his surviving friends about his *bodies* resting place on earth; was brought at last, by water (in a chest like those for sugar, fild up with sand, and lodged at a Grocers) there to deposite the *remaines of death*, where the *service of his life* had been devoted.[3]

However, even here there is nothing about the cause and circumstances of the death of this Baptist pastor from Abingdon.

Fortunately, within the Bodleian Library in Oxford there is a manuscript which contains an intriguing note about the death of Pendarves. This manuscript consists of various papers of the Baskerville family collected and bequeathed to the library by Ralph Rawlinson in 1756. Disappointingly, the eight-line note, apparently written by a contemporary witness, is unsigned and undated. Nevertheless, it does give the first substantial clue in these matters; it reads:

> About ye beginning of September 1656
> The famous preacher Mr Pendarvis of Abington
> died at London of ye plague in ye gutts and
> likewise John Prince died suddenly and our Hutchins
> died suddenly in Abington.
>   Ye new Church yard or Cimitary for his
> church then was made and goodman Tomkins
> children was first there buried.[4]

Meeting place and Market place, for seeking the Lord, and bearing our Testimony to the Kingdom of our Lord Jesus Christ in and over the nations'.
  [3]   William Hughes, *Munster and Abingdon* (Oxford, 1657), pp. 85-86.
  [4]   *MS Rawlinson D 859*, folio 162. It is possible that Anthony Wood himself wrote this note. It should be compared with the entry contained in one of the volumes of

As far as I am aware, the first person to call attention to this intriguing piece of contemporary seventeenth-century evidence was B.S. Capp.[5] His lead was followed up by B.R White, who refers to the note in what is generally regarded as the fullest study of the life of Pendarves thus far published.[6] However, what precisely is meant by 'the plague in the guts' is difficult to ascertain—the phrase is so enigmatic that it offers little of real substance. Nevertheless, the details contained within *MS Rawlinson D 859* do give us some help with the overall dating of the note itself. For example, we note the reference to John Prince dying suddenly, presumably of the 'plague' as had Pendarves. Fortunately the Oxford antiquarian Anthony Wood (1632–95) offers assistance here, providing an interesting note about John Prince. Prince, he says, was an innkeeper who ran the Magpie Inn along Grope Lane near Merton College in Oxford; he died suddenly on 26 October 1673 and was buried in St John the Baptist churchyard the following day.[7] This information gives us an indication that the comment about Pendarves was written at least seventeen years after Pendarves himself had died. This indicates something of the enduring impact that John Pendarves left in the memories of those who followed; his untimely death, and the politically-charged funeral were still being remembered a generation later.

Fortunately, there is one bit of additional evidence, apparently hitherto completely unnoticed, which sheds light on Pendarves's death. This is contained within a book published by a London-based Dutch physician named Gideon Harvey (1640?–1700?). It was entitled *Morbus Anglius: or, the Anatomy of Consumptions* (1666), and was one of the early medical books describing the causes, effects, and cures of tuberculosis (see Figure #1). Dr Harvey became a well-known figure within the medical world of seventeenth-century London, and rose to hold several

---

the parish register of St Helen's church in Abingdon (*Burials, Baptisms and Marriages 1653–1665, 1682–1688*, folio 20 verso):
    'Sept[ember] xiiith [1656]—was buryed Grace the daughter of John
    Tomkins and Martha his wife
    was buryed Benjamin the sonne of the
    said John Tomkins and Martha his wife
    in the Ock Sreeete as it is reported.'

[5] B.S. Capp, *The Fifth Monarchy Men: A Study in Seventeenth-century English Millenarianism* (London: Faber and Faber, 1972). The note from *MS Rawlinson A 859* is discussed on p. 144.

[6] B.R. White, 'John Pendarves, the Calvinistic Baptists and the Fifth Monarchy', *Baptist Quarterly* 25.6 (1974), p. 264. Elsewhere, based on this note, White states, 'Pendarves died of the plague in London'. See 'Pendarves (or Pendarvis), John (c.1623–1656)', in Richard L. Greaves and Robert Zaller (eds), *Biographical Dictionary of British Radicals in the Seventeenth Century. Volume III: P-Z* (Brighton: Harvester Press, 1984), p. 21.

[7] *MS Wood E 33*, folio 64 recto.

positions of responsibility within the royal courts of both Charles II and William and Mary. Harvey studied medicine at various places on the continent, including Leyden and Paris. He settled in England after the Restoration, having been granted his denization by Charles II on 11 December 1661,[8] and spent most of his medical career in London. Most of what we know about him comes through his own writings, although we get a glimpse of the man himself through the fine engraving of him done by Pierre Philippe in 1663 (Figure #2).[9]

Harvey wrote books on an astonishingly wide range of medical subjects, a matter which illustrates something of his eclectic interests as well as his innate curiosity about diseases and afflictions suffered by seventeenth-century Londoners. It is worth recording the titles of some of these works for they help set the context for his remarks about John Pendarves. Harvey's publications were written in both Latin and English, and many of them went into several editions. These include: *A Discourse of the Plague* (London, 1665, 1673) (which dealt with the nature, cause, signs and treatment for plague in London); *Little Venus Unmask'd: or, a Perfect Discovery of the French Pox* (London, 1670) and *Great Venus Unmasked: or a more Exact Discovery of the Venereal Evil, or French Disease* (London, 1672) (both of which dealt with various venereal diseases and their treatment); *The Accomplisht Physician, the honest Apothecary, and the skilful Chyrirgeon* (London, 1670); *A Theoretical and Chiefly Practical Treatise of Fevors* (London, 1674); *Casus Medico-Chirurgicus:, or, A Most Memorable Case of A Noble-Man Deceased* (London, 1678) (which dealt with his attempt to cure a man who was mortally wounded in a sword-fighting duel); *The Family-Physician and the House-Apothecary* (London, 1676, 1678) (which gave advice about medicines, their costs, and preparations, etc.); *The Conclave of Physicians* (London, 1683, 1686) (which dealt with the intrigues, frauds and plots used by physicians against their patients); *The Disease of London: or a New Discovery of the Scorvey* (London, 1684) (which dealt with scurvy, palsies, convulsions, rheumatisms, etc.); *A New Discourse of the Smallpox and Malignant Fevers* (London, 1685); *The Art of Curing Diseases by Expectation* (London, 1689); *A Treatise of the Small-Pox and Measles* (London, 1696); and *A Particilar Discourse on Opium* (London, 1696). Early in his life, as a result of his initial studies at university, he even published a volume dealing with the relationship between philosophy and metaphysics entitled *Archelogia Philosophica Nova, or, New Principles of Philosophy* (London, 1663). This was followed up later in his life by *The Vanities of Philosophy and Physick* (London, 1699, 1700, 1702).

---

[8] *State Papers* 44/5, p. 84.
[9] The engraving was published as a frontpiece to Harvey's *Archelogia Philosophica Nova, or, New Principles of Philosophy* (London, 1663).

These publications also list some of his professional and royal positions: he was a Fellow of the College of Physicians in The Hague during the Civil War; Physician to Charles II's army in Flanders; Physician in Ordinary to His Majesty Charles II; and Physician of the Tower to William and Mary. In short, he seems to have been a man who moved readily within the established medical circles of the day. It is also known that he was in London during much of the Commonwealth period, and that on 6 July 1659 he was nominated by the Committee of Safety to go as physician to Dunkirk.[10] This may help account for the fact that he apparently had access to information about the medical condition of John Pendarves when he died back in September of 1656. It also helps make sense of the description of Pendarves given by Wood above which notes that his body was 'embowelled and wrap'd up in Sear-cloth'. The fact that Wood says the body was 'embowelled' suggests that it was dissected in some way, although this has always remained a point of conjecture. However, Gideon Harvey's *Morbus Anglicanus: or, The Anatomy of Consumptions* helps solve the mystery for us, confirming that the body of Pendarves had indeed been subjected to a dissection in London.[11]

Pendarves is mentioned twice within this book, which was first published in 1666 and then went into a second edition in 1672. The first mention of him occurs in chapter five which is entitled 'Of the Nature of a Proper and True Consumption'. Here he cites the classical writer Galen's definition of the disease: 'A Consumption is the dying of a living Creature through dryness', and goes on to relate this to problems with the lungs which by their very nature are parts of the body 'not at all disposed to suscept any dryness'. This is followed by a sentence which notes John Pendarves as a case study:

> But on the contrary, it's ordinary for Smiths, Cooks, and others, whose imployment is conversant about the Fire, to incurre such an extreme dryness of their Lungs; the like observation you'l read below touching the withered Lungs of one *Pendarves*.[12]

The case of Pendarves is returned to in chapter 10 of the book which is entitled 'Of a Studious Consumption'. Here Harvey argues that too much 'toyl of the mind' can lead to an imbalance of the spirits of the body and a want of nutriments to the various organs; this he calls 'Studious Bastard

---

[10] *State Papers 25/128*, page 24. The suggestion came from John Desborough (1608–80), a member of the Committee.

[11] This also helps explain the long delay between his death 'about the beginning of September' (so Wood) and his burial a month later on 2 October. The performance of a dissection seems to have considerably delayed the movement of his body to Abingdon.

[12] Gideon Harvey, *Morbus Anglicus: or, The Anatomy of Consumptions* (London, 1666), p. 29. Italics original.

Consumption'. It is compounded by the sedentary life-style of students which causes 'crushing of the bowels, and for want of stirring the body, suffers the spirits to lye dormant and dull'. This, Harvey argues, causes 'head-ach, flushing of the blood to the head, feavers, loss of appetit, and disturbance of Concoction'. As his supreme case in point of 'Studious Bastard Consumption' Harvey turns to John Pendarves, issuing warnings about the effects of a life of study for the development of consumption:

> It is beyond imagination to conceive the sudden destructive effects of a Studious life; some eight or ten years since there dyed at *Abington* one *Pendarves*, an incomparable hard Student, and Minister of that Town, who being dissected, his Lungs were found to be withered and dryed up into an exact resemblance of an ordinary Spunge in point of substance and bigness.
>
> The like Emblems we find frequently in Universities, where Scholars daily drop away from Consumptions.
>
> Neither is it an extraordinary observation, to see Consumptions in the Faces of hundreds of the late Preaching Divines; witness else their thin Jaws and number of Caps.[13]

The example of Pendarves as a warning against an overly studious life is reproduced in the second edition of Harvey's book with only minor modifications (notably, that the word 'incomparable' is dropped in the description of him).[14] Perhaps more interesting is the fact that the third paragraph, with its reference to 'hundreds of the late Preaching Divines' as other cases of 'Studious Bastard Consumption', is dropped altogether in the second edition of the book. Why this line is dropped is unclear, but it may have something to do with the change of religious attitudes and the issuing of the *Declaration of Indulgence* in 1672. In any event, the image of Pendarves as an obsessive student who contracted consumption as a result of sitting too many hours in the library of Exeter College in Oxford (Figure #3) is an evocative one. We know that Pendarves was a student there from 1637–42, although there is no indication of his suffering with ill health at the time. The Exeter College records show that Pendarves was a 'poor scholar' (*paupere scholari*) of the college from 11 December 1637 to 14 July 1642 (Figure #4).[15]

---

[13] Harvey, *Morbus Anglicus* (1666), pp. 62-63.
[14] Gideon Harvey, *Morbus Anglicus: or, The Anatomy of Consumptions* (London, 2nd edn, 1672), pp. 15, 28-29.
[15] *Liber Cautionum Collexion 30 May 1629–17 July 1686* (A.I.22), p. 57. According to Charles William Boase, *Registrum Collegii Exoniensis: An Alphabetical Register of the Commoners of Exeter College, Oxford* (Oxford: W. Pollard, 1894), p. 247, John Pendarves matriculated on 9 February 1638 at the age of fifteen. His brother Ralph matriculated on the same day, aged nineteen. Anthony Wood, *Fasti Oxonienses*

The reference to Exeter College, Oxford, also provides one final link between Pendarves and Harvey and helps answer the question why the physician was so interested in the case of Pendarves. Gideon Harvey himself was admitted to Exeter College as a visitor or 'sojourner' (*ad mensam sojournariorum admisso*) on 23 May 1655 and remained a member of the college until 13 September 1658 (Figure #5).[16] In other words, it appears that Harvey was interested in Pendarves because he was a fellow alumnus from his *alma mater* in Oxford.

In conclusion, this new piece of evidence, contained within a medical book published only ten years or so from the date of his death and written by a physician apparently well-placed to know about a post-mortem dissection which was performed upon him, suggests that Pendarves had tuberculosis. That does not, of course, preclude the possibility that the overly-studious, lung-withered Pendarves might have contracted some other illness which was the immediate cause of his death.[17] It does, however, raise the real possibility that he died directly as a result of complications associated with tuberculosis, or, as Harvey described it 'Studious Bastard Consumption'.

(Oxford, 1692), p. 687, states that Pendarves took his BA on 3 March 1642. The Exeter College manuscript *Summary of Bursars' Accounts—1631–1797* (A.IV.10), folio 21 verso, records that 3s 4d was paid for his admission to the BA degree on 16 July 1642.

[16] *Liber Cautionum Collexion 30 May 1629–17 July 1686* (A.I.22), p. 152. Boase, *Registrum Collegii Exoniensis*, pp. 144-45, records that Harvey matriculated on 31 May 1655. Harvey himself describes his study in Oxford in *Casus Medico-Chirurgicus: or, A most Memorable Case of a Noble-Man, Deceased* (London, 1678), pp. 140-41: 'The *Latine* and *Greek* Tongues I attained in the *Low-countries*; then was placed in *Exeter*-College in *Oxford*, Doctor *Conant* being at that time Rector, where I studied Philosophy several years.'

[17] Pendarves was in sufficient enough a state of health to have preached a sermon to the church in Petty France in London on 10 August 1656. This was later printed as *The Fear of God* (London, 1657), with a dedication by John Cox which is directed to the Baptist church in Abingdon. There is no indication of ill health within the sermon itself, although Cox does describe Pendarves at one point within the dedication as 'your dying pastor' (A3).

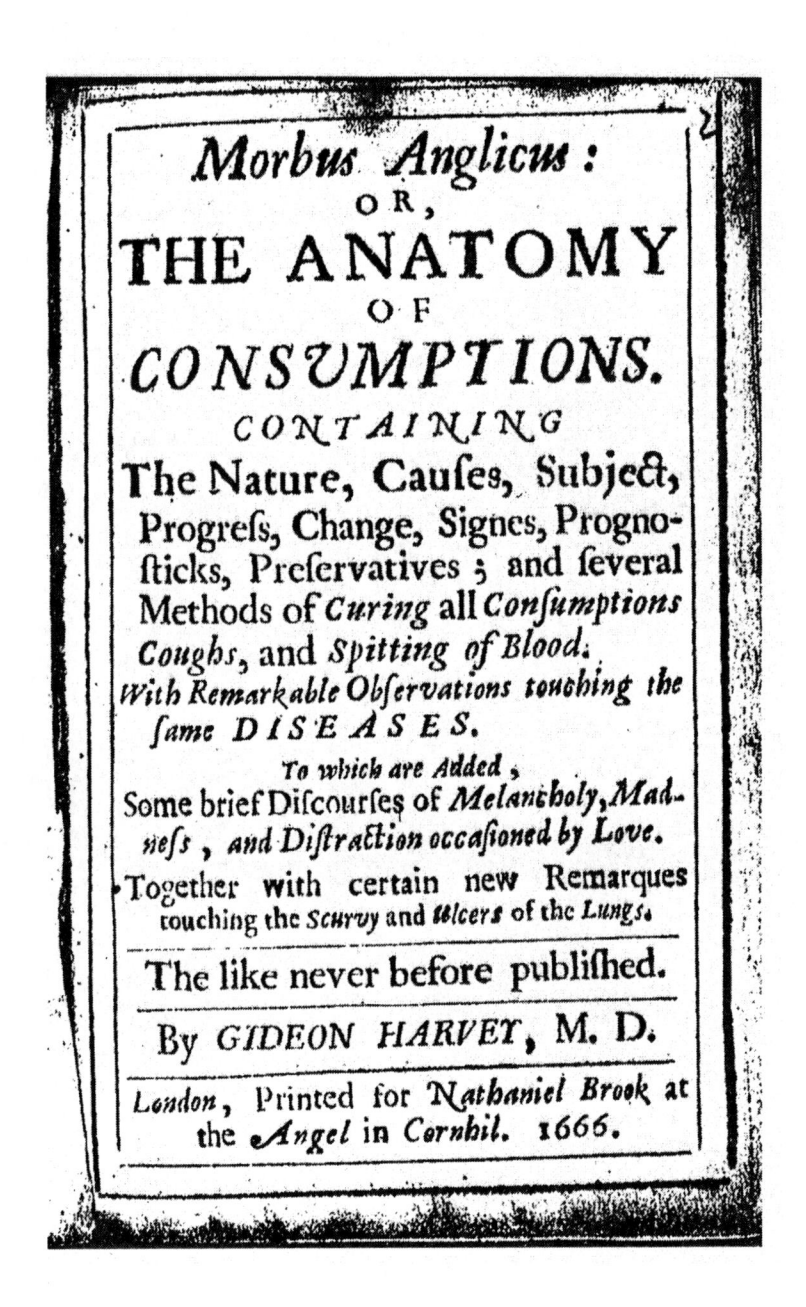

Figure #1: Title Page of Gideon Harvey's *Morbus Anglicus: or, The Anatomy of Consumptions* (London, 1666)

Figure #2: Gideon Harvey from an engraving made in 1663.

Figure #3: A view of Exeter College, Oxford, from David Loggan's *Oxonia Illustrata* (Oxford, 1675). John Pendarves matriculated as a student here in 1637, and Gideon Harvey in 1655.

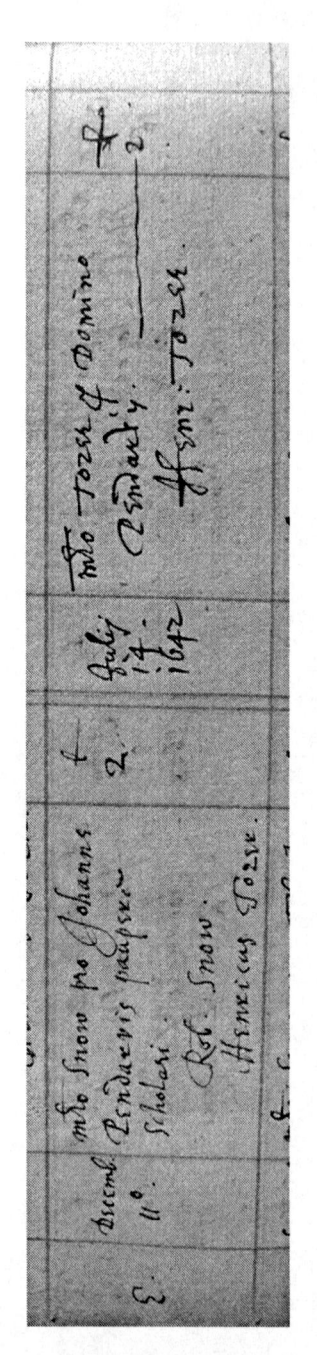

Figure #4: Exeter College record of John Pendarves as a student of the college from 1637–42.

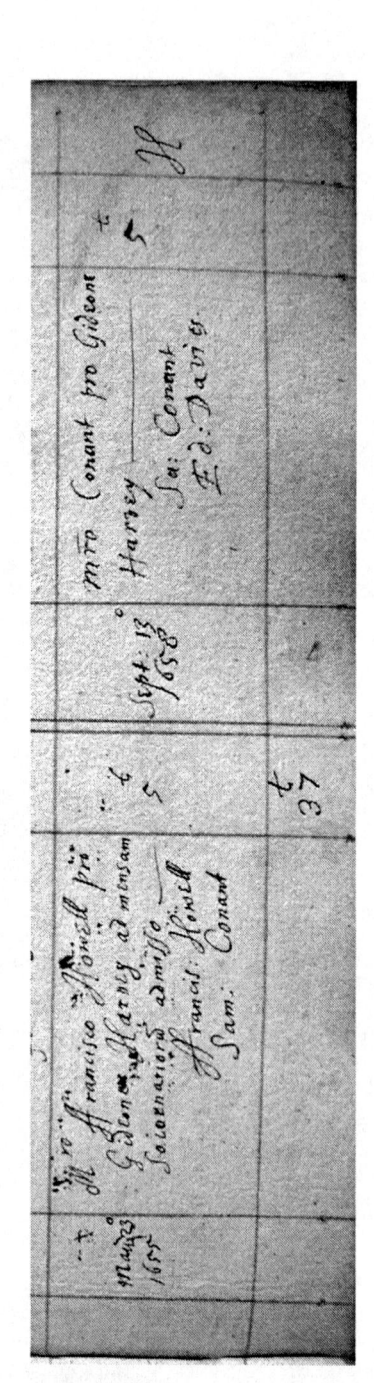

Figure #5: Exeter College record of Gideon Harvey as a student of the college from 1655–58.

CHAPTER 12

The Myth of High-Calvinism?

Clive Jarvis

Introduction

It has long been received wisdom that English Particular Baptist churches in the early to mid-eighteenth century were in a period of rampant stagnation and decline. Ken Manley, former Principal of Whitley College, Melbourne, on the opening page of his recently published book on John Rippon (1751–1836) maintains this position when he states that mid-eighteenth-century Calvinisitc Dissenters 'lacked vitality and were in numerical decline'. Manley acknowledges in passing a variety of causes but states, 'the main religious blame has usually been laid on the widely-adopted High Calvinism which was especially influential among the Calvinistic or Particular Baptists'.[1] This is by no means a modern assumption for as early as 1815 Elie Halévy was convinced that Baptists in the run up to 1770 were on the verge of extinction.[2]

The explanation for this decline in the case of the General (Arminian) Baptists was that they were moving from evangelical orthodoxy to Unitarianism. As evidence of the decline amongst General Baptists Michael Watts cites the Kent General Baptist Assembly which, in 1704, 1711, 1714, 1719, and 1724, referred to the decaying state of religion and called for days of prayer and fasting to halt the decline.[3] There is little doubt that in the case of the General Baptists the picture of decline is essentially a correct one and, in fact, for many General Baptist churches the slide into Unitarianism was not halted and to all intents and purposes they became extinct as Baptist causes.[4] General Baptist fortunes would

---

[1] Ken R. Manley, *'Redeeming Love Proclaim': John Rippon and the Baptists* (Studies in Baptist Thought and History, 12; Carlisle: Paternoster Press, 2004), p. 1.
[2] Elie Halévy, *A History of the English People in 1815* (London: Penguin, 1924), p. 355. See also Alan D. Gilbert, *Religion and Society in Industrial England: Church, Chapel and Social Change, 1740–1914* (London: Longman, 1976), p. 32.
[3] Michael R. Watts, *The Dissenters: Volume I. From the Reformation to the French Revolution* (Oxford: Clarendon Press, 1978), p. 384.
[4] By the time of the 1851 Religious Census this has progressed to the point that General Baptists are designated by Horace Mann, the compiler of the official report, as

take a marked upturn with the establishment in 1770 of the New Connexion of General Baptists,[5] but throughout they were outnumbered by some 7:1 by Particular Baptist churches and 5:1 by Baptist churches that did not affiliate to either of the two main groups.[6] Their decline in the early to mid-1700's did little to prevent a prevailing story of growth, as we shall see.

It is also said that a passion for mission was replaced by a passion for theological disputation, and that by distancing themselves from the Methodist, or Wesleyan Revival, Baptists appeared to cut themselves off from the one obvious means of re-establishing their fortunes.[7] W.R. Ward writes: 'few Englishmen had ever cherished the scruples which sent the Dissenters into the wilderness, and, despite the multiplication of chapels, their numbers probably diminished throughout the first half of the eighteenth century'.[8] Alan Gilbert provides evidence of the growth in chapel numbers for Baptist churches using the returns for 'Dissenter places of worship certified by the Registrar General'.[9] The nature of dissenting church life in 1689[10] meant that the majority of these licences were for temporary places of worship in homes or pre-existing public buildings, such as the Guild Halls in London, as few purpose built chapels were in existence.[11] However, Gilbert is convinced of the decline, stating that between 1700 and 1740 the numbers associated with dissenting communities halved to 150,000 (2.5% of the population).[12]

Unitarians, cf. *Census of Great Britain 1851: Religious Worship in England and Wales*, abridged from the official Report (London: G. Routledge, 1854). PP, 1851 Census, vol 33, p. lix.

[5] On the New Connexion, see Frank Rinaldi, *'The Tribe of Dan': A Study of the New Connexion of General Baptists 1770–1891* (Studies in Baptist History and Thought, 10; Milton Keynes: Paternoster, 2006).

[6] Given the slide of General Baptists into Unitarianism the undefined churches might be assumed to be mainly Calvinistic in theology but unwilling to be identified directly in association with other Particular Baptist churches.

[7] Clive Jarvis, 'Growth in English Baptist Churches 1770–1830: With Special Reference to the Northamptonshire Particular Baptist Association' (PhD thesis, University of Glasgow, 2001), ch. 2: 'English Baptist Churches, the Methodist Revival, and the Protestant Awakening', pp. 34-48, and Appendix 1, 'Comparative Tables for all Churches and for Baptist Church Lists', pp. 248-68.

[8] W.R. Ward, 'The Evangelical Revival in Eighteenth-Century Britain', in S. Gilley and W. J. Sheils (eds), *A History of Religion in Britain: Practice and Belief from Pre-Roman Times to the Present* (Oxford: Blackwell, 1994), p. 269.

[9] Jarvis, 'Growth in English Baptist Churches', Appendix 1, Table 19, 'All Dissenting meeting-house Registrations 1691–1850', p. 256.

[10] It was only with the 1689 Toleration Act that Dissenters were afforded the right to register their meeting places

[11] See Watts, *Dissenters*, I, pp. 303-304

[12] Gilbert, *Religion and Society in Industrial England*, p.16.

The 'myth' I wish to challenge here does not concern the existence of a theology which we many call high-Calvinism, for that is beyond doubt. John Ryland, Jr, (1753–1825), aware of the writings of earlier 'evangelical Calvinists',[13] chose initially, though briefly, a high-Calvinist stance. He writes in 1817–18, 'when I first entered on the work of the ministry, though I endeavoured to say as much to sinners as my views on this subject would allow, yet I was shackled by adherence to a supposed systematic consistency, and carefully avoided exhorting sinners to come to Christ for salvation'.[14] Andrew Gunton Fuller's memoir of his father, Andrew Fuller, records him as writing of the 'system of doctrine' that he had been used to hear from his youth: 'it was in the high Calvinistic, or hyper-Calvinistic[15] strain, admitting nothing spiritually good to be the duty of the unregenerate, and nothing to be addressed to them in a way of exhortation, excepting what related to external obedience... Nothing was said to them from the pulpit in the way of warning them to flee from the wrath to come, or inviting them to apply to Christ for salvation.'[16]

The doyen of theological high-Calvinism was the Northampton born John Gill (1697–1771), who left the town of his birth and upbringing to become a Baptist minister in London.[17] Gill is charged with responsibility for the wide acceptance of a theology that caused English Particular Baptists to decline in the early- to mid-eighteenth century. Gill's ministry lasted from September 1719 to his death in 1771, and it is with this period we are concerned. Michael Haykin quotes Benjamin Godwin, writing in 1819, as evidence of Gill's influence, when, in reference to attitudes in the 1780s, Godwin commented that 'amongst Calvinistic Dissenters there was an extreme jealousy of orthodoxy; so that any modification of the views of Dr. Gill...was considered as a certain mark of heterodoxy'.[18] Haykin accepts that high-Calvinism's principal exponent was John Gill when he writes, 'The marked failure of many early

---

[13] I apply the term retrospectively.

[14] Timothy Whelan, 'John Ryland at School: Two Societies in Northampton Boarding Schools', *Baptist Quarterly* 40.2 (April, 2003), p. 96. It is interesting to note that Ryland makes mention of John Brine but not John Gill in the fuller quote he gives.

[15] A.G. Fuller clearly sees the terms high or hyper-Calvinism as interchangeable and this would also be my understanding of their use. Attempts to use the latter term to define a form of high-Calvinism that includes antinomianism do not convince.

[16] Andrew Gunton Fuller, *The Principal Works and Remains of the Rev. Andrew Fuller, With a Memoir of His Life by His Son the Rev. A.G. Fuller* (London: Henry G. Bohn, London, 1852), p. 19.

[17] John Brine (1703–65), another native of Northampton, a contemporary and life long friend of Gill, also left Northampton for a London pastorate at the Curriers' Hall church. He was another very significant figure in this debate.

[18] Michael A.G. Haykin, *One Heart and One Soul: John Sutcliff of Olney, His Friends and His Times* (Durham: Evangelical Press, 1994), p. 368 n. 4.

eighteenth century Baptist churches to evangelise aggressively in the way that their seventeenth century forebears had done was thus traced primarily to the flawed thinking of John Gill about evangelism.'[19]

What I want to address here is whether there was such a period of decline and stagnation amongst Particular Baptists. The term 'high-Calvinism' has come to describe the 'stagnation of mid-eighteenth century English church life', not just Baptist church life, but I believe that this widely accepted consensus needs to be challenged. To this end, it is necessary first to define high-Calvinism and understand the role of John Gill, and second to challenge the thesis of decline.

Where this understanding was accepted the consequence was the absence of any need to preach the gospel or to seek to win converts until an individual showed signs of repentance. This was not purely a Baptist issue and Nuttall indicates that the matter was as virulently fought out amongst Congregationalists as amongst Baptists.[20] Roger Hayden traces its roots amongst Baptists to posthumously published sermons (c.1690) of the antinomian Tobias Crisp (1600–43), in the reaction to the Independent Richard Davis of Rothwell (1658–1714) and the significant effect of the former Presbyterian turned Independent Joseph Hussey (1660–1726), minister in Cambridge, on the Baptist minister John Skepp (1675–1721) and subsequently on the aforementioned Baptist divine, John Gill and his colleague John Brine (1703–65).[21] Yet, as Peter Toon writes, 'Crisp's method of preaching seems to have been to offer Christ freely to men and to invite them to find in Him their forgiveness and eternal life. He had little sympathy for those preachers who waited for signs of repentance before offering grace.'[22]

The difficulty in making 'evangelistic activity' the means by which the orthodoxy of Gill or any other eighteenth-century Calvinist may be judged is that even among 'evangelical Calvinists' their commitment to the doctrine of predestination placed severe limits on their understanding of the term. One can hardly expect Gill to prove his Calvinistic orthodoxy

---

[19] Cf. Haykin, *One Heart and One Soul*, pp. 17-19.

[20] Geoffrey F. Nuttall, 'Northamptonshire and The Modern Question: A Turning Point in Eighteenth-Century Dissent', Journal of Theological Studies 16.1 (April, 1965), pp. 102-11.

[21] Roger Hayden, 'Evangelical Calvinism among Eighteenth Century Particular Baptists with Particular Reference to Bernard Foskett, Hugh and Caleb Evans and the Bristol Baptist Academy 1690–1791' (PhD thesis, Keele University, 1991). p. 323. Cf. Toon, *Emergence of Hyper-Calvinism*, pp. 49-50, who also traces high-Calvinism to Crisp (d.1642). The sermons were published under the title *Christ Alone Exalted: being the compleat works of Tobias Crisp D.D. containing fifty-two sermons to which are now added notes explanatory with some memoir of the doctor's life by John Gill, D.D.* (London, 1755)

[22] Toon, *Emergence of Hyper-Calvinism*, p. 63.

by demonstration of an Arminian approach to evangelism. High-Calvinism evolved because it was a viable extension of the Calvinistic position, a variant of it, even if we judge it to have become a heresy, a judgement which may prove to be overly harsh.

We should also note that not all writers consider John Gill guilty of the charge of arch-high-Calvinist. In particular, George Ella argues that Gill should rather be seen as 'a great Reformed, eighteenth century defender of orthodoxy'.[23] The heart of the issue, as Ella is right to spell out, is whether Gill's views meant that he and the churches that looked to him for leadership lost 'their evangelistic impulse'.[24]

The problem is perhaps seen clearly in the following quote from Gill that Ella uses to substantiate his view that Gill was not a high-Calvinist:

> The Gospel is indeed ordered to be preached to every creature to whom it is sent and comes; but as yet, it has never been brought to all the individuals of human nature; there have been multitudes in all ages that have not heard it. And that there are universal offers of grace and salvation made to all men, I utterly deny; nay, I deny that they are made to any; no, not to God's elect; grace and salvation are provided for them in the everlasting covenant, procured for them by Christ, published and revealed in the Gospel, and applied by the Spirit.[25]

There is certainly an incongruity in this quote from Gill that makes the kind of firm conclusion drawn by Ella hard to substantiate. The first sentence, alluding presumably to Matthew 28.19-20, acknowledges the 'command' to preach the gospel to the entire world and notes it is unfulfilled. The second sentence, however, appears to limit the understanding of preaching the gospel to exclude offers of salvation. Such offers are unnecessary even for the elect who will be saved in God's good time, regardless of anything. The question now arises as to whether the notion that it is possible to preach the gospel without 'offering salvation' to the hearer is a legitimate one. In reality, the way this question is answered goes a long way to distinguishing between an Arminian and a Calvinist. Ella writes that Gill 'believes that there is a two-fold call in evangelism. First there is the internal effectual call which is the "powerful operation of the spirit of God on the soul," which cannot be resisted, then there is the external call by the ministry of the Word which "may be resisted, rejected and despised, and become useless."' Such teaching Ella concludes reflects fully the heart of Calvinism,[26] however, it

---

[23] George M. Ella, 'John Gill and the Charge of Hyper-Calvinism', *Baptist Quarterly* 36.4 (October, 1995), p. 160.
[24] Ella, 'John Gill', p. 162.
[25] Ella, 'John Gill', p. 167; Ella is quoting from Gill, *A Collection of Sermons and Tracts* (Streamwood, IL: Primitive Baptist Library, 1981 [1814]), III p. 117.
[26] Ella, 'John Gill', pp. 167-68.

is not in doubt that Gill was a Calvinist, the question at hand is whether he was truly a high-Calvinist? Robison's conclusion as to Gill's attitude toward evangelism is blunt: 'Apart then, from some of his own homiletical admonitions, Gill's theological writings present a formidable argument against open evangelism.'[27] Yet, by contrast Ella writes, 'It is difficult to conceive that anyone familiar with the ministry of John Gill could accuse him of being without vigour in preaching the Gospel to sinful man.'[28]

The issue can perhaps be explained by viewing preachers rather like the pieces on a chess-board which all belong to the chess master and simply wait to be set in motion, and will be set in motion when the chess master—God—determines to do so. The movement of the other pieces on the board is irrelevant as only the chess master can set a piece in motion, and, indeed, the other pieces on the board are incapable of setting each other in motion.

This last point, the belief that only God can make the moves and that what preachers do is irrelevant, is the crux of the issue. Yet, if this is high-Calvinism *per se* it is clear that few believed it, certainly not Gill or Brine. Whatever their beliefs on the issues of free will and predestination they did believe in the efficacy of preaching. It was on the question of salvation alone that they maintained their high-Calvinisitic beliefs. Where evangelical Calvinists drew back from their high-Calvinist brethren was in the matter of the efficacy of their actions. To continue the chess analogy, it was as if whilst accepting that the chess master alone could move the pieces they understood that the pieces did not move at random but in conjunction with each other. So, without denying the controlling hand of God in all their actions they believed that what they did mattered, as part of the schema of God, and that inaction was not a proper response. The distinctions it must be understood were very subtle ones and people could and did accept the same doctrinal positions only to respond differently to them. In the end, the true difference between a high-Calvinist and an evangelical Calvinist may be one of comparative response rather than doctrine. Both can believe in a particular or limited atonement, and both can believe that only the activity of God can lead a man or woman to faith, but where the high-Calvinist might conclude that nothing is expected of them the other evangelical Calvinists will conclude that everything is demanded of them regardless of any response perceived. We mentioned earlier that we are attempting here to distinguish shades of grey not primary colours and this becomes apparent when we consider that Gill's *Declaration of Faith and Practice*, while thoroughly

---

[27] O.C. Robison, 'The Legacy of John Gill', *Baptist Quarterly* 24.3 (July, 1971), p. 120.

[28] Ella, 'John Gill', p. 173.

Calvinistic, contains no hint of the high-Calvinism of which he is accused.[29] Indeed, according to Robison it differs in no material degree from the *Rules and Articles of the Particular Baptist Church* published in 1855,[30] containing no hint of the antinomianism of which high-Calvinists are often accused, nor mention of the doctrine of reprobation. Asking what the difference was between Calvinism and high-Calvinism Robison writes, 'It lay primarily in emphasis and interpretation.'[31]

This was an era when John Wesley and others were, at the end of their sermons, calling men and women to respond there and then to the gospel, with astounding results, but high-Calvinists refused to follow suit, although an evangelical Calvinist like George Whitefield could do so. We may be on solid ground to say that high-Calvinists did not give altar calls, but then again, apart from the preachers of the Methodist Revival, who did? We possess printed sermons aplenty from the mid- to late-1800s but not descriptions of services. Did Fuller, Ryland and Sutcliff make 'altar calls'? We simply don't know. Can the difference between high-Calvinists and moderate or evangelical Calvinists be so small in practice? W.R. Ward[32] describes how difficult it is to distinguish between high-Calvinism and what came to be known as Fullerism (evangelical Calvinism). He writes, 'I doubt whether the difference between the highs and the Fullerites will yield to a structural theological analysis.'[33]

The idea that John Gill, because he was a high-Calvinist, did not preach the gospel simply is untrue. George Ella is ultimately unconvincing in his attempt to prove that Gill was not a high-Calvinist, but he scores well in his attempt to present evidence from Gill's public sermons listing a series of texts that any evangelist would be pleased to preach from.[34] Peter Toon similarly in describing Richard Davis as the champion of Crisp's high-Calvinism points out that the complaints against Davis were as much, if not more, for his aggressive evangelistic methods, than his theology. Fifty years before the staunchly Arminian Wesley criss-crossed the nation on horseback, Davis travelled across the South Midlands on horseback preaching the gospel wherever opportunity arose.[35] Not, one would have thought, the actions of a convinced high-Calvinist, yet Davis, as we have

---

[29] John Gill, *Declaration of the Faith and Practice of the Church of Christ in Carter-Lane, Southwark, underthe pastoral care of J.G.; read and assented to at the admission of members* (London, 1771)

[30] *Rules and articles of the Particular Baptists Church* (London: Alabaster and Passmore, 1855)

[31] Robison, 'Legacy of John Gill', p. 115.

[32] Ward, 'The Evangelical Revival', pp. 167-84.

[33] W.R. Ward, 'The Baptists and the Transformation of the Church, 1780–1830', *Baptist Quarterly* 25.4 (October, 1973), p. 168.

[34] Ella, 'John Gill', pp. 173-75.

[35] Toon, *Emergence of Hyper-Calvinism*, pp. 51-52.

noted, is credited by many as being the father of high-Calvinism. John Collett Ryland, pastor of College Street Baptist Church, Northampton, an old reactionary and supporter of Gill if ever there was one, wrote in 1758 a description of the quintessential preacher: 'It is in the "Persuasive Part of his Discourse" that the great preacher principally shines so that, "...when he came to make his Attack and storm the Soul with all his Force, it was difficult to resist; yea when GOD's Arm attended the Word, it was impossible to hold out against his strong and tender Persuasions."'[36] Here and elsewhere Ryland, Sr, exhibits his immense passion for people's souls, a passion shared by Gill and indeed by all eighteenth-century Particular Baptists. They desired, above all else, for people to find faith in Christ and for their churches to grow, and considered it failure if they did not. A preacher can believe that a person's salvation is determined fully and completely by God and, at the same time, accept that the moment God chooses to enact that salvation follows the preaching of an 'evangelistic sermon'. There need be no summoning of people to conversion; no expectation that a man or woman would be transformed by the preacher or their preaching and no suggestion that the sermon makes the difference, only recognition that it was at such times that God, in his sovereignty, chose to act. It was never part of the tenets of high-Calvinism that churches would fail to grow and that men and women would fail to find faith, in fact the opposite.

By placing the emphasis on the action of God and not people's inaction, high-Calvinism recedes from the extremes to which some writers have sentenced it, without necessarily denying its tenets. In fairness, one would be hard put to use the word 'inaction' in any sense when applied to the life, work, writings, and preaching of John Gill. This argument holds more import if, when we look at the relative strength of English Baptists in the mid-eighteenth century, we were to discover they were not in stagnation but were enjoying a measure of growth. It is to this question we must soon turn.

By 1771 both Gill and Brine had died and their cause, if in truth there was one, did not survive them. They did not hold Particular Baptists enslaved to high-Calvinism, they were rather the main advocates of an identifiable theological strain amongst English Particular Baptists that we may identify as high-Calvinist and which those involved referred to as 'The Modern Question'. No great debate followed their demise; Gill was succeeded at Horsley Down by John Rippon, an evangelical Calvinist, and Gill's written works remained the staple diet of Bristol students well into the nineteenth century. If we look back and see stark differences between high and evangelical Calvinists it is not apparent that these distinctions divided them while they were alive.

---

[36] John Collett Ryland, *The Christian Preacher Delineated* (London, 1758), p. 4.

Our approach thus far has been to question the reality of high-Calvinism and our conclusion is that it is far less distinct than has often been argued. At the same time we must also question the extent to which high-Calvinism can be said to have been the prevailing theology among English Calvinists in the early- to mid-eighteenth century. We must be aware of the counter theological position of evangelical Calvinism which Roger Hayden is right to argue was predominant in the influential Western Association from where it spread into other associations,[37] not least through the ministers trained at the Bristol Baptist Academy.[38] Joshua Thomas' list of Bristol students makes clear that they fanned out from the college as far as Northampton and London, even Norwich, but the majority of those who did not remain in the Western Association returned either to Wales or went to the West Midlands. There is no doubt that a very significant part of the denomination espoused evangelical rather than high-Calvinist principles diminishing with each increasing part the importance we give to high-Calvinism. It is equally apparent that within an association like the Northamptonshire Association[39] high-Calvinists and evangelical Calvinists could co-exist in harmony, and that within a decade of the death of Gill and Brine high-Calvinism had receded to the margins of English Particular Baptist church life.

The Evidence

So we come to the very heart of the issue, as it must be acknowledged that the importance of high-Calvinism as a doctrine is measured only in as much as it is an explanation for the decline of English Particular Baptists in the early to mid-eighteenth century. Thus we must ask, having seen the lack of strong difference between high-Calvinism and evangelical Calvinism, whether there was indeed such a decline among Baptists as is often assumed. As we approach the statistical evidence we do so with some caution for statistics prior to 1750 are vague and difficult to come by. The primary sources available for investigation are the Evan's List of 1715, and the Josiah Thompson Lists of 1772–73. The focal point of our survey will be the churches contained with the boundaries of the Northamptonshire Particular Baptist Association (NPBA), which, at its peak, included member churches from nine surrounding counties. The formation of the NPBA in 1765 and the availability of statistical

---

[37] See Hayden, 'Evangelical Calvinism'. This is Hayden's general thesis and so I refer you to the whole volume.
[38] MS 'The Joshua Thomas list of students at Bristol Baptist College with a Biography of Bernard Foskett (1685–1758)', The Angus Library, Regents Park College, Oxford, England
[39] Though long before the Association formed in 1765 it was from the Kettering church that both Gill and Brine had originally been sent into ministry

information make the Association an excellent case study. As both John Gill and John Brine were natives of Northampton and the College Street church there is something appropriate about making this Association our focal point.

The Evan's List

The Evans List[40] was compiled following a correspondence set in motion by the 'Committee of the General Body of Protestant Dissenting Ministers of the Three Denominations in and about the Cities of London and Westminster'.[41] The three denominations in question were the Baptists, the Presbyterians, and the Independents/Congregationalists. The *List* was compiled in the handwriting of John Evans who was minister of the Presbyterian church in Hand Alley, London, and a member of the Committee of the Three Denominations.

The Evans List itself provides a very limited amount of information and cannot be regarded in the same light as more recent attempts at compiling statistics. Evans relied on correspondents around the country to send him the desired information. A footnote from Evans appears on the Northamptonshire statistics stating he is unsure of the accuracy of returns from four churches, but no reason for this is given. Some of the returns show the deficiencies of Evans' correspondents as Lincolnshire, Yorkshire, Northumberland and Durham are indicated as having no Baptist presence. However, according to the *Baptist Union Directory* these counties had eighteen churches which existed prior to and including 1715.[42] It is possible that some of these churches were not Baptist churches when the *List* was compiled. However, it is also the case that the *Baptist Union Directory* does not list churches that may have been established prior to 1715 but have since closed, or those churches which may have then been designated as Baptist but are not now in membership of the Baptist Union of Great Britain. It is likely that these absences result from the information provided to Evans by his mainly Presbyterian correspondents. Evans continued to amend the list until 1729 (he died in 1730), though mostly only in respect of changes of ministry.

The average number of hearers for the 151 churches reporting their total is 197.[43] What we do not know is how the statistics sent to Evans were compiled, nor what instructions, if any, he sent out regarding their

---

[40] MS John Evans, *The Evans List of Dissenting Congregations and Ministers, 1716–1718* held in the Dr Williams's Library, London.

[41] Hereafter the Committee of the Three Denominations.

[42] See *The Baptist Union Directory, 1996–1997* (Didcot: Baptist Union of Great Britain, n.d.).

[43] Hearers not members. According to the 1851 Religious Census the number of hearers in Baptist churches exceeded the number of members by a multiple of four.

compilation. Did responding churches simply add up the number of adults attending all of their services on a given Sunday regardless of duplicate attendance? Is it only the main service that is considered or is it an estimated average adult attendance? No separate information regarding the number of children in attendance is given so we have no certain way of knowing if they are counted as hearers or not, though the likelihood is they were not. The absence of any description of the method of compiling the statistics would tend to point to a very informal method of gathering information by estimation and possibly hearsay. The fact that statistics are unreported for 39% of the identified Baptist churches also strongly suggests that methods less than what we now regard as scientific were in operation.

The Josiah Thompson List of Dissenting Congregations

Josiah Thompson who compiled his list[44] in 1772-73 was at the time of its compilation retired from the Baptist ministry, which would suggest that he was a man of some independent means. The list was occasioned by the passing through Parliament in 1772 of a bill designed to relieve dissenting ministers from the modified subscription required of them by the Toleration Act of 1689. Although the matter was not resolved by Parliament until 1779 the information in the *Thompson List* was provided to aid the passage of the bill by supplying evidence of the strength of Dissenters in England and their support for the bill. Thompson arranges his list by counties and provides information about the numbers of congregations, some limited information about individual church origins and present status, and those ministers in each county who signed a petition supporting the 1772 bill. As with the *Evans List* few churches make it clear if they are General Baptist, Particular Baptist, or Independent Baptist.

Unlike the *Evan's List*, the *Thompson List* did not come into existence as a survey of dissenting church life in England and Wales, so while Thompson provides fairly comprehensive information about the location and number of churches and ministers the information about the size of congregations is incidental. Only the churches in Bedfordshire have reported with any consistency the number of attenders. Bedfordshire's seventeen churches indicate a total attendance of 4,160 at an average of 245.

---

[44] Josiah Thompson, 'A View of English Nonconformity in 1773', *Transactions of the Congregational Historical Society* 5 (1911–1912), pp. 205-22, 261-77 and 372-85.

A Comparison of the Evans and Thompson Lists[45]

Whilst it would not be wise to draw detailed conclusions from the two lists they do provide, as Table 3 shows, a clear picture of growth in the total number of churches. Tables 3 and 4 are concerned only with growth in the number of churches and not the number of members. Whereas some attempt to calculate the number of churches is possible, it is not possible to do this for church membership or attendance as the statistics become increasingly less available as we travel backwards in time, accelerating beyond 1770. English Baptist church membership peaked in 1906 at 434,710 with 590,321 scholars, but the numbers of churches did not peak until 1951 at 3,351, by which time membership had fallen to 335,630 and scholars to 320,898.[46] This indicates that an increase in the number of churches does not *per se* equate to an increase in church members. However, such a picture might be expected at the end of a long period of sustained growth or revival, and is almost certainly to be reflected in other such circumstances. This was not the situation in the early- to mid-eighteenth century and an increase in the number of churches can more fairly be seen as an increase in the number of members, particularly in the absence of evidence to the contrary.

Table 1 indicates that the nine counties of England who would have churches in membership of the NPBA at its peak increased between 1715 and 1773 by nineteen churches, an increase of 33%, while in Northamptonshire the number of Baptist churches decreased by seven, a decrease of 31%. This decline against the trend might also offer some explanation of the motivation of those Northamptonshire ministers and churches of the late 1760s as they formed their association.[47]

Table 2 was compiled using the 2002–2003 Baptist Union of Great Britain *Handbook* and refers, therefore, only to churches still in existence

---

[45] See Table 1

[46] Ernest A. Payne, *The Baptist Union: A Short History* (London: Baptist Union of Great Britain and Ireland, 1959), Appendix IV 'Statistics', p. 268. Members here refers to those on the church membership roll while scholars refers to those who attended Sunday School which, alongside the development of state education post-1870, became increasingly a children's activity. Initially Sunday Schools were attended by all age groups and were schools on a Sunday.

[47] Most of the Baptist Associations produced annual reports following their annual assembly and in the eighteenth century these came to take a common format. These *Circular Letters* as they were known were published but can now mainly be found only in archives. The *Circular Letters* of the Northamptonshire Particular Baptist Association 1766–1815 can be found in the archives of Kettering Baptist Church, the Northampton County Records Office, and The Angus Library, Oxford. The British Library also possesses a cross section of *Circular Letters*. All of the Northamptonshire Letters contain a section on the 'state of the churches' in which annual returns for membership gains and losses are given

The Myth of High-Calvinism?

and in membership with the Baptist Union. This provides a simple and effective means of demonstrating the growth in the number of Baptist churches during a period usually characterized by decline. London presents an interesting study as only three churches remain that were formed prior to 1770, whereas Thompson reported the existence in 1773 of 104 London churches.[48] The explanation lies not in church failure but in the constantly shifting population and the expansion of the city. Table 2 also helps to illustrate some of the weaknesses in the *Evans List* for we can see that where Evans records for Yorkshire and Lancashire only one Baptist church in 1715,[49] the *Directory* notes ten in those two counties increasing by a further twelve by 1770. Nevertheless, compared with 118 churches formed in the 165 years between 1550 and 1715 (1550 being the oldest recorded church date in the *Handbook*[50]) some sixty-six churches were formed between 1715 and 1770, with slightly more than half being formed in the period 1715–50. Again the evidence is of growth and Table 3 shows the extent of that growth using the two lists.

We have noted already the paucity of statistical information available for individual churches prior to 1770. My research within the Northamptonshire Association has provided only two churches for which a useful series of figures can be established; Olney from 1738–49 (see Table 5) and College Lane, Northampton, from 1759–80 (see Table 6) during the pastorate of J.C. Ryland. In a book held in the archives of the Olney church, entitled *Index of Burials 1738–1826*, the opening page contains the names of the thirteen individuals who on 15 November 1738 formed the Baptist church there. The book records, 'Our beginning is small so that we may greatly increase.' By July 1742 the membership had increased to forty-six, and by 1749 to fifty-four. Olney was a new church that from small beginnings showed steady and consistent growth throughout the period when John Gill was at his most influential, despite the fact that throughout this period the church only once had a pastor and then for only one year, between 1742 and 1743. An unsettled period for the church followed this initial pastorate that was not wholly overcome

---

[48] See Table 4

[49] On Table 2 North West essentially equates to Lancashire. It must, however, be noted that not all the churches listed in the *Directory* might have declared themselves as Baptists in 1715, and whilst the *Directory* gives the date of a church's formation it does not give the date at which they became Baptist in name, or by joining an Association. However, from 1715 onwards it is probable that all but a few of the churches were Baptist at their formation.

[50] Churches formed prior to the 1600's will not have originated as Baptist churches but as Independent congregations (Separatist congregations from within the Church of England) who later came to hold Baptist views and consider themselves Baptist. This etymology would remain common for the next century in Baptist church life.

by the arrival of William Walker as pastor in 1753 even though Walker remained at Olney for over twenty years. In fact both Walker's arrival and departure from the church were troublesome and the church's archive contains a wallpaper bound volume written by Walker himself detailing what took place. The account of his arrival he entitles *A true Representation of the Case of the Church at Olney*[51] and it is a 'from the heart' and devastating indictment of those at Olney who had given him such trouble. High-Calvinism appears to have figured prominently in the antagonism. When Caleb Evans, the principal at Bristol, sent John Sutcliff to preach at Olney he warned him of those in the congregation with high-Calvinist sentiments, and it seems they gave Sutcliff as many initial problems as they had given Walker.[52] However, the presence of an influential group of high-Calvinists did not prevent the church growing.

A list of members is maintained in the Olney church book dated 1752–1854 and shows that during his troubled ministry Walker admitted some seventy-five individuals into membership, but, despite this, when his successor John Sutcliff arrived the church had only fifty-four members. However, Walker was involved in two events of note during his time at Olney. The first was the building in 1763, at a cost of £250, of a new church building, always a sign of life and good health in a church. More significant, though on a wider scale, was Walker's presence on 17 October 1764 at the meeting at Kettering to establish the NPBA. On 14–15 May 1765 Olney became one of the six founding members of the Association.

In commending Olney to John Sutcliff, Evans had informed him that there was a considerable interest there with 'a large house and a large congregation'.[53] John Ryland, Jr, who would become a lifelong friend, was more precise informing Sutcliff he would be preaching to a congregation in the afternoon and evening of 300-400 people.[54] Certainly the evidence of the 1851 Census[55] is that Baptist church congregations were three to four times the size of the membership and we should note that membership growth is only one indicator of a healthy and growing church. It is not impossible that the thirteen members recorded at the founding of the Olney church in 1738 also constituted, in

---

[51] Maurice Hewitt, who was minister at Olney from 1925–31, wrote an unpublished history of the church (c.1930) possibly intended for its bi-centenary in 1938, and the manuscript remains in the church's archive.
[52] Haykin, *One Heart and One Soul*, p. 114.
[53] Haykin, *One Heart and One Soul*, p. 97.
[54] Haykin, *One Heart and One Soul*, p. 98.
[55] On the Census, see, e.g., K.S. Inglis, 'Patterns of Religious Worship in 1851', *Journal of Ecclesiastical History* 11.1 (April, 1960), pp. 74-86; and, specifically as it reflected Baptist life, John H.Y. Briggs, *The English Baptists of the Nineteenth Century* (A History of English Baptists, 3; Didcot: Baptist Historical Society, 1994), pp. 258, 261, 264-68, 272 and 298.

the main, the entire congregation (children almost certainly were not counted) and therefore that by the time of Sutcliff's arrival the real growth that had occurred was enormous.

Michael Haykin also mentions the revival that occurred in Bourton-on-the-Water in 1741 during which John Collett Ryland was converted along with forty others through the preaching of Benjamin Beddome (1717–95), who was pastor there from 1743–95. A graduate of the Bristol Academy and an evangelical Calvinist he joined a church with 100 members. By 1763 the church had grown to 183 members and Beddome had conducted 200 baptisms. A further feature of this exciting church in a small Cotswold village during this period was the number of men, including John Collett Ryland, it sent into the Baptist ministry.[56] Once again we must wonder at the precise nature of the distinction and question the reality of any supposed theological gulf between high-Calvinists and evangelical Calvinists!

What is apparent from Tables 1 to 4 is that the number of Baptist churches in England continued to grow through the period 1715–73 at the not insignificant rate of 66% or 2.94 new churches per year. The nineteenth century is widely acknowledged as a period of great Baptist church growth in England and it is interesting to note that the available statistics for 1798–1866 indicate a rate of growth in number of churches of 371%, and the period 1866–1906, when growth peaked, at 25.6%.

The Northamptonshire Association and Church Growth in the Late Eighteenth Century

London and Bristol had long been the two significant centres of Baptist influence, but for a brief period toward the end of the eighteenth century the focus switched to the Baptists of central England. It began in 1765 with the formation of the Northamptonshire Particular Baptist Association (NPBA).[57] The formation of Particular Baptist churches into an association was by no means new, yet, as it was some seventy to eighty years since the formation of the first, the Western Association, it cannot be argued that Northamptonshire was simply following the trend. Nor is it true to argue that the NPBA was only formed when there were sufficient churches for it to do so. Two of the original member churches are no longer in existence and the date of their formation is unknown. Of the remaining six Walgrave, which formed in 1700, is the youngest.[58]

---

[56] Haykin, *One Heart and One Soul*, p. 70, lists four.
[57] See T.S.H. Elwyn, *The Northamptonshire Baptist Association: A Short History 1764–1964* (London: Carey Kingsgate Press, 1964).
[58] *Baptist Union Directory 2001–2002* (Didcot: Baptist Union of Great Britain, n.d.), p. 149

The eight churches that formed the Association from Leicestershire and Northamptonshire were Sheepshead, Arnsby, Foxton, Kettering, Walgrave, Olney, Carlton and Northampton. What was their motivation for forming their association? Moses Deacon (d.1773), minister at Walgrave,[59] wrote in the first *Circular Letter* of the Association in 1766: 'it is a day of small things, and religion at a low ebb, yet be not discouraged, the Lord you know is a Sovereign, he hath his set times to favour Zion: It is a mercy your Church state is continued, that you have yet a few names, and a little strength, though not so spiritual, lively and active, as you could wish; 'tis well that your love and unity still subsists, though prosperity, with respect to increase, is much wanting.'[60] It is hard to deny the clear sense of failing churches expressed by these comments and to conclude that this association formed to combat the perceived decline of religion is inescapable. In the case of the Northamptonshire churches we see from Table 1 there is evidence of this decline but the reverse was true for Leicestershire. The evidence for the growth of the two churches for which statistics are available (Olney and College Street, Northampton) has already been presented. This atmosphere of doom was most prevalent at the 1784 Association Assembly following three successive years of decline in the Association's membership.[61] These are not large numbers, but following sixteen years of consistent growth we may perhaps appreciate how they impacted upon the leadership of the Association.

There is something intensely pragmatic about their concerns for numerical growth and, of course, it was no part even of high-Calvinistic theory that Christ would not bring about the extension of his church. The high-Calvinist belief that God did not need the church to bring men and women to a living faith never supposed that without their activity men and women would not come to faith. A further indication of the importance of the numerical state of the churches is revealed by the fact that from their very first gathering in 1766 they kept records of their progress.[62] From 1766 to 1784 the Association records an annual increase in membership, the rate of which is in fact greater than later periods more usually considered a time of Baptist church growth.

In fact, as Table 8 shows, throughout the period 1766–1831 the average increase in church membership is a relatively low 1.73 members, but when it is considered that the gain is an average over the period of

---

[59] Deacon had been at Walgrave as pastor prior to 1738, for at one time he had pastoral oversight for the newly formed Olney church

[60] See *Circular Letter*, NPBA (1766), pp. 1-2.

[61] See Table 7 the years 1782–1784, also 1785

[62] By contrast the 2004–05 *Handbook for the Southern Counties Baptist Association* includes no membership statistics. (n.p.: Southern Counties Baptist Association, n.d.).

The Myth of High-Calvinism? 247

112 members per church it can be seen to be far more significant. Table 9 shows the rate of growth for selected periods in other associations indicating on the whole slightly higher rates of growth than experienced in the NPBA again awareness of this within the NPBA may explain their occasional anxiety about 'the state of religion' as they perceived it.[63]

One might have assumed they were reacting at least in part to the success of the Methodist Revival, and the lack of direct comment in circular letters about the Methodist Revival might seem surprising, but the letters were not intended as commentaries on anything except the life, mission and ministry of Northamptonshire Baptists. The 1798 *Circular Letter* by Brother Burton on 'Experimental Religion' is perhaps the clearest reference. Burton writes: 'By experimental religion we do not mean any of those extacies, visions, or revelations, which, though they have existed in the Church of God, yet were of an extraordinary kind, and peculiar to the days of inspiration. For such revelations in the present day we have no foundation in the sacred writings. We pretend to nothing of the kind ourselves, and consider those who do as under the influence of enthusiasm. The Christian experience of which we speak may be found in all the devotional parts of scripture, particularly in the Psalms of David.'[64] The Revival is not mentioned in any direct way and Burton writes six years after the death of John Wesley and some fifty years after the outbreak of the Revival.

The decline of 1782–84 drew two immediate responses from the Association. The first is the issuing by John Sutcliff, of his now famous 'Call to Prayer'. The second is the decision taken at the 1784 Assembly to ask Andrew Fuller, recently installed as minister at Kettering, to prepare the next *Circular Letter* on the theme 'Decline and Revival'. In the opening to this letter Fuller writes: 'Tis true we have reason to bewail our own and other's declensions, yet we are not, upon the whole, discouraged. It affords us with no little satisfaction to hear in what manner the monthly prayer meetings which were proposed in our letter of last year, have been carried on, and how God has been evidently present in those meetings, stirring up the hearts of his people to wrestle hard with him for the revival of his blessed cause. Though as to the number of members, there is no increase this year, but something of the contrary; yet a spirit of prayer in some measure being poured out, more than balances in our account for this defect. We cannot but hope, wherever we see a spirit of earnest prayer

---

[63] Note that in considering rates of annual membership growth per church we have not here accounted for the increase in the number of churches, which is much more difficult to quantify in isolated associations, but was overall extremely significant. At its height in 1851 the nine counties covered by the NPBA had 239 Particular Baptist churches, whereas in 1765 the NPBA had begun with just eight member churches, and in 1773 Thompson identified sixty-two Baptist churches in the Central Region.

[64] *Circular Letter*, NPBA, 1798, p. 2.

generally and perseveringly prevail, that God has some good in reserve, which in his own time, he will graciously bestow.' This depth of concern for the unconverted appears again and again in the *Circular Letters* and the breviates of the Assembly meetings and becomes for the generation of Baptists represented in men like John Sutcliff, John Ryland, Jr, and Andrew Fuller the motivation for their adoption of an evangelical Calvinism that encouraged proactive evangelistic endeavours. They did not abandon their strongly held Calvinistic beliefs, but they did abandon the extremes of high-Calvinism for an openly evangelistic and moderate Calvinism. However, we would be quite wrong to assume that this motivation did not fuel the faith and actions of John Gill, John Collett Ryland and the like.

The change in Association fortunes from 1785 onward was dramatic with the decline by thirty-seven members of 1772–85 restored by a gain of sixty-two members in 1786, and a further run of regular increases in total membership and in numbers of member churches. By 1827 the number of member churches was such that the Association began to break down into smaller more manageable county units when the church at St Albans left to join with other Hertfordshire churches. As a result, by 1837 the membership of the NPBA itself had diminished to twenty-two churches from three counties (nineteen from Northamptonshire) with a membership in the region of 2,200, and yet more growth to follow. In 1851 the government implemented the first Religious Census held in Great Britain, the main purpose of which appears to have been the desire to ensure that the country's churches provided sufficient 'sittings' (space/seats) to accommodate its population. There are four main groupings of Baptist churches identified by the Census: Particular Baptists, New Connexion of General Baptists (founded as a movement in 1770), General Baptists, and Undefined Baptists (those admitting membership to none of the established groups). Tables 10–13 show the respective numbers of Baptist churches in the NPBA counties in 1851 and all the information is gleaned from the Census reports. These clearly demonstrate the enormous growth that had occurred since 1770 when compared to the Thompson List.[65] By 1851 the nine counties of the NPBA contained more Baptist churches than did the entire country in 1773.

It was part of the purpose of the Census to identify the different religious groupings in Great Britain. The Census records sixty-three Particular Baptist churches in Northamptonshire, while the Association records for 1851 reveal the returns for only thirty-seven churches. The conclusion that most of the twenty-six churches unaccounted for in the records of the Association were not, therefore, in membership is

---

[65] See Table 3.

inescapable. Also inescapable is the parallel conclusion that this is consistently so in the period from 1765 onwards and that the real growth amongst Particular Baptist is much greater than revealed within the NPBA statistics.

The decline throughout the eighteenth century in General Baptist churches has been acknowledged, but even this should not be overstated. Evans shows fifty-seven Baptist churches in the NPBA counties and Thompson eighty-six, and whilst neither consistently differentiates between the churches' affiliations the general assumption of one General Baptist church to seven Particular Baptist churches pertains. On either count, it seems probable that the 1851 Census reveals an increase in the number of General Baptist churches in the nine counties. There is, of course, a question as to the genuine Baptist credentials of these churches and we have already noted that in his report on the 1851 Census Horace Mann considered General Baptists to be synonymous with Unitarians.

Who were these undefined Baptist churches? By definition it is clear that they were not New Connexion churches as membership of this grouping defines their identity. We have noted already that it was more than possible to be identified as a Particular Baptist church and not be in membership of any Association and so we cannot simply assume that these churches are Calvinistic Baptist churches who did not wish to be identified as such. The same point is true from a General Baptist stance. We are left with the reality of a significant group of independent churches which identified themselves as Baptist but could or would not associate themselves with any of the three distinct groupings in existence, nor presumably with each other. The twenty-three independent churches in Northamptonshire alone is equal to the number of churches in total within the county identified by Evans and more than those counted by Thompson.

Conclusion

Explaining High-Calvinism

The statistical evidence presented does not lend support to the commonly expressed view that English Baptists in the mid-eighteenth century were in a state of stagnation, despite the drift of the General Baptists toward Unitarianism and the claimed prevalence among Particular Baptists of high-Calvinism. In fact, the figures as presented would tend to suggest the opposite, that English Baptists during this period experienced steady and continuous growth. Allowance must be made especially for the weaknesses inherent in the *Evans List*, but notwithstanding these the picture is one of growth and not decline throughout the middle sixty years of the century.

Andrew Fuller looked back disparagingly on the high-Calvinism of his upbringing, but he did so not only as one who had abandoned high-Calvinism for evangelical Calvinism, but as the one who championed the cause of evangelical Calvinism to the extent that it was renamed Fullerism, at least in its Baptist form. He looked back also from a time when the gains made by Baptists from 1770 onwards far outstripped anything that had occurred between 1715 and 1770. And he addressed the situation from the standpoint of a Northamptonshire minister, which was one of the few counties in England in which there may have been some evidence of decline. One more question must be raised which is to ask whether the high-Calvinism of Fuller's upbringing was the same in every detail as that of John Gill. Given the connection between Gill and Kettering, the influence of Gill's writings and his position as the foremost high-Calvinist of the eighteenth century we might assume the answer must be yes. However, one of Fuller's main concerns was that in the preaching of high-Calvinists nothing was said to the unregenerate 'in the way of warning them to flee from the wrath to come', yet Ella has demonstrated from his detailed analysis of Gill's surviving sermons that this was far from the case.[66] John Gill was a man esteemed during his life-time and long afterwards as an energetic minister, much sought after and well traveled. He was not only the principal dissenting theologian of the eighteenth century, he was read long after his death. Whatever criticism would later be made of high-Calvinism, it never extended to criticism of Gill personally.

What is without doubt is that from 1770 there is an increasingly clearer commitment from English Baptists to mission. In the breviates of the 1779 NPBA Assembly we are told that the gathered ministers and messengers from the churches agreed together 'to promote village preaching as being a likely method to spread divine knowledge among multitudes who are ignorant; to encourage the catechizing of children; and to print the articles of the association'.[67] Five years before Fuller completed his *Gospel Worthy of all Acceptation*[68] it is evident that his own Association, in promoting such an overtly evangelistic policy, had abandoned any commitment to the supposed tenets of high-Calvinism. Ward suggests that 'the shift arose from a transformation of the church partly affected, and partly evoked, by the transformation of the context in

---

[66] Jarvis, 'Growth in English Baptist Churches', p. 64.
[67] *Circular Letter*, NPBA, 1779 cf. section entitled 'Breviates'.
[68] Andrew Fuller, *The Gospel Worthy of all Acceptation: or the Obligations of Men fully to Credit, and Cordially to Approve, whatever God makes Known. Wherein is considered the Nature of Faith in Christ, and the duty of those where the Gospel comes in that Matter* (Northampton, 1785), located in British Library, Rare Books, 4255.aaa.1.[1].

The Myth of High-Calvinism?

which it operated, and that the new frame of mind owed much to the effort to understand that transformed context'.[69]

The question is, if this is not the heretofore clearly understood significant shift from a rigid high-Calvinism to a more moderate evangelical Calvinism what was it? Ward's explanation of this transformed context would be the shift in the world-view of Particular Baptists encouraged by the writings of Jonathan Edwards exemplified in *The Millennial significance of the Indian missions of Elliot and Brainerd*[70] and William Carey's call to overseas mission fulfilled in 1792.[71] There is no doubt that many Particular Baptists under the influence of Edward's writings adopted a more expansive outlook, which within the NPBA resulted in the birth of the Baptist Missionary Society in 1792.[72] What is unclear is what constitutes this 'transformed context?' Clearly English society in 1770 had moved on from 1689 and from 1730 there is the effect of rationalism to consider, the impact of the Evangelical Revival, the industrial revolution and the accession of the house of Hanover. It is also possible that Ward has in mind the specific context of the local church, freed from the excesses of the Clarendon Code, enjoying the benefits of new premises which have a greater impact on how we conduct 'church' than is often realised. However, does any of this merit the dramatic language of transformation that Ward employs, or, significant though they may be in themselves, do they amount to nothing more than the evolution of society that might be expected over any fifty to a hundred year period? In reality, does the change in approach among English Baptists following the death of Gill involve no more than a slight shift of application and in theological principle? How truly dramatic is a shift that essentially moves from passionate preaching of the gospel that expects the Spirit to move people to conversion, to passionate preaching of the gospel that concludes with encouraging people to make a response of faith to Christ; when in each case the assumption of the passionate preacher is that the Spirit will move men and women to faith in Christ through the preaching of the gospel?

---

[69] Ward, 'Baptists and the Transformation of the Church', p. 167.

[70] Ward, 'Baptists and the Transformation of the Church', p. 170. Jonathan Edwards, *An account of the Life of the late Reverend Mr. David Brainerd missionary to the Indians chiefly taken from his own diary, and other private writings* (Boston, 1749)

[71] William Carey, *An Enquiry into the Obligations of Christians to Use Means for the Conversion of the Heathens. In which the religious state of the different nations of the world. The success of former undertakings, and the practicability of further undertakings are considered* (Leicester, 1792).

[72] See Brian Stanley, *The History of the Baptist Missionary Society 1792–1992* (Edinburgh: T&T Clark, 1992), e.g., ch. 1 'The Origins and Early Domestic History of the Society', pp. 1-35.

By 1810 the matter appears finally settled beyond dispute and Andrew Fuller can write in the NPBA *Circular Letter* on 'The Promise of the Spirit' that, 'We take for granted that the spread of the Gospel is the great object of your desire. Without this it will be hard to prove that you are Christian Churches.'[73] Indeed, few English Baptist churches would take issue with Fuller on this, however he does later go on to write, 'There are those, on the other hand, who abuse the doctrine by converting it into an argument for sloth and avarice. God can convert sinners, say they, when he pleases, and without any exertions, or contributions of ours.'[74]

What is being questioned here is whether John Gill really held to a more rigid form of Calvinism than did those who succeeded him. If so, was it as distinctive as has been stated, and was it as significant in its effect on the life of mid-eighteenth-century English Baptists as has been claimed? In answer to the first question it seems likely that the Calvinism of John Gill was more rigid than the likes of Fuller, Sutcliff and John Ryland, Jr, as representatives of those who succeeded him. It was distinct enough to be recognized, but not so distinct as to cause dissension and division among Particular Baptists, all of whom considered themselves Calvinists, and all of whom held John Gill and his writings in high regard. High-Calvinism was not as significant as claimed on two grounds. The first is that throughout the century there were a sufficient number of Particular Baptists who were evangelical Calvinists to question the apparent total dominance of the high-Calvinists. The second is that if the effect of high-Calvinism is considered to have been the stagnation of English Particular Baptist church life there is little support to be found for this charge, and ample evidence to the contrary that this was a period of steady growth and advance.

We must face the possibility that later theologians, in an attempt to explain a falsely perceived decline in Baptist fortunes in the mid-eighteenth century, latched on to an existing strain of Calvinism, which emphasized the role of God in bringing people to salvation, but pushed it to an extreme it did not occupy at the time in order to prove their views. Set against the backcloth of the Evangelical Revival we may be able to perceive that what concerned the high-Calvinists was the evangelistic methods of the Wesley's (whose Arminian theology equally failed to commend them and their methods to the Particular Baptists), the apparent emphasis on emotion and experience, and the calling of people to respond to their message. Gill, Brine, John Collet Ryland and their like may have rejected those methods, but to conclude they were passionless preachers unconcerned for the souls of their hearers is to misrepresent them.

---

[73] *Circular Letter*, NPBA, 1810, p. 2
[74] *Circular Letter*, NPBA, 1810, p. 3

John Gill was the foremost dissenting theologian of the eighteenth century, possibly the foremost theologian *per se*. At a time when the church was assailed from within by a drift to Unitarianism and from without by the challenge of Rationalism, John Gill more than any other kept the Particular Baptists true to their biblical and Calvinistic heritage. If in doing this he held more rigidly to his doctrines than those who followed him, and was more concerned with doctrine than evangelism, perhaps he may be forgiven. To charge him with responsibility for the stagnation of a people when, by his tireless work, he perhaps preserved them for a more glorious future, would seem somewhat churlish.

The Real Transformation of English Baptists

The language of transformation when applied to English Particular Baptists in the last third of the eighteenth century is rendered redundant in the sense it has usually been applied. The theological shift from high-Calvinism to evangelical Calvinism, or Fullerism, is less theologically dramatic than has been supposed, as the acceptance of high-Calvinism was less widespread than has been acknowledged, and the stagnation and decline in Baptist church life it spawned is an interpretation which, I believe, is in need of revision.

It is doubtful that English Particular Baptists ceased to increase their numbers from their advent in the country early in the 1630s until they reached their peak in 1906, but rather experienced 300 years of sustained growth. That this growth gained increasing momentum through the years should not be surprising and that from 1770 onwards this attained revival proportions among Particular Baptists, as it had thirty years earlier among Anglicans through the Wesleyan Revival, may in one sense be seen as a natural evolution of events.

In purely Baptist terms the focal point for a short period of time at the end of the eighteenth century ceased to be the great cities of London and Bristol, settling instead upon the Northamptonshire Association, whose foundation in 1765 signalled this shift of focus. At the heart of this shift was not theology but people, and in particular the advent of a group of brilliant, strong, like-minded ministers who would bring their boundless energy and commitment to one another to bear on the church they served locally, regionally, nationally and internationally. The leading figures were Sutcliff, Fuller, Ryland, Jr, and Carey, but there were others such as Robert Hall, Jr, and Samuel Pearce who added their own abilities to the mix. They found encouragement in the great Elijah figure that was Robert Hall, Sr, and, to a lesser extent, from John Collett Ryland, who encouraged his son to be his own Elisha, and surpass his master. They were the new guard who loved and respected the old, found strength and support from one another and determined together to make a difference.

They began by shaping an association of churches, overseeing it through a time of growth, giving authority to the change in emphasis that moved those Particular Baptists who adhered to a restrictive form of high-Calvinism to a mission-oriented evangelical Calvinism, or Fullerism as it was termed.[75] They ended by shaping a denomination and, through the establishment of the Baptist Missionary Society, gave rise to a missionary movement that has impacted the entire world. It is difficult to overstate the significance of these men and their influence upon a whole generation of British Baptists. Just one such example is found in William Knibb (1803–45) who grew up in Fuller's Kettering church before becoming a missionary in Jamaica with the Baptist Missionary Society, and was the man who, in the end, did more than any other to ensure Britain abolished slavery in its Empire.[76]

Though my primary interest is in the Particular Baptists of the Northamptonshire Association it is something perhaps more than an amazing coincidence that it was within the same boundaries that the story of the New Connexion of General Baptists unfolded. For all that Dan Taylor came from Yorkshire and was brought into the Baptist fold via Lincolnshire's General Baptists, it was within the Barton Fabis churches in Leicestershire that the New Connexion of General Baptists was born.

The real transformation that had come to English Baptists by 1800 is not that of a frog becoming a prince, but of a child maturing into wondrous adulthood. They did not become something they were not, they simply grew up, maturing into what they were supposed to be. If the child had been a little shy and unsure of itself, the adult was strong, powerful, attractive and charismatic, and would continue to be so for a century or more.

---

[75] There is no doubt the writings of Jonathan Edwards arrived at an opportune time to give fresh inspiration to Ryland, Jr, and Sutcliff in particular, but they had formed their views before they read his works. Fuller, famously confused the American Edwards with an English writer with the same name, and had written his treatise before he read the 'real' Edwards. On the influence of Edwards on Fuller, see Peter J. Morden, *Offering Christ to the World: Andrew Fuller (1754–1815) and the Revival of Eighteenth Century Particular Baptist Life* (Studies in Baptist History and Thought, 8: Carlisle: Paternoster Press, 2003), pp. 40-51.

[76] See John Howard Hinton, *Memoir of William Knibb, Missionary in Jamaica* (London: Houlston and Stoneman, 1849), and Philip Wright, *Knibb, 'the Notorious': Slaves' Missionary 1803–1845* (London: Sidgwick & Jackson, 1973).

Tables

County	Evan's List 1715–17 number of churches	Thompson List 1773 number of churches
Bedfordshire	18	17
Derbyshire	4	3
Hertfordshire	12	8
Leicestershire	9	21
Lincolnshire	—	17
Northamptonshire	23	16
Nottinghamshire	1	9
Rutlandshire	1	3
Staffordshire	1	—
NBPA Totals	57	86
Whole Country	249	414

Table 1: Comparative Numbers of Churches 1715 and 1773 for NPBA Counties

Region	1550–1715	1715–50	1750–70
Central	16	1	2
East Midland	19	2	11
Eastern	15	3	2
Heart of England	9	3	1
London	2	1	—
North West	5	1	5
Northern	5	1	—
South East	3	5	3
South West	10	4	—
Southern	17	1	1
West of England	12	5	1
Yorkshire	5	6	4
Total	**118**	**33**	**30**
% Increase		**28%**	**25%**

Table 2: Dates of Existing Baptist Church Formation[77]

---

[77] *The Baptist Union Directory, 2002–2003* (Didcot: Baptist Union of Great Britain, n.d.). Under the entry for each of the remaining churches is given the date of its formation.

Date	Source	Number of churches	Change	% Growth	Annual increase
1717	Evan's List	249	—	—	—
1773	Thompson List	414	+165	+66%	2.94

Table 3: Growth in Baptist Church Numbers 1717–73

Area (county)	Evan's List 1715–17: number of churches	Thompson List 1773: number of churches	Rate of growth
South West: (Devon and Somerset)	20	32*	60%
West: (Gloucestershire, Wiltshire, and Worcestershire)	29	51	37%
Central: (Bedfordshire, Hertfordshire Northamptonshire, and Leicestershire)	62	62	0%
London: (London, Middlesex, Surrey, Kent and Sussex)	62	104	68%
North: (Yorkshire and Lancashire)	1	35	3500%
TOTALS	162	282	—
% of total churches	65%	70%	—

Table 4: Evans and Thompson: A Comparison of Areas of Concentrated Baptist Strength in England in 1715 and 1773 (* includes Cornwall)

The Myth of High-Calvinism? 257

Date or Year	New Members	Membership[78]
15 November 1738	13	13
1738–41	4	
4 November 1741	16	
11 November 1741	1	33
14 January 1742	5	
1 April 1742	1	
29 May 1742	3	
4 July 1742	2	46
19 March 1745 or 6	3	
20 July 1746	3	51
24 February 1748	1	
18 March 1749	1	54

Table 5: Olney Baptist Church: Membership Growth 1738–49[79]

Year	Men	Women	Members
5 October 1759	13	29	42
6 November 1760	23	33	56
6 November 1762	30	63	93
6 October 1765	37	54	91
21 July 1766	42	55	97
24 September 1767	48	60	108
5 August 1768	49	65	114
19 May 1769	52	71	123
23 May 1770	56	78	134
7 August 1772	68	91	159
10 May 1776	84	137	221
1780	96	149	245[80] (205)

Table 6: College Lane Membership Statistics during the Pastorate of J.C. Ryland[81]

---

[78] It is possible because of the records from 1738–49 for membership, exclusions and deaths to calculate accurately the total membership as indicated. After 1749 the records become unusable for this purpose until 1776.
[79] The Information in this table is taken from the Olney Church Book.
[80] The summary of J.C. Ryland's ministry from 1759–81 when his son became joint pastor with him indicates only 202 members in 1780 not 245 and the Annual Letter written by College Street to the NPBA Assembly for 1780 indicates 205 members. A large collection of such Annual Letters form part of the NPBA archive material held by the Northampton Public Record Office for the Association

Year	Increases			Decreases			Totals	
	N	R	DtA	D	DfA	E	MC	LC
1766	19	—	—	5	—	2	13	8
1767	50	—	—	27	—	2	21	8
1768[82]	60	2	—	19	—	6	37	11 (3)
1769	56	1	—	12	3	3	38	11
1770	89	2	—	17	1	7	66	12 (1)
1771	61	8	—	15	3	10	41	14 (2)
1772	48	3	—	20	4	13	14	15 (1)
1773	73	2	1	19	6	10	41	12
1774	42	—	—	23	7	4	8	14
1775	160	2	—	16	3	6	137	17 (2)
1776	69	4	—	28	1	7	37	16
1777	56	—	13	29	9	14	17	17
1778	59	—	3	24	1	14	23	17
1779[83]	75	10	20	13	23	6	53	17 (1)
1780	75	1	5	32	3	13	33	17
1781	59	—	6	25	5	18	17	16
1782	39	1	7	25	13	17	(8)	16
1783	24	1	1	19	6	7	(7)	16
1784	31	0	2	34	5	2	(8)[84]	16

[81] The Information in this table is taken from the College Lane Church Book.

[82] It is unclear from the statistics whether the increase in membership of the Association included the members of new churches admitted to the Association. It would appear unlikely, as the addition of three new churches in 1768 does not result in an unusually large increase in the number of new members for that year. The large increases of 1775 might be explained if the total membership of the two new churches were included. However, neither Soham nor Spalding were likely to have been large churches. From 1813 onward the statistics appear in tabular form listing each church's statistics separately. In 1814 Blaby and Southwell joined the Association and there is no question that the total membership of these two churches of 100 is not added to the 'Increases' column, only their respective increase of six and two. This balance of probability is such that the practice of 1813 was a continuation of the practice established since 1767, but this cannot be established with certainty.

[83] In 1779 the Association began a work at Clipstone to which eighteen members of the Association were sent and they are included in the respective figure for members dismissed from and members dismissed to the Association.

[84] In the wake of three consecutive decreases Sutcliff offered his 'Call to Prayer' to the association, and the agreed subject for the following *Circular Letter* in 1785 was

The Myth of High-Calvinism?

1785	25	—	1	23	3	14	(14)	16
1786	82	7	4	20	5	6	62	19 (2)
1787	79	2	18	31	19	5	44[85]	22 (3)
1788	116	3	12	27	10	12	82	22

Table 7: NPBA Membership Statistics and Changes 1766–1888

Table 7 Key:
N   = New members.
R   = Restored.
DtA = Dismissed to the Association. (The term dismissed is not a negative one: its modern equivalent is transferred. These are members who have left one church to join another with the blessing of their original church.)
D   = Deaths.
DfA = Dismissed from the Association.
EX   = Exclusions.
MC   = Membership change. (The figures for most years do not give a total of the membership only the increase or decrease in total. The figures in parentheses indicate an overall decrease in the Association's membership.)
LC   = Listed Churches. (The figure in parentheses is the number of new churches that appear in any annual list.)

Years	Membership Increase	Number of churches	Average increase in actual members per church
1766–81	579	206	2.81
1786–95	359	222	1.62
1796–1805	396	233	1.70
1806–15	469	296	1.58
1816–25	737	322	2.29
1826–31	220	170	1.29
1766–1831	1409	815	1.73

Table 8: NPBA Average Increases in Membership

'Decline and Revival' to be prepared by Andrew Fuller: *Circular Letters of the Northamptonshire Particular Baptist Association 1766–1815*.
[85] The increase included the addition of ten new members at Codnor and Guilsborough not included in the original statistics but noted below them.

Association	Period	Membership increase	Number of churches	Average increase in actual members per church
Western	1774–83	339	326	1.04
Kent and Sussex	1781–88	278	75	3.71
Western	1786–95	849	304	2.79
Midlands	1789–98	509	146	3.49
Norfolk and Suffolk	1817–25	632	191	3.31

Table 9: Other Associations Average Increase in Membership

County	NC	AA	Particular Baptist Attendance			S[86]
			morning	afternoon	evening	
Bedfordshire	47	17,205	8,811	8,140	7,628	13,935
Derbyshire	7	2,089	961	619	1,404	2,108
Hertfordshire	28	9,625	4,902	4,123	4,725	9,452
Leicestershire	25	5,827	3,665	1,752	2,907	7,349
Lincolnshire	22	2,775	1,777	1,014	1,173	4,786
Northamptonshire	63	16,664	8,031	8,219	7,556	20,066
Nottinghamshire	14	3,646	2,013	823	2,372	4,885
Rutlandshire	7	1,055	533	493	481	1,331
Staffordshire	26	6,126	3,948	1,931	2,872	8,561
Totals	239	65,012	34,641	27,114	31,118	72,473
Average per church		272	145	113	130	303

Table 10: 1851 Census: Particular Baptist attendance and Sittings in the NPBA Counties

---

[86] 'Sittings' literally refers to the number of seats available in each church as concern that the nation's churches had sufficient space to accommodate the population was one of the reasons for the conducting of the Census.

The Myth of High-Calvinism? 261

Table 10 Key:
NoC = Number of Churches.
AA = Actual Attendance.
S   = Sittings.

County	NoC	AA	General Baptist Attendance			S
			morning	afternoon	evening	
Bedfordshire	1	295	145	217	60	260
Derbyshire	11	1,994		847	587	1,431
Hertfordshire	3	1,267	522	401	887	950
Leicestershire	10	788		663	463	1,530
Lincolnshire	3	269	92	67	110	316
Northampton-shire	1	188	100	60	45	100
Nottinghamshire	14	1,934	112	1,323	1,330	2,320
Rutlandshire						
Staffordshire						
Totals	43	5,622	971	3,578	3,482	6,907
Average per church		131	23	83	81	

Table 11: 1851 Census: General Baptist Attendance and Sittings in the NPBA Counties

Table 11 Key:
NoC = Number of Churches.
AA = Actual Attendance.
S   = Sittings.

County	NoC	AA	New Connexion Attendance			S
			morning	afternoon	evening	
Bedfordshire						
Derbyshire	16	4,327	1,947	1,266	2,969	5,274
Hertfordshire						
Leicestershire	45	11,701	5,933	3,249	7,534	1,422
Lincolnshire	31	5,953	3,385	1,479	3,640	7,948
Northampton-shire						
Nottingham-shire	23	4,827	1,979	1,732	3,185	5,633
Rutlandshire	4	363	286	36	196	490
Staffordshire	4	552	357	44	388	726
Totals	123	27,724	13,887	7,806	17,912	21,493
Average per church		225	113	63	146	

Table 12: 1851 Census: New Connexion Attendance and Sittings in the NPBA Counties

Table 12 Key:
NoC = Number of Churches.
AA = Actual Attendance.
S = Sittings.

The Myth of High-Calvinism?

County	NoC	AA	Undefined Baptist Attendance			S
			morning	afternoon	evening	
Bedfordshire	7	855	114	265	476	707
Derbyshire	5	2,070	702	356	1,012	1,851
Hertfordshire	13	2,506	603	811	1,092	1,667
Leicestershire	5	702	94	178	430	700
Lincolnshire	6	345	100	125	120	570
Northamptonshire	23	3,869	1,235	1,329	1,305	3,034
Nottinghamshire	2	401	30	213	158	370
Rutlandshire	1	220	80	20	120	120
Staffordshire	5	932	290	325	317	770
Totals	67	11,900	3,248	3,622	5,030	9,789
Average per church		177	48	54	75	

Table 13: 1851 Census: Undefined Baptist Attendance and Sittings in the NPBA Counties

Table 13 Key:
NoC = Number of Churches.
AA = Actual Attendance.
S   = Sittings.

CHAPTER 13

Eighteenth-Century Calvinistic Baptists and the Political Realm, with Particular Reference to the Thought of Andrew Fuller

Michael A.G. Haykin

> Bliss was it in that dawn to be alive,
> But to be young was very heaven!—Oh! times...
> When Reason seemed the most to assert her rights
> When most intent on making of herself
> A prime Enchantress—to assist the work
> Which was then going forward in her name![1]

Thus did William Wordsworth (1770–1850), the English writer whose poetry is central to the canon of British Romanticism, describe the headiness of the early days of the French Revolution. Wordsworth was actually resident in France for a month or so in the fall of 1790, and he informed his sister Dorothy that 'the whole nation was mad with joy, in consequence of the revolution'.[2]

This naïve enthusiasm for what was happening in France was shared by a number of sectors of English society, in particular, English Dissent, which, ever since the reaction against Puritanism after the restoration of the monarchy in 1660, had suffered from profound civil and legal discrimination. For instance, Joseph Kinghorn (1766–1832), who became the pastor of St Mary's Baptist Church, Norwich, only a few months before the opening salvos of the Revolution in June and July of 1789, wrote to his father, David Kinghorn (d. 1822), in August 1789, the month

---

[1] W. Wordsworth, 'French Revolution as it appeared to Enthusiasts at its Commencement', in W. Wordsworth, *Poems* (London: Longman, Hurst, Rees, Orme and Brown, 1815), pp. 69-70. For a critical edition of this poem, which eventually became a part of Wordsworth's posthumously published *Prelude*, see W.J.B. Owen (ed.), *The Fourteen-Book Prelude* (*The Cornell Wordsworth*; Ithaca, NY: Cornell University Press, 1985), p. 218. The lines cited above can be found at *Prelude* xi.108-109, 113-116.

[2] Letter to Dorothy Wordsworth, 6 and 16 September, 1790, in Ernest de Selincourt (ed.), *The Letters of William and Dorothy Wordsworth* (8 vols; rev. Chester L. Shaver; Oxford: Clarendon Press, 2nd edn, 1967), I, p. 36.

after the storming of the Bastille (July 14): 'I rejoice with all my heart at the destruction of that most infamous place the Bastille.'[3] Another Norwich Calvinistic Baptist minister, Mark Wilks (d. 1819), began a sermon on 14 July 1791, the second anniversary of the storming of the Bastille, with the provocative statement, 'Jesus Christ was a Revolutionist'. He went on to inform his congregation that the French Revolution 'is of God and that no power exists or can exist, by which it can be overthrown'.[4] Robert Hall, Jr. (1764–1831), the most famous Calvinistic Baptist preacher in the early nineteenth century, was equally enthralled by what was taking place in France. In a famous tract that went through a number of pirated editions, *Christianity Consistent with a Love of Freedom* (1791), Hall stated:

> Events have taken place of late, and revolutions have been effected, which, had they been foretold a very few years ago, would have been viewed as visionary and extravagant; and their influence is yet far from being spent... The empire of darkness and of despotism has been smitten with a stroke which has sounded through the universe.[5]

Again, one finds a similar attitude to the Revolution expressed in a circular letter of the Northamptonshire Baptist Association written between 1 June and 3 June 1790. Associations of churches in geographical proximity had been a regular feature of Calvinistic Baptist life since the denomination's seventeenth-century beginnings. By the last half of the eighteenth century these associations were holding annual meetings at which representatives of the churches in these associations, usually the pastors and elders, were meeting for a couple of days. These

---

[3] Cited C.B. Jewson, 'Norwich Baptists and the French Revolution', *Baptist Quarterly* 24.5 (January, 1972), p. 209. On Kinghorn's life and ministry, see Dean Olive, 'Joseph Kinghorn (1766–1832)', in Michael A.G. Haykin (ed.), *The British Particular Baptists, 1638–1910* (3 vols; Springfield, MO: Particular Baptist Press, 1998–2003), III, pp. 84-111. This biographical piece does not discuss Kinghorn's political views.

[4] Mark Wilks, *The Origin and Stability of the French Revolution* (Norwich, 1791), pp. 5-7, cited by Robert Hole, 'English sermons and tracts as media of debate on the French Revolution 1789–99', in Mark Philip (ed.), *The French Revolution and British Popular Politics* (Cambridge: Cambridge University Press, 1991), pp. 23-24.

[5] R. Hall, *Christianity Consistent with a Love of Freedom*, in Olinthus Gregory and Joseph Belcher (eds.), *The Works of the Rev. Robert Hall, A.M.* (4 vols; New York: Harper & Brothers, 1854), II, p. 37. For an excellent summary of Hall's life and ministry, see W.H. Brackney, 'Hall, Robert, Jr', in Timothy Larsen (ed.), *Biographical Dictionary of Evangelicals* (Downers Grove, IL: InterVarsity Press, 2003), pp. 284-86. For a study of Hall's attitude to the French Revolution, see especially Dominc Aidan Bellenger, 'The Persecution Chalice: Three Reactions to the French Revolution', in Dominc Aidan Bellenger (ed.), *Opening the Scrolls: Essays in Catholic History in Honour of Godfrey Anstruther* (Bath: Downside Abbey, 1987), pp. 154-59.

annual meetings would be marked by times of corporate prayer, sweet fellowship, and occasions for the public preaching of the scriptures. At some point in the two-day meeting one of the pastors would be chosen to write a letter to all of the churches in the association on behalf of the association itself. It would be ratified, printed after the annual meeting, and sent out as a circular letter. In the 1790 circular letter of the Northamptonshire Association there is this appended paragraph:

> The astonishing Revolution in France, and the increasing thirst among the nations after *civil* and *religious* Liberty, should greatly encourage us to pray, that they also may enjoy *spiritual and evangelical* Liberty, or the glorious Liberty of the Children of God!... May the ravenous *Beast* DESPOTISM, which has so long supported the *Harlot* FALSE RELIGION, be shortly slain, by the well-tempered, great and strong sword of Jehovah![6]

Such sentiments proved to be utterly naïve and uninformed, as we shall see. But it needs to be noted, though, that there were legitimate attempts to alleviate the political position of the Dissenters—Baptists included. In 1787, 1789 and 1790 there were three distinct attempts to secure the parliamentary repeal of the Test and Corporation Acts, passed respectively in 1673 and 1661, which required all holders of military and civic office to receive the Lord's Supper at the hands of an Anglican clergyman. The attempts would prove to be unsuccessful, the one in 1789 failing only by twenty votes. In 1789, the Northamptonshire Association thanked those involved in these attempts:

> The cordial and unanimous thanks of this association, were voted to the *committee of the three denominations of Protestant Dissenters in London*, for their exertions in attempting to procure a repeal of the *Test* and *Corporation Acts*; of which the *moderator* was desired to inform their *secretary*, and that we hope they will not be discouraged by the late failure, from using every wise and legal effort to obtain a desirable end. We cannot but think that the abolition of those laws [is] an object that deserves the concurrence of every friend to liberty and religion, not only that protestant dissenters in general, who have ever approved themselves sincere friends to the present Royal Family, and our happy constitution of government, may no longer be debarred from the full possession of those privileges which ought to be open to all good and faithful subjects, but especially that a stop may be put to the awful *prostitution* of a *divine institution*, which we cannot but consider as a national SIN of enormous magnitude.[7]

---

[6] Cited by Thornton Elwyn, 'Particular Baptists of the Northamptonshire Baptist Association as reflected in the circular letters, 1765–1820', http://www.rpc.ox.ac.uk/bq/elwyn_2.htm, accessed November 13, 2004. Italics original.

[7] Cited by Elwyn, 'Particular Baptists of the Northamptonshire Baptist Association'. Italics original.

Here the Northamptonshire Baptists expressed their loyalty to the British government and the royal family, but they protested the disabilities under which they, along with other Dissenting bodies, had to labour.

While political matters like the one referred to above had their place, many of the Baptists of this era would have agreed with the Northamptonshire Baptist theologian Andrew Fuller (1754–1815) when he told John Fountain (1767–1800), a missionary to India, 'All political concerns are only affairs of this life with which he that will please him, who hath chosen him to be a soldier, must not entangle himself.'[8] William Steadman (1764–1837) well summed up this view in his ordination sermon *The Christian Minister's Duty and Reward* (1807) when he advised the man being ordained, Richard Pengilly (1782–1865), 'I do not wish you to be wholly ignorant of the political state of your country…but do not, I beseech you, let politics engross so much of your thoughts, or your conversation, as to cause the duties of the citizens to interfere with those of the preacher'.[9]

'Tyrants not the deliverers'

Such Baptist sentiments in the early says of the Revolution proved to be utterly naïve and uninformed, for right from the start the powerhouse behind the Revolution had been violence. As one of the moderate revolutionaries had remarked, 'There must be blood to cement revolution.'[10] In 1793 and 1794 the Revolution descended into a vortex of unspeakable violence and terror. During this period, known to history as the Reign of Terror, at least 300,000 were arrested with some 17,000 people being executed by the guillotine. Many others died in prison or were simply killed without the benefit of a trial. French revolutionary armies sought to spread the ideals of the Revolution to neighbouring nations. What they exported, though, was 'unprecedented destruction and warfare'[11] to the rest of Europe, and so plunged the Continent into a war

---

[8] Letter to John Fountain, 25 March 1796, cited Michael A.G. Haykin, *One Heart and One Soul: John Sutcliff of Olney, His friends, and His Times* (Darlington: Evangelical Press, 1994), p. 247.

[9] W. Steadman, *The Christian Minister's Duty and Reward* (Gateshead: J. Marshall, 1807).

[10] Attributed to Manon Philipon Roland; see Simon Schama, *Citizens: A Chronicle of the French Revolution* (New York: Alfred A. Knopf, 1989), p. 859. I am indebted to Schama's perspective on the Revolution, especially the summary in *Citizens*, pp. 851-61.

[11] These words are those of Mark A. Noll in his discussion of the French Revolution as a turning-point in the history of Christianity, see his *Turning Points: Decisive Moments in the History of Christianity* (Grand Rapids, MI: Baker Books, 1997), p. 251.

that more or less lasted until 1815. Not surprisingly Baptists like Kinghorn and Hall became increasingly critical of what was taking place in France. By April of 1798, Kinghorn was convinced that 'all those notions of liberty which the French Revolution very generally raised a few years ago are at an end, they [that is, the rulers of France] are the tyrants not the deliverers of men'.[12]

Hall's views had likewise been transformed. In a sermon entitled *Modern Infidelity Considered, with respect to its Influence on Society* (1800), a work that made Hall something of a celebrity in England, Hall spoke of divine revelation having undergone 'a total eclipse' in France,

> while atheism, performing on a darkened theatre its strange and fearful tragedy, confounded the first elements of society, blended every age, rank, and sex in indiscriminate proscription and massacre, and convulsed all Europe to its centre...[13]

Hall was now convinced that at the root of the sanguinary violence of the Revolution—what he rightly described as 'atrocities...committed with a wanton levity and brutal merriment'—lay the skepticism and rationalism of *les philosophes*, men like Voltaire (1694–1778), Jean-Jacques Rousseau (1712–78), and Denis Diderot (1713–84).[14] 'Settle it therefore in your minds, as a maxim', he told his hearers, 'that atheism'—he is referring to the rationalism of *les philosophes*—'is an inhuman, bloody, ferocious system...: its first object is to dethrone God, its next to destroy man'.[15] In another sermon preached two years later in 1802 entitled *Reflections on War*, Hall expressed the opinion that the French Revolution was also in part God's judgement on the French nation for their brutal persecution in the previous century of the Huguenots, French believers who shared Hall's Calvinistic worldview.[16]

Not only these Baptists, but the vast majority of British men and women were horrified by the Reign of Terror during the Jacobin dictatorship and the wars accompanying and following it. Wordsworth, writing in 1805, expressed the fears of many at that time:

> Through months, through years, long after the last beat
> Of those atrocities, the hour of sleep
> To me came rarely charged with natural gifts,

---

[12] Cited by Jewson, 'Norwich Baptists and the French Revolution', p. 215.

[13] R. Hall, *Modern Infidelity Considered, with respect to its Influence on Society*, in *Works of the Rev. Robert Hall*, I, p. 47.

[14] Hall, *Modern Infidelity Considered*, p. 38.

[15] Hall, *Modern Infidelity Considered*, p. 39. On the atheism, actual and implicit, of Voltaire and Diderot, see James M. Byrne, *Religions and the Enlightenment: From Descartes to Kant* (Louisville, KY: Westminster John Knox Press, 1996), pp. 124-43.

[16] R. Hall, *Reflections on War*, in *Works of the Rev. Robert Hall*, I, pp. 69-70.

Such ghastly Visions had I of despair
And tyranny, and implements of death,
And innocent victims sinking under fear,
And momentary hope, and worn-out prayer,
Each in his separate cell, or penned in crowds
For sacrifice, and struggling with forced mirth
And levity in dungeons where the dust
Was laid with tears. Then suddenly the scene
Changed, and the unbroken dream entangled me
In long orations which I strove to plead
Before unjust tribunals—with a voice
Labouring, a brain confounded, and a sense
Death-like of treacherous desertion, felt
In the last place of refuge, my own soul.[17]

Given such depth of anxiety and fear among the English, it is not surprising that large numbers volunteered to defend their island from possible invasion. As Linda Colley has recently noted, the prime incentive between 1798 and 1805 for Englishmen to join the armed forces was simply fear of invasion.[18]

Sermons preached in England during this time of war and horror that touched upon the realm of politics were frequently centred around the duties of believers to the government and the importance of loyalty.[19] An excellent example of such a sermon is one entitled *Christian Patriotism* that was preached in 1803 by Andrew Fuller, pastor of Kettering Baptist Church, Northamptonshire, a man who has been well described as 'the soundest and most creatively useful theologian' the English Calvinistic Baptists have ever had.[20]

Christian Patriotism

Not long before Fuller's delivery of *Christian Patriotism*, the treaty of Amiens (27 March 1802), which had secured an uneasy peace in Europe for close to fourteen months, collapsed as open hostilities resumed between France and Great Britain. Almost immediately Napoleon

---

[17] W. Wordsworth, *Prelude* x.399-415, in Owen (ed.), The *Fourteen-Book Prelude*, p. 208.

[18] Linda Colley, *Britons: Forging the Nation 1707–1837* (London: Vintage, 1996 [1992]), pp. 317-26.

[19] For Baptist examples of such sermons and tracts, see Samuel Pearce, *Motives to Gratitude* (Birmingham: James Belcher, 1798); and Thomas Blundel, *The Duty of Christians to Civil Government* (Dunstable: J.W. Morris, 1804).

[20] A.C. Underwood, *A History of the English Baptists* (London: Carey Kingsgate Press, 1956), p. 164.

Bonaparte (1769-1821) and his French generals committed themselves to extensive preparations for the invasion of Britain. Although these preparations would occupy much of Napoleon's energy for the next two years, events were at their most critical during the latter months of 1803, when invasion seemed an imminent certainty. Fuller's sermon, based upon Jeremiah 29:7 ('Seek the peace of the city whither I have caused you to be carried away captives, and pray unto the Lord for it; for in the peace thereof shall ye have peace', KJV) sought to help the members of his congregation determine their Christian duty during a time of grave national crisis.

The first section of the sermon is devoted to outlining the historical context in which the prophet Jeremiah spoke these words. The Babylonian king Nebuchadnezzar had taken away into captivity a significant number of the nobility of Judah along with their king Jeconiah (aka Jehoiachin). Certain false prophets who had also been taken into captivity were encouraging the king and his nobles to expect a speedy return to the land of Palestine. Jeremiah, though, knew differently. Seventy years were to elapse before the return of the captives. Meanwhile, they should accept their lot, put down roots in their new home, and above all seek and pray for the peace of Babylon. If such was God's intent for men and women who were enslaved by the very nation for which they were to pray, then, Fuller asked his congregation, ought not they to seek the good of their native land, a land where they were protected by 'mild and wholesome laws, administered under a paternal prince; a land where civil and religious freedom [were] enjoyed in higher degree than in any other nation under heaven?'[21]

Fuller understood God's command to his ancient people to 'seek the peace' (or 'prosperity', as Fuller translated the word *shalom*) of Babylon to be a call to British Christians of his day to be 'patriots, or lovers of our country'. Such patriotism, the Baptist theologian was at pains to emphasize, was not of the sort that sought the prosperity of Great Britain at 'the expense of the general happiness of mankind'. To those men and women in Fuller's day, for instance, who argued that the prosperity of the British Empire was intrinsically bound up with the shameful institution of what he calls 'negro slavery', Fuller vehemently replied, 'if my country cannot prosper but at the expense of justice, humanity, and the happiness of mankind, let it be unprosperous!' His ultimate concern, he went on to say, was 'to cultivate that patriotism which harmonizes with good-will to men'.[22] However, what did this sort of patriotism actually involve when the French army was massed at Boulogne, preparing to embark on an

---

[21] A. Fuller, *Christian Patriotism*, in Joseph Belcher (ed.), *The Complete Works of the Rev. Andrew Fuller* (3 vols; Harrisonburg, VA: Sprinkle Publications, 1988 [1845]), I, pp. 202-203.

[22] Fuller, *Christian Patriotism*, pp. 203-204.

invasion of Great Britain? Well, in such 'cases of imminent danger' it meant the willingness to risk one's life in the defence of one's nation. Fuller was conscious that there were some in his day, notably the Quakers, who would cite Matthew 5:39a ('resist not evil') in support of a position of total pacifism. 'Jesus taught his disciples not to resist evil', Fuller quoted them as saying, 'and when Peter drew his sword, he ordered him to put it up again; saying, "All they that take the sword shall perish with the sword" [Matthew 26:52].'[23] To such pacifists, Fuller gave a series of replies. He began by asking his hearers to recall that he had always deprecated war as one of life's 'greatest calamities'. The Christian faith is indeed 'a religion of peace'. Yet, he stressed, this did not mean that he considered war in every instance to be 'unlawful'. As he once wrote to his close friend William Carey (1761–1834), 'Bro[the]r Carey hates war; so do I, excepting what is purely defensive.'[24] More specifically, he noted that Christ's command in Matthew 5 not to resist evil informs believers that they should never 'retaliate from a principle of revenge' and that 'if an adversary 'smite us on one cheek' we had better 'turn to him the other also' [Luke 6.29; Matthew 5.39b], than go about to avenge our own wrongs'. Fuller saw Christ's words as a vivid contrast to the mores of his society. For instance, the lifestyle of the upper class in eighteenth-century Britain was ruled by a code of honour that frequently involved the men in duelling, something that Fuller could only consider as being in 'direct opposition to the laws of Christ'. Then, with regard to nations, Fuller understood Matthew 5.39a to mean that countries should 'never engage in war but for [their] own defence; nor for that, till every method of avoiding it had been tried in vain'. When it came to Christians, Christ's injunction further entailed a refusal to respond with force when they are persecuted for the gospel's sake: 'no weapon is admissible in this warfare but truth'. Those Christians who followed this command while being subjected to persecution have found that 'the more they have been afflicted, the more they have increased'. On the other hand, those Christian bodies who have acted differently and taken up the sword in their own defence, like the Huguenots in sixteenth- and seventeenth-

---

[23] Fuller, *Christian Patriotism*, p. 205. See also Andrew Fuller, 'Mr. Bevan's Defence of the Christian Doctrine of the Society of Friends', in *Works*, III, p. 759. For some of what follows, I am drawing upon my '"RESISTING EVIL": Civil Retaliation, Non-resistance, and the Interpretation of Matthew 5:39a among Eighteenth-century Calvinistic Baptists', *Baptist Quarterly*, 36.5 (January, 1996), pp. 212-227. Used by permission.

[24] Fuller, *Christian Patriotism*, p. 205; Letter to William Carey, 1 March 1811 (Letters of Andrew Fuller, typescript transcript, Angus Library, Regent's Park College, Oxford University).

century France, have ultimately perished by it—'overcome by their enemies, and exterminated'.[25]

Fuller's point here was part and parcel of the entire Baptist approach to church and state. The church should not employ the state to help in the defence of the truth. Now, one of the great challenges to biblical Christianity in the 1790s was Socinianism. Should the state's power be used to curb its advance? As Fuller would argue, absolutely not. As the Northamptonshire Association put it in their circular letter of 1790, part of which has already been cited above:

> The sword of the Spirit which is the Word of God is enough for them [that is, the Socinians]. Away with all other means of defending evangelical truth. Let us use no weapons in God's cause, but what are taken from his own Armoury... The *testimony of Scriptures* and *sound Reason* are the arms of our Warfare.[26]

Nonetheless, Fuller was not convinced that Matthew 5.39a should be taken 'literally and universally' and that Christians can never bear arms. To argue otherwise would be to imply that the Apostle Paul was wrong to remonstrate with the Philippian magistrates over the illegal beating which he received at their hands (Acts 16.35-39) and that Christ himself erred when he reproved the individual who smote him during his trial before Annas (John 18.19-23). And in the case at hand, the defence of Great Britain against unlawful invasion, there were other texts that needed to be taken into account. There was, for example, Romans 13, which expressly urged believers to support the state and which 'authorized the legal use of the sword' by state magistrates. Fuller reasoned that if it is right for these magistrates to bear the sword against evil-doers within the country, surely 'it cannot be wrong to use it in repelling invaders from without' who have shown themselves to be an 'unprincipled and brutal soldiery' bent on Britain's destruction?[27] As Fuller asked, 'Is it right that any one nation should seek absolutely to ruin another, and that other not be warranted, and even obliged to resist it?'[28]

Here Fuller is drawing upon the *Second London Confession* (1677/1689), a major text in his Calvinistic Baptist heritage, in which the magistrate's use of the sword for national defence had been affirmed.

---

[25] Fuller, *Christian Patriotism*, pp. 205-206.

[26] Cited by Elwyn, 'Particular Baptists of the Northamptonshire Baptist Association'. Italics original. For a study of Fuller's opposition to Socinianism, see Tom J. Nettles, 'Christianity Pure and Simple: Andrew Fuller's Contest with Socinianism', in M.A.G. Haykin (ed.), *'At the Pure Fountain of Thy Word': Andrew Fuller as an* Apologist (Studies in Baptist History and Thought, 6; Carlisle: Paternoster Press, 2004), pp. 139-73.

[27] Fuller, *Christian Patriotism*, pp. 205-206 and 208.

[28] Fuller, *Christian Patriotism*, p. 207.

First issued in 1677 and then adopted twelve years later as the doctrinal standard of Calvinistic Baptists in England and Wales, this confession unequivocally affirmed that it is entirely 'lawful for Christians' to be involved in the political affairs of the nation, in particular, 'to Accept, and Execute the Office of a Magistrate'.[29] By the nature of their office, however, rulers from time to time must employ coercive power and engage in acts of war. So, along with this affirmation of the possibility of being a Christian magistrate was an affirmation of the use of the sword. God himself, the *Second London Confession* asserted, has armed magistrates 'with the power of the Sword, for defence and encouragement of them that do good, and for the punishment of evil doers'. Furthermore, this document declared, Christian magistrates 'may lawfully wage war upon just and necessary occasions'.[30]

In support of this position, the Baptist framers of this confession turned to passages such as Romans 13.4, where the Apostle Paul notes that God has bestowed upon civil authorities the military power necessary to quell resistance to their decrees, and even Luke 3.14, where a group of soldiers are advised by John the Baptist not to abuse the privileges of their occupation, but receive no demand to quit their form of employ. Thus, Fuller believed that if it is right for the magistrate to use the sword in this way, it is not improper for him to expect help and support from those under his authority, 'Otherwise, his power would be merely nominal, and he would indeed "bear the sword in vain" [Romans 13.4].'

Although Fuller believed that the day in which he was living called for British Christians to be actively involved in repelling a French invasion, he was not about to endorse carte blanche every war in which his country engaged. As he declared near the close of his sermon, 'If my country were engaged in an attempt to ruin France, as a nation, it would be a wicked undertaking; and if I were fully convinced of it, I should both hope and pray that they might be disappointed.'[31]

The Political Duty of Prayer

Finally, Fuller argued that there is one other duty believers of his day owed to the British state and that was to pray for the safety of their nation.

---

[29] *The Second London Confession*, XXIV.2, in William L. Lumpkin, *Baptist Confessions of Faith* (Philadelphia, PA: Judson Press, rev. edn 1969), p. 284. The way in which eighteenth-century Baptists were far from being politically quietistic is detailed in James E. Bradley, *Religion, Revolution, and English Radicalism: Nonconformity in Eighteenth-Century Politics and Society* (Cambridge: Cambridge University Press, 1990).

[30] *Second London Confession*, XXIV.1 and 2, in Lumpkin, *Baptist Confessions of Faith*, p. 284.

[31] Fuller, *Christian Patriotism*, pp. 206-207.

You are aware that all our dependence, as a nation, is upon God; and, therefore, [we] should importune his assistance. After all the struggles for power, you know that in his sight all the inhabitants of the world are reputed as nothing: he doth according to his will in the army of heaven, and among the inhabitants of the earth; and none can stay his hand, or say unto him, What doest thou?...but in general the great body of a nation, it is to be feared, think but little about it. Their dependence is upon an arm of flesh. It may be said, without uncharitableness, of many of our commanders, both by sea and land, as was said of Cyrus, God hath girded them, though they have not known him [see Isaiah 45.5]. But by how much you perceive a want of prayer and dependence on God in your countrymen, by so much more should you be concerned, as much as in you lies, to supply the defect. 'The prayer of a righteous man availeth much' [James 5.16].[32]

Fuller was very conscious that the safety of the British people did not depend on their military might, even though many of Fuller's fellow citizens believed it did and were trusting in their armed forces. No, it is a sovereign God who rules over the affairs of people and nations and all of his holy purposes will stand. This lack of a genuine dependence upon God on the part of many of the British, though, should not lead believers to stand aloof from their neighbours and merely condemn them as godless. Rather, Fuller argued, they should give themselves even more assiduously to prayer.

Another motivation for believers to intercede for their nation's welfare was, Fuller said, 'the load of guilt that lies upon your country'. Earlier in the sermon, when he had made mention of 'negro slavery', he had exclaimed,

> O my country, I lament thy faults! Yet, with all thy faults, I will seek thy good; not only as a Briton, but as a Christian...[33]

In fact, Fuller went on,

> I acknowledge myself to have much greater fear from this quarter than from the boasting menaces of a vain man. If our iniquities provoke not the Lord to deliver us into his hand, his schemes and devices will come to nothing. When I think, among other things, of the detestable traffic before alluded to [that is, the slave trade], in which we have taken so conspicuous a part, and have shed so much innocent blood, I tremble! When we have fasted and prayed, I have seemed to hear the voice of God, saying unto us, 'Loose the bands of wickedness, undo the heavy burdens, let the oppressed go free, and break every yoke!' Yet, peradventure, for his own name's sake, or from a regard to his own cause, which is here singularly protected, the Lord may hearken to our prayers, and save us from deserved ruin.[34]

---

[32] Fuller, *Christian Patriotism*, p. 208.
[33] Fuller, *Christian Patriotism*, p. 204.
[34] Fuller, *Christian Patriotism*, p. 208.

Fuller admits to being afraid, but it is not from 'the boasting menaces of a vain man', namely Napoleon Bonaparte. Rather, his anxiety stemmed from Britain's iniquitous participation in the 'detestable' slave trade. England's entry into the slave trade may be dated from 1562 when the Elizabethan adventurer Sir John Hawkins (1532–95) took a shipload of 300 West Africans and sold them to the Spanish in what is now the Dominican Republic. Elizabeth I (r.1558–1601), though, was not impressed with his actions, and called them 'detestable', an attitude towards the slave trade that appears to have generally prevailed among the English into the first few decades of the seventeenth century.[35] Yet, by the time of the Restoration of Charles II (r.1660–85) the English had begun to ferry slaves regularly across the Atlantic for sale in America and the West Indies. By the mid-eighteenth century they had become the leading slave-traders in the world. And in the final decades of that century they were engaged in transporting around 45,000 slaves a year from the West African coast to the American South and the Caribbean. Throughout their rapacious slave-trading history, the British were responsible for transporting some 3 million enslaved Africans to the New World.

English involvement in the slave trade was primarily linked to their desire to encourage the rapid economic development of their colonies in the New World. The key event that drew England into this pernicious trade was the introduction of sugar plantations to the West Indies. The English had tried to grow sugar without any real success in Bermuda and Virginia in the first few decades of the seventeenth century. The turning-point came on Barbados, which the English settled in 1625. Within thirty years they had made sugar a thriving industry on the island and set the course of development for the rest of their island holdings in the Caribbean. Sugar soon became the main export of these islands. By 1730 the English were annually importing 100,000 hogshead of sugar to satisfy what would become known as their 'sweet tooth'.

The growing and harvesting of sugar, though, required prodigious numbers of workers, and England soon followed the example of the Spanish and Portuguese in manning their sugar plantations with armies of black slaves taken from West Africa. Slave ships sailing from London, Bristol, and especially Liverpool, made their way down to the west coast of Africa where they bought slaves from African middlemen and chiefs in exchange for metal goods, woollens, cotton, beads, mirrors, even gunpowder and firearms—the sort of things the Africans did not possess and which were often of extremely poor quality. Many of these cheaper goods were made in Birmingham and were known as 'Brummagem

---

[35] In the words of C.M. MacInnes, 'Bristol and the Slave Trade', in P. McGrath (ed.), *Bristol in the Eighteenth Century* (Newton Abbot: David & Charles, 1972), p. 162: 'It was the proud boast of Englishmen in the opening decades of the seventeenth century that, whatever other nations might think or do, they abhorred the trade in human flesh.'

ware'.[36] Initially the slaves were prisoners of tribal wars, but then as the demand for slaves grew in the eighteenth century, they were more frequently the captives of slave-raiding parties. Those who were captured by such raids into the African interior sometimes spent months being taken to the coast, where for the first time in their lives they saw white men. While this trek to the Atlantic was itself a traumatic experience, it could hardly compare to what followed.

After they had been bought, the slaves were thrust into the hold of the slave ship and the ship set out on what was called 'the Middle Passage', that is the voyage across the Atlantic. Here many of them died in the squalid, fetid quarters that they had to inhabit for up to three or four months while the ship made the crossing. Such an environment, where the sick and the dying might remain shackled to the healthy and living for weeks on end and where they were given little opportunity for exercise, was a breeding ground for epidemic diseases. Those slaves who survived the voyage faced even more trauma in the New World as they might be sold and re-sold a number of times before finally arriving at their final destination.[37] Upwards of twenty-five per cent of the Africans would die within three years of their arrival in America or the Caribbean.

All of this human suffering, which escapes the power of the historian to describe in its enormity and hideousness, ultimately served two chief ends: to produce luxury goods so as to satisfy the palate and fill the pockets of British consumers, and support the lifestyle of the affluent in the Southern American states. As William Cowper (1731–1800) incisively lampooned this real reason for the continuance of the slave trade in his poem 'Pity for Poor Africans':

> I pity them greatly, but I must be mum,
> For how could we do without sugar and rum?
> Especially sugar, so needful we see!
> What! Give up our desserts, our coffee and tea![38]

Britain was thus far from guiltless—she too had shed innocent blood and had been an oppressor. Such social sins deserved judgement and ruin. But Fuller hoped that the Lord, for the sake of his glory or his cause, which had flourished in Great Britain under the banner of Evangelicalism, would hearken to their prayers.

---

[36] On the impact of the slave trade on Bristol and Liverpool, see respectively MacInnes, 'Bristol and the Slave Trade', pp. 161-84; and Ramsay Muir, *A History of Liverpool* (London: Williams & Norgate, 1907), pp. 190-206.

[37] Cf. A.B. Pinn, *Terror and Triumph: The Nature of Black Religion* (Minneapolis, MN: Fortress Press, 2003), pp. 27-51.

[38] W. Cowper, 'Pity for Poor Africans', in W.M. Rossetti (ed.), *The Poetical Works of William Cowper* (London: Griffith Farran Okeden & Welsh, n.d.), pp. 370-71.

Undergirding Fuller's argumentation is also the conviction that, as he said in another sermon preached a couple of years before *Christian Patriotism*, 'religion is not a matter to be cooped up in a closet, nor yet in a place of worship'.[39] Fuller well knew that the Christian faith has implications for every sphere of human existence for Jesus Christ is the Lord of all life.

Fuller was not a lone Baptist voice in his strident criticism of slavery. In the previous dozen or so years there had been a growing chorus of opposition among British Baptists to what Fuller called 'a detestable traffic'. Other Baptist preachers like Robert Robinson (1735–90), Abraham Booth (1734–1806), and James Dore (d.1825) had published sermons that ably argued the case for the abolition of slavery.[40] And over the next forty years, the British Baptist community would come to play a decisive political role in the emancipation of the slaves in the British Empire.[41] This political involvement, in both the struggle against the slave trade and the fight for the freedom of the slaves, surely illustrates that the late eighteenth-century British Baptist community cannot be regarded as wholly apolitical. As Robert Robinson once noted, the conviction that 'Christians,...and particularly ministers of religion, have nothing to do with what they call politics' is nothing more than a 'groundless opinion'.[42]

Praying for the French

There is one area that Fuller does not mention in his sermon and that is prayer for the enemy. However, one of his closest friends, Samuel Pearce (1766–99), pastor of Cannon Street Baptist Church, Birmingham, shows that Fuller would have considered such very appropriate. Fuller wrote Pearce's memoirs after the latter's death from tuberculosis in the autumn

---

[39] Fuller, *Paul's Prayer for the Philippians, Works*, I, p. 360.

[40] Robert Robinson, *Slavery Inconsistent with the Spirit of Christianity* (London, 1788); Abraham Booth, *Commerce in the human species, and the enslaving of innocent persons, inimical to the laws of Moses and the gospel of Christ* (London, 1792); James Dore, *A Sermon on the American Slave Trade* (London, 1788). On the opposition to the slave trade by the various Baptist associations, see the references in Olin C. Robison, 'The Particular Baptists in England 1760-1820' (DPhil thesis, Regent's Park College, Oxford University, 1963), p. 437 n. 1.

[41] See, for example, the correspondence of a group of London pastors to Baptists of America in 1833 in Robert Baker, *A Baptist Sourcebook* (Nashville, TN: Broadman Press, 1966), pp. 87-88, and the life of William Knibb (1803-45): e.g., J.H. Hinton, *Memoir of William Knibb, Missionary in Jamaica* (London: Houlston and Stoneman, 1849), and P. Wright, *Knibb, 'the Notorious': Slaves Missionary 18-3-1845* London: Sidgwick & Jackson, 1973).

[42] R. Robinson, *Christian Submission to Civil Government* (1780), in his *Sermons*, p. 21.

of 1799. In Fuller's account of his friend's life he particularly stressed Pearce's remarkable piety in which Pearce's concern for the salvation of the lost was prominent.

Pearce had caught a chill in October 1798 and had not taken care of himself. The chill went deep into his lungs and by mid-December 1798 Pearce could not converse for more than a few minutes without losing his breath. In one of the last sermons that Pearce ever preached, on a day of public thanksgiving for Horatio Nelson's victorious annihilation of the French Fleet at the Battle of the Nile (1798) and the repulse of a French invasion fleet off the coast of Ireland in the same year, Pearce pointedly said,

> Should any one expect that I shall introduce the *destruction* of our foes, by the late victories gained off the coasts of Egypt and Ireland, as the object of pleasure and gratitude, he will be disappointed. The man who can take pleasure at the destruction of his fellow men, is a cannibal at heart;...but to the heart of him who calls himself a disciple of the merciful Jesus, let such pleasure be an everlasting stranger. Since in that sacred volume, which I revere as the fair gift of heaven to man, I am taught, that 'of one blood God hath made all nations,' [Acts 17.26] it is impossible for me not to regard every man as my brother, and to consider, that national differences ought not to excite personal animosities.[43]

A few months later, when he was desperately ill, he wrote a letter to William Carey telling him of his plans for a missionary journey to France. 'I have been endeavouring for some years', he told Carey, 'to get five of our Ministers to agree that they will apply themselves to the French language,...then we [for he was obviously intending to be one of the five] might spend two months annually in that Country, and at least satisfy ourselves that Christianity was not lost in France for want of a fair experiment in its favour: and who can tell what God might do!'[44] Unlike the hatred that gripped many of his fellow citizens when they thought of France, Pearce was gripped by the priorities of the kingdom of Christ.

God would use British Evangelicals, notably Pearce's Baptist contemporary Robert Haldane (1764–1842), to take the gospel to Francophones on the Continent when peace eventually came, but Pearce would play no part in that great work. Yet his ardent prayers on behalf of the French, and those of other believers in England, could not have been without some effect. As Fuller had quoted, 'The prayer of a righteous man availeth much' (James 5.16).

---

[43] S. Pearce, *Motives to Gratitude* (Birmingham: James Belcher, 1798), pp. 18-19. Italics original.

[44] Cited by S. Pearce Carey, *Samuel Pearce, M.A., The Baptist Brainerd* (London: Carey Press, 3rd edn, n.d.), p. 189.

CHAPTER 14

Episcopacy in the Baptist Tradition

Valdis Teraudkalns

The Baptist tradition has so emphasized the principles of the priesthood of all believers, egalitarian relationships in the church and the freedom of local churches that Baptists have rightly been criticized for being too atomistic an approach to ecclesiology, would probably be the last place to look for an episcopal tradition. But, as will be shown in this paper, such an assumption is too simplistic and serves as an example of the tendency to create denominational identity by excluding minority perspectives and practices that challenge a dominant view. We should also take into account the fact that the historical episcopacy, which has legitimized the rights of a 'divinely' appointed class of leadership to rule the church and has served as an important element of the inclusion–exclusion mechanism of religious power discourse, has been severely criticized not only by the Free Churches but from all Christian traditions. In contemporary societies, which are at least trying to be open and democratic, a governing authority structure based on a medieval view of hierarchical social relationships looks odd.

Following the Second Vatican Council, some Catholic theologians have also made this criticism. For example, Leonardo Boff offers an interpretation of what he believes was the ecclesiastical paradigm shift of the Council—in which the old model was replaced by one in which all are involved—lay people, priest, bishop—in a more integrative way.[1] He then elaborates the theological framework for such a model: 'by baptism an entire people becomes priestly'.[2] Catholic author John McKenzie has criticized the prevailing traditional concept of authority by arguing that 'authority in the New Testament is conceived in a way which must be called democratic rather than absolute. Authority in the Church belongs to the whole Church and not to particular officers.'[3] From another wing

---

[1] L. Boff. *Ecclesiogenesis: The Base Communities Reinvent the Church* (London: Collins, 1986), pp. 30-33.
[2] Boff. *Ecclesiogenesis*, p. 69.
[3] J.L. McKenzie, *Authority in the Church* (London: Geoffrey Chapman, 1966), p. 85.

of the theological spectrum, feminist theologians are proposing ecclesiastical models alternative to ones grounded in the medieval social order/hierarchy. Authority is modelled as partnership, not as pyramidal structure. Letty M. Russel pictures Christian leadership as a rainbow which 'consists of a wider variety of colors, and it gains its beauty as more of the color and more of the entire circle may been seen. The rainbow appears most often in the midst of a storm, and this is appropriate for portraying a new reality in the midst of struggling with the old.'[4]

With their emphasis on horizontal relationships based on mutual respect and the principle of covenant, Baptists can make a good contribution to the current ecumenical debate. But any interdenominational dialogue always includes in itself denominational debate calling for critical reappraisal of one's own tradition. It is too idealistic and naive to ignore the fact that in many cases strong personalities have ruled local Baptist churches and the pious slogan of 'looking for the mind of Christ' in church meetings has been used to cover manipulative actions. This is part of the constant struggle within every religion. The institutionalization and bureaucratization of religious groups create the rank of 'experts', which are often very resistant to attempts to limit its rights. As Paul Tillich said:

> The ambiguity of leadership is closely connected with the ambiguities of inclusiveness and of equality, for it is the leading groups that exclude and produce inequality, even in the relation to God. Leadership and its ambiguities belong to the life of every historical group... Religious leadership has the same profane and demonic possibilities as every other leadership.[5]

In this article I will mainly concentrate on an historical analysis of the British and Latvian Baptist traditions. It is worth mentioning that today the Baptist unions of Georgia and Moldova also have the office of bishop. Moldavian Baptists elect their bishop for four years in the Congress of the Union where representatives of all local churches are present. In their case 'bishop' is not considered a separate rank in the pastoral ministry, therefore he is not consecrated by a special act (the laying on of hands) as occurs in the ordination of a presbyter. Thus, Moldavian Baptists are trying to avoid being perceived as imitating the hierarchical structure of the Orthodox Church.[6] The newly formed Federation of Evangelical Christians, founded by those Evangelical

---

[4] L.M. Russel, *Household of Freedom: Authority in Feminist Theology* (Philadelphia: The Westminster Press, 1987), p. 35.
[5] P. Tillich, *Systematic Theology* (3 vols; Chicago: University of Chicago Press, 1963), III, p. 207.
[6] V. Gileckij in a letter to the author, 28 January 2002.

Christians in the Far East of Russia who have separated from Baptists, has also appointed a bishop.[7]
Georgian Baptists use the title 'bishop' because they believe that

> this is a biblical word while president or chairman is not in the Bible. But this is a minor reason. The second reason is more important. In a country like Georgia people will only understand titles which they know from their religious life. So in order to be acceptable for the people they use this word and not only for the Presiding Bishop but also for the regional leaders.[8]

This development is part of the efforts of local Baptist leaders to contextualize the gospel and to diminish the negative effect of stereotyping which have occurred in the past. In the Assembly of Georgian Baptist churches in October 2001 presiding Bishop Malkhaz Songulashvili said, 'It is my great desire and intention to help our churches and the union to get out of the corner of having a sectarian image'.[9] There is no surprise that Georgian Baptists have developed warm relationships with the Church of England. Anglican representatives view this Baptist group as 'a church in the liberal Baptist tradition, reflecting many attributes of Anglicanism apart from the discipline on baptism itself'.[10] Georgian Baptists are not unique among Free Churches in their interest in church tradition. From time to time in the former USSR one encounters Protestant groups experimenting with high church liturgy, historical church offices and/or spiritual heritage of apostolic fathers. For example, a national Komi Evangelical Church, founded as an independent Baptist church in the 1960s and finally registered in 1992, combines charismatic liturgy with an interest in Russian Orthodoxy.[11]

The long-term exclusion of Baptists in former USSR from full participation in the international arena did cause damage, but it also had a positive side in that local religious identities have developed in a way which is primarily concerned with the local context and not so much with conforming to what is perceived by many to be *the* Baptist way. With new openness comes also greater social pressure to 'fit in the accepted picture'.

It should be added that bishops and archbishops (both male and female) are also part of the church order of Spiritual Baptists (Shouters)

---

[7] K. Rösler, '"Breakup of the Unions" or increased co-operation across all borders?', *European Baptist Press Service* (January 20, 2005), www.ebf.org.
[8] K.H. Walter in a letter to V. Teraudkalns, 19 December 2001.
[9] Walter, letter to V. Teraudkalns.
[10] http://orders.anglican.org/tssf (20 August 2003)
[11] X. Dennen, 'Russia's Far North: Christianity Today in the Komi Republic', *Frontier* 7 (Winter 2005), p. 6.

popular among Caribbean people.[12] Because of the highly syncretistic nature of their faith (a mixture of Protestantism, Catholicism, African polytheism, Islam etc.) and the indigenous character of opposing western Baptists this group is usually excluded from the books on Baptists. For the researcher, however, it provides valuable material how floating and multiple religious identities can be.

Moving between Denial and Acceptance: British Baptist Experience of Episcopacy

By the middle of the seventeenth century the term 'messenger' was used by both General and Particular Baptists to designate a person commissioned by one church to preach and form new churches, and as a title for the person sent by one church to another to deal with ecclesiastical matters. General Baptists in the Midlands and in Kent used it of a specific office separate from that of elders.[13] This ministry has been described as 'trans-local—giving a focus to *episkopé between* churches rather than *over* them'.[14] The General Baptist *Orthodox Creed* issued in 1679 by fifty-four representatives of local churches outlines a three-fold pattern of ministry—bishops/messengers, elders/pastors and deacons/overseers. The *Orthodox Creed* describes the process of election and ordination of the bishop and its main responsibilities:

> That he be chosen thereunto by the common suffrage of the church, and solemnly set apart by fasting and prayer, with imposition of hands, by the bishops of the same function, ordinarily, and those bishops so ordained, have the government of those churches, that had suffrage in their election, and no other ordinarily; as also to preach to word, or gospel, to the world, or unbelievers.[15]

We can find the justification of the bishop's office in the work written in 1671 by Thomas Grantham, *A Defence of the Office of Apostles and of Continuance Thereof in the Church till the End.* Grantham argued that apostles still exist (though not in the sense of the twelve) in the office of bishops in three ways: in respect of the lawful power or authority to preach the gospel; in unwearied diligence in teaching and strengthening

---

[12] See, e.g., www.raceandhistory.com/historicalviews/africanspirit.htm (3 March 2003); www.shouterbaptist.org (3 January 2003).

[13] J.F.V. Nicholson, 'The Office of "Messenger" amongst British Baptists in the Seventeenth and Eighteenth Centuries', *Baptist Quarterly* 17.5 (January, 1958), pp. 210-11.

[14] P.C. Bouteneff and A.D. Falconer (eds), *New Experiences of Episkopé and Episcopacy, Episkopé and Episcopacy and the Quest for the Visible Unity* (Geneva: WCC Publications, 1999), p. 16.

[15] W.J. McGlothlin, *Baptist Confessions of Faith* (Philadelphia: American Baptist Publication Society, 1911), p. 147.

both pastors and churches in all council of God; and in being set for a defence of the gospel or doctrine once delivered.[16] During this same period Particular Baptists continued using the title for the representative of a church, though they denied the existence of a third order of ministry.[17]

By the second half of eighteenth century the General Baptist messenger acted primarily as a bishop comparable to those in the Church of England, whose primary role was no longer as an evangelist but in ordaining, visiting, remedying abuses and presiding at associations and assemblies.[18] Later, with the decline of old General Baptists, the office of messengers also disappeared. The rise of the Oxford movement among members of the Church of England in the nineteenth century deepened British Baptist suspicion of church offices and of symbolic acts setting people apart for a particular office, such as ordination. This reaction created a long-standing fear of being 'infected' by High Church ideology. The 1994 Baptist Union discussion document on forms of ministry stated that 'there is a fear that singling out one kind of ministry as the "ordained ministry" not only suppresses the ministry of the whole people of God in their daily life in the world, but also fails to give proper recognition to other kinds of service in the church to which people are called to give their primary commitment—for example as a youth leader of evangelist.'[19] The twentieth-century Area Superintendent (now replaced by Senior Regional Ministers) effectively revived the earlier office of bishop. Superintendents cared for the pastors and churches in the geographical areas they were appointed to oversee. This innovation was introduced by John Howard Shakespeare (Secretary of the Baptist Union from 1898–1924) who had as his ultimate goal union of the Free Churches with the Church of England under the episcopal system. The term 'superintendent' was probably borrowed from the German Lutherans and was used as an alternative to 'bishop'. However J.H. Shakespeare did not object when in public or mass media superintendents were called bishops.[20]

Many British Baptist theologians have been careful to avoid any episcopal connotations regarding the Area Superintendent. Paul Beasley-Murray argues that 'the most important reason for not referring to

---

[16] N. Wright, *Challenge to Challenge: A Radical Christian Agenda for Baptists* (Eastbourne: Kingsway, 1991), p. 180.
[17] Nicholson, 'The Office of "Messenger"', p. 213.
[18] Nicholson, 'The Office of "Messenger"', p. 220.
[19] *Forms of Ministry among Baptists: Towards an Understanding of Spiritual Leadership* (Didcot: Baptist Union of Great Britain, 1994), p. 21.
[20] P. Shepherd, *The Making of a Modern Denomination: John Howard Shakespeare and the English Baptists 1898–1924* (Studies in Baptist History and Thought, 4; Carlisle: Paternoster Press, 2001), pp. 80, 83.

superintendents as Baptist "bishops" is found in the unhelpful associations connected with the Anglican and Roman Catholic doctrine of the "historic episcopate"... This understanding of episcopacy is a direct denial of the Baptist understanding of the church.'[21] This is quite a weak argument because not only does he admit that 'there are similarities in role',[22] but, I believe, misconceptions arising from the associations linked to a term used by other traditions cannot provide a sufficient ground for balanced argumentation. It would be just as rhetorical as stating that the Bible as a sacred text of Christianity should be abolished because some people have abused it.[23] One of the tasks of theology is to question assumed definitions and provide the Christian Community with alternative meanings. The broad semantic field of theological terms, formed not only by the nature of language but also by the polycentric character of the Christian scriptures, has enough space for new meanings attached to terms packed with disputable perspectives. In spite of attempts of denominational leaders 'to domesticate' theology in such a way that it serves the needs of legitimized theological discourse (recent controversies in the Southern Baptist Convention is example of that), theology should act as a constructive disturber of such discourse. Theologians are restricted by experience and their cultural framework, but at the same time they will have a courage and knowledge to look beyond the grammar of faith constructed by any particular tradition.

The growth of the ecumenical movement has raised the debate over episcopacy to a new level. In 1941, the Baptist minister Dr Hugh Martin,[24] one of the first secretaries of ecumenical organization The Friends of Reunion, published the book *Christian Reunion*. It was written as an apologetic for the ecumenical movement. This book is interesting for its analysis of the Baptist attitude to the episcopal tradition because it deals, among other issues, with the Anglican demand for episcopacy one of the bases of unity. Denying re-ordination and apostolic succession, Martin

---

[21] P. Beasley-Murray, *Radical Believers: The Baptist Way of Being the Church* (Didcot: Baptist Union of Great Britain, 1993), p. 97. See also his statement that 'The fact is that "episcopacy" is alien to Baptist ecclesiology and should not be encouraged in any shape or form'. P. Beasley-Murray, 'Concern over "Episcope"', *Baptist Times*, 21 July 1994, p. 6.

[22] Beasley-Murray, *Radical Believers*, p. 97.

[23] In a similar way, the contributors to A.R. Cross and P.E. Thompson (eds), *Baptist Sacramentalism* (Studies in Baptist History and Thought, 5; Carlisle: Paternoster Press, 2003), have sought to reclaim the term 'sacrament' in Baptist theology despite widespread Baptist antipathy to it.

[24] See the three-part series of articles on Hugh Martin by A.R. Cross, 'Revd. Dr. Hugh Martin', *Baptist Quarterly*: 'Publisher and Writer. Part 1', 37.1 (January, 1997), pp. 33-49; 'Ecumenist. Part 2', 37.2 (April, 1997), pp. 71-86; 'Ecumenical Controversialist and Writer. Part 3', 37.3 (July, 1997), pp. 131-46.

acknowledges that 'the historical objection of the Free Churches is not against episcopacy but against prelacy... But the bishop need not be an autocratic prelate. He can be the father of his people and *pastor pastorum*.'[25] In the 1946 sermon by the Archbishop of Canterbury, Geoffrey Fisher, suggested that the Free Churches should consider taking episcopacy into their systems.[26] Later in his retirement he changed his views and argued for developing the already existing 'organic' union that Christians possess through their common baptism.[27] However, keeping in mind that historically Nonconformity had suffered at the hands of the Established Church, this statement from the side of the Church of England generated a considerable amount of negative reaction. A number of Free Church scholars, which included Robert L. Child, Principal of Regent's Park College, and Ernest A. Payne, Senior Tutor of Regent's Park College, presented a report to the Archbishop of Canterbury, Dr Fisher, defending the Protestant view of authority and arguing for the recognition of ecclesiastic plurality, which, they observed, also existed within the Church of England.[28]

In the Baptist Union of Great Britain and Ireland's statement 'The Baptist Doctrine of the Church', issued in March 1948, the section on 'The Structure of Local Baptist Churches' deals with the interdependence of local churches and officers appointed to carry out tasks related to strengthening fellowship among the churches. After mentioning messengers and the contemporary ministry of General Superintendents, the report sets out the theological background for such ministry:

> we believe that a local church lacks one of the marks of a truly Christian community if it does not seek the fellowship of other Baptist churches, does not seek a true relationship with Christians and churches of other communions and is not conscious of its place in the one catholic Church.[29]

In the following section on 'The Ministry', the report ensures that the Baptist understanding of ministry is not dependent on episcopal

---

[25] H. Martin, *Christian Reunion: A Plea for Action* (London: SCM Press, 1941), p. 154.
[26] He was not the first and only Anglican archbishop who has made such a suggestion. It should be noted that the 1888 Lambeth Quadrilateral proposed four points—the Holy Scripture, the Apostles' Creed, the two sacraments and the historical episcopate—as the bases for relationships between Anglicans and the Free Churches.
[27] W.M.S. West, 'Archbishop Fisher: His Own Man', *Baptist Times*, 23 July 1992, p. 11.
[28] R.N. Flew and R.E. Davies (eds), *The Catholicity of Protestantism: Being a report Presented to His Grace the Archbishop of Canterbury by a Group of Free Churchmen* (London: Lutterworth Press, 1950).
[29] E.A. Payne, *The Fellowship of Believers: Baptist Thought and Practice Yesterday and Today* (London: Carey Kingsgate Press, enlarged edn, 1952), p. 157.

succession and affirms 'to our non-episcopal communities' that 'the gifts of the Spirit and the power of God are freely given'.[30]

At the end of twentieth century Britain experienced a new era of ecumenical projects.[31] When, in 1990, the Baptist minister, Hugh Cross, was appointed by the Milton Keynes Christian Council to the post of Ecumenical Moderator, the *Baptist Times* noted that 'in episcopal terms, Mr. Cross will be a Bishop in all but name'.[32] A number of Baptist churches in Wales have gone a step further and adopted a project of the appointing an ecumenical bishop in Wales. Behind this project stands a conviction that 'Christian unity will most effectively be expressed if we embrace a concept of shared episcopacy'.[33] In Great Britain, then, projects which bring together episcopal and non-episcopal churches are part of an ecclesiastical renewal looking for patterns which transcend existing denominational boundaries.

Practice Still Waiting for Reflection: The Latvian Baptist Experience of Episcopacy

The Latvian experience is instructive for our study as it allows us to see how a Baptist fellowship has understood and employed the office of bishop in various ways and under various historical circumstances. The Latvian Baptist movement started in the middle nineteenth century. One of the founders of the movement, Adams Gertners, was called the bishop of churches of Kurzeme and was in this office from 1866 to 1874 (at the same time he continued to pastor local churches), only resigning because of illness. However, it is not known whether he himself used that designation.[34] We do not have information available about origins of that title among Latvian Baptists. What we know is that Gertners acted as overseer of churches, visiting them and giving advice on matters relating to their buildings and addressing spiritual questions, as well as baptizing new converts which he managed to do during the night while being under house arrest. In the Book of Minutes of the Ziru church we read the following summary of his visitation:

---

[30] Payne, *Fellowship of Believers*, p. 158.

[31] See A.R. Cross, *Baptism and the Baptists: Theology and Practice in Twentieth-Century Britain* (Studies in Baptist History and Thought, 3; Carlisle: Paternoster Press, 2000), pp. 289-315. On ecumenical developments in the latter third of the century, see pp. 244-318.

[32] 'Unique city post creates Baptist "Bishop"', *Baptist Times*, 22 November 1990, p. 1.

[33] G. Abraham-Williams, *Towards the Making of an Ecumenical Bishop in Wales* (Penarth: Covenanted Churches in Wales, 1998), p. 2.

[34] J. Tervits. *Latvijas baptistu vesture* [*History of Baptists of Latvia*] (Riga: Latvijas Baptistu Draudzu Savieniba, 1999), p. 56.

The chair and Bishop of the Baptist church of Venta and Aizpute district A. Gertners found that the Ziru Mission is in good standing. He checked according to the Holy Scripture its chair and workers and church and found them in good standing. There are no complaints found against anybody, all are in peace.[35]

After his resignation and later death, in 1875, Latvian Baptist representatives from twenty-four churches gathered in congress in October 1875 and appointed the Missions Committee that elected as their Chairman Janis Rumbergs. The title of bishop, however, was no longer used, probably due to the fact that after Gertners' death the Baptists had no charismatic leader to replace him, but also because of the process of homogenization of Baptist identity where local practices were influenced by internationally dominant ecclesiastical standards. In spite of the fact that from 1879 Latvian Baptists were independent from their German co-believers and were to construct the history of their origins in such a way as to minimize foreign influence—and in so doing emphasizing the role of divine providence in establishing their movement as well as presenting Baptists as a genuinely Latvian movement—nevertheless the German impact is undeniable.[36] Local churches followed the pattern of their German counterparts. The German Baptist Union, formed in 1848, accepted as its doctrinal foundation the Confession of Faith which was the revision of the document drafted by J.G. Oncken and J. Köbner. The confession recognized the offices of elders, preachers and deacons (servants). Its authors believed that there is no 'distinction in rank among elders and preachers, but hold that the designations of holy Scripture: Bishops, presbyters, etc., do not indicate distinctions in rank'.[37] This understanding certainly had an affect on Latvian Baptists because some of first Latvian pastors studied in Germany.

The office of bishop was not reintroduced during Latvia's short independence in the inter-war period, 1918–40. As a result of some debate during the early 1920s, the title of bishop came into use by the newly established Latvian Lutheran Church but it did not affect Baptist understanding. Latvian expatriate communities show varied patterns. For example, Latvian Baptists in Brazil and the USA did not have bishops either. The title was, however, used by Latvian Baptists in the district of Novgorod, Russia, an area to which Latvians had emigrated in the

---

[35] Tervits, *Latvijas baptistu vesture*, p. 56.
[36] See R.V. Pierard, 'Germany and Baptist Expansion in Nineteenth-Century Europe', in D.W. Bebbington (ed.), *The Gospel in the World* (Studies in Baptist History and Thought, 1; Carlisle: Paternoster Press, 2002), pp. 190-208; I.M. Randall, '"Every Apostolic Church a Mission Society": European Baptist Origins and Identity', in A.R. Cross (ed.), *Ecumenism and History: Studies in Honour of John H.Y. Briggs* (Carlisle: Paternoster Press, 2002), pp. 281-301.
[37] McGlothlin, *Baptist Confessions of Faith*, pp. 333-34.

nineteenth century. The Union of Latvian Baptist Churches of Novgorod was formed in 1907 and before the First World War it followed general practice and had a chairman as moderator of its work After the war, however, pastor Julijs Alfreds Kalnins served the local churches from 1924 to 1930 and was called the 'bishop'.[38] After a period of relative freedom given to Protestant minorities—the communists regarding them, like Marxists, as those persecuted during the rule of the tsars—persecutions started and the Union was abolished. In such a situation the continuation of inter-church co-operation depended on those ready to take on this role and who were unofficially recognized as such by others. In this sense the title of bishop fitted well in the situation. Later Kalnins was deported and from 1948 he lived in Latvia and served as elder in one of the local churches.

Ecclesiastical practice in Latvia changed at the end of the Second World War when Baptists started to renew their work in the context of the second Soviet occupation and the Soviet authorities pressuring them to come under auspices of the All-Union Council of Evangelical Christians-Baptists (AUCECB), a structure which was organized in 1944 when the Soviet government decided to allow some religious freedom but under the strict control of its security service.[39] This was not an easy process because of the political background and the cultural differences between Slavonic and Baltic Baptists. The Latvian Baptist Congress, which met before the end of the war in April 1945, accepted the resolution but included among its preconditions to joining the Union the demand that Latvian Baptists should in future be led by a bishop who, like his assistant, should be Latvian and who is elected by the Baptist pastors of Latvia.[40] Karlis Laceklis, who from 1944 was the Chairman of the Interim Council of the Union of Baptist Churches of Latvia, became the first bishop. During the meeting of the AUCECB leadership with representatives of Latvian Baptists in Moscow, August 1945, agreement between two sides was reached and Latvian Baptist churches were incorporated in the Union of Evangelical Christians and Baptists. The minutes of this meeting reveal an interesting aspect of the issue of bishops. The meeting decided

> to appoint brother K. Laceklis as the Senior Presbyter of Evangelical Christian and Baptist Churches of Latvia, however, because the Latvian translation of the Bible

---

[38] Tervits, *Latvijas baptistu vesture*, p. 218.
[39] On the background to Baptists during this period, see M. Dowling, 'Baptists in the Twentieth-Century Tsarist Empire and the Soviet Union', in Bebbington (ed.), *The Gospel in the World*, pp. 209-32.
[40] Tervits, *Latvijas baptistu vesture*, p. 144.

does not have the word 'presbyter' it is allowed to call the brother in Latvian language the 'Bishop'.[41]

The choice of the title 'bishop' depended on the prevailing literal understanding of the Bible among Latvian Baptists. The influence of other Free Churches in the former USSR who had started to use the title, or at least the existence of parallel developments in several territories, should be taken into consideration. For example, the Pentecostal historian Vladimir Franchuk notes that during the German occupation in the Second World War, Ukrainian Pentecostals started to use the title of bishop in the hope that it would be more acceptable to Nazi officials who were used to the Lutheran hierarchical system.[42]

The bishop's activities were controlled by the AUCECB's plenipotentiary in the Baltic republics Nikolay Levindanto, who remained in this post until his death in 1966, worked in constant tension with the local church leaders. The Soviet authorities replaced democratic Baptist principles with a Soviet-type Baptist system where denominational leadership played a crucial role. Church leaders were faced with a difficult choice: they could refuse to submit to the demands of the state and face the consequences, or they could collaborate with the hope of personal and denominational survival. The former often meant imprisonment, which was the fate of K. Laceklis and many others. A travel report of AUCECB Chairman J.I. Zidkov visiting Estonian and Latvian Baptists published in AUCECB journal *Bratskij Vestnik*[43] is a typical example of the Soviet-type Baptist approach. Zidkov wrote it in the form of a summary of the formal visitation of an authoritarian leader who expressed anger with those who were not supportive of official policies, which included Pentecostals being forced to join Baptists and some local Baptist churches who expressed their opposition by withdrawing financial support for denominational structures. During worship services he received special gifts from 'grateful' congregations, participated in the election of a new bishop (in accordance with Soviet traditions such election was unanimous), and fulfilled the task assigned by governmental authorities to close some congregations, explained as bringing various wings of the denomination together and cutting down expenses. Instead of the title 'bishop', Zidkov used the title traditional to Slavonic Baptists, 'Senior Presbyter'. The Senior Presbyter in the Slavonic Baptist tradition performed episcopal functions, but was not

---

[41] Tervits, *Latvijas baptistu vesture*, p. 145.
[42] V. Franchuk, *Prosila Rossija Dozdja u Gospoda* [*Russia Asked for Rain from the Lord*] (Mariupolj: Gazeta 'Priazovskij Rabochij', 1999), p. 287.
[43] J.I. Zidkov, 'Poseschenije estonskih i latvijskih obschin' ['Visiting Estonian and Latvian congregations.'], *Bratskij Vestnik* [*The Brotherly Messenger*], No. 2 (1949), pp. 70-80.

theologically defined. For example, the Confession of Faith accepted by the Congress of Evangelical Christians-Baptists in USSR in 1985 formally concentrates on the local church and only briefly mentions 'presbyters, deacons and others'.[44]

Restrictions formally imposed by the government after the Second World War were presented as a decision of the denominational leadership only created further tension between leaders of the denomination and local churches. There were cases when the office-holder (as in the case of Peteris Egle who was bishop from 1966 to 1977 was well respected and because of his personality) served as a spiritual adviser to pastors and churches in general. By the time the hierarchical structure had been reformed in the 1970s by the appointment of the Bishop's Council, the existing system was challenged by a proposal submitted by a number of pastors and other well-known congregational leaders. This was partially caused by the leadership style of Bishop Janis Tervits (in office from 1977-90) who was a gifted but forceful personality. Among the issues raised there was no proposal to abolish existing denominational offices but rather a more general call for congregational democracy. We should not portray the authors as free-thinkers striving for an inclusive church, but the impact of Soviet authoritarianism and religious conservatism is clearly seen in this declaration where its signatories are were under the obligation 'to fight against the penetration of modernist teachings in local churches'.[45]

Major changes started to occur in the 1990s with the collapse of USSR. In 1990 Latvian Baptists re-established an independent Union. The office of bishop was included in the by-laws of the Union (the title 'president' appears immediately in parentheses) and according to them bishop has a representative function (particularly in its relation to the Baptist World Alliance), leads the work of the Union's Council and has rights to be the first signature on representative documents (though not financial) of the Union.[46] The Baptist bishop exercises all three aspects of episcopacy— personal (one person to whom people can point as a denominational leader), collegial (he works in good relationships with the bishops of other churches and thus is related to the wider church) and communal (accountability to people who have elected him). The bishop often

---

[44] S.V. Sannikov, *Istorija Baptisma* [*Baptist History*] (Odessa: Bogomislije, 1996), p. 467.

[45] Latvijas baptistu draudzu ieksejas atjaunosanas kustibas programma [Programme of the Movement for Inner Renewal of the Baptist churches of Latvia], 11 October 1975. File 'Biskapa parvalde. Sanaksmes. Kongresi' ['Bishop's administration. Meetings. Congresses'], *Historical Archive of the Union of the Baptist Churches of Latvia*.

[46] J. Tervits, *Latvijas Baptistu Draudzu Savienibas draudzes pasreiz* [*Churches of the Union of the Baptist Churches of Latvia Today*] (Riga: Latvijas Baptistu Draudzu Savieniba, 1995), p. 129.

presides at ordinations, though this is not mandatory, because accreditation is in hands of the Collegium of the Brotherhood of Clergy, an organization which unites all ministers.[47] The continuation of episcopacy in Latvian Baptist churches is linked not only with the past but also with the striving for acceptance and recognition as a 'traditional' religion alongside with large churches (Catholic, Lutheran, Orthodox) which have episcopacy. The bishop's office (and with it the visible symbols such as the bishop's purple, collared shirt) is understood as a symbol of tradition and respect. According to this view, the titles 'president' and 'general secretary' sound too secularized and devoid of any sacredness. However, in some cases denominational leadership has been inconsistent. For example, the consecration of Bishop Janis Smits in 2002 was called an inauguration, a term which for many has political overtones. The bishop's role has been weakened by the fact that most of the bishops during their term of office have continued to work as pastors in local churches and also the diminishing the role of denominational structures.

Baptists are not the only Protestant minority in Latvia that have introduced the bishop's office. From the mid-1980s, the title bishop started to be used Latvian Pentecostals and more recently it has also been applied to the President of local Seventh Day Adventist Union, but so far it has been possible to use it unofficially because of the centralized international structure of the Adventist Church. Free Churches, which in Latvia are using the title bishop, still have to deal theologically with the meaning of that office and the role it can play in the nation's fragmented religious life.

Conclusion: A Way Forward

The church exists as a social reality and therefore its structures are expressions of a particular period of time. Instead of looking for 'pure' forms of Christian leadership which would correspond to an assumed golden age of Christianity we should strive to develop forms of ministry which, according to the perspective of a particular church and association of churches in a given geographical area, would be most appropriate for Christian ministry and would also be perceived as such by wider society. In the words of the Anglican–Reformed International Commission,

> the particular ministerial structures which are now embodied in our different communions cannot claim the direct authority of Scripture. The New Testament cannot be held to prescribe a three-fold ministry of bishops, priests and deacons, a

---

[47] The patriarchal name of that institution is a reflection of the reality that currently all accredited Latvian Baptist ministers are male (in the past there were also some female ministers).

presbyterian or congregational form of government, or the primacy of the see of Rome. All attempts to read off one divinely authorised form of ministry from the New Testament are futile.[48]

Scholarly research challenges assumptions often made by defenders of the historical episcopacy showing that the episcopate depicted by Ignatius is not as monarchical as some have supposed it to be. He calls on the people to obey not only bishops but also presbyters, he does not say that presbyters lie under his command. 'Ignatius may have influenced the new nomenclature, but it was not his letters alone which shifted the lever of power.'[49]

Baptists are more at home with a functional episcopacy—'concerned above all with providing for the church forms of ministry which enable it to fulfill itself in the service of God'[50]—than with historical episcopacy. Baptists do believe in apostolic succession but for them it is not succession of offices but succession of Christian beliefs. This dynamic process includes not only preserving but also of letting go, even if the latter sometimes has been no less difficult as for Roman Catholics. Functional episcopacy does not exclude personal *episkope* as a way of governing the denomination. Recognition of the office of bishop does not depend on a three-fold or two-fold order that churches choose to follow. We can agree with American Lutheran theologian Ted Peters that

> Bishops should be considered a subclass within the more inclusive category of ordained pastors. What distinguishes a Bishop is the particular function he or she performs, not the task of shouldering apostolic succession for the rest of the church.[51]

Rather in the debate for or against episcopacy we can interact with the richness of traditions representing episcopacy. It means not only consulting early church and Reformation period heritage, but also with the past of these groups which like Baptists usually are not in favor of episcopacy. There can be unexpected surprises. For example, the episcopal order is employed by the Hungarian Reformed Church and Romanian Unitarians. In the age of the information-society episcopacy may have additional value because the media are looking for the person representing the church and terminology of the bishop's office is still known in the wider, secularized society. We also should consider the

---

[48] *God's Reign and Our Unity* (London: SPCK/Edinburgh: Saint Andrew Press, 1984), pp. 48-49.
[49] J.T. Burtchaell, *From Synagogue to Church: Public Services and Offices in the Earliest Christian Communities* (Cambridge: Cambridge University Press, 1992), p. 311.
[50] Wright, *Challenge to Challenge*, p. 174.
[51] T. Peters, *God—The World's Future* (Minneapolis, MN: Fortress Press, 1992), p. 304.

weaknesses of the collegial exercise of *episkope* commonly practised in Free Churches. Spiritual oversight can easily be lost in jungles of denominational bureaucracy. A balance needs to be kept:

> Personal oversight apart from the wisdom of a corporate body is apt to become arbitrary and erratic; oversight by a corporate body without a personal pastor is apt to become bureaucratic and legalistic.[52]

It is not the office itself but the personality of its holder, the charisma of serving the wider church and society in general which can make the difference. A bishop should be one of chief guardians of safe space for various wings of the denomination to co-exist in peace. He or she cannot create such a space alone because it comes with a long process of nurturing tolerance and skills of dialogue. But the bishop can exercise a spirituality of weakness which would replace a dominant spirituality of power. This is the only way how this office can function without becoming a watchdog of some kind of threatened and therefore defendable identity. The bishop's office should also serve as a symbol of the inter-dependency, not dependency, of local churches on meta-structures or strict dogmatic framework. We must keep in mind that the church is not united around or dependent on its forms of ministry. 'There is a diversity of function, but only one Church. The life of the Church is not in its structure, but its structure either upholds or restricts its life.'[53]

---

[52] *God's Reign and Our Unity*, p. 73.
[53] R.M.C. Jeffery, *Case Studies in Unity* (London: SCM Press, 1972), p. 108.

CHAPTER 15

Strict Baptists and Reformed Baptists in England, 1955–76

Tim Grass

Introduction

To an outsider surveying the English ecclesiastical landscape, Strict Baptists and Reformed Baptists appear very similar. Both are firmly committed to Calvinist doctrine, and both remain aloof from the ecumenical movement. However, this apparent similarity belies the existence of considerable differences in outlook which have at times caused considerable tension, not least because many members of these groups were also under the impression that there were no significant differences between them and were therefore perplexed to discover that this was not the case. This paper offers some suggestions as to why, in spite of a shared commitment to Calvinistic doctrine and the gathered church, these two groups did not really coalesce as one movement.[1]

The period covered by this paper is bracketed by two significant conferences. The first was held in November 1955 and considered one of the most intractable problems facing Strict Baptist churches, that of 'Pastorless Churches and the Itinerant Ministry'. The second was the first Assembly of Baptised Churches holding the Doctrines of Grace (later known as Grace Baptist Assembly), which took place in May 1976 and which was the first to draw together Reformed and Strict Baptists in significant numbers. What we see taking place between them is a transformation of many Strict Baptist churches, partly due to the wider Reformed resurgence, and partly due to other evangelical trends, and the emergence of a new constituency of Reformed Baptist churches. These developments will be outlined before a sustained comparison is undertaken.

---

[1] I am indebted at many points to those who read and commented on a draft of this paper, Dr Kenneth Dix, Pastor Erroll Hulse and Dr Ian Randall.

A Sketch of the Strict Baptists

Strict Baptists have their roots in the older Particular Baptist tradition, although they originated in a move away from this in reaction against what they saw as unbiblical modifications to Calvinist teaching being propagated in Particular Baptist circles by Andrew Fuller[2] and others. The two doctrinal issues which had precipitated the formation of the first Strict Baptist Association (the Suffolk and Norfolk, in 1829) had been the free offer of the gospel to all and the obligation of all to repent and believe. Both of these were denied by high Calvinists.

The denomination continued to adhere to Calvinistic doctrine, interpreted in a fairly experientially-orientated manner, and itself divided during the mid-nineteenth century over differing attitudes to 'experimentalism'.[3] The more introverted party was led by J.C. Philpot (1802-69) and became known as Gospel Standard churches, from the title of their magazine. They maintained an increasing separation from all other Strict Baptist churches and agencies, ostensibly because they alleged that these tolerated the denial of the eternal sonship of Christ, but in reality the division had more to do with differing conceptions of the nature of spiritual experience. During the 1870s, the Gospel Standard churches adopted certain articles of faith to which other Strict Baptists objected, the most controversial of which denied the legitimacy of taking the evangelistic addresses of the book of Acts as precedents for contemporary preaching.[4] The separation was maintained with increasing firmness during the inter-war period, culminating in the 'God-Honouring movement' of 1934, which called churches, ministers and officers to reaffirm their allegiance to Gospel Standard principles and practice.[5] Although the focus in this paper is on the non-Gospel Standard churches, the ghosts of this controversy continued to haunt the Strict Baptists during this period, and to influence how they were perceived by outsiders.

---

[2] See Peter Morden, *Offering Christ to the World: Andrew Fuller (1754-1815) and the Revival of Eighteenth Century Particular Baptist Life* (Studies in Baptist History and Thought, 8; Carlisle: Paternoster Press, 2003).

[3] For a discussion of this division, see K. Dix, *Strict and Particular: English Strict and Particular Baptists in the Nineteenth Century* (Didcot: Baptist Historical Society, 2001).

[4] For a study of one Gospel Standard Baptist pastor's opposition to these articles of faith, namely Joseph Wiles, see M. Wiles, *Scholarship and Faith: A Tale of Two Grandfathers* (Cambridge: Biograph, 2003), pp. 60-63.

[5] See J.H. Gosden, *Valiant for Truth: Memoir and Letters of J.K. Popham* (introduction by J.R. Broome; Harpenden: Gospel Standard Trust, 1990), pp. xxi-xxii, 232-36; Ian M. Randall, *Evangelical Experiences: A Study in the Spirituality of English Evangelicalism 1918-1939* (Studies in Evangelical History and Thought; Carlisle: Paternoster Press, 1999), ch. 6.

In 1947, there were 256 Gospel Standard churches, approximately half of all Strict Baptist churches. Of the non-Gospel Standard churches, about two hundred belonged to regional associations. These were the Suffolk and Norfolk Association (f. 1829), the Metropolitan Association (hereafter referred to as MASBC; f. 1871), and the Cambridgeshire and East Midlands Union (f. 1927). There was also a Northern Federation, but this appears to have died out by the 1950s. One 'umbrella' body was the National Strict Baptist Federation (NSBF), inaugurated in 1946. In the end, although it sought to draw all sections of the denomination together, it found itself without a job to do. It never attracted many more than a hundred churches into membership, and thus remained a minority body, merging with the National Assembly of Strict Baptist Pastors and Deacons in 1969.

However, there were other means by which a measure of cohesion was provided, including several periodicals and a range of service agencies. Three monthlies reflected different shades of Strict Baptist opinion: *The Christian's Pathway*, privately owned and serving 'same faith and order' churches; *The Gospel Herald*, the organ of the Metropolitan Association and serving churches which in general admitted 'all baptized believers' to communion; and *The Gospel Standard*.[6] To these we must add *The Free Grace Record*, a quarterly published by the Strict and Particular Baptist Society (from 1958 the Trust Corporation) and devoted to more substantial theological and historical articles and often including comment on contemporary theological issues such as the Fundamentalist debate and the Reformed revival of the 1950s. Under the editorship of John Doggett, this acquired a wide readership outside Strict Baptist circles who valued its thoughtful, penetrating and outward-looking presentation of a moderate position.

For a small denomination, Strict Baptists were united at a national level by an extensive range of support agencies, most of which came into existence from 1920 onwards. The Strict Baptist Mission (f. 1861) was the most important, not only by virtue of its ability to draw support from various outlooks, but also through its annual meetings in London. These were the social occasion of the year for many Strict Baptists, and drew large crowds. The Strict and Particular Baptist Trust Corporation (incorporated in 1958 and taking over the Strict and Particular Baptist Society [f. 1911]) acted as a trustee for property and provided financial assistance to pastors and churches. There were also agencies connected with work among the young: the National Strict Baptist Sunday School

---

[6] Peter Toon, 'English Strict Baptists', *Baptist Quarterly* 21.1 (January, 1965), pp. 30-31. The same division is made by John Doggett, 'Reformation According to the Word of God', *Free Grace Record* 3.6 (Spring, 1964), pp. 142-46; Doggett also notes the rise of a fourth group, comprising Particular Baptist churches adhering to the 1689 Confession and not practising closed communion. These will be discussed below.

Association (f. 1939) and the Fellowship of Youth (f. 1934), and groups catering for particular interests, such as the Strict Baptist Historical Society (f. 1960), the National Strict Baptist Women's Federation (f. 1949), the Strict Baptist Open-Air Mission (f. 1923), the Strict Baptist Bible Institute (SBBI, f. 1923) and the Strict and Particular Baptist Ministers' Fellowship (f. 1943).

The busy round of meetings organized by these agencies and the associations, as well as the constant stream of anniversaries of pastors, churches and Sunday Schools, filled the advertisement and report pages of the periodicals. Yet, underneath the activity, there was a nagging sense that things were very far from what they should be. By the 1950s, many in the denomination were expressing concern at its condition. Among the reasons given for this were prayerlessness; the lack of full-time pastors, the unwillingness of some churches with pastors to provide adequate financial support, and the willingness of many churches to rely upon the 'supply system' in which the pulpit was supplied by a different visiting preacher each week;[7] an over-emphasis on congregational independency which resulted in churches dying out while their neighbours were forced to stand by unable to assist because uninvited; and a fatalistic refusal to engage in evangelistic activity.[8] On a practical level, one writer listed reasons which included lack of observance of the Lord's Table (presumably he was referring to its infrequency rather than to non-observance), unconcern regarding the Second Coming, neglect of the needs of children, inadequate noticeboards and advertising, and uncleaned chapels.[9] From a more traditionally-minded standpoint, James Payne of Brighton listed the denomination's sins as neglect of the scriptures, fraternization with enemies of the cross (presumably in ecumenical contact), magnifying small differences while letting heresies gain entrance, and a complacency and lethargy regarding its condition.[10] Such introspection should not be seen as the fruit of high-Calvinist spirituality, for it was shared by other denominations at the time, notably the Brethren,[11] who also felt that they were missing a golden opportunity

---

[7] Of course, some churches genuinely could not afford to support a pastor, and saw no alternative to the use of lay or visiting preachers.

[8] See, e.g., 'The State of our Churches', *Gospel Herald* 123 (1955), pp. 70-71; L.R. G[arrard]., 'The State of our Churches', *Gospel Herald* 125 (1957), pp. 129-31; P.H. Crees, 'The Strict Baptist Denomination: Its Position and Problems', *Gospel Herald* 126 (1958), pp. 3-7; Editorial, *The Christian's Pathway* n.s.30 (1962), pp. 283-84.

[9] An Itinerant Minister, 'Some Denominational Maladies', *The Christian's Pathway* n.s.26 (1958), pp. 149-50.

[10] *The Christian's Pathway* n.s.30 (1962), p. 115.

[11] See Roger Shuff, *Searching for the True Church: Brethren and Evangelicals in Mid- Twentieth-Century England* (Studies in Evangelical History and Thought; Carlisle: Paternoster, 2005).

to grow by accessions from the wider evangelical world because of their own spiritual condition.

A landmark in the process of self-examination had been the conference held at Chadwell Street, London, on 8 November 1955. This had attracted over 150 attenders, and passed some potentially revolutionary resolutions. Pastorless churches were recommended to secure a measure of continuity by booking the same preacher for several successive Sundays, and it was suggested that experienced pastors could, with the consent of local congregations, take the oversight of a group of churches rather than restricting themselves to one church.[12] However, it is doubtful whether these resolutions made much difference in practical terms; Strict Baptists seem to have been good at airing the problems and deciding how to deal with them, but weak on taking practical action. Tradition may have given rise to a considerable degree of inertia in this respect.

Similar concerns were raised at a conference of representatives from the main Strict Baptist agencies which was held on 17 April 1962, at the invitation of the MASBC; the issues included shortage of ministers, division within the denomination, the low state of many churches, and the recent closure of the college, all at a time when there were signs elsewhere of a resurgence of belief in the doctrines for which the Strict Baptists stood.[13] What was not always recognized by insiders, however, was that often the doctrines of grace were not in fact what marked out the Strict Baptists; rather, they were seen by outsiders as standing for strict communion coupled with a distinctive type of introspective spirituality.

Reports of a further conference on 11 September indicated that a major obstacle to denominational unity was presented by differences in communion practice. Deadlock was resolved by the recognition that the principle of congregational church order allowed each church freedom to decide this matter for itself, within the overall affirmation of believer's baptism by immersion as a prerequisite to membership and the Lord's Supper. Building on this consensus at a further meeting on 27 November, a committee was formed to oversee the preparation of a new confession of faith acceptable to all Strict Baptists, as well as arranging further meetings for mutual consultation.[14]

---

[12] G.E. G[ould]., 'Conference Chronicle', *Gospel Herald* 123 (1955), p. 200; 124 (1956), pp. 14-15.

[13] The letter inviting to this meeting was printed in *The Christian's Pathway* n.s.30 (1962), pp. 88-89, and as 'Steps Towards Denominational Unity', *Gospel Herald* 130 (1962), p. 70.

[14] 'Report of the Strict Baptist Prayer/Conference Held on September 11th, 1962', *Gospel Herald* 130 (1962), pp. 205-208; also in *The Christian's Pathway* n.s.30 (1962), pp. 285-87.

A prayer conference on 15 October 1963 called for a meeting of pastors and deacons to examine the differences and difficulties, out of which emerged the first National Assembly of Strict Baptists on 25 April 1964. Papers would be presented on the New Testament teaching concerning inter-church fellowship, and the practical outworking of such principles. The conference attracted 177 pastors and deacons from eighty-three churches, and a committee was appointed to continue the work.[15] This became known as the '22 committee' (from its size), and included a variety of perspectives in its membership. At the Assembly's 1965 meeting, it was decided to arrange a conference for humiliation and prayer in view of the denomination's serious condition.[16] Almost sixty ministers came together for a weekend at Leicester from 23-26 July 1965.[17] Although the conference issued a 'A Message to our Churches and People', and a number of follow-up prayer meetings took place in the succeeding months, its long-term effects appear to have been minimal, and it was not repeated. Looking back ten years later, one of the prime movers, Frank Ellis, lamented the lack of response from Gospel Standard churches, but rejoiced in the greater measure of mutual trust and willingness to work together.[18]

Signs that the denomination was becoming more outward-looking began to appear. In 1967, a Strict Baptist Festival was held at St John's Wood, London, largely the inspiration of the younger element. For a week, denominational organizations mounted displays and presentations concerning their work and the challenges facing the churches. On the mission front, Frank Ellis became secretary of the SBM in 1969 and carried though a major reshaping in the process of which it moved from the old society-orientated approach to a much more church-based approach, in which the mission was seen as a service agency for the churches, on whom rested the primary responsibility for sending and

---

[15] 'A National Assembly of Strict Baptists', *The Christian's Pathway* n.s. 31 (1963), pp. 325-26; L.S. Hill and B.F. Ellis, 'National Assembly of Pastors and Deacons of Strict Baptist Churches 1964', *Gospel Herald* 132 (1964), pp. 159-60; *The Christian's Pathway* n.s.32 (1964), pp. 214-15; and *Free Grace Record* 3.7 (Summer, 1964), pp. 295-321 (a fuller account, including the text of the papers).

[16] 'National Assembly of Strict Baptist Pastors and Deacons', *Gospel Herald* 133 (1965), pp. 109-10.

[17] B.F. Ellis, 'The Story of Leicester', *Gospel Herald* 133 (1965), pp. 167-69; *The Christian's Pathway* n.s.33 (1965), pp. 231-33; and *Free Grace Record* 3.12 (Autumn, 1965), pp. 530-39 (a fuller account, which indicates that a letter was sent to 'Gospel Standard' pastors and others not involved, expressing sorrow for causes of division which had arisen); Editorial, *The Christian's Pathway* n.s.33 (1965), p. 227. During the early 1960s, Surrey Strict Baptists, Gospel Standard and others, had united for days of prayer arising from similar concerns.

[18] Frank Ellis, 'Leicester Remembered', *Grace* 58 (July–August, 1975), pp. 8-10.

supporting missionaries. The previous focus on a defined area of work in India and Malaya was replaced by a willingness to support churches in sending out members anywhere in the world. The initial catalyst for this appears to have been changing government attitudes in India towards missionaries, but it quickly became a reality as missionaries were sent to countries in Western Europe.

Erroll Hulse, pastor of the church at Cuckfield, Sussex, had observed in 1962 that 'it does not help to be continually harping on our weak condition'.[19] He saw the crucial issue as the health of each local church, which could only be secured by heaven-sent revival; formation of larger bodies was not the answer, as the career of the Baptist Union had shown. During the late 1960s, an increasing number of pastors came to share his vision, but they coupled this with energetic work which did much to renew the denomination's outlook and activity. The panel producing a new confession of faith issued *We Believe* in 1966, which was widely acclaimed within and beyond Strict Baptist circles. This adopted a generally similar position to the Particular Baptist *1689 Confession of Faith*, but included expanded coverage of the Christian life and adopted an explicit strict-communionist position. It was followed in 1974 by *A Guide to Church Practice*.

During the late 1960s, economic pressures and the concern for denominational unity resulted in talks to replace the magazines by one which would also speak to the new constituency of Reformed Baptist churches outside the denomination.[20] In the event, *The Christian's Pathway* was forced to cease publication before the merger could be implemented, but *The Gospel Herald* and *The Free Grace Record* were replaced in 1970 by *Grace*.

The Emergence of a Distinct Reformed Baptist Constituency

In the 1950s, there had been a remarkable reawakening of interest in Reformed theology in Britain, extending well beyond evangelicalism. Within the evangelical sphere, this expressed itself in terms of a rediscovery of the writings of the Puritans and, to a lesser extent, the sixteenth-century Reformers. One highly-visible aspect of this resurgence was the formation of the Banner of Truth Trust in 1957, to publish works advocating the 'doctrines of grace': its books and its magazine were soon being read by young preachers in many denominations.

Curiously, the Strict Baptists were in effect sidelined when the doctrines of grace were rediscovered, in part because the movement associated with

---

[19] 'Meeting for Strict Baptist Unity', *The Christian's Pathway* n.s. 30 (1962), p. 172.

[20] Cf., *Gospel Herald* 137 (1969), pp. 51, 88; 'The Future of Our Magazine', *Gospel Herald* 138 (1970), pp. 38-40.

the Banner of Truth was dominated by Paedobaptists.[21] It is also difficult to establish how many Strict Baptists read the Puritan writers whose rediscovery excited so many elsewhere, although this changed once Banner of Truth commentaries became available at very reasonable prices. At the beginning of the period, the indications are that ministerial reading did not differ all that much from that of other evangelical pastors. There was one significant exception, Ernest F. Kevan (1903–65), who as Principal of London Bible College, produced an important doctoral thesis on the Puritans and was a longstanding friend of Martyn Lloyd-Jones. Kevan's absence from the pages of *Banner of Truth*, which might have been expected to welcome his researches, may have been due to Lloyd-Jones' estrangement from the college from 1958, which arose from his concerns at its quest for academic respectability, which he feared would lead to injurious spiritual results,[22] and at Kevan's intent to produce men who would be loyal to their (theologically mixed) denomination as ministers, which he regarded as incipient compromise.[23] Nevertheless, John Doggett asserted that the availability of Banner of Truth publications had stimulated some Strict Baptist ministers to question received tradition and move from hyper-Calvinism to a more orthodox Particular Baptist position.[24]

It is against the background of this widespread interest in Reformed theology that the emergence of Reformed Baptist churches as a distinct constituency should be seen. The chief architect of this development was Erroll Hulse, a South African who pastored the church at Cuckfield. An old-established Strict Baptist cause, it closed briefly but was refounded in 1957 with support from the church at Brighton Tabernacle. It is surely significant that Hulse, although he had served as a pastor among the Strict Baptists and had been fully involved in denominational life as the last editor of *The Christian's Pathway*, dropped these connections from 1970, and associated thereafter with Reformed Baptists. Other reasons for his apparent preference for striking out on a fresh path would have included his passion for evangelism, something for which Strict Baptists had not generally been noted; in a letter to his church, he expressed the belief that

---

[21] K. Dix to author, 3 August 2002.

[22] See John Brencher, *Martyn Lloyd-Jones (1899–1981) and Twentieth-Century Evangelcalism* (Studies in Evangelical History and Thought; Carlisle: Paternoster Press, 2002), pp. 84-85.

[23] See Brencher, *Lloyd-Jones*, p. 199. The Banner of Truth also turned down two works by Kevan on the Puritans and the Law (Iain H. Marray, *David Martyn Lloyd-Jones: The Fight of Faith 1939-1981* [Edinburgh: Banner of Truth, 1990], 462). For the estrangement, see also Ian Randall, *Educating Evangelicalism: The Origins, Development and Impact of London Bible College* (Carlisle: Paternoster Press, 2000), pp. 104-107.

[24] John Doggett, 'Where we Stand', *Free Grace Record* 4.6 (Spring, 1967), p. 243.

the Reformed movement in England was also deficient in this respect.[25] Cuckfield were involved in assisting nearby Strict Baptist chapels at Barcombe (from 1969) and Crawley (reopened in 1971),[26] both of which rapidly established themselves as viable churches, but Hulse had had a negative experience trying to assist a Gospel Standard cause during the 1960s.[27]

Another factor would have been that, humanly speaking, he was a man who could 'think big' and secure the co-operation of others to turn his dreams into reality. Such a man could not have fitted easily within the confining structures and procedures of an established denomination. An example of this is his vision for literature, which found expression in the founding of Carey Publications in 1971 to fill the gap left by the demise of the Baptist publisher Carey Kingsgate Press.[28] The new company was an outgrowth of *Reformation Today*, which was launched in 1970 as the magazine of the Cuckfield church. From the start it was clearly aimed at a wider constituency, and it rapidly developed into a solid and well-produced periodical serving Reformed Baptists.[29] Compared with most Strict Baptist productions, especially pre-1970, *Reformation Today* is noticeably more concerned to engage with contemporary social and intellectual trends, as well as offering considerably more demanding articles, historical, ecclesiological and doctrinal. It also reflects the emergence of an international network of Reformed Baptists, something which contrasts with the distinctly English ethos of Strict Baptist churches: associate editors were located in various countries, overseas authors contributed articles, and Reformed Baptist conferences abroad were reported in detail. In some ways its ethos is reminiscent of that of the *Free Grace Record*, and of the latter issues of *The Christian's Pathway*.

There are indications in *Reformation Today* that Hulse was somewhat disillusioned with his former colleagues. In an editorial in its first issue, he commented that 'some churches have become traditional to the extent that self-criticism is no longer possible'.[30] Sketching Particular Baptist history, he went even further, describing Strict Baptists as excessively introspective, dependent on itinerant ministry, lacking pastoral leadership,

---

[25] 'A Message from Pastor Hulse', *Free Grace Record* 4.9 (Winter, 1967–68), pp. 391-94.
[26] 'Renewal at Cuckfield', *Evangelical Times* (September, 1969), p. 10; *Grace* 19 (January, 1972), p. 16.
[27] *The Christian's Pathway* n.s.37 (1969), p. 151.
[28] *Grace* 27 (October, 1972), p. 14.
[29] It thus represents an implicit distancing of himself from the *Banner of Truth* wing of Reformed Christianity, which was dominated by Paedobaptists and in which Hulse had also been involved from the late 1950s.
[30] 'Editorial', *Reformation Today* 1 (Spring, 1970), p. 6.

and exclusive.[31] In the next issue he redressed the balance somewhat, acknowledging that some churches 'provide a fine example of evangelistic enterprise' and that most did not subscribe to the Gospel Standard 'added articles'; on the other hand, he complained, some Suffolk churches were more Arminian than Reformed.[32] However, a few years later, he appeared to be adopting a more conciliatory line; rejecting a suggestion that his church might share in forming a new association, he pointed to the existence of Strict Baptist agencies designed to help needy causes, and encouraged readers to strengthen what remained rather than starting something new.[33]

Hulse was also an instigator of the residential Carey Conference, which took place from 1970 onwards, initially under the aegis of the Cuckfield church. This proved highly successful, with its combination of solid papers dealing with doctrinal, historical, ecclesiological and pastoral topics with time for healthy recreation and informal fellowship. Wishing to avoid competing with other initiatives, he had consulted with both the Baptist Revival Fellowship (a fellowship of conservative evangelical Baptist ministers and others, mostly from the Baptist Union, concerned for a revival of spiritual life) and the National Assembly of Strict Baptist Pastors and Deacons.[34] He need not have worried; Strict Baptists had nothing like it, and some began to attend, as did men from Brethren and Arminian churches, among others. Such conferences and ministers' fraternals (Hulse founded one of those as well, the Whitefield Fraternal) went a long way to providing the cohesion and fellowship felt desirable by Reformed Baptist churches.

Another figure who was to achieve prominence in Reformed Baptist circles, but who appears to have pursued a more independent line, was Peter Masters. He was the first editor of *Evangelical Times*, a monthly founded in 1967 as a voice for those independent churches which wished to stand apart from the ecumenical movement. In 1970 he became pastor of the Metropolitan Tabernacle, leading it out of the Baptist Union the following April. 1975 saw the commencement of the London Reformed Baptist Seminary, which aimed to train pastors and church officers by means of guided reading, assignments and monthly study days. The full development of Masters' work (and it has grown considerably, including a publishing company, a bookshop and a resurrected version of Spurgeon's magazine, *Sword and Trowel*) postdates this study, but he and Hulse appear always to have worked largely in independence of one

---

[31] E. Hulse, 'Baptist Heirs of the Reformation', *Reformation Today* 1 (Spring, 1970), pp. 22-23.
[32] E. Hulse, 'Editorial', *Reformation Today* 2 (Summer, 1970), pp. 7-8.
[33] Editorial, *Reformation Today* 27 (September–October, 1975), pp. 1-2.
[34] 'Reformed Baptist Newsletter', March 1969 (Baptist Revival Fellowship Archives, Spurgeon's College).

another. Indeed, Masters worked independently of most people, and the ethos of his work is reminiscent of North American separatist fundamentalism.

The work of such men and many others was essential to the emergence of the Reformed Baptist movement, but it was outside events which were to secure them an interested audience. In 1965, Peter Toon (then a Strict Baptist, but later to become an Anglican clergyman) had asserted that

> The terminology used by all Strict Baptists may be described as Calvinistic yet one rarely hears sermons of really systematic doctrinal content, and because of this all sections are poorly instructed in the Calvinistic Faith which the term 'Particular' implies... If these Churches are to give the world a valid reason for their separate existence outside the Baptist Union, something very drastic needs to happen.[35]

Toon conceived of this in terms of a return to the doctrines of the Particular Baptist 1689 Confession of Faith. Something 'very drastic' did indeed happen to give them such a reason for continued separate existence, but outside the Strict Baptists rather than among them.

From about 1965, a steady trickle of churches seceded from the Baptist Union. Until 1971, they tended to be motivated by concerns over the ecumenical policy of the Union leadership, and in particular by the conviction that this involved compromise with Rome and with non-evangelicals; other factors included perceived marginalization of evangelicals and concern to maintain the independence of the local church over against what were seen as centralizing tendencies in the Union's thinking about such matters as ministerial accreditation.[36] The lines had been drawn more sharply following Martyn Lloyd-Jones' speech to the National Assembly of Evangelicals in 1966,[37] which not only shaped but also reflected increasing polarization on this issue. In a trenchant address to the Baptist Revival Fellowship Conference in 1967 reviewing past doctrinal controversies within Baptist circles and the way in which they were dealt with, David Kingdon had argued that 'Evangelicals within the Union are in a position of great embarrassment, and indeed of profound inconsistency.' Themselves loyal to the faith once delivered to the saints, they were associated with some who denied its fundamentals. If they were to remain in the Union, it could only be because they sought reform according to the word of God; if this was not part of their

---

[35] Toon, 'English Strict Baptists', p. 35.

[36] Paul Beasley-Murray, *Fearless for Truth: A Personal Portrait of the Life of George Raymond Beasley-Murray* (Carlisle: Paternoster Press, 2002), p. 142. For a concise account of the concern regarding ecumenism at this time, see Ian M. Randall, *The English Baptists of the Twentieth Century* (A History of the English Baptists, 4; Didcot: Baptist Historical Society, 2005), pp. 337-45 and 382-88.

[37] See Brencher, *Lloyd-Jones*, pp. 92-106.

thinking, then they were implying that evangelicalism was merely one point of view among many, rather than being itself the historic Christian faith. The choices open to them were inaction, reform (the possibility of which Kingdon doubted), or separation.[38]

Secessions after 1971, while continuing to be motivated in part by such concerns, also represented a protest at the Union's apparent willingness to tolerate fundamental error within its circles. This, it was asserted, was shown by its failure to discipline the Principal of the Northern Baptist College, Michael Taylor. He delivered an address at the 1971 Assembly advocating a 'Christology from below', refusing to call Jesus 'God' and questioning the traditional understanding of the divinity of Christ. During the bitter and long-drawn-out controversy which resulted, several dozen churches, and rather more ministers, withdrew from the Union. According to *Evangelical Times*, 140 protests were received before the end of the year: including three from area associations, six from districts, thirty-six from churches and sixty-three from ministers.[39]

Some churches formed a short-lived Association of Evangelical Baptist Churches (AEBC) in 1972. This originated in a decision by the Baptist Revival Fellowship whose 1969 conference voted 101-59 to explore the possibility of forming a group of evangelical Baptist churches as an interim measure.[40] The AEBC was intended to have a ten-year life span, and appears to have been modelled on the Evangelical Fellowship of Congregational Churches, formed in 1967 by those who wished to remain out of the proposed merger with the Presbyterians; this too was seen as an interim body. The hope was that in time churches would be able to join some kind of broader evangelical fellowship. The AEBC adopted a modified form of the Inter-Varsity Fellowship doctrinal basis, and purposely set out to make do with a minimum of organization, as its intent was to foster fellowship rather than become a body which dictated to the churches.[41] Paradoxically, its appeal was limited by the breadth of its doctrinal basis, which allowed Arminian as well as Calvinist churches to join. There were also initial questions concerning its alleged tolerance of annihilationism, which stirred spectres of the 'Downgrade' controversy in the minds of some critics; although this charge was rebutted by the

---

[38] David Kingdon, *Baptists at the Crossroads: Past and Present* (n.p.: Baptist Revival Fellowship, 1968), pp. 10-11.

[39] 'Baptist Union Goes Comprehensive', *Evangelical Times* (January, 1972), p. 2. For a fairly full account of events, see Beasley-Murray, *Fearless for Truth*, pp. 145-65.

[40] David Potter, 'Revival and Ecumenism at the Baptist Revival Fellowship', *Evangelical Times* (December, 1969), p. 1.

[41] 'Not Going In', *Evangelical Times* (April, 1971), p. 2; M.C. B[uss]., 'Out for Truth—but Keeping Together', *Evangelical Times* (February, 1972), pp. 1-2; 'Independent Baptist Churches form New Fellowship', *Evangelical Times* (November, 1972), p. 1.

organizers, the damage was done. Eleven churches joined at its inception, but its membership never rose above a couple of dozen and it folded before the expiry of its intended ten-year lifespan. The problem was that seceders from the Union were united in opposing its toleration of the views of Michael Taylor and its ecumenical involvement, but divided over the positive matter of developing some means of fellowship and mutual support, as well as representing a range of evangelical doctrinal perspectives.

A number of seceding ministers would take up pastorates among the Strict Baptists, but whilst a considerable number of those churches which seceded were Calvinistic in doctrine (some rediscovering their old Particular Baptist trust deeds during the process), none joined the Strict Baptist associations, although it had been hoped that they would.[42] Rather, they provided a massive injection of personnel into the Reformed Baptist movement. Others became charismatic congregations, and a number would later link up with the Restorationist movement (and especially that stream of it led by Terry Virgo, which would become known as New Frontiers).[43] Some churches joined the Fellowship of Independent Evangelical Churches (f. 1922): this offered a broader basis of union, and avoided entanglement in issues of church order.[44] Many churches, aware of difficulties over trust deeds and other matters which had soured relationships with the Baptist Union, were apprehensive about joining anything, a case of 'once bitten, twice shy'.

Relationships between Strict Baptists and Reformed Baptists

Close examination of both constituencies indicates that there were a number of differences between them; these may be divided into differences of ethos, of doctrine and of practice. Related to these, and to some extent accounting for them, is the fact that the Strict Baptists were an old-established movement which in some areas had become an accepted part of the ecclesiastical landscape, whereas many Reformed Baptists had seceded from other denominations and were still in the throes of developing a distinctive identity.

---

[42] According to John Doggett, 'Baptists Under Stress', *Free Grace Record* 4.2 (Spring, 1966), pp. 57-58, Strict Baptists were receiving overtures from churches not in the Baptist Union or which were in it but considering secession, regarding the possibility of linking up with them.

[43] Although outside the scope of this paper, it is worth noting that both the Reformed and the Restorationist groupings demonstrated an ecclesiological idealism which sought to recover what they perceived as the divinely-revealed principles according to which churches should be ordered.

[44] Oral information, M. Laver, 17 February 2003.

Differences of Ethos

The rather undoctrinal nature of the Strict Baptist ethos contrasts with the more sharply-defined nature of Reformed Baptists. To some extent this may reflect the experiential emphasis of many Strict Baptists: this tended to displace doctrine in preaching, with the result that many members would have been well-schooled in the kind of experience which was regarded as evidence of a work of grace, but unable to offer a clear statement of their doctrinal beliefs as Strict Baptists. Furthermore, the focus on experience may have meant that they felt they had much in common with others who shared that experience, even if they differed to some extent doctrinally: this would have been reinforced as the distinctiveness of Strict Baptist spirituality weakened into a sort of mildly Calvinistic pietism which had much in common with the relatively undoctrinal evangelicalism which was dominant during the 1940s and early 1950s. A sense of kinship with other evangelicals would have been facilitated by contacts through such agencies as London Bible College: the appointment of the ex-Strict Baptist pastor Ernest Kevan as Principal from 1946 (and of another Strict Baptist, Donald Guthrie, as a lecturer from 1949, though he later joined the Baptist Union) proved an attraction to a number of Strict Baptist students, especially after their own college closed in 1962.[45]

Strict Baptists were also given coherence by a network of intermarriage, facilitated by inter-church activities such as attending one another's anniversaries (this formed a major part of Strict Baptist social life, and the lavish teas provided opportunities for informal conversation), and camps and house parties for young people. Often it was moving in these circles, rather than believing certain doctrines, which often served to identify an individual as Strict Baptist. By contrast, new Reformed Baptist churches were often isolated and unknown.

There were differences regarding the legitimacy of ecumenical contact. Strict Baptist churches were often present in parts of the country where they were long-established and had achieved a measure of acceptance, especially in Suffolk, where they outnumbered members of Baptist Union churches. It was not uncommon for such churches to engage in joint activities with other denominations at a local level, some even joining local Free Church councils. At the Suffolk and Norfolk Association

---

[45] In an attempt to increase the size of its student body, and in response to awakening interest in the doctrines of grace outside the Strict Baptists, it had previously opened its doors to non-baptistic Calvinists from 1958 as the Calvinistic Theological College (W.C. Plail, 'Calvinistic Theological College', *The Christian's Pathway* n.s.26 (1958), 235). Two factors which hastened its demise were the appearance on the scene of other Calvinist colleges and the continuing refusal of some churches and ministers to accept that any kind of training was needed (*Free Grace Record* 4.8 (Autumn 1967), 349-50).

meetings each year greetings would be brought by a representative of the Suffolk Baptist Union. The NSBF had even been represented at the Baptist World Alliance jubilee celebrations in 1955.[46] By contrast, Reformed Baptists drew the lines much more clearly; secession from existing denominations (especially the Baptist Union) was often a costly matter, entailing the possible loss of premises, wider support and fellowship, and required a depth and clarity of conviction which many Strict Baptists did not have.

It may have been a sense of isolation resulting from their secession which meant that Reformed Baptists appeared much more aware of their place in history, or at least much more interested in discovering historical precedents, than Strict Baptists. Hulse defined Reformed Baptists as characterized by a heart experience of grace, a return to Puritan practice, and a belief in the doctrines of the Reformers.[47] They also had a much stronger perception of themselves as part of a worldwide movement.

Cultural differences may also have existed. *Reformation Today* welcomed the writings of Francis Schaeffer, whose attempts from the late 1960s to offer a Christian perspective on culture caught the imagination of many evangelicals looking for something more world-affirming than traditional pietist spirituality. For rural Strict Baptists, though, such issues were a world away from their own concerns, not least because they tended to be drawn from a somewhat lower social class, in which the literary, musical and artistic pursuits discussed by Schaeffer did not feature very prominently and were often categorized as worldly (although it must be said that they had their own chapel-centred musical culture).

Differences of Doctrine

From time to time articles appeared in the Strict Baptist press reiterating the denomination's distinctive high Calvinist position. However, the mere fact that such articles were felt necessary, coupled with the way that some were angled, indicates that these distinctives were being challenged by advocates of a more moderate Calvinism. A high-profile challenge to the denial of the obligation of all to repent and believe (an idea often described by Strict Baptists as 'duty-faith') was issued around 1960 by Hulse in *The Christian's Pathway*. Before this, the question of warrants to believe had been raised in *Banner of Truth* circles, although this would have been with primary reference to the Scottish context. The Strict and Particular Baptist Ministers' Fellowship remained strongly opposed to

---

[46] *Gospel Herald* 123 (1955), pp. 112, 145.
[47] E. Hulse, 'What it is to be Reformed', *Reformation Today* 10 (Summer, 1972), pp. 20-24.

duty-faith.[48] Charles Breed (d.1967), who had been principal of the SBBI, denied the free offer and duty-faith, and had reservations concerning the post-war renewal of interest in Calvinism.[49] *We Believe*, seeking to unite all sections of the denomination (though never accepted by Gospel Standard churches), was silent on the duty-faith issue, although some in the denomination continued to inveigh against 'Fullerism', which in their opinion had opened the door to doctrinal decline among nineteenth-century Particular Baptists. Both duty-faith and the free offer of the gospel gradually became accepted by most Strict Baptist churches, and, by the mid-1980s, the denial of duty-faith would be deleted from the doctrinal basis of all three associations. This was, however, too late for many Reformed Baptists; by that stage their constituency had already become established as a distinct entity with its own publications, conferences and support networks.

Differences of Practice

Church order was another major area of difference. Strict Baptists practised a congregational order with strong inter-church links. Reformed Baptists often adopted an order with presbyterian elements, but shorn of the formal links of presbytery and synod; their vigorous espousal of plural eldership did not sit well with what the Strict Baptist associations' doctrinal bases called 'the congregational order of the churches inviolable'.[50] Moreover, if those elders were earnest young men with clear doctrinal convictions but little experience of pastoral work, eldership was unlikely to be seen at its best in practice.

Another problem was caused by differences over communion practice. There was the question of who should be welcomed to the Lord's Table, an issue which above all others defined Strict Baptists as a constituency, in

---

[48] Oral information from K. Dix, 24 April 2003. Cf., Stephen T. Hover, 'The Offers of the Gospel', *Gospel Herald* 128 (1960), pp. 130-33 (also in *The Christian's Pathway* n.s.28 [1960], pp. 120-22), which drew a rejoinder from Erroll Hulse arguing that the Puritans offered Christ to sinners without implying human ability to close with Christ (*Gospel Herald* 128 [1960], pp. 193-95). Hover accused Hulse of subtlety, and explained that in rejecting 'offers' he did not reject the practice of warning and exhorting sinners to turn to Christ (*Gospel Herald* 129 [1961], pp. 35-36). It would appear that there was relatively little difference between their positions, as another correspondent, E.J. Wood, pointed out (*Gospel Herald* 129 [1961], p. 50). Another debate over these issues was sparked off by L.F. Lupton and carried on in the pages of *The Christian's Pathway* during 1964–65.

[49] Obituary by John Doggett, *Free Grace Record* 4.8 (Autumn, 1967), pp. 349-50.

[50] This phrase formed part of the doctrinal basis of (for example) the Suffolk and Norfolk Association of Strict Baptist Churches, as read out at its annual meetings and printed in its annual handbooks.

that they united on the importance of restricted communion even though they disagreed about how far the restriction should go. But there were also such matters as when it should be held (following a public service or at a different time altogether) and how frequently; a number of Reformed Baptist churches, sometimes influenced by Brethren or Scotch Baptist practice, adopted weekly communion, sometimes including a period of Brethren-style open worship, whereas Strict Baptists, like other English Baptists, tended to hold the Lord's Supper monthly or twice-monthly.

Strict Baptists were known for their practice of strict communion, and indeed many members would have cited this, rather than Calvinistic doctrine, as the denomination's primary distinguishing feature. It is not always recognized, however, that in fact it caused deep tensions within the denomination, as well as between it and other denominations, since the principle was applied in a variety of ways. Differences of communion practice were frequently cited in the calls to repentance, prayer and reconciliation issued during the 1960s, these being seen as a hindrance to blessing. Where visitors were concerned, some would have welcomed 'all baptized believers' (that is, those baptized by immersion on profession of faith), while others would have restricted their table fellowship to members of churches sharing the 'same faith and order'; a minority of churches rejected all forms of transient communion, restricting the Lord's Table to members of that particular church.

Reformed Baptists tended to espouse open communion, coupled with closed membership, and saw themselves as following Spurgeon in this. Undoubtedly they were also influenced by the depth of their fellowship with Reformed Paedobaptists through the 'Banner' movement: shared Calvinism was more important than shared baptismal practice. In this, they represented one wing of the older Particular Baptist tradition. Brethren practice also shaped the thinking of some: one pastor with a Brethren background, John Davison of Perth, defended open communion, and suggested that if Strict Baptists did not change, they would be left behind by Reformed Baptists and disappear in the same way that the Scotch Baptists had done.[51] Significantly, a Strict Baptist correspondent in the same issue of the *Free Grace Record*, David Smith of Eden, Cambridge, admitted that he did not bar godly Paedobaptists from the Lord's Table.[52] This more open approach would become more widespread among Strict Baptists, but not until the 1980s.

Evangelism was another area where differences of outlook are discernible. From the 1930s to the 1950s, Strict Baptists were perhaps catching up with other denominations, following them in such matters as youth work and open-air work. By contrast, Reformed Baptists were

---

[51] *Free Grace Record* 4.10 (Spring, 1968), pp. 466-70.
[52] *Free Grace Record* 4.10 (Spring, 1968), p. 472.

thinking out every aspect of church life from the foundation up.[53] Many Strict Baptists, while not uncritical of aspects of the conduct of the Billy Graham missions, nevertheless welcomed his bold proclamation of the gospel and rejoiced in the blessing which they saw as resulting. Reformed Baptists, on the other hand, tended to be quite critical of such missions. They looked not only at the message, but also at the methods, and found a great deal which they considered did not match the New Testament pattern of local church evangelism. Erroll Hulse and his wife had been involved in the 1954 Wembley crusade and reacted strongly against what they had seen. He even issued a book, *Billy Graham: The Pastor's Dilemma*, which sold 20,000 copies in a very short period. Reviewing it in the *Gospel Herald*, L.R. Garrard acknowledged that the 1966 Earl's Court campaign had introduced disturbing new features, such as the profile given to liberal sponsors, though he considered that for many the opportunities still outweighed the objections.[54]

Strict Baptists were perceived by Reformed Baptists as slack concerning their evangelistic responsibilities. There was a measure of truth in this: the Strict Baptist Open-Air Mission had to disband in 1966 due to lack of support. Many Reformed Baptists went on to lump all Strict Baptists together (somewhat unfairly) as introspective, hyper-Calvinistic, traditionalist and unconcerned about evangelism, blaming this state of affairs on their rejection of the free offer. One factor influencing them was that one centre of gravity of the newer movement lay in Sussex. Local Strict Baptist churches were mostly of the Gospel Standard variety, and, at the first Carey Conference, Bernard Honeysett shared how in 1967 he had resigned as pastor of a Gospel Standard church in Tenterden, Kent, and founded a Reformed Baptist church in the same town.[55] His story would have reinforced negative perceptions of the Strict Baptists, as would his subsequent explanation of the history and import of the added articles.[56] However, his experience was not typical of the associated Strict Baptists. During the 1950s and 1960s they engaged in vigorous open-air work using several 'Mobile Units' (vans fitted out with loudspeakers). Some churches held evangelistic campaigns and children's missions, and a number circulated their locality regularly with the chapel magazine, the

---

[53] Oral information from K. Dix, 24 April 2003.

[54] L.R. G[arrard]., 'The Pastor's Dilemma', *Gospel Herald* 134 (1966), pp. 57-58; cf. also his 'Earls Court', *Gospel Herald* 133 (1966), p. 105, in which he warned against Strict Baptists becoming known for isolationism, and 'Earls Court, 1966', *Gospel Herald* 133 (1966), 151-52.

[55] Selwyn Morgan, 'The Carey Conference', *Reformation Today* 1 (Spring, 1970), p. 4. For a full account, see Bernard Honeysett, *'The Sound of His Name'* (Edinburgh: Banner of Truth, 1995).

[56] Bernard Honeysett, 'The Ill-Fated Articles', *Reformation Today* 2 (Summer, 1970), pp. 23-30.

content of which included an evangelistic element. Pastors may not always have 'offered' the gospel, but it would have been rare to find one among these churches who did not 'present' it, seizing whatever opportunities arose to do so.

Reformed Baptists also criticized Strict Baptist dependence on itinerant ministry as unable to build up the flock and contrary to New Testament teaching about the need for elders to shepherd them.[57] Reformed preachers would not always have been full-time, especially in churches with a plurality of elders, but they would usually have come from within the membership of the church where they preached. More generally, the two streams appear to have differed somewhat in their attitudes to ministerial preparation. Hulse was not uncritical of the institution where he had trained (London Bible College), but he applauded the historic Presbyterian ideal of an educated ministry.[58] Reformed Baptist pastors were usually well-educated (not always in theology), and many had received formal training in their previous denominations. Strict Baptists, by contrast, had many pastors who were self-taught 'men of the soil'[59] and their experimentalism made many stress the need for the Spirit's unction rather than (and possibly at the expense of, or opposed to) preparation and study. Where they had been trained, however, it was often at the SBBI, London Bible College or South Wales Bible College. Related to this may be a difference in predominant preaching styles. Through the influence of Lloyd-Jones in particular, Reformed Baptists had espoused an expository approach to preaching, in which preachers often worked through a particular book of the Bible passage by passage and week by week; this approach had experienced something of a revival during the post-war period. Strict Baptists by and large remained wedded to a textual approach which focused on one verse or phrase (this approach had, incidentally, been that preferred by Spurgeon), often lifted out of context; many were thus averse to the preaching of series of sermons as this hindered the freedom of the Spirit to guide the preacher.

Association was another area of difference, arguably one of the most significant in practice. Denominational thinking was much stronger among Strict Baptists, since the denomination (or the local association) held them together and often kept smaller causes alive. During the 1950s,

---

[57] Erroll Hulse, *An Introduction to the Baptists* (Worthing and Haywards Heath: Henry E. Walter and Carey Publications, 1973), p. 36.

[58] E. Hulse, 'Baptist Heirs of the Reformation', *Reformation Today* 1 (Spring, 1970), pp. 23-24; cf. also his *Introduction to the Baptists*, p. 37.

[59] A.J. Klaiber, *The Story of the Suffolk Baptists* (London: Kingsgate Press, n.d. [1931]), p. 84, quoted in S. Wolstenholme, *These 150 Years: A Commemorative Memento of the Suffolk and Norfolk Association of Strict Baptist Churches* (n.p: Suffolk and Norfolk Association of Strict Baptist Churches, 1980). p. 9, who notes the increasing proportion of men receiving formal training.

bodies such as the NSBF and the MASBC had also shown evangelistic vision, negotiating with the authorities to secure sites for churches in the new towns of Basildon and Hemel Hempstead, and on a large new housing estate in Aylesbury. The first proved a remarkably successful church-plant, and the third resulted in a new lease of life for a long-established town centre congregation. By contrast, for most Reformed Baptists the denomination was, in their experience, a major part of the problem. They were often vociferously independent, possibly by way of a reaction against the perceived influence of denominational mechanisms. What was welcomed by Strict Baptists as sensible rationalization which avoided duplication of effort would have been seen by Reformed Baptists as evidence of a dangerous ecumenical-style tendency to centralization. Those who had previously belonged to the Baptist Union were also aware of twentieth-century developments in the realm of association, which they interpreted as tending to erode the autonomy of the local church and as linked with a move away from viewing the New Testament as providing a sufficient guide to the principles and pattern of church life.[60]

Reformed Baptists were thus conscious of the tendency of denominational structures to take on a life of their own and become self-perpetuating institutions, hindering churches from exercising their freedom to think and act radically when necessary. Such bodies, with the lists of member churches, excluded as well as included; were churches in association to part fellowship with other gospel churches?[61] Hulse advised against the formation of new Reformed associations on the grounds that Strict Baptist bodies already existed, and the Strict Baptists had thought through the issues relating to association developing useful agencies such as the Trust Corporation and the SBM. With an eye on the wider scene, he advised against restricting association to a limited group of churches and thus depriving others of much-needed fellowship and support; 'should we not seriously question an approach which automatically cuts off all fellowship with ministers who are in the Ecemunical [sic] Movement?'[62] In this, he was of a different opinion from Peter Masters, who would advocate just such a separation.

The fact that no Reformed churches joined the Strict Baptist associations does not mean that they lacked sympathy for the doctrinal position of the latter; indeed, it was asserted that demand for *We Believe* was higher outside Strict Baptist churches than within them.[63] Similarly,

---

[60] For an influential expression of concern over this issue, see *Liberty in the Lord: Comment on Trends in Baptist Thought Today* (London: Baptist Revival Fellowship, 1964), pp. 24-25.

[61] H. Carson, 'Doctrinal or Doctrinaire?', *Reformation Today* 27 (September–October, 1975), pp. 23-24.

[62] *Reformation Today* 30 (March–April, 1976), pp. 40-41.

[63] *Grace* 35 (June, 1973), p. 16.

many Reformed churches were happy to adopt *Grace Hymns*, compiled by a committee of Strict Baptists and published in 1975. They also sought listing in the *Grace Directory*, a publication which continued the *Christian's Pathway* tradition of maintaining a directory of churches, giving details of preachers and times of services. It would seem, then, that the doctrinal differences were not felt to be that significant; more to the point were probably the differing attitudes to associating and to church polity (especially communion practice). Some Strict Baptists tried to downplay the importance of strict communion as a denominational distinguishing mark, and saw themselves as merely a part of the older Particular Baptist tradition,[64] but this perspective did not find favour among most; if it had, the story of relations between these two groups might have been rather different.

Signs of Hope?

However, there were some signs of a *rapprochement*. In 1975, it was noted that Reformed Baptists joined Strict Baptists at the National Assembly.[65] As a barrister, John Doggett pointed out that the old Particular Baptist denomination still existed in law and in fact, and thus disapproved of references to Strict Baptists as themselves constituting a denomination; he therefore welcomed an initiative for a conference to draw Reformed and Strict Baptists together in the quest for more tangible expressions of fellowship.[66] Reporting the meeting in Birmingham which ensued, he noted that many Reformed churches were well aware of their isolation and wanted fellowship, but they were cautious about committing themselves to new arrangements after extricating themselves from the Baptist Union; furthermore, they were unhappy about certain aspects of the Strict Baptist ethos, such as the hyper-Calvinism and lack of concern for sound doctrine. Nevertheless, they recognized that the two streams had much in common. Although one Strict Baptist commentator would express equal unhappiness with aspects of the Reformed Baptist ethos (such as an alleged downplaying of experience and an undue emphasis on reformation of church structures),[67] Strict Baptists at the meeting were willing to do what they could, and the result was that the convenors were

---

[64] E.g., John Doggett, 'Editorial', *Free Grace Record* 4.1 (Winter, 1965–66), pp. 8-10. Doggett also advocated union of all 'free grace' churches, whether Baptist or Paedobaptist, and denied that strict communion was explicitly taught in the New Testament ('Schism, Separation and Segregation', *Free Grace Record* 4.7 [Summer, 1967], pp. 290-97.

[65] J.C. Doggett, 'Assembly 1975', *Grace* 57 (June, 1975), p. 18.

[66] John Doggett, 'Time to try to pick up the pieces?', *Grace* 60 (October, 1975), pp. 1-3.

[67] Letter from Arthur Stone in *Grace* 64 (February, 1976), p. 12.

invited to explore the possibility of calling an assembly in 1976.[68] That May, Strict and Reformed Baptists shared in the Assembly of Baptised Churches holding the Doctrines of Grace. A Strict Baptist speaker, Frank Ellis, expounded the New Testament practice of association (for purposes of mission, expression of concern over social issues and mutual consultation) and churches were invited to consider whether they wished to be included on a list of baptized churches holding the doctrines of sovereign grace.[69] Although this assembly never quite achieved its organizers' hopes, in that many Strict Baptists (especially in churches belonging to the regional associations) did not participate, it would remain the most significant place for contact between the two streams.

Conclusion

There appear to have been several main reasons why, in spite of apparent similarities, the two streams remained separate:

1. *Differing attitudes to denominational structures.* For Reformed Baptists, these were a major part of the problem; for Strict Baptists, they were often a lifeline, as well as serving to initiate church-planting activity.

2. *Differing ways of applying biblical authority to church polity.* Generally speaking, it appears that Reformed Baptists were more radical in their application of scripture to church polity, probably because in many cases they were starting new churches and therefore had no inheritance of tradition with which to contend. Communion practice and evangelism were two particularly important areas of difference.

3. *Different stages in their existence.* Reformed Baptists were a young movement, sharply defined and vigorous in outreach; the Strict Baptists were older, more settled and with a strong sense of tradition, and had often reached a measure of accommodation with other local churches. Their tradition was a mixed blessing to them; as one Strict Baptist writer put it, 'Perhaps the greatest failure in our denomination has been the inability to distinguish between that which is definitely and permanently Scriptural, and that which is merely traditional.'[70] In the end, it did much to shape outside perceptions of them, and thus to deter potential accessions, even though they were already shedding some of the aspects to which outsiders objected.

Like the tributaries of the Amazon, the different streams can still be distinguished years later. There is no immediate likelihood of their merging, but hopefully an awareness of the dynamics of their relationship during two formative decades may contribute to a deeper mutual respect

---

[68] J.C. Doggett, 'Feeling towards the future', *Grace* 62 (December, 1975), p. 11.
[69] John Doggett, '"Ransomed Souls the Tidings Swell"', *Grace* 68 (June, 1976), pp. 1-2.
[70] L.R. G[arrard]., 'The State of our Churches', *Gospel Herald* 125 (1957), p. 131.

and acceptance between churches which, for all their differences, have so much in common.

General Index

Abingdon Association 46, 208-16
Abingdon Baptist Church 221
Act of Toleration, 1689, The 31
Adventist Church 291
Affirmation of Faith, The 36
Albury Circle, The 11
All Saints' Church, Monkwearmouth 113
All-Union Council of Evangelical Christians-Baptists 288, 289
American Baptist Churches 35
American Baptist Churches in the USA 184
American Baptist Convention 35
amnesia xvi, 189, 190, 198, 199
Anabaptists 93, 148
Ancient Church, the (Holland) 75
Anderson, F. 187, 191, 194
Anglicans/Anglicanism 1, 5, 7, 8, 9, 11, 12, 15, 88, 115, 116, 122, 134, 150, 253, 281, 284, 304
Anglican Reformed International Commission 291
Anglo-Catholics/Anglo-Catholicism 124, 147
Angus Library, Regent's Park College, Oxford 209, 210, 211
Angus, Amelia Gurney 168, 177
Angus, Edith 177
Angus, J. 177
anti-Catholicism 151
Anti-Corn Law League 17
anti-creedalism xvi
anti-denominationalism 25
anti-establishmentarianism 11
Antipaedobaptists 145
anti-sacramentalism 54, 128-62
Apostles' Creed, The 186, 205, 285
Aquinas, T. 71
archbishops 281
Area Superintendents 283, 284
Aristotle 70

Arminian Baptists 231
Arminians/Arminianism 5, 22, 91, 204, 235, 237, 252, 303, 305
Asad, T. 58
Ash, J. 169
Asquith, Lord 181
Assemblies of God 114
Assembly of Baptised Churches holding the Doctrines of Grace 294, 315
Association of Evangelical Baptist Churches 305
atonement 100, 102, 236
Aubrey, M.E. 124, 127
autonomy 25, 26, 27, 28, 29, 35, 36, 37, 38, 39, 41, 42, 44, 45, 46, 48, 49

Backus, I. 91, 92, 189
Balandier, G. 198
Baltic Baptists 288
Band of Hope 172
Banner of Truth Trust 300, 301, 308
baptism 3, 5, 9, 10, 21, 23, 43, 59, 63, 65, 74, 93, 97, 99, 101, 101, 102, 113, 125, 128-62, 166, 169, 204, 205, 281, 310
baptism of the Spirit 108
baptismal practice(s) 43, 76
baptismal regeneration 131, 134, 137, 146, 148, 151, 154, 155
Baptist Bible Union 34
Baptist Church House 21
Baptist Convention of Ontario and Quebec 25
'Baptist Doctrine of the Church, The' 37, 155, 285
Baptist Evangelical Society 147
Baptist Faith and Message, The 28, 204
Baptist historiography 68
'Baptist Manifesto, The' 52, 53

Baptist Missionary Auxiliary 172
Baptist Missionary Society 5, 10, 16, 18, 19, 115, 141, 168, 174, 175, 177, 179, 251, 254
Baptist Revival Fellowship 38, 303, 304, 305
Baptist State Convention of North Carolina 48
Baptist Union of Great Britain (and Ireland) 16, 17, 18, 19, 23, 37, 38, 108, 112, 119, 121, 125, 126, 129, 130, 147, 151, 153, 154, 155, 172, 176, 177, 179, 213, 240, 242, 243, 283, 285, 300, 303, 304, 305, 306, 307, 308, 313
Baptist Union Discipleship Group 127
Baptist Union of Ireland 17
Baptist Union of Wales 179
Baptist Union's Spiritual Welfare Committee 125
Baptist Women's Home Auxiliary 177
Baptist Women's League 177, 178, 179, 180, 182
Baptist Women's Missionary Association in Wales 179
Baptist World Alliance 1, 19, 173, 178, 186, 290, 308
Baptist World Alliance Congress 19
Baptist Zenana Mission, the 175, 176
Barcombe Strict Baptist Chapel 302
Barfoot, T. 211
Barnes, M.C. 66
Barth, K. 153
Beasley-Murray, G.R. 131, 158
Beasley-Murray, P. 283
Bebbington, D. 89
Beddome, B. 139, 245
Bedfordshire Union of Christians 20
Belcher, J. 17
Bellah, R. 193
Benevolent Society, the 172
Berger, P. 15
Berkshire Association 208, 210, 211
Berry, W. xv, xviii
Bethesda Free Church, Sunderland 113

Bible College, Dunoon 121
Bible Training College, London 123
biblical authority 93
Binkley Memorial Baptist Church, Chapel Hill, NC 48
Birrell, C.M. 176
Birt, I. 5
bishops 33, 34, 279-93
Blair, J. 80
Blair, R. 47
Bloomsbury Central Baptist Church, London 111
Boddy, A. 113
Boddy, Mary 113
Boff, L. 279
Bogue, D. 6
Bonaparte, N. 269, 274
Boobyer, G.H. 120
Book of Common Prayer, The 13, 146
Booth, A. 12, 139, 276
Booth, C. 109
Booth, J. 194, 199
Brainerd, D. 171
Breed, C. 309
Brethren 21, 310
Briggs, J.H.Y. 149, 152
Brighton Tabernacle 301
Brine, J. 141, 233, 234, 236, 238, 239, 240, 252
Bristol Baptist College/Academy 18, 120, 142, 238, 239, 244, 245
British and Foreign Bible Society 9, 10
British Council of Churches 157
British Women's Temperance Association 180
Broadmead Baptist Church, Bristol 168
Broughton Baptist Church, Hampshire 169
Brownism 73
Brunner, E. 153
Buchanan, C. 8, 9
Buchman, F. 117, 118, 119, 120, 121
Bucknell University 179
Bunting, J. 2

General Index

Bunyan, J. 106
Burns, D. 21, 176
Burns, Mrs Dawson 176
Burton, Brother 247
Butterfield, H. xviii, xx
Butterworth, John 5
Butterworth, Joseph 5

'Call to Prayer, The' 247, 258
Calvin, J. 137
Calvinistic Baptists xvii, 165, 231, 264-78
Calvinistic Dissenters/Dissent 146, 231, 233
Calvinistic pietism 307
Calvinists/Calvinism 14, 16, 22, 20, 88, 90, 91, 96, 97, 101, 140, 142, 148, 234, 235, 237, 252, 254, 294, 295, 304, 305, 306, 308, 309
Cambridge Inter-Collegiate Christian Union 120
Cambridge University 119
Cambridgeshire and East Midlands Union 296
Campbell, R.J. 109
Cannon Street Baptist Church, Birmingham 277
Capp, B.S. 222
caravan mission 177
Cardiff Women Citizen's Association 181
Carey Kingsgate Press 302
Carey Publications 302
Carey, W. 4, 5, 7, 8, 9, 10, 12, 171, 174, 251, 253, 271, 278
Carmichael, Miss 169
Casey, E.S. 199
Catholic Apostolic Church 11
Catholic Revival 148, 152
Cavanaugh, W. 58, 59
Chadwick, Rosie 207
Chamberlain, J. 9
Chambers, Biddy 123
Chambers, O. 120, 121, 122, 123
charismatic liturgy 281
charismatics/charismatic movement/renewal 51, 107, 124
Charles II 223, 224, 274

Charlotte Chapel, Edinburgh 17, 117
Child, R.L. 285
Christ Church, Lambeth 110
Christendom 5, 6
Christian Endeavour 172
christoformation 202, 204
Christology 95, 96, 98, 99, 104
christomonism 63
Church Missionary Society 9, 10
Church of England 14, 15, 20, 75, 88, 115, 134, 143, 144, 152, 243, 281, 283, 285
Church of Scotland 143
Churches of Christ 20
Churches Together in Britain and Ireland 157
church–sect 14, 22
church–state 93
City Temple, London 109
Civil Rights movement 59
Clark, N. 38, 111, 158
clergy 54
Clifford, Hettie Rowntree 123
Clifford, J. 18, 109, 125
close(d)/strict comunnion 13, 147, 151, 296
closed membership 151
Coffey, D. 158
Coggins, J.R. 75
College Street Baptist Church, Northampton 238, 240, 243, 246, 257, 258
Colley, Linda 269
Collins, W. 135
Colwell, J.E. 131
common baptism 285
communion 7, 12, 144, 146, 147, 149, 151, 157, 162, 309, 310, 315
communion service 110, 111
Conder, J. 16
Confession of Faith (1689), *The* 300, 304
Congregational Board 20
congregational principle 17
Congregational Union 20, 21
Congregationalists/Congregationalism 7, 9, 20, 21, 76, 109, 110, 154, 240

Congress of Evangelical Christians-
  Baptists in USSR 290
connectionalism 27, 29, 36, 38, 44,
  79
Conner, W.T. 187
conservative theology 50
conservative-evangelicals/
  evangelicalism 26, 28, 29, 38, 303
conversion/conversionism 69, 71, 78,
  85, 87, 88, 89, 90, 91, 99, 103,
  104, 132, 150, 159, 162, 204, 238
Coombe, Brother 212
Corporation Act, 1661, the 266
Corrie, D. 9
Council of Churches for Britain and
  Ireland 157
Countess of Huntingdon Connexion
  2
covenant 75, 76, 83, 86, 88, 93, 94,
  97, 98, 102, 103, 104, 105, 138,
  160, 161, 164, 167, 280
Cowper, W. 276
Cox, F.A. 12
Cox, J. 226
Crawley Strict Baptist Chapel 302
creedalism 29, 57
Creighton, H. 14
Crisp, T. 234, 237
Crosley, D. 139
Cross, H. 286
Crozer Theological Seminary 69
Cuckfield Strict Baptist Chapel 300,
  301
Cuff, W. 109, 121
Curriers' Hall Baptist Church,
  London 233

Davies, H. 108, 109, 110
Davis, R. 234, 237
Davison, J. 310
Deacon, M. 246
Deaconess Order 177
deaconesses 123, 168, 178
deacons 33, 34, 164, 165, 168, 172,
  282, 290 291
deathbed testimonies 169, 170, 171

*Declaration of Faith of English
  People Remaining in Amsterdam,
  A* 96, 97, 164
Deism 144
denominations/denominationalism 1,
  5, 6, 11, 25
Derrida, J. 205
Descrates, R. 70
devotional reading 136
Deweese, C.W. 191
Diderot, D. 268
Disciples of Christ 20
discipline 76, 78, 80, 82, 148
Dissenters/Dissent 2, 8, 9, 11, 146,
  207, 232, 241, 264, 266, 267
Dix, K. 17
doctrinal supersessionism 201, 202
Doddridge, P. 169
Doggett, J. 296, 301, 306, 314
Dorcas Society 172
Dore, J. 276
Dover Association, Virginia 80
Downgrade controversy 305
Drake, J. 176
Draper, J.T. 26
Drummond Streeet Mission,
  Hampstead 177
Duckett Road Baptist Church,
  Harringay, London 114
Duncan, G. 148
Duncan, W.C. 190, 194
Dutton, Anne (Williams) 140, 143,
  168, 169
Dutton, B. 168

East India Company 8, 14
Eastern Association 6
Eastern Orthodoxy 1
ecclesiology 1-24, 13, 25-49, 50-66,
  67-83, 88, 92, 93, 98, 101, 145,
  165, 298, 306
Ecumenical Moderator 286
ecumenism/ecumenical movement 6,
  8, 37, 38, 151, 153, 158, 280,
  284, 286, 294, 297, 304, 306, 313
Eden Baptist Church, Cambridge 310
Edgerton, C. 85, 92
education 40

General Index 321

Edwards, J. 254
Edwards, Lilian 163, 169
Edwards, Sarah Ann 163, 179, 180, 181, 182
Edwards, W. 163, 179, 181, 182
Egle, P. 290
elders 33, 41, 42, 165, 282, 287
election 88, 96, 101
Elizabeth I 274
Ella, G.M. 235, 236, 237, 250
Ellis, C.J. 158, 159, 160
Ellis, F. 299, 315
Eltham Park Baptist Church, London 122
Elyett, Mary 170
Enlightenment, the 70, 81, 92, 192, 196, 203
Enlightenment rationalism 187
episcopacy 18, 23, 51, 52, 279-93
Episcopalians/episcopalianism 7, 200
eschatology 43, 94, 102, 195
Established Church 285
Estonian Baptists 289
eucharist 62, 201
European Baptist Federation 19
Evangelical Alliance, the 13, 14, 21
evangelical Anglicans 5, 11, 12, 14
evangelical Arminians 20
evangelical Calvinists/Calvinism 34, 141, 204, 233, 236, 237, 238, 239, 245, 248, 250, 251, 253, 254
Evangelical Christian and Baptist Churches of Latvia 288
Evangelical Fellowship of Congregational Churches 305
evangelical Nonconformity 21
Evangelical Revival 6, 13, 14, 77, 144, 152, 251, 252
evangelicals/evangelicalism 9, 10, 11, 12, 13, 14, 16, 22, 25, 38, 47, 86, 87, 89, 90, 106, 107, 113, 116, 117, 119, 131, 146, 169, 170, 186, 189, 231, 239, 272, 276, 278, 294, 298, 300, 304, 305, 307
evangelism 13, 40, 91, 93, 117, 118, 234, 235, 236, 301, 310
Evans, C. 169, 244

Evans, J. 240, 241, 242, 243, 249
Evans, Sarah Ann (Edwards) 163, 179, 180, 181, 182
Ewing, J.W. 112
ex opere operato 143, 152
Exeter College, Oxford 225, 226, 229, 230
experimentalism 295

Faith and Order Movement 154, 157
Faith and Practice of Thirty Congregations, The 98
Farrer, Ellen Margaret 176
Farrer, W. 176
Federal Council of the Evangelical Free Churches 154
federalism 21
Federation of Evangelical Christians 280
Fellowship of Evangelical Baptist Churches in Canada, The 25, 36, 44
Fellowship of Independent Baptist Churches in Canada 25
Fellowship of Independent Evangelical Churches 306
Fellowship of Youth 297
Fiddes, P.S. 65, 86, 98, 102, 103, 104, 160, 161
Fifth Monarchists 220
Finley, M. 196
Finney, C.G. 90
First Baptist Church, Jackson, Mississippi 59
First London Confession, The 30, 76, 97, 98
Fisher, G. 18, 284
five-point Calvinists 51
Forde, G. 92
formal traditionalism 198, 199
Fountain, J. 267
Fowler, S.K. 132, 133, 134, 135, 139, 140, 141, 142, 143, 152
Franchuk, V. 289
Free Church Fellowship, The 124, 125
Free Church Retreat movement 108
Free Churches Group 6

Free Churchmen/Free Churches 6, 21, 23, 107, 109, 115, 124, 157, 180, 279, 281, 285, 288, 291, 293, 307
Freeman, C.W. 52
Freewill Baptists xvii
French Revolution 264, 265, 266, 267, 268
Frere, W.H. 126
Friends of Reunion, the 284
Fuller, A. 4, 5, 7, 8, 9, 12, 13, 140, 141, 204, 233, 237, 247, 248, 250, 252, 253, 267, 269, 270, 271, 272, 273, 274, 276, 277, 278, 295
Fuller, A.G. 233
Fullerism 5, 237, 250, 254, 309
Fullerton, W.Y. 115, 116
fundamental traditionalism 198
fundamentalist–modernist controversy 199
fundamentalists/fundamentalism 28, 34, 35, 44, 296

Gadsby, W. 18
Gainsborough 75
Garner, R. 139
Garrard, L.R. 311
Gates, Edith 122
Gaustad, E.C. xvi, 91, 92
Gee, D. 114
General Association of Regular Baptist Churches (USA) 44
General Baptist Missionary Society 5
General Baptists 3, 4, 6, 32, 33, 59, 73, 75, 76, 94, 95, 101, 133, 135, 136, 139, 144, 165, 231, 241, 248, 249, 254, 261, 262, 282, 283
General Body of Protestant Dissenting Ministers 240
General Superintendents 285
George, T. 57, 61
Georgian Baptists 280, 281
German Baptists 287
Gertners, A. 286, 287
Gilbert, A.D. 14, 15, 232

Gill, J. 139, 141, 233, 234, 235, 236, 237, 238, 239, 240, 243, 248, 250, 251, 252, 253
Gilmore, A. 38
Girls' Hostel, London, the 180
Gladstone, W.E. 14, 15
glorification 101
Glover, T.R. 119, 120
gnosticism 63, 64
God's Bible School, Cincinnati 123
Godwin, B. 233
Gorham case, the 146
Gospel Standard Aid societies 18
Gospel Standard Articles of Faith 18
Gospel Standard Baptists 131, 295, 296, 299, 302, 303, 309, 311
Gould, G. 210
Gould, G.P. 210
Grace Baptist Assembly 294
Grace Baptists 130
Graham, B. 311
Grantham, T. 4, 59, 60, 136, 137, 138, 139, 203, 204, 282
Graves, J.R. 43, 195
Great Awakening, the 78, 79
Great Gransden Baptist Church, Huntingdonshire 168
Greenfield, W. 9
Grenville Congregational Church 176
Grenz, S.J. 89, 185
Griffiths, Mr 110
Guthrie, D. 307

Halbrooks, G.T. 186
Haldane, R. 278
Halévy, E. 231
Hall, Jr, R. 9, 12, 147, 148, 149, 253, 265, 267, 268
Hall, Sr, R. 253
Harford-Battersby, T.D. 115
Harris, H. 169
Harris, Mary 122
Harris, R.R. 122, 123
Hartford Theological Seminary 118
Harvey, B. 52
Harvey, G. 222, 223, 224, 225, 226, 227, 228, 230
Hatch, N. 195

General Index 323

Hauerwas, S. 56
Hawkes, B. 47
Hawkins, J. 274
Hawkins, W. 150
Hayden, R. 207, 208, 209, 210, 216, 234, 239
Haykin, M.A.G. 233, 245
Haymes, B. 22, 63
Heath Street Baptist Church, Hampstead, London 125, 167, 168, 176, 177, 178
Heber, Bishop 7, 8
Hedger, Violet 122
Helwys, T. 3, 75, 96, 164, 165
Hempton, D. 11
Hervey, J. 14
Hervieu-Léger, Danielle 192, 193, 196, 197, 198, 199
Hewitt, M. 244
high-Calvinists/high-Calvinism 21, 139, 141, 143, 152
High Churchmen/High Church/High Anglicanism 11, 109
Highams Park Baptist Church, London 126
high-Calvinists/high-Calvinism 231-63, 297
Hill, R. 5
Hinson, E.G. 53, 54, 106, 185, 186, 190
Hiscox, E. 46
historiography xx, 43
Hoad, J. 130
Hobbes, T. 70
Hobbs, H. 51, 68, 69
Hoffman, B. 107
holiness 104, 112, 123
Holmes, S.R. 185, 186
Home Work Fund 177
Honeysett, B. 311
Hooker, Joan 123
Horsey, Esther 170
Horsey, J. 170, 171
Hosley Down Baptist Church, London 238
Hudgins, D. 59
Hudson, W.S. 69, 73, 74, 75, 76, 92

Hughes, W. 221
Huguenots 268, 271
Hulse, E. 130, 300, 301, 302, 303, 308, 309, 311
Hume, D. 70
Hungarian Reformed Church 292
Huntingdonshire Union of Independent and Baptist Churches 20
Hussey, J. 234
hymns/hymn-singing 34, 109, 110, 169
hyper-Calvinism 233, 301, 311, 314

Ignatius 292
immersion 3, 10, 93, 135, 140, 143, 145, 152, 153, 157, 298, 310
incarnation 63, 64, 66, 96
independency 25, 27, 29, 34, 39, 44, 46
Independent Baptists 130
independent churches 24
Independents 5, 73, 74, 234, 240, 243
individualism 46, 51, 52, 53, 54, 55, 59, 67-83, 91, 92, 111, 132, 149, 151, 192, 193, 203
inerrancy 51, 59
infallibility 47
infant baptism 9, 13, 39, 51, 52, 134, 142, 143, 144, 145, 161, 221
initiation 64, 97, 137, 140
institutionalism 23
Intentionalism 53
inter-communion 1
interdependence 17, 38, 46
Interim Council of the Union of Baptist Churches of Latvia, the 288
Inter-Varsity Fellowship 305
Ivimey, J. 12, 171

James, Isabel Riley 172, 178
James, J.A. 21
Japan Holiness Church 123
Jefferson, T. 78, 195
Jenkins, C.A. 188
Jenson, R. 63
Jessey, H. 74

Johnson, E. 64
Jones, J.A. 171
Jones, K. 158
Jones, R.B. 112, 113
Jones, R.P. 191, 205
Jordan, C. 57, 58
Jordan, R. 57
Jung, C. 205
justifiation by faith 52, 85, 86, 90, 92, 94, 95, 96, 97, 98, 100, 101, 102, 103, 104, 152, 169

Kalnins, J.A. 288
Kammen, M.G. 188, 189, 195, 196, 197, 198, 199
Kant, I. 70
Keach, B. 34, 135, 136, 137, 139
Keach, E. 34
Keble, J. 15
Kempis, T. à 125
Kennedy, Lt Col. 9
Kent General Baptist Assembly 231
Kerfoot, F.H. 26
Keswick Convention 114, 115, 116, 117, 118, 119, 123, 126
Keswick Group 121
Kettering Baptist Church 239, 242, 247, 254, 269
Kevan, E.F. 301, 306
Keymer, W. 211
Kingdon, D. 304, 305
Kinghorn, D. 265
Kinghorn, J. 12, 147, 264, 267
Knibb, W. 254, 277
Köbner, J. 287
Komi Evangelical Church 281
Kreitzer, L.J. xx

Laceklis, K. 288, 289
Ladies Association for the Support of Zenana Work and Bible Women in India 175
Lambeth Appeal, The 154
Lambeth Quadrilateral, the 285
Landmarkism 27, 34, 35, 40, 43, 199, 201
Lane, E. 130
Langley, A.S. 129

Latvian Baptist Congress, the 288
Latvian Baptists 280, 286-91
Latvian Lutheran Church 287
Latvian Pentecostals 291
Lawrence, H. 139
laying on of hands 59, 156, 157
legends xviii, xix, xx
Leland, J. 67, 78, 79, 80, 81, 91, 92, 203
Leonard, B.J. 87, 88, 90, 91
Levindanto, N. 289
Lewis, Marianne 175
liberal theology 29, 44, 47
liberalism 1, 38
Liberation Society, the 11
Little Tew and Cleveley, Oxfordshire 122
liturgical renewal 107
liturgy 62, 110, 111, 126, 281
Lloyd-Jones, D.M. 301, 304, 312
Locke, J. 70, 78
London Baptist Area (Metropolitan) 112
London Baptist Association 114
London Bible College 301, 306, 312
London Confession, The 3, 74
London Missionary Society 6, 10
London Reformed Baptist Seminary 303
London Road Baptist Church, Lowestoft 111
Lord's Supper 1, 59, 76, 80, 107, 124, 131, 133, 135, 136, 138, 144, 148, 149, 155, 156, 157, 201, 204, 266, 310
Lovegrove, D.W. 17
Lupton, L.F. 309
Luther, M. 2, 24, 61, 63, 107, 130
Lutherans/Lutheranism 107, 118, 283, 291, 292

MacIntyre, A. 70
Madison, J. 78
Malone, F.A. 27
Manchester Baptist College 126
Manley, K.R. 231
Mann, H. 231, 249
Mansfield College, Oxford 120, 124

General Index 325

Marlowes Baptist Church, Hemel Hempstead 172
Marshall, Molly 85
Marshall, N.H. 125
Marshman, J. 7, 8, 9, 174
Martin, H. 284, 285
Martin, R.H. 11, 12, 13
Martyn, H. 7, 8, 9
Mass, the 146
Masters, P. 303, 304
Maternal Society, the 172
Mathews, D. 77, 78, 79, 82
McBeth, H.L. 68, 75
McCaig, A. 112
McClendon, Jr, J.W. 52, 54, 87, 185, 194, 198
McGill Baptist Church, Concord, NC 48
McGrath, A.E. 106
McKenzie, J. 279
McLaren, A. 21
McNutt, W.R. 69, 72
means of grace 136, 137, 152, 153, 154, 155, 159
Medley, E. 176
Medley, M.S. 185
Medley, Mrs Edward 176
Melbourne Hall, Leicester 113, 115
membership 107, 151, 157, 161, 162, 166, 167, 298
memory xv, xvi, xvii, xviii, xix, 193, 197, 198, 199, 202, 204, 205
Mennonites 19, 134
Meredith, A. 27
messengers 33, 42, 282, 283
Methodist Revival 232, 237, 247
Methodists/Methodism 2, 5, 20
Metropolitan Association of Strict Baptist Churches 296, 298, 312
Metropolitan Community Baptist Church, Toronto 46, 47
Metropolitan Tabernacle, London 17, 112, 303
Meyer, F.B. 110, 112, 113, 115, 116, 117, 118, 119, 121, 126
Middlebrook, J.B. 120, 127
Midnight Mission, the 180

Midwestern Baptist Theological Seminary 28
Miller, P. 88
Milton Keynes Christian Council 286
Mirfield community 126
mission 27, 93, 94, 96
Mitchell, W. 139
mode of baptism 40
moderate Calvinism 34
moderate theology 50
modern missionary movement 6
modernist–fundamentalist controversy 35
modernity 193, 197, 198
'Modern Question, the' 238
Moldovan Baptists 280
monarchical episcopate 42
Moody, D. 48
Moody, D.L. 117, 118
Moral Re-Armament 117
Moss Side Baptist Church, Manchester 176
Moulden, J. 210
Moule, H.C.G. 116
Mullins, E.Y. 51, 52, 54, 59, 61, 62, 69, 187, 191, 195, 201, 202
myths xx, 29, 46, 86, 95, 184, 185, 231

Nakada, J. 123
National Assembly of Evangelicals 304
National Assembly of Strict Baptist Pastors and Deacons 296, 303
National Assembly of Strict Baptists 299
National Association of Baptist Professors of Religion 186
National Free Church Council 6
National Strict Baptist Federation 296, 313
National Strict Baptist Sunday School Association 296, 297
National Strict Baptist Women's Federation 297
Neely, A. 28
Nelson, H. 277

New Connexion of General Baptists 5, 18, 21, 23, 139, 232, 248, 249, 254
New England Puritans 88
New Frontiers 306
New Hampshire Confession, The 34, 35, 36
New North Road Baptist Church, Huddersfield 120
New Road Baptist Church, Oxford 207
New Theology 109
Newman, Elizabeth 52
Newman, J.H. 10, 126
Newman, S. 204
Newsome, D. 11
Newton, J. 5, 12
Niebuhr, H.R. 14, 15, 22
Noel, B.W. 150
Nonconformists/Nonconformity 6, 111, 144, 147, 150, 220, 285
non-creedalism 57
Norman, R.S. 184, 185, 196
North Rocky Mount Baptist Church, NC 48
Northamptonshire Association 12, 14, 17, 239, 240, 242, 243, 245-49, 250, 251, 253, 254, 257, 258, 265, 266, 271
Northern Baptist College 305
Northern Baptist Convention 35
Northern Federation 296
Northfield Student Conferences 117, 118
Norwich Chapel Case, the 147
Nozick, R. 70
Nuttall, G.F. 234

Oakes Baptist Church, Lindley, near Huddersfield 148
Ohlmann, E. xviii, 86, 93, 94, 190
Old General [Unitarian] Baptists 22
Olney Baptist Church 243, 244, 246, 257
Oncken, J.G. 19, 287
open Brethren 21
open communion 7, 9, 12, 13, 147, 152, 310

open membership 147 151, 152
ordinance(s) 34, 96, 99, 129, 130, 135, 136, 140, 142, 143, 152, 162
ordo salutis 94
Oriental Orthodoxy 1
Orissa 5
Orthodox Church(es)/Orthodoxy 1, 62, 104, 201, 280, 291
Orthodox Creed, The 3, 32, 95, 101, 102, 103, 133, 136, 282
Overseas Missionary Fellowship (China Inland Mission) 22
Owen, J. 3
Owen, O. 112
Oxford Group, the 117, 120, 121, 126
Oxford Movement, the 147, 148

pacifism 270
Paedobaptists/Paedobaptism 10, 133, 135, 142, 143, 145, 149, 151, 150, 152, 153, 301, 302, 310, 314
pan-evangelicalism 11-14
paramnesia 199, 200, 203, 205
Parker, J. 21
Particular Baptists 5, 3, 6, 18, 30, 31, 32, 34, 73, 74, 75, 76, 97, 98, 135, 136, 139, 141, 142, 143, 144, 152, 165, 231, 232, 233, 234, 238, 239, 241, 248, 249, 251, 252, 253, 254, 264-78, 282, 283, 295, 296, 300, 301, 302, 306, 310, 314
pastors 33, 34, 136, 165
patriotism 269-73, 276
Patterson, P. 26, 27, 28, 35
Patterson, T. 126
Payne, E.A. 3, 17, 108, 156, 157, 158, 178, 210, 213, 285
Payne, J. 297
Pearce Gould, Miss K.M. 168
Pearce, S. 253, 277, 278
Pelikan, J. 2, 24
Pendarves, J. 220-30
Pendleton, J.M. 43
Pengilly, R. 267
Penn-Lewis, J. 113, 118
Pennsylvannia State College 118

General Index

Pentecostal League of Prayer 122, 123
Pentecostals/Pentecostalism 113, 114, 117, 123, 289
Perkin, J.R.C. 145, 149, 150
perseverance 97, 99
Peters, T. 292
Philadelphia Association 34, 74
Philadelphia Confession of Faith, The 34, 74, 81
Philippe, P. 223
Phillips, T. 111
Philpot, J.C. 18, 295
Pietists/Pietism 87, 88, 89, 91, 103
Pike, J.B. 18
Pike, J.D.G. 5
Plymouth Brethren 21
pneumatology 101, 125
Pontypool Baptist College 163, 179
Popery 21
Porton Calvinistic Baptists, Wiltshire 165
post-denominationalism 1
post-Englightenment 149
Poteat, W.H. 54
Potts, E.D. 8
predestination 96, 101
Presbyterians/Presbyterianism 73, 154, 234, 240
Pressler, P. 50, 51
Price, Ann 171
priesthood of all believers, the 50-66, 68, 279
Primitive Baptists xvii, 40
Prince, J. 221, 222
Priory Street Baptist Church, York 117
'Probus' 166
Protestants/Protestantism 1, 106, 194, 195, 200, 201, 281, 285
Psalsm and Hymns Trust 110
pseudo-traditionalism 198, 199
Pullen Memorial Baptist Church, Raleigh, NC 48
Puritan Independents 73
Puritans/Puritanism 2, 73, 87, 88, 89, 90, 73, 91, 93, 94, 97, 103, 134, 170, 171, 264, 300, 301, 309

Puritan-Separatists 165
Puseyism 21

Quakers 53, 144, 270

Radlett Fellowship, the 129
Radner, E. 200, 201, 206
Raine, Sarah Ann (Mrs John [Annie] Drake) 176
Randall, I.M. 107
rantism 143
rationalism 92, 253, 268
Rauschenbusch, W. 189, 191
Rawdon College, Leeds 18, 120, 125
Rawlinson, R. 221
Rawls, J. 70
Rees, Jean 116
Reformation, the xix, 108, 144, 194, 196, 292
Reformed Baptists 32, 294-316
Reformed Churches 158
Reformed tradition 21, 39, 130, 142
regeneration 89, 93, 137, 142, 155
Regent's Park Chapel, London 118, 119
Regent's Park College, Oxford 18, 107, 120, 122, 125, 176, 179, 210, 285
Regular Baptists 81
regulative principle, the 39, 40
Religious Census 1851 231, 244, 248, 249, 260, 263
religious freedom 288
religious liberty 93, 199, 266
religious toleration 58, 165
Religious Tract Society, the 12
Renault, J.O. 79, 80
Reno, R.R. 200, 201, 202, 203
Rescue Home, Cardiff 180
restorationism 306
revisionism 191
revivalism 90, 103, 132
Richmond, L. 12
Ridgelands Bible College, London 123
righteousness 95, 96
Riley, A.F. 172
Rippon, J. 19, 231, 238

ritualism 148
Roberts, E. 111, 113
Robinson, H.W. 107, 125, 126, 158
Robinson, R. 12, 276, 277
Robison, O.C. 236, 237
Rogers, A. 51
Roman Catholics/Roman Catholicism/Roman Catholic Church 11, 20, 52, 53, 54, 88, 106, 124, 143, 158, 161, 200, 201, 202, 279, 282, 284, 291, 292
Romanian Unitarians 292
Romanticism 264
Romsey Baptist Church, Hampshire 166
Rose, C.S. 177
Rose, Doris 177
Rosman, Doreen 170
Rouse, Ruth 12
Rousseau, J.-J. 268
Rumbergs, J. 287
Rushbrooke, J.H. 158
Russel, Letty M. 280
Rye Lane Baptist Church, Peckham, London 122
Ryland, J.C. 12, 238, 243, 245, 248, 252, 253, 257
Ryland, Jr, J. 140, 141, 142, 233, 237, 244, 248, 252, 253, 254, 257

sacerdotalism 129
sacramentalism 11, 38, 64, 88, 91, 128-62
sacraments 52, 54, 65, 90, 128-62, 202, 203, 285
Saffery, Maria 149
Sale, Elizabeth 175
Salisbury Baptist Church 170
Salvation Army 110
sanctification 86, 89, 90, 93, 94, 95, 96, 97, 98, 99, 100, 101, 102, 103, 104, 108, 122
Sandford, F.D. 122
Savoy Declaration, the 73
Saxby, A. 114
Scarborough, G. 48
scepticism 144
Schaeffer, F. 308

Schleiermacher, F.D.E. 59
Schmemman, A. 62, 65
Scotch Baptists 21, 310
Scott, T. 5
Scroggie, W.G. 113, 114, 116, 117, 123
se-baptism 3
Second London Confession, The 31, 32, 33, 34, 37, 76, 100, 101, 135, 201, 272, 273
Second Vatican Council 279
Semple, R.B. 81
Senior Regional Ministers 283
Separate Baptists 72, 73, 77, 78, 79, 80, 81, 83
Separatists/Separatism 44, 73, 74, 75, 76, 97, 74, 243
Serampore College 5, 7, 9
Serampore Trio 9, 10, 174
Seventh Day Adventist Union 291
Shaftesbury, Lord 14
Shakespeare, J.H. 18, 20, 22, 23, 37, 125, 154, 172, 173, 178, 182, 283
Sheldrake, P. 106, 107
Shepherd, P. 22, 23
Sherman, C. 195
Shoreditch Tabernacle, London 109, 121
Short Confession of Faith 95, 164
Short Confession of Faith, A 96, 97, 164
Shurden, W. 51, 52, 53, 54
Simmons, P. 55, 56
Skepp, J. 234
skepticism 268
slavery 82, 83, 254, 274, 275, 276, 277
Slavonic Baptists 288
Smith, D. 310
Smits, J. 291
Smyth, J. 3, 75, 95, 96
Smyth-Helwys Baptists 75
Socinianism 144, 271, 272
sola scriptura 194, 196
Somerset Confession, The 30, 98, 99, 167
Songulashvili, M. 281

General Index

soteriology 84-105, 132, 154, 155, 161
soul competency 50, 51, 52, 55, 56, 59, 63, 64, 69, 92, 93, 187, 191, 201, 202
soul freedom 55
soul liberty 27, 48, 50
South Wales Baptist College 163, 179, 180
South Wales Bible College 312
Southern Baptist Theological Seminary, Louisville, KY 69
Southern Baptists/Southern Baptist Convention xvii, 1, 26, 27, 28, 35, 36, 43, 48, 50, 51, 59, 68, 184, 196, 197, 199, 201, 284
Southwell, Clara 168
Southwestern Baptist Theological Seminary, Fort Worth, TX 26
sovereignty of God 96, 100
Speer, R. 118
Spirit-baptism 114, 126, 130
spiritual journals 172
spirituality 106-27, 171, 297
sprinkling 143
Spurgeon, C.H. 13, 14, 303, 312
Spurgeon's College (Pastor's College) 112, 117
Spurgeonic Baptists 18, 21
Spurr, F.C. 119, 124, 125
St Andrew's Street Baptist Church, Cambridge 124
St Mary's Baptist Church, Norwich 264
St. Amant, C.P. xvii
Standard Confession, The 94, 95, 101
Stanley, B. 175
Steadman, W. 267
Stearns, S. 77
Steele, Anne (Froud, 'Theodosia') 163, 169
Steele, W. 169
Stevens, W. 209, 210, 215
Stinton, B. 210
Stockford, Mrs 176
Stout, J. 70
Stovel, C. 149

Strict and Particular Baptist Ministers' Fellowship 297, 308
Strict and Particular Baptist Society 296
Strict and Particular Baptist Trust Corporation 296
Strict and Particular Baptists 22, 147
Strict Baptist Association 295
Strict Baptist Bible Institute 297, 309, 312
Strict Baptist Festival 299
Strict Baptist Historical Society 297
Strict Baptist Mission 296, 299, 313
Strict Baptist Open-Air Mission 297, 311
Strict Baptists 17, 18, 21, 22, 130, 294-316
strict communion 18, 298, 300, 310, 314
Student Christian Movement 120
subjectivism 148, 152
successionism 40
Sudan Inland Mission 22
Suffolk and Norfolk Association of Strict Baptist Churches 16, 296, 307, 308, 309
Suffolk Baptist Union 308
Sunday schools 169, 172
Surrey Strict Baptists 299
Sutcliff, J. 237, 244, 245, 247, 248, 252, 253, 254, 258
Sutton, Katherine 168
Swidler, Anne 197

Tabernacle Welsh Baptist Church, the Hayes, Cardiff 180
Taylor, A.J.P. xviii, xix, xx
Taylor, C. 70
Taylor, D. 254
Taylor, M. 305, 306
temperance 111, 180, 181
Tenterden Gospel Standard Baptist Church, Kent 311
Tervits, J. 290
Test Act, 1673 266
Thirty-Nine Articles 133
Thomas, J. 14, 239
Thomason, T. 9

Thompson, D.M. 11, 13, 143, 144, 146
Thompson, J. 239, 241, 242, 243, 247, 249, 248
Thompson, P.E. 52, 53, 132, 133, 136, 137, 138
Thornton, H. 5
Thorp, Jennifer 211
Three English Baptist Associations in South Wales and Monmouthshire, the 181
Tidmarch, R. 213
Tillich, P. 280
Tisdale, T. 213
Toleration Act, 1689 241
Tomkins 221
tongues 117, 122
Toon, P. 234, 237, 304
Torrance, J. 61
Townsend, H. 126
Tract Society 172
Tractarianism 147
tradition xv, xvi, xvii, 183-206
Training College for Baptist deaconesses 178
transubstantiation 146
Tredegarville Baptist Church, Cardiff 179
Trinity, the xv, 60, 63, 64, 65, 66, 103, 104, 105, 140
True Gospel-Faith Declared, The 135
Turner, D. 12

Ukranian Pentecostals 289
Underhill, E.B. 175
Union of Evangelical Christians and Baptists 288
Union of Latvian Baptists Churches of Novgorod, the 288
Union of Regular Baptist Churches of Ontario and Quebec 25
Unitarians/Unitarianism 33, 61, 139, 144, 231, 232, 249, 253
United Free Church 22, 23
United Reformed Church 21
University of Wales 179

Vedder, H. 188

Victorian Road Church, Leicester 113
Virginia Baptists 82
Virgo, T. 306
Voltaire, F.M.A. 268
voluntaryism/voluntarism 14, 27, 28, 35, 36, 53, 54, 57, 67-83, 85, 103, 132

Wacker, G. 113
Walgrave Baptist Church 246
Walker, M.J. 107, 108, 148, 149, 150, 151
Walker, W. 244
Ward, R.H. 11
Ward, W. 7, 9, 174
Ward, W.R. 13, 232, 250, 251
Wardin, A.W. 128
Waterlander church 3
Watson, G.D. 122
Watson, Joann Ford 169
Watts, M.R. 231
Wayland, F. 187, 188, 190, 193, 197
Welsh Revival, the 111, 112, 113, 118
Wesley, J. 14, 89, 169, 237, 247, 252
Wesleyan Revival 232, 253
Wesleyanism 89, 122, 123
West Ham Central Mission 123
West, W.M.S. 38, 158
Westbourne Park Baptist Church, London 109, 125
Western Association 239, 245
Westminster Confession, The 100
Westminster divines 73
Whitby, F.F. 129
White, B.R. 209, 222
White, R.E.O. 131, 158
Whitefield Fraternal 303
Whitefield, G. 2, 14, 169, 237
Whitley College, Melbourne 231
Whitley, W.T. 129, 163, 210, 211, 215
Wilberforce, W. 5
Wilken, R.L. xv
Wilks, M. 265
William and Mary 223, 224
William Jewel College 179

General Index

Williams, C. 20, 129
Williams, D.H. 189
Williams, R. 64
Wilson, J.B. 5
Wilson, Linda 170
Winward, S.F. 38, 108, 126, 156, 157
Witney Baptist Church, near Oxford 211
Wittgenstein, L. 56, 61
Wolterstorff, N. 192
women 122, 123, 163-83, 281, 291
Women's Liberal Association, Cardiff 181
Wood, A. 220, 221, 222, 224
Wood, E.J. 309
Woolwich Tabernacle 110
Wordsworth, Dorothy 264

Wordsworth, W. 264
World Council of Churches 1, 155, 158
World Evangelization Crusade 22
worship 108, 109, 110

YMCA 118, 123
Young Baptist and Forward Movement 112
Young Women's Committee 182
Young Women's Guilds 176

Zenana Mission Fund 172
Zidkov, J.I. 289
Zizioulas, J. 104, 105
Zoar Baptist Church 179
Zwingli, H. 130, 147,
Zwinglianism 132, 148

Studies in Baptist History and Thought

(All titles uniform with this volume)
Dates in bold are of projected publication
Volumes in this series are not always published in sequence

David Bebbington and Anthony R. Cross (eds)
Global Baptist History
(SBHT vol. 14)
This book brings together studies from the Second International Conference on Baptist Studies which explore different facets of Baptist life and work especially during the twentieth century.
2006 / 1-84227-214-4 / approx. 350pp

David Bebbington (ed.)
The Gospel in the World
International Baptist Studies
(SBHT vol. 1)
This volume of essays from the First International Conference on Baptist Studies deals with a range of subjects spanning Britain, North America, Europe, Asia and the Antipodes. Topics include studies on religious tolerance, the communion controversy and the development of the international Baptist community, and concludes with two important essays on the future of Baptist life that pay special attention to the United States.
2002 / 1-84227-118-0 / xiv + 362pp

John H.Y. Briggs (ed.)
Pulpit and People
Studies in Eighteenth-Century English Baptist Life and Thought
(SBHT vol. 28)
The eighteenth century was a crucial time in Baptist history. The denomination had its roots in seventeenth-century English Puritanism and Separatism and the persecution of the Stuart kings with only a limited measure of freedom after 1689. Worse, however, was to follow for with toleration came doctrinal conflict, a move away from central Christian understandings and a loss of evangelistic urgency. Both spiritual and numerical decline ensued, to the extent that the denomination was virtually reborn as rather belatedly it came to benefit from the Evangelical Revival which brought new life to both Arminian and Calvinistic Baptists. The papers in this volume study a denomination in transition, and relate to theology, their views of the church and its mission, Baptist spirituality, and engagements with radical politics.
2007 / 1-84227-403-1 / approx. 350pp

July 2005

Damian Brot
Church of the Baptized or Church of Believers?
A Contribution to the Dialogue between the Catholic Church and the Free Churches with Special Reference to Baptists
(SBHT vol. 26)

The dialogue between the Catholic Church and the Free Churches in Europe has hardly taken place. This book pleads for a commencement of such a conversation. It offers, among other things, an introduction to the American and the international dialogues between Baptists and the Catholic Church and strives to allow these conversations to become fruitful in the European context as well.

2006 / 1-84227-334-5 / approx. 364pp

Dennis Bustin
Paradox and Perseverence
Hanserd Knollys, Particular Baptist Pioneer in Seventeenth-Century England
(SBHT vol. 23)

The seventeenth century was a significant period in English history during which the people of England experienced unprecedented change and tumult in all spheres of life. At the same time, the importance of order and the traditional institutions of society were being reinforced. Hanserd Knollys, born during this pivotal period, personified in his life the ambiguity, tension and paradox of it, openly seeking change while at the same time cautiously embracing order. As a founder and leader of the Particular Baptists in London and despite persecution and personal hardship, he played a pivotal role in helping shape their identity externally in society and, internally, as they moved toward becoming more formalised by the end of the century.

2006 / 1-84227-259-4 / approx. 324pp

Anthony R. Cross
Baptism and the Baptists
Theology and Practice in Twentieth-Century Britain
(SBHT vol. 3)

At a time of renewed interest in baptism, *Baptism and the Baptists* is a detailed study of twentieth-century baptismal theology and practice and the factors which have influenced its development.

2000 / 0-85364-959-6 / xx + 530pp

July 2005

Anthony R. Cross and Philip E. Thompson (eds)
Baptist Sacramentalism
(SBHT vol. 5)
This collection of essays includes biblical, historical and theological studies in the theology of the sacraments from a Baptist perspective. Subjects explored include the physical side of being spiritual, baptism, the Lord's supper, the church, ordination, preaching, worship, religious liberty and the issue of disestablishment.
2003 / 1-84227-119-9 / xvi + 278pp

Anthony R. Cross and Philip E. Thompson (eds)
Baptist Sacramentalism 2
(SBHT vol. 25)
This second collection of essays exploring various dimensions of sacramental theology from a Baptist perspective includes biblical, historical and theological studies from scholars from around the world.
2006 / 1-84227-325-6 / approx. 350pp

Paul S. Fiddes
Tracks and Traces
Baptist Identity in Church and Theology
(SBHT vol. 13)
This is a comprehensive, yet unusual, book on the faith and life of Baptist Christians. It explores the understanding of the church, ministry, sacraments and mission from a thoroughly theological perspective. In a series of interlinked essays, the author relates Baptist identity consistently to a theology of covenant and to participation in the triune communion of God.
2003 / 1-84227-120-2 / xvi + 304pp

Stanley K. Fowler
More Than a Symbol
The British Baptist Recovery of Baptismal Sacramentalism
(SBHT vol. 2)
Fowler surveys the entire scope of British Baptist literature from the seventeenth-century pioneers onwards. He shows that in the twentieth century leading British Baptist pastors and theologians recovered an understanding of baptism that connected experience with soteriology and that in doing so they were recovering what many of their forebears had taught.
2002 / 1-84227-052-4 / xvi + 276pp

July 2005

Steven R. Harmon
Towards Baptist Catholicity
Essays on Tradition and the Baptist Vision
(SBHT vol. 27)
This series of essays contends that the reconstruction of the Baptist vision in the wake of modernity's dissolution requires a retrieval of the ancient ecumenical tradition that forms Christian identity through rehearsal and practice. Themes explored include catholic identity as an emerging trend in Baptist theology, tradition as a theological category in Baptist perspective, Baptist confessions and the patristic tradition, worship as a principal bearer of tradition, and the role of Baptist higher education in shaping the Christian vision.
2006 / 1-84227-362-0 / approx. 210pp

Michael A.G. Haykin (ed.)
'At the Pure Fountain of Thy Word'
Andrew Fuller as an Apologist
(SBHT vol. 6)
One of the greatest Baptist theologians of the eighteenth and early nineteenth centuries, Andrew Fuller has not had justice done to him. There is little doubt that Fuller's theology lay behind the revitalization of the Baptists in the late eighteenth century and the first few decades of the nineteenth. This collection of essays fills a much needed gap by examining a major area of Fuller's thought, his work as an apologist.
2004 / 1-84227-171-7 / xxii + 276pp

Michael A.G. Haykin
Studies in Calvinistic Baptist Spirituality
(SBHT vol. 15)
In a day when spirituality is in vogue and Christian communities are looking for guidance in this whole area, there is wisdom in looking to the past to find untapped wells. The Calvinistic Baptists, heirs of the rich ecclesial experience in the Puritan era of the seventeenth century, but, by the end of the eighteenth century, also passionately engaged in the catholicity of the Evangelical Revivals, are such a well. This collection of essays, covering such things as the Lord's Supper, friendship and hymnody, seeks to draw out the spiritual riches of this community for reflection and imitation in the present day.
2006 / 1-84227-149-0 / approx. 350pp

Brian Haymes, Anthony R. Cross and Ruth Gouldbourne
On Being the Church
Revisioning Baptist Identity
(SBHT vol. 21)
The aim of the book is to re-examine Baptist theology and practice in the light of the contemporary biblical, theological, ecumenical and missiological context drawing on historical and contemporary writings and issues. It is not a study in denominationalism but rather seeks to revision historical insights from the believers' church tradition for the sake of Baptists and other Christians in the context of the modern–postmodern context.
2006 / 1-84227-121-0 / approx. 350pp

Ken R. Manley
From Woolloomooloo to 'Eternity': A History of Australian Baptists
Volume 1: Growing an Australian Church (1831–1914)
Volume 2: A National Church in a Global Community (1914–2005)
(SBHT vols 16.1 and 16.2)
From their beginnings in Australia in 1831 with the first baptisms in Woolloomoolloo Bay in 1832, this pioneering study describes the quest of Baptists in the different colonies (states) to discover their identity as Australians and Baptists. Although institutional developments are analyzed and the roles of significant individuals traced, the major focus is on the social and theological dimensions of the Baptist movement.
Vol. 1 2006 / 1-84227-194-6 / approx. 450pp
Vol. 2 2006 / 1-84227-404-X / approx. 450pp

Ken R. Manley
'Redeeming Love Proclaim'
John Rippon and the Baptists
(SBHT vol. 12)
A leading exponent of the new moderate Calvinism which brought new life to many Baptists, John Rippon (1751–1836) helped unite the Baptists at this significant time. His many writings expressed the denomination's growing maturity and mutual awareness of Baptists in Britain and America, and exerted a long-lasting influence on Baptist worship and devotion. In his various activities, Rippon helped conserve the heritage of Old Dissent and promoted the evangelicalism of the New Dissent
2004 / 1-84227-193-8 / xviii + 340pp

July 2005

Peter J. Morden
Offering Christ to the World
Andrew Fuller and the Revival of English Particular Baptist Life
(SBHT vol. 8)
Andrew Fuller (1754–1815) was one of the foremost English Baptist ministers of his day. His career as an Evangelical Baptist pastor, theologian, apologist and missionary statesman coincided with the profound revitalization of the Particular Baptist denomination to which he belonged. This study examines the key aspects of the life and thought of this hugely significant figure, and gives insights into the revival in which he played such a central part.
2003 / 1-84227-141-5 / xx + 202pp

Peter Naylor
Calvinism, Communion and the Baptists
A Study of English Calvinistic Baptists from the Late 1600s to the Early 1800s
(SBHT vol. 7)
Dr Naylor argues that the traditional link between 'high-Calvinism' and 'restricted communion' is in need of revision. He examines Baptist communion controversies from the late 1600s to the early 1800s and also the theologies of John Gill and Andrew Fuller.
2003 / 1-84227-142-3 / xx + 266pp

Ian M. Randall, Toivo Pilli and Anthony R. Cross (eds)
Baptist Identities
International Studies from the Seventeenth to the Twentieth Centuries
(SBHT vol. 19)
These papers represent the contributions of scholars from various parts of the world as they consider the factors that have contributed to Baptist distinctiveness in different countries and at different times. The volume includes specific case studies as well as broader examinations of Baptist life in a particular country or region. Together they represent an outstanding resource for understanding Baptist identities.
2005 / 1-84227-215-2 / approx. 350pp

James M. Renihan
Edification and Beauty
The Practical Ecclesiology of the English Particular Baptists, 1675–1705
(SBHT vol. 17)
Edification and Beauty describes the practices of the Particular Baptist churches at the end of the seventeenth century in terms of three concentric circles: at the centre is the ecclesiological material in the Second London Confession, which is then fleshed out in the various published writings of the men associated with these churches, and, finally, expressed in the church books of the era.
2005 / 1-84227-251-9 / approx. 230pp

Frank Rinaldi
'The Tribe of Dan'
A Study of the New Connexion of General Baptists 1770–1891
(SBHT vol. 10)
'The Tribe of Dan' is a thematic study which explores the theology, organizational structure, evangelistic strategy, ministry and leadership of the New Connexion of General Baptists as it experienced the process of institutionalization in the transition from a revival movement to an established denomination.
2006 / 1-84227-143-1 / approx. 350pp

Peter Shepherd
The Making of a Modern Denomination
John Howard Shakespeare and the English Baptists 1898–1924
(SBHT vol. 4)
John Howard Shakespeare introduced revolutionary change to the Baptist denomination. The Baptist Union was transformed into a strong central institution and Baptist ministers were brought under its control. Further, Shakespeare's pursuit of church unity reveals him as one of the pioneering ecumenists of the twentieth century.
2001 / 1-84227-046-X / xviii + 220pp

July 2005

Karen Smith
The Community and the Believers
A Study of Calvinistic Baptist Spirituality in Some Towns and Villages of Hampshire and the Borders of Wiltshire, c.1730–1830
(SBHT vol. 22)

The period from 1730 to 1830 was one of transition for Calvinistic Baptists. Confronted by the enthusiasm of the Evangelical Revival, congregations within the denomination as a whole were challenged to find a way to take account of the revival experience. This study examines the life and devotion of Calvinistic Baptists in Hampshire and Wiltshire during this period. Among this group of Baptists was the hymn writer, Anne Steele.

2005 / 1-84227-326-4 / approx. 280pp

Martin Sutherland
Dissenters in a 'Free Land'
Baptist Thought in New Zealand 1850–2000
(SBHT vol. 24)

Baptists in New Zealand were forced to recast their identity. Conventions of communication and association, state and ecumenical relations, even historical divisions and controversies had to be revised in the face of new topographies and constraints. As Baptists formed themselves in a fluid society they drew heavily on both international movements and local dynamics. This book traces the development of ideas which shaped institutions and styles in sometimes surprising ways.

2006 / 1-84227-327-2 / approx. 230pp

Brian Talbot
The Search for a Common Identity
The Origins of the Baptist Union of Scotland 1800–1870
(SBHT vol. 9)

In the period 1800 to 1827 there were three streams of Baptists in Scotland: Scotch, Haldaneite and 'English' Baptist. A strong commitment to home evangelization brought these three bodies closer together, leading to a merger of their home missionary societies in 1827. However, the first three attempts to form a union of churches failed, but by the 1860s a common understanding of their corporate identity was attained leading to the establishment of the Baptist Union of Scotland.

2003 / 1-84227-123-7 / xviii + 402pp

Philip E. Thompson
The Freedom of God
Towards Baptist Theology in Pneumatological Perspective
(SBHT vol. 20)
This study contends that the range of theological commitments of the early Baptists are best understood in relation to their distinctive emphasis on the freedom of God. Thompson traces how this was recast anthropocentrically, leading to an emphasis upon human freedom from the nineteenth century onwards. He seeks to recover the dynamism of the early vision via a pneumatologically-oriented ecclesiology defining the church in terms of the memory of God.
2006 / 1-84227-125-3 / approx. 350pp

Philip E. Thompson and Anthony R. Cross (eds)
Recycling the Past or Researching History?
Studies in Baptist Historiography and Myths
(SBHT vol. 11)
In this volume an international group of Baptist scholars examine and re-examine areas of Baptist life and thought about which little is known or the received wisdom is in need of revision. Historiographical studies include the date Oxford Baptists joined the Abingdon Association, the death of the Fifth Monarchist John Pendarves, eighteenth-century Calvinistic Baptists and the political realm, confessional identity and denominational institutions, Baptist community, ecclesiology, the priesthood of all believers, soteriology, Baptist spirituality, Strict and Reformed Baptists, the role of women among British Baptists, while various 'myths' challenged include the nature of high-Calvinism in eighteenth-century England, baptismal anti-sacramentalism, episcopacy, and Baptists and change.
2005 / 1-84227-122-9 / approx. 330pp

Linda Wilson
Marianne Farningham
A Plain Working Woman
(SBHT vol. 18)
Marianne Farningham, of College Street Baptist Chapel, Northampton, was a household name in evangelical circles in the later nineteenth century. For over fifty years she produced comment, poetry, biography and fiction for the popular Christian press. This investigation uses her writings to explore the beliefs and behaviour of evangelical Nonconformists, including Baptists, during these years.
2006 / 1-84227-124-5 / approx. 250pp

Other Paternoster titles relating to Baptist history and thought

George R. Beasley-Murray
Baptism in the New Testament
(Paternoster Digital Library)
This is a welcome reprint of a classic text on baptism originally published in 1962 by one of the leading Baptist New Testament scholars of the twentieth century. Dr Beasley-Murray's comprehensive study begins by investigating the antecedents of Christian baptism. It then surveys the foundation of Christian baptism in the Gospels, its emergence in the Acts of the Apostles and development in the apostolic writings. Following a section relating baptism to New Testament doctrine, a substantial discussion of the origin and significance of infant baptism leads to a briefer consideration of baptismal reform and ecumenism.

2005 / 1-84227-300-0 / x + 422pp

Paul Beasley-Murray
Fearless for Truth
A Personal Portrait of the Life of George Beasley-Murray
Without a doubt George Beasley-Murray was one of the greatest Baptists of the twentieth century. A long-standing Principal of Spurgeon's College, he wrote more than twenty books and made significant contributions in the study of areas as diverse as baptism and eschatology, as well as writing highly respected commentaries on the Book of Revelation and John's Gospel.

2002 / 1-84227-134-2 / xii + 244pp

David Bebbington
Holiness in Nineteenth-Century England
(Studies in Christian History and Thought)
David Bebbington stresses the relationship of movements of spirituality to changes in their cultural setting, especially the legacies of the Enlightenment and Romanticism. He shows that these broad shifts in ideological mood had a profound effect on the ways in which piety was conceptualized and practised. Holiness was intimately bound up with the spirit of the age.

2000 / 0-85364-981-2 / viii + 98pp

July 2005

Clyde Binfield
Victorian Nonconformity in Eastern England 1840–1885
(Studies in Evangelical History and Thought)
Studies of Victorian religion and society often concentrate on cities, suburbs, and industrialisation. This study provides a contrast. Victorian Eastern England—Essex, Suffolk, Norfolk, Cambridgeshire, and Huntingdonshire—was rural, traditional, relatively unchanging. That is nonetheless a caricature which discounts the industry in Norwich and Ipswich (as well as in Haverhill, Stowmarket and Leiston) and ignores the impact of London on Essex, of railways throughout the region, and of an ancient but changing university (Cambridge) on the county town which housed it. It also entirely ignores the political implications of such changes in a region noted for the variety of its religious Dissent since the seventeenth century. This book explores Victorian Eastern England and its Nonconformity. It brings to a wider readership a pioneering thesis which has made a major contribution to a fresh evolution of English religion and society.
2006 / 1-84227-216-0 / approx. 274pp

Edward W. Burrows
'To Me To Live Is Christ'
A Biography of Peter H. Barber
This book is about a remarkably gifted and energetic man of God. Peter H. Barber was born into a Brethren family in Edinburgh in 1930. In his youth he joined Charlotte Baptist Chapel and followed the call into Baptist ministry. For eighteen years he was the pioneer minister of the new congregation in the New Town of East Kilbride, which planted two further congregations. At the age of thirty-nine he served as Centenary President of the Baptist Union of Scotland and then exercised an influential ministry for over seven years in the well-known Upton Vale Baptist Church, Torquay. From 1980 until his death in 1994 he was General Secretary of the Baptist Union of Scotland. Through his work for the European Baptist Federation and the Baptist World Alliance he became a world Baptist statesman. He was President of the EBF during the upheaval that followed the collapse of Communism.
2005 / 1-84227-324-8 / xxii + 236pp

Christopher J. Clement
Religious Radicalism in England 1535–1565
(Rutherford Studies in Historical Theology)
In this valuable study Christopher Clement draws our attention to a varied assemblage of people who sought Christian faithfulness in the underworld of mid-Tudor England. Sympathetically and yet critically he assess their place in the history of English Protestantism, and by attentive listening he gives them a voice.
1997 / 0-946068-44-5 / xxii + 426pp

July 2005

Anthony R. Cross (ed.)
Ecumenism and History
Studies in Honour of John H.Y. Briggs
(Studies in Christian History and Thought)
This collection of essays examines the inter-relationships between the two fields in which Professor Briggs has contributed so much: history—particularly Baptist and Nonconformist—and the ecumenical movement. With contributions from colleagues and former research students from Britain, Europe and North America, *Ecumenism and History* provides wide-ranging studies in important aspects of Christian history, theology and ecumenical studies.
2002 / 1-84227-135-0 / xx + 362pp

Keith E. Eitel
Paradigm Wars
The Southern Baptist International Mission Board Faces the Third Millennium
(Regnum Studies in Mission)
The International Mission Board of the Southern Baptist Convention is the largest denominational mission agency in North America. This volume chronicles the historic and contemporary forces that led to the IMB's recent extensive reorganization, providing the most comprehensive case study to date of a historic mission agency restructuring to continue its mission purpose into the twenty-first century more effectively.
2000 / 1-870345-12-6 / x + 140pp

Ruth Gouldbourne
The Flesh and the Feminine
Gender and Theology in the Writings of Caspar Schwenckfeld
(Studies in Christian History and Thought)
Caspar Schwenckfeld and his movement exemplify one of the radical communities of the sixteenth century. Challenging theological and liturgical norms, they also found themselves challenging social and particularly gender assumptions. In this book, the issues of the relationship between radical theology and the understanding of gender are considered.
2005 / 1-84227-048-6 / approx. 304pp

David Hilborn
The Words of our Lips
Language-Use in Free Church Worship
(Paternoster Theological Monographs)
Studies of liturgical language have tended to focus on the written canons of Roman Catholic and Anglican communities. By contrast, David Hilborn analyses the more extemporary approach of English Nonconformity. Drawing on recent developments in linguistic pragmatics, he explores similarities and differences between 'fixed' and 'free' worship, and argues for the interdependence of each.
2006 / 0-85364-977-4

Stephen R. Holmes
Listening to the Past
The Place of Tradition in Theology
Beginning with the question 'Why can't we just read the Bible?' Stephen Holmes considers the place of tradition in theology, showing how the doctrine of creation leads to an account of historical location and creaturely limitations as essential aspects of our existence. For we cannot claim unmediated access to the Scriptures without acknowledging the place of tradition: theology is an irreducibly communal task. *Listening to the Past* is a sustained attempt to show what listening to tradition involves, and how it can be used to aid theological work today.
2002 / 1-84227-155-5 / xiv + 168pp

Mark Hopkins
Nonconformity's Romantic Generation
Evangelical and Liberal Theologies in Victorian England
(Studies in Evangelical History and Thought)
A study of the theological development of key leaders of the Baptist and Congregational denominations at their period of greatest influence, including C.H. Spurgeon and R.W. Dale, and of the controversies in which those among them who embraced and rejected the liberal transformation of their evangelical heritage opposed each other.
2004 / 1-84227-150-4 / xvi + 284pp

July 2005

Galen K. Johnson
Prisoner of Conscience
John Bunyan on Self, Community and Christian Faith
(Studies in Christian History and Thought)
This is an interdisciplinary study of John Bunyan's understanding of conscience across his autobiographical, theological and fictional writings, investigating whether conscience always deserves fidelity, and how Bunyan's view of conscience affects his relationship both to modern Western individualism and historic Christianity.
2003 / 1-84227- 151-2 / xvi + 236pp

R.T. Kendall
Calvin and English Calvinism to 1649
(Studies in Christian History and Thought)
The author's thesis is that those who formed the Westminster Confession of Faith, which is regarded as Calvinism, in fact departed from John Calvin on two points: (1) the extent of the atonement and (2) the ground of assurance of salvation.
1997 / 0-85364-827-1 / xii + 264pp

Timothy Larsen
Friends of Religious Equality
Nonconformist Politics in Mid-Victorian England
During the middle decades of the nineteenth century the English Nonconformist community developed a coherent political philosophy of its own, of which a central tenet was the principle of religious equality (in contrast to the stereotype of Evangelical Dissenters). The Dissenting community fought for the civil rights of Roman Catholics, non-Christians and even atheists, on an issue of principle which had its flowering in the enthusiastic and undivided support which Nonconformity gave to the campaign for Jewish emancipation. This reissued study examines the political efforts and ideas of English Nonconformists during the period, covering the whole range of national issues raised, from state education to the Crimean War. It offers a case study of a theologically conservative group defending religious pluralism in the civic sphere, showing that the concept of religious equality was a grand vision at the centre of the political philosophy of the Dissenters.
2007 / 1-84227-402-3 / x + 300pp

July 2005

Donald M. Lewis
Lighten Their Darkness
The Evangelical Mission to Working-Class London, 1828–1860
(Studies in Evangelical History and Thought)
This is a comprehensive and compelling study of the Church and the complexities of nineteenth-century London. Challenging our understanding of the culture in working London at this time, Lewis presents a well-structured and illustrated work that contributes substantially to the study of evangelicalism and mission in nineteenth-century Britain.
2001 / 1-84227-074-5 / xviii + 372pp

Stanley E. Porter and Anthony R. Cross (eds)
Semper Reformandum
Studies in Honour of Clark H. Pinnock
Clark Pinnock has clearly been one of the most important evangelical theologians of the last forty years in North America. Always provocative, especially in the wide range of opinions he has held and considered, Pinnock, himself a Baptist, has recently retired after twenty-five years of teaching at McMaster Divinity College. His colleagues and associates honour him in this volume by responding to his important theological work which has dealt with the essential topics of evangelical theology. These include Christian apologetics, biblical inspiration, the Holy Spirit and, perhaps most importantly in recent years, openness theology.
2003 / 1-84227-206-3 / xiv + 414pp

Meic Pearse
The Great Restoration
The Religious Radicals of the 16th and 17th Centuries
Pearse charts the rise and progress of continental Anabaptism – both evangelical and heretical – through the sixteenth century. He then follows the story of those English people who became impatient with Puritanism and separated – first from the Church of England and then from one another – to form the antecedents of later Congregationalists, Baptists and Quakers.
1998 / 0-85364-800-X / xii + 320pp

Charles Price and Ian M. Randall
Transforming Keswick
Transforming Keswick is a thorough, readable and detailed history of the convention. It will be of interest to those who know and love Keswick, those who are only just discovering it, and serious scholars eager to learn more about the history of God's dealings with his people.
2000 / 1-85078-350-0 / 288pp

July 2005

Jim Purves
The Triune God and the Charismatic Movement
A Critical Appraisal from a Scottish Perspective
(Paternoster Theological Monographs)
All emotion and no theology? Or a fundamental challenge to reappraise and realign our trinitarian theology in the light of Christian experience? This study of charismatic renewal as it found expression within Scotland at the end of the twentieth century evaluates the use of Patristic, Reformed and contemporary models (including those of the Baptist Union of Scotland) of the Trinity in explaining the workings of the Holy Spirit.
2004 / 1-84227-321-3 / xxiv + 246pp

Ian M. Randall
Evangelical Experiences
A Study in the Spirituality of English Evangelicalism 1918–1939
(Studies in Evangelical History and Thought)
This book makes a detailed historical examination of evangelical spirituality between the First and Second World Wars. It shows how patterns of devotion led to tensions and divisions. In a wide-ranging study, Anglican, Wesleyan, Reformed and Pentecostal-charismatic spiritualities are analysed.
1999 / 0-85364-919-7 / xii + 310pp

Ian M. Randall
One Body in Christ
The History and Significance of the Evangelical Alliance
In 1846 the Evangelical Alliance was founded with the aim of bringing together evangelicals for common action. This book uses material not previously utilized to examine the history and significance of the Evangelical Alliance, a movement which has remained a powerful force for unity. At a time when evangelicals are growing world-wide, this book offers insights into the past which are relevant to contemporary issues.
2001 / 1-84227-089-3 / xii + 394pp

Ian M. Randall
Spirituality and Social Change
The Contribution of F.B. Meyer (1847–1929)
(Studies in Evangelical History and Thought)
This is a fresh appraisal of F.B. Meyer (1847–1929), a leading Free Church minister. Having been deeply affected by holiness spirituality, Meyer became the Keswick Convention's foremost international speaker. He combined spirituality with effective evangelism and socio-political activity. This study shows Meyer's significant contribution to spiritual renewal and social change.
2003 / 1-84227-195-4 / xx + 184pp

July 2005

Geoffrey Robson
Dark Satanic Mills?
Religion and Irreligion in Birmingham and the Black Country
(Studies in Evangelical History and Thought)
This book analyses and interprets the nature and extent of popular Christian belief and practice in Birmingham and the Black Country during the first half of the nineteenth century, with particular reference to the impact of cholera epidemics and evangelism on church extension programmes.
2002 / 1-84227-102-4 / xiv + 294pp

Alan P.F. Sell
Enlightenment, Ecumenism, Evangel
Theological Themes and Thinkers 1550–2000
(Studies in Christian History and Thought)
This book consists of papers in which such interlocking topics as the Enlightenment, the problem of authority, the development of doctrine, spirituality, ecumenism, theological method and the heart of the gospel are discussed. Issues of significance to the church at large are explored with special reference to writers from the Reformed and Dissenting traditions.
2005 / 1-84227330-2 / xviii + 422pp

Alan P.F. Sell
Hinterland Theology
Some Reformed and Dissenting Adjustments
(Studies in Christian History and Thought)
Many books have been written on theology's 'giants' and significant trends, but what of those lesser-known writers who adjusted to them? In this book some hinterland theologians of the British Reformed and Dissenting traditions, who followed in the wake of toleration, the Evangelical Revival, the rise of modern biblical criticism and Karl Barth, are allowed to have their say. They include Thomas Ridgley, Ralph Wardlaw, T.V. Tymms and N.H.G. Robinson.
2006 / 1-84227-331-0

July 2005

Alan P.F. Sell and Anthony R. Cross (eds)
Protestant Nonconformity in the Twentieth Century
(Studies in Christian History and Thought)
In this collection of essays scholars representative of a number of Nonconformist traditions reflect thematically on Nonconformists' life and witness during the twentieth century. Among the subjects reviewed are biblical studies, theology, worship, evangelism and spirituality, and ecumenism. Over and above its immediate interest, this collection provides a marker to future scholars and others wishing to know how some of their forebears assessed Nonconformity's contribution to a variety of fields during the century leading up to Christianity's third millennium.
2003 / 1-84227-221-7 / x + 398pp

Mark Smith
Religion in Industrial Society
Oldham and Saddleworth 1740–1865
(Studies in Christian History and Thought)
This book analyses the way British churches sought to meet the challenge of industrialization and urbanization during the period 1740–1865. Working from a case-study of Oldham and Saddleworth, Mark Smith challenges the received view that the Anglican Church in the eighteenth century was characterized by complacency and inertia, and reveals Anglicanism's vigorous and creative response to the new conditions. He reassesses the significance of the centrally directed church reforms of the mid-nineteenth century, and emphasizes the importance of local energy and enthusiasm. Charting the growth of denominational pluralism in Oldham and Saddleworth, Dr Smith compares the strengths and weaknesses of the various Anglican and Nonconformist approaches to promoting church growth. He also demonstrates the extent to which all the churches participated in a common culture shaped by the influence of evangelicalism, and shows that active co-operation between the churches rather than denominational conflict dominated. This revised and updated edition of Dr Smith's challenging and original study makes an important contribution both to the social history of religion and to urban studies.
2006 / 1-84227-335-3 / approx. 300pp

David M. Thompson
Baptism, Church and Society in Britain from the Evangelical Revival to *Baptism, Eucharist and Ministry*
The theology and practice of baptism have not received the attention they deserve. How important is faith? What does baptismal regeneration mean? Is baptism a bond of unity between Christians? This book discusses the theology of baptism and popular belief and practice in England and Wales from the Evangelical Revival to the publication of the World Council of Churches' consensus statement on *Baptism, Eucharist and Ministry* (1982).
2005 / 1-84227-393-0 / approx. 224pp

Martin Sutherland
Peace, Toleration and Decay
The Ecclesiology of Later Stuart Dissent
(Studies in Christian History and Thought)
This fresh analysis brings to light the complexity and fragility of the later Stuart Nonconformist consensus. Recent findings on wider seventeenth-century thought are incorporated into a new picture of the dynamics of Dissent and the roots of evangelicalism.
2003 / 1-84227-152-0 / xxii + 216pp

Haddon Willmer
Evangelicalism 1785–1835: An Essay (1962) and Reflections (2004)
(Studies in Evangelical History and Thought)
Awarded the Hulsean Prize in the University of Cambridge in 1962, this interpretation of a classic period of English Evangelicalism, by a young church historian, is now supplemented by reflections on Evangelicalism from the vantage point of a retired Professor of Theology.
2006 / 1-84227-219-5

Linda Wilson
Constrained by Zeal
Female Spirituality amongst Nonconformists 1825–1875
(Studies in Evangelical History and Thought)
Constrained by Zeal investigates the neglected area of Nonconformist female spirituality. Against the background of separate spheres, it analyses the experience of women from four denominations, and argues that the churches provided a 'third sphere' in which they could find opportunities for participation.
2000 / 0-85364-972-3 / xvi + 294pp

Nigel G. Wright
Disavowing Constantine
*Mission, Church and the Social Order in the Theologies of
John Howard Yoder and Jürgen Moltmann*
(Paternoster Theological Monographs)
This book is a timely restatement of a radical theology of church and state in the Anabaptist and Baptist tradition. Dr Wright constructs his argument in dialogue and debate with Yoder and Moltmann, major contributors to a free church perspective.

2000 / 0-85364-978-2 / xvi + 252pp

Nigel G. Wright
Free Church, Free State
The Positive Baptist Vision
Free Church, Free State is a textbook on baptist ways of being church and a proposal for the future of baptist churches in an ecumenical context. Nigel Wright argues that both baptist (small 'b') and catholic (small 'c') church traditions should seek to enrich and support each other as valid expressions of the body of Christ without sacrificing what they hold dear. Written for pastors, church planters, evangelists and preachers, Nigel Wright offers frameworks of thought for baptists and non-baptists in their journey together following Christ.

2005 / 1-84227-353-1 / xxviii + 292

Nigel G. Wright
New Baptists, New Agenda
New Baptists, New Agenda is a timely contribution to the growing debate about the health, shape and future of the Baptists. It considers the steady changes that have taken place among Baptists in the last decade – changes of mood, style, practice and structure – and encourages us to align these current movements and questions with God's upward and future call. He contends that the true church has yet to come: the church that currently exists is an anticipation of the joyful gathering of all who have been called by the Spirit through Christ to the Father.

2002 / 1-84227-157-1 / x + 162pp

Paternoster
9 Holdom Avenue,
Bletchley,
Milton Keynes MK1 1QR,
United Kingdom
Web: www.authenticmedia.co.uk/paternoster

July 2005